Klairi Lykiardop

# SPIRITUAL HEALING

*A human potential
in theory and practice*

**MEGAS SEIRIOS**
Publications

ISBN 978-960-7350-26-8

© 2010 Servers' Society
All rights reserved. No part of this publication may be reproduced, stored in a retrieval system, or transmitted, in any form or by any means, electronic, mechanical, photocopying, recording or otherwise, without the prior permission of the publishers.

This book is published by **Megas Seirios Publications**, which are founded under the auspices of **Omilos Eksipiretiton – Servers' Society Spiritual Centre**, a non-profit organization. All sales income goes to publishing, printing and distributing of the books in order to disseminate spirituality. No royalties are paid on the books. To find more information about the mission, works and activities of the Society and/or to place an order, please visit our website: **www.megas-seirios.com**

or contact us at:
9, Sarantaporou Street, Athens, Greece, P.O.: 111 44
*e-mail:* info@megas-seirios.gr
*Tel.:* +30 210 20 15 194
*Tel./Fax:* +30 210 22 30 864

Translation from Greek: Geoffrey Cox

Cover/jacket photo: Kostas Tzioumakas
(appearance of a rainbow during a seminar of the Servers' Society at Ypati, Greece)

Design: Marianna Smyrniotou

*This book is dedicated
to the spiritual healer Kiki Keramida
who bravely stood up to her health
problems, contributed to the structuring
of the healing section of Omilos
Eksipiretiton and dedicated herself
to its task with the guidance
of the Master.*

༃

# CONTENTS

| | |
|---|---|
| FOREWORD TO THE ENGLISH EDITION | 9 |
| NOTE | 13 |
| FOREWORD | 17 |
| THE FIRST LESSON IN SPIRITUAL HEALING | 29 |
| WHAT ILLNESS IS | 37 |
| ILLNESS: A UNIVERSAL PHENOMENON | 51 |
| THE HUMAN BEING AND ITS BODY | 63 |
| SOUL AND BODY | 73 |
| THE ENERGY CENTRES | 83 |
| THE SPIRITUAL HEALER | 97 |
| METHODS AND TECHNIQUES OF SPIRITUAL HEALING | 105 |
| THE HEALER AND THE SPIRITUAL FIELDS | 117 |
| MEDICAL SCIENCE AND SPIRITUAL HEALING | 127 |
| SELF-HEALING | 139 |
| ILLNESS: AN INCENTIVE FOR EVOLUTION | 149 |
| POSITIVE AND NEGATIVE ATTITUDE OF PATIENTS | 159 |

| | |
|---|---|
| PARENTS, CHILDREN AND ILLNESSES | 169 |
| ILLNESSES AND THE COUPLE | 183 |
| NEGATIVE THOUGHTS AND EMOTIONS | 197 |
| ABUSE – PASSION – POSSESSION | 207 |
| THE IMPORTANCE OF RELAXATION | 221 |
| SINGING – RITUALS – CHORODROMENA (RITUAL DANCING) | 231 |
| COLOURS AND HEALING | 241 |
| SERVICE | 249 |
| THE DIVINE HUMAN BODY | 259 |
| POSSIBILITIES AND LIMITATIONS OF SPIRITUAL HEALING | 267 |
| THE HEALING SECTION OF THE SERVERS' SOCIETY | 275 |
| A HEALING CENTRE FOR THE FUTURE | 281 |
| EPILOGUE | 291 |
| LETTERS OF THANKS FROM PATIENTS | 295 |
| REVIEWS | 309 |

# FOREWORD TO THE ENGLISH EDITION

At the time when the book "Spiritual Healing" was being translated into English, one of the longest-serving members of our Spiritual Centre reread a copy of the second edition in Greek, which came out in 1995. When she finished studying it, she had formed the following opinion, which she passed on to me and certain other members of the Society:

> *"I think that in this book's translation, as well as in all of its editions, in Greek or in any other language, it must be made abundantly clear that the work of spiritual healing is still being carried on at the present day, both by yourself*

*– the author of the book – and by other healers. Without this explanation, the reader may not realise that the Servers' Society's healing section still exists today, constantly working on the healing of patients seeking its help. We shouldn't forget that this book was first published in 1987 and that – naturally – the information it contains on spiritual healing and specifically on the Society's healing work, was relevant up to that year. I therefore believe that all current knowledge should also be mentioned in the new editions, either by including it, or by referencing the books containing it."*

I considered this opinion valid, and I was glad that it had been voiced before the book's publication, as I was given time to write this foreword and clarify that the Society's healing work continues to this day – something that had not previously crossed my mind. I shall not go into details about what has happened since the book was published. I will simply note that the interest in spiritual healing had been continuously increasing and that is the reason why those of us healers who constituted the original healing team have seen our numbers steadily grow with the passage of time.

I think it is important to emphasize that in the course of the 29 years since the Society's founding, there have always been spiritual healers working for the healing of the sick. Even during difficult times, such as when the Master Dimitris Kakalidis was gravely ill, or even after his death, the healings still continued.

Practice has shown that the success of spiritual healing relies on the constant work of the healer. The Master himself was an example of steadfastness and this is what he always taught us, by expressing a genuine interest in each and every patient. Mrs Kiki Keramida generously responded to the task of the healing section by contributing to its organisation and by working as a healer to the sick. Many details of her work are included in the book she wrote on her experiences as a spiritual healer*.

The Master's teaching on spiritual healing has been given in specific written texts. These are taught every week to the group of healers in training, consisting of members of the Society who wish to give expression to their healing capabilities by taking part in the group healings carried out by the healing section. Some of the Master's lessons are included in the fourth volume of the series 'The Master', with the subtitle 'Accomplishment – Spiritual Healing'**. In these lessons it is stressed that illness is not just a health problem, but also anything that

---

*Kiki Keramida, 'Experiences of a Spiritual Healer', Athens: Megas Seirios 2014, translated and published in English.
** Klairi Lykiardopoulou, 'THE MASTER, Accomplishment-Spiritual Healing', Athens: Megas Seirios, 2nd edition, published in Greek.

causes pain, unhappiness, poverty, and the like. Consequently, healing is any positive power, will, thought or action which reduces and eventually heals the cause of this pain.

The methods and techniques applied by the healers for the healing of those seeking help from the healing section are all necessary. However, over and above the implementation of these methods, one thing the healer is called upon to do, and this, the Master says, is to recognise that the one true Healer of all is God. This recognition leads to the corresponding faith in Him, whose love the healer asks for and receives, in order to convey it to the patient, with absolute trust in its divine healing power.

*Klairi Lykiardopoulou, author*
*2009*

# NOTE

*The aim of this book is to give an account of the spiritual potential inherent in human beings as a means of healing physical illnesses as well as other adversities they undergo in their lives which affect their psychosomatic condition. It delves into the positive and negative human functions and offers ways and methods of changing them for the better.*

*Spiritual healing does not oppose classical medical science in any way, in fact, it is recognised and studied by all spiritual healers, in order to acquire a general or more specialised training. It is clear that the medical profession has worked with great conscientiousness and success, and is constantly enhanced with the help of technology and the development of laboratory research. Spiritual healers do not intervene in the work of the doctors, whose vocation often requires great personal sacrifices. Indeed, they often encourage patients to seek medical aid, while at the same time contributing to their health's improvement by invoking the power of the Spirit.*

*The following texts are a comprehensive and concise study of human potential, which, when employed correctly, can change the flow of life, thus reducing pain and illness. The subject is certainly broad, and what is stated here should be regarded merely as the fundamental facts in an introductory book. To cover this vast subject, it is necessary for more books to be written, possibly with the collaboration of several spiritual healers or specialists dealing with classical medicine, psychiatry and other methods of healing.*

*The reader will notice that the content of the following chapters is not just a philosophical approach. It is principally based on the personal experiences of spiritual healers and of patients who have received help. It provides specific examples that confirm the abilities of spiritual healing, while at the same time describing its difficulties and failures due to various reasons, each of which is respectively explained.*

*Every subject is dealt with in a simple and explanatory way, making it comprehensible to everyone, even to those*

# NOTE

*who have no prior knowledge of it. If the contents of this book provide certain stimuli and serve as motivation for a fresh enquiry into the nature of the human self, its aim will have largely been achieved. Further study and work on the improvement of human health is a purely personal matter that concerns each person individually.*

*The Author*

# FOREWORD

Life is a miracle. An endless, everyday miracle unfolding around us and within us every second. The flight of a bird, the lapping of the waves, the sun blazing blindingly above us, giving us the gift of life – they are all a miracle. The human organism is itself a miracle. Even if we contemplate only the mechanism of breathing, we shall be astonished by the complexity of its functions.

Included within the marvelous expression of life is the miracle of death, the end of existence, the decomposition of form. The creation of a material appearance is as superb as its dissolution. Decay conceals the mystery of life, the transmutation of matter. Through it a new form is born, a new cycle of existence begins. An eternal cycle of synthesis and dissolution, the inviolable law of all Creation.

Humans live within this miracle; they are themselves an expression of that miracle. They do not, however, always recognise this. They often forget it, regarding it as something so simple, so natural, as to seemingly ignore its existence. And so they cease to consciously and willingly give expression to it. They lose its wonderful beauty, and attempt to discover it in certain particular events. They seek the truth elsewhere. They search for strength in the unusual. They expect love from others. They do not see that their own self is the truth, the strength and the love!

The light of true life is lost this way, making human beings seemingly live in darkness. Of course, there are moments when a flash of lightning passes through their minds and hearts. Moments when the vision of another reality is revealed to their hypnotized consciousness. Humans then experience true ecstasy, briefly discovering themselves, becoming that which they truly are. They become a creation endowed with awareness that consciously participates in its own creation!

The inability of humans to recognise, always and everywhere, the existence of this miracle, constantly distances them from it. Thus, they strive in their isolation or attempt to find the truth with other fellow humans.

They build worldviews and adopt dogmatic positions, approving and rejecting. They classify and rank things in the light of their own criteria. They measure life in terms of intelligence, reputation, money or even health. They divide the planet up into continents, countries, cities and villages. They separate humankind into races; dissecting religion, rating faith at different levels, starting with non-belief. They fragment the one and only Truth of life into the tiniest of pieces, truncated and weak.

All this, all human functions are nothing more than an attempt to unite with the Truth. They simply reveal the conscious or unconscious need for the revelation of the essence of life. The means used by each of us in finding our way are not important. Even the mistakes that are made along this path are parts of it. These are only but a few of the notes in a world symphony played by the Universe itself. Humans suffer for their mistakes because they portray them as mistakes. They do not see them as part of the whole, balanced out of their own accord. They identify with their imperfections and suffer for it, until the pain makes them ill, disables them and eventually leads them to an untimely death, severing their natural cycle of life.

Beyond the human attitude, individual evolution and endless doubts, the miracle of Existence continues, because it is the work of the power of Creation, the power of the Supreme Mind, of God, who has created everything. Some claim that the beginning of the world was a particle of matter which self-evolved and continues to multiply, whereas others maintain that it was a formless, diffuse essence. It is not important. Power is power, and the magnitude or the form in which it manifests does not alter the reality of the miracle it expresses.

If we suffer from pain, distress and illness, this is because we have not yet realised what we are: a part of God's miracle. If we are not aware of this truth, it is natural that we should not manifest it. It is natural that we should not know how to balance the opposing facets within us and around us. We cannot turn illness into health and distress into joy, because we think that all these things lie outside our jurisdiction, beyond our selves. Our self, though, has the power to accomplish the miracle every second, to turn darkness into light, to express the magic of the soul.

Humankind has not been abandoned to its fate and its torments. The power that created it oversees its course and works on its evolution. It gives it endless opportunities to understand who it is and what it can do. Through the ages, there have been examples of this dynamic mentoring, which has shaken people into seeing the Light. Evolved beings, whom we call God-men, Adepts and Masters convey a message, a new current for human life. They speak of the Truth, they live the Truth, because they themselves are what they teach. They are united with the miracle and for that reason they perform it simply, on a daily basis, with their every movement, with their every word.

People hear and, to a greater or lesser extent, believe. They understand, to a degree, what they are taught, or sometimes misinterpret it. They begin to give expression to what they learn, or they limit it only to the person who taught it to them. Often, however, the teaching of love and of knowledge is turned by humankind into yet another limiting schema. Dogmatic differences and personality cults are constructed which are vastly distant from the teachings of the Wise, the true Masters. No Master asks of us to worship him as a human. He only asks of us to worship God, whom he places before us through his acts and words. If we are still in need of the presence of new Masters, if we still seek the return of Christ, this is because we have not yet assimilated the essential part of what past generations were taught. We are in the darkness that hides the light and the magic of our own soul. We restrict the teaching to one Master, religion to one dogmatic faith, Truth to only one of its forms.

A Master does not consider himself only human. He knows that he is part of God, and remains consciously united with Him. He naturally has a human body, but he considers it also as part of the Divine Existence. A corruptible body like those of all humans, but also an immortal consciousness, united with the immortality of God. A Master who comes to bring light to the souls will not talk of himself as a God, because he has understood that our human nature is created 'in the image and likeness of God'. This understanding is conveyed to those who are willing to hear him, through his work and his very existence. He teaches and performs the miracle which he has recognised within himself and which he absolutely believes in. Jesus spoke of the power of the miracle when he said that one who has faith can move mountains. He accomplished the miracle with the innumerable healings which he carried out to those who sought help and believed in the power of God. His presence in the world was a healing of the bodies and souls from humanity's countless diseases.

Every incarnated Master does the same. He cures humankind's sufferings, in whatever form they materialise. His presence gives power and health to those who receive it without resistance, because the power flows from within him and is radiated all around him. His objective is not only to cure an organic disease, but to actually transform the patients into healers. To give them features which they lack, so that they can express the magic of the Light, the power of the soul that dissolves the darkness of ignorance and pain.

A Master validates the truth with his actions. He also validates it through the actions of his disciples, as they begin expressing what they have been taught. The Masters' message is neither difficult nor complicated. On the contrary, it is quite simple – just as any truth is simple. But humans, having forgotten their true nature, have difficulty in rediscovering it. They do not remember that everything is part of God; they ignore that fact that He is 'Omnipresent', and so remain in ignorance. They retain only a disconnected individual existence and do not integrate it into the whole of Creation as an integral part of it.

People who encounter a Master in their life and decide to serve a discipleship with him are called upon to abandon their personal doubts and resistances and to unite themselves with the teaching, for the truth and power to be revealed to them. They are called upon to give expression to this power and to realise it day by day. The disciples' progress passes through many stages, as ignorance, doubt and resistance interfere with the new current inundating them. There is a period of attachment or of resistance to the Master's person. The discipleship passes through the very fluctuations of their souls, until a steady balance is achieved. They put into practice some of the things they are taught, until they are convinced that every such realisation is itself a continuation of their soul's expression. They only have to make the decision in order to become what they are by nature, assimilated to the power of God – to become, that is, an expression of truth, of light, of health in everyone and everything.

The Master's miracle lies precisely in this transformation, which comes to all those who draw near to him. Every teaching must be authenticated in humans; its truth must be recognised, and then it must be proved in practice. It is only then that the inner change will come, and this will be externalised around them. Then the disciples of truth will become truth and the light of their soul will shine all around them.

In conclusion to this foreword, I shall speak on a personal level, as this is the way in which all of the following chapters have been written. Six years ago, in June of 1980, I had the good fortune of becoming acquainted with a Master, a person who is consciously united with God and teaches this union with all his being. At that time I had no idea what a 'Master' was, and, naturally, a long time had to pass for me to understand it – or, to be more precise, to understand only as much as my soul's present state permits.

Like everyone else, I too had my difficulties. What brought me close to him was the quest for knowledge which I hoped would help in the improvement of my life. Knowledge is not acquired without personal sacrifices, because knowledge means union, and union presupposes dissolution of the personal ego and a new synthesis. A synthesis of the divine element within the human; it is only when this is accomplished that the truth arises. In the course of my discipleship up to the present day, I have seen the miracle taking place before my eyes. I too have learnt to heal – first myself and then others. I have seen people with psychological problems recover their power and become creative members of the society. Drug addicts have been rehabilitated simply by being close to the Master, immature individuals have developed, family problems have been resolved. But the most important part has been the power which I have received from his radiance that has led me to a new manner of existence. The hope for the improvement of my life has been fulfilled and I know that the power to improve it as much as I wish rests in my own hands. I have been taught to experience the everyday miracle and to continuously give expression to it. My discipleship continues, because union must be externalised in all areas equivalently without inhibition and in this I am constantly being educated.

I have resolved to writing this book in the first person, because, in doing so, the way in which the Master works will become apparent. My own initial reactions will also become apparent, as I received and progressively understood his teachings. It is not possible for me to cover the full range of the lessons I have received, as they have been filed in a large number of binders in the form of a diary. From these I have chosen only the extracts concerning the subject of spiritual healing.

Today I am the President of the Servers' Society and in charge of its healing section. Our spiritual centre was set up in 1980, with the aim of disseminating the teachings regarding the spiritual development of humans. Included among its activities is spiritual healing for all patients seeking our help. I shall use examples from the section's work in the following chapters, but I will not confine myself to the description of the specific cures which have been accomplished by the healers. My aim is to illustrate the fact that healing means differentiating the function of the soul, thus firmly consolidating health in human beings, a health of 'soul and body' alike. As the Master says, there is no benefit in patients merely recovering from illness. If they have not understood what they must do in order to maintain their health, then they are always at risk from a new illness which will make its appearance as a result of the same erroneous functioning. Naturally, healers work alike on all cases, in the belief that only their own healing intervention can reveal the truth to their patients and gradually turn them into healers towards themselves and others. To make them, that is, a living expression of the power of life that, equipped with the relevant knowledge, will handle the energies of the soul for the common good.

## FOREWORD

The readers already familiar with spiritual healing may not find new information in this book. However, as I am addressing those who are uninformed, as I also was six years ago, or those who have only a minimal knowledge of it, I shall present the subject in simple terms, as I was taught it at the beginning of my discipleship. I shall include analyses of the healing power in order to explain its operation. The knowledge which I have acquired from the Master's lessons, my personal experiences and the books which I have studied will constitute the content of the chapters which follow. In this way an initial picture of such an important subject – the potential of healing through union with the spiritual power and faith in God – will be formed.

Master Dimitris Kakalidis

# THE FIRST LESSON
# IN SPIRITUAL HEALING

"Let me introduce you to the Master, Mrs Klairi", said the young man, who had accompanied me to his house on that day in June. I looked at the man who was standing before me and was taken by surprise. He was at least ten years younger than me. I had imagined him an old man with a white beard, as the wise men of antiquity are portrayed. "What can this man teach me?" I wondered, "He is not even forty years old!"

I didn't have time for further thought, when his wife and two children also appeared. Another surprise for me. The Master was a family man and not a loner, an ascetic, as I had supposed. Something inside me fell apart. Had

I made a mistake? Was I wasting my time and should I better make up some kind of excuse and leave? No, my upbringing would not allow me to do so. Besides, a certain curiosity had begun building within me. And so I sat down beside them and we started talking. I had nothing to lose... And then – who knows? – perhaps Masters were just like everybody else. In any case, I had never met one before and had no idea what they taught.

A discussion on multiple topics began. I felt very much at ease, and I talked, listened and answered, as if I was in a very familiar environment. As time passed, our conversation flowed in a new direction. I was suddenly aware that I was saying very little, that I had become absorbed, without realising it, in the Master's answers and in his analyses of every subject. His words expressed confidence, knowledge and power that held me rooted in my spot.

Six years have now passed, and I still feel the same way when listening to him. Even though the subjects we discuss are usually familiar to me by now, there is, nevertheless, a special quality in his manner which makes me feel that an unshakeable truth emanates from his every word; a truth about life, about the world, about love, about God.

That day we talked about so many things that I was not able to assimilate them all. Later on, I asked again about everything that I had not understood, and continued to do so, until the concepts cleared up in my mind. The Master always answers, even if he has said the same thing ten times over. He explains it in a different way each time, so that understanding eventually comes to the disciples, helping them change their approach and their attitude towards their problems.

The discussion was nearing its conclusion. We had talked about my personal issues, my children, my husband, my job. We had touched on existential matters, such as the meaning of the 'soul', and what life energies and forces are. I realised that it would soon be time to leave. And I was, in fact, in a hurry to be on my own and to mentally classify what I had heard. I wanted to go home and write down my impressions. But the Master still had something more to say to me, something to teach me. This 'something', as I later discovered, is the basis of spiritual healing. It is the prerequisite for anyone wanting to become a healer. Up to that moment the subject had not come up, nor had I been informed that the Master was a spiritual healer. This I only found out on the second or third time that we met.

As I was getting ready to leave, he told me to sit down in my seat, to relax and to begin feeling the weight of my body and a restfulness overwhelming me. When I did as he told me, closing my eyes and waiting, he began to give me specific instructions. It was then that I received my first lesson in relaxation and meditation. The course of that lesson had various stages, which are not necessary to be mentioned here. I shall describe only two main points which have a direct bearing on spiritual healing.

As calmness increasingly overwhelmed me, the Master told me to focus my attention on my feet and feel them being flooded with the power of life. What happened was so unexpected that I opened my eyes in astonishment: a powerful current, which I was totally unprepared for, burst through them, making me spring up, as if I had received an electric discharge. But I carried on, as instructed, and started following this current as it rose up to my calves, my body, my head. In a short while, the whole of my being had changed, it had come to life as never before. It seemed to me that, for the first time in my life, my body was an organism fully alive, with its every point vibrant with the pulsations of life.

I didn't understand at that time what had happened, and a long time had to pass for me to realise the significance of the event. In a later chapter I shall go into details about this life force which flows within us, even though we don't feel it all the time. Knowledge and correct use of psychic energy are essential conditions for becoming a healer. But on that occasion I was simply amazed by its revelation and the difference it brought to my organism.

When this first stage of meditation was completed, the Master told me to focus on one of my internal organs.

Then came the second revelation. The organ which I had concentrated my attention on suddenly presented itself with perfect clarity before me, as if I was seeing it with open eyes. And yet it was one of the organs which are well hidden inside our body. At first it was the heart, then the stomach, then the intestines, then the brain – every one of them... I was unexpectedly presented with new, inner vision, giving me the ability to penetrate the shell of the external form and see what is hidden beneath it. As is only natural, my surprise was entirely justified. Of course, I was not able at that time to explain this fact either, and it was only later, after a great deal of study, that I discovered what happens during such moments. However, as I have said, I shall explain all this at greater length in the following chapters. Here, particular emphasis is placed on the way in which I felt my body being activated, giving me the ability to see it internally – a way that was simple and direct.

At the end of this contemplation, the Master asked me to describe to him what had happened. I began telling him everything that had occurred, still surprised by the new facts that I had discovered. When I finished my description, he instructed me to repeat the same exercise every day until we met again and to make a record of the results of my work. He also noted that by studying my body in this way, I should be able to discern any illness or anything abnormal within it. He added that whenever

I became aware of any disorder in my organism, I should simply visualise that there was nothing wrong and that it was completely healthy. This way of thinking would be enough for healing to occur.

Before going home, filled with impressions and reflections which I wanted to classify, I received one more instruction: to read the book of the well-known British healer Harry Edwards\*, which explains what spiritual healing is and how it functions. I did not understand why he recommended this book to me, nor did this suggestion arouse any particular curiosity in me at the time. Naturally, I read it all, but my mind did not concern itself with it all that much. At that time I was more concerned with various personal issues as well as with the new experience of meditation. However, perhaps the Master had sufficient indications that I could become a healer if I wanted to. Possibly the ease with which I was able to see my internal organs and to feel the current flooding me were factors that were favourable for a future healer. In spite of this, together with all the other matters which were of interest to me at the time, I began progressively applying all the things that I was hearing about spiritual healing. It took me quite a while, though, before I began devoting a number of hours to the matter, as there were still other unmet needs to which I gave priority.

---

\*Edwards, H. "Spirit Healing" The Harry Edwards Spiritual Healing Sanctuary Trust, Surrey: Burrows Lea 1960.

My first contact with the Master finished with the completion of the meditation and the discussion surrounding everything I had experienced through it. The rest of the things that were said that day have no direct connection with spiritual healing. They were part of a much more composite teaching, and an account of them cannot be given in this book which deals with a specific subject. Nevertheless, because this teaching is closely linked to the healing abilities, I shall frequently refer to the Master's lessons, whenever I deem it necessary, thus illustrating the comprehensive approach which must be taken to an issue as substantial as human health, of both the body and the soul.

As the weeks and months passed, I continued to meditate and my healing power was increasingly revealed to me. I began to exercise it of my own accord – just as I was taught to. Furthermore, without anyone's suggestion, I began reading books on the subject. I was perplexed by many matters having to do with the existence of illness, its causes, and the ways of dealing with it. I shall speak of these in the following chapters, giving examples of cures whenever necessary.

# WHAT ILLNESS IS

*"All disease is the result of inhibited soul life, and that is true of all forms in all kingdoms".*

**Alice A. Bailey***

As the days passed following the Master's first lesson, I began noticing certain changes in my body and in my state of mind. I felt stronger, more powerful, as if I was not squandering my powers on pointless matters. My work seemed easier, I slept less and I felt a general renewal that was unexpected at my age.

I began to wonder what had brought this about. Was it meditation? Was it the new attitude I had adopted towards life following the Master's lessons? I observed myself as if for the first time, because every so often a new

---
*Bailey, A., 'Esoteric Healing', London: Lucis Trust 1953.

power would emerge, a power which up to then seemed to have been asleep, buried amidst a thousand hindrances. As my general disposition was improved by this power, the question of illness and its causes gave rise to a strong interest in me. What, ultimately, is illness, and what is it that affects human health?

My observations were not confined to myself. The people around me, relatives and friends, began to be revealed to me in a different light. Each of their actions seemed to externalise something; something much deeper, a state of the soul, often hidden behind their words and movements. I was particularly concerned with people who were experiencing health problems at the time. I began to record my observations, as they seemed to be leading me to very important conclusions.

> *17.7.80 "I observe Ms. M. She is definitely in need of help. She is sadly obsessed with her body and in constant fear of becoming ill. She fears for her life, even though she finds it unbearable and boring. She is constantly feeling unwell. Her body hurts, she complains about everything, she finds no true interest in anything. Her relationship with her husband makes things difficult, as he is authoritarian and selfish, being no help to her at all. But people re-*

*gard them as an ideal couple, because they put up a perfect social façade. They themselves do not understand what is happening to them. It is as if they are blind... ".*

*25.7.80 "From the moment that Mr P entered our house, I was greatly disturbed. He came like a whirlwind and unloaded his problem on to us. At first I was stifled, but, in turn I calmed down and began to observe him. Through his every word could see that he was suffering. And the more he suffered, the angrier he became. He screamed, shouting absurdities, breathing hostility towards the world. Every so often, he becomes ill, sometimes with stomach cramps and other times with migraines. But how could he possibly be well when he finds fault in everything, when he is critical of everyone?"*

All these observations led me to the conclusion that the state of the soul and the health of the body are inextricably connected. In most cases, behind the illness I saw a resistance, a negative attitude towards life. There was nobody around me who was completely healthy, although some only suffered from minor, everyday afflictions. These are so common that we rarely stop to wonder why we have been taken ill, or why illness exists in the first place.

## SPIRITUAL HEALING

Before I began dealing with this subject, I considered it completely natural for myself to become ill, just like everybody else. But the Master, every time I was not well, would ask me the following question: "Why have you fallen ill, Mrs Klairi?" He also asked what I was doing or thinking about at the time when my illness manifested itself. This question challenged me all the more to search for the cause of sicknesses, not only mine, but of others, too. Could it be that eventually there is a genuine correlation between illness and the disposition of the soul?

The Master says that humankind's sicknesses are those that affect not only the body, but also the mind, or manifest themselves as mental illnesses. 'Sicknesses' are all the negative currents which overwhelm humans and tie them down. Hatred, malice, envy, obsession and any other negative thought or feeling is a sickness. Because one who is governed by fear, for example, is not free to express oneself. Similarly, a person who feels hatred often externalises the powers of one's soul in a reverse manner. In both cases, the energy of life does not penetrate the whole of the body as it should, revitalising and maintaining it in good condition. It will charge one area more, but leave another barely energised at all. This results in an incorrect distribution of the powers of the soul, leading to an imbalance in the body.

Human beings have recognized, up to a point, the interrelation of health and their psychological state. Medical science has proven this direct connection on numerous cases. Even unconsciously, people tend to avoid certain unpleasant conflicts, which could affect them and lead them to illness.

All this, however, is not sufficient to improve human health. In this day and age in particular, there has been an onset of diseases, with many of them being new physical ailments which were previously unknown. The knowledge that anxiety, for example, causes ulcers does not teach us how to avoid anxiety, and its subsequent effects on the stomach. Distancing ourselves from unpleasant contacts does not relieve us of all the unwelcome events happening around us daily. The solution to the problems of life lies not in the withdrawal from life, but in dealing with it dynamically.

A dynamic person is one who fearlessly lets oneself function freely at every moment; a person who does not imprison the energies of the soul within one's body for fear of losing something, for fear that others might exploit or suck out one's very lifeblood. Certainly, to a greater or lesser extent, all of us at times are like vampires, wrongdoers and victims who constantly want to take something from life. We close ourselves off because of fear and in doing so we turn into lifeless, dead beings; dead in the heart, in the mind, and emotionally; playing no part in the flow of events and often aggressive towards the situations which challenge us every day to do something about them, to settle them in the best way possible.

The greatest fear of human beings is death. Death not only of the body, but of all the simple things they have filled their lives with. But do we do anything else but die every moment? If today did not die, tomorrow would not be born. If the child did not die, the adolescent would not be born. We must accept this of every situation. A relationship is lost for another to come along, or, perhaps, for us to be alone for a while, which is also an experience. We lose a sum of money, usually as a result of a mistaken action, but the loss is not a disaster. Life goes on, we learn not to make the same mistake again, but to find something to replace that which is lost. People who no longer have a certain object or a loved one at their side are not lost. But if a loss succeeds in taking away the power of their soul, weakening them, and eventually sending them to their sickbed, then they are the lost ones.

Barricading oneself behind certain 'possessions' is merely an attempt at reducing one's fear and insecurity. A husband wants his wife to be his property and a wife wants something else from him. A mother wants her child to love her, as if it is the reason she gave birth. Everybody wants only beautiful and pleasant things, leaving the ugly things to their fate or unloading them on to those who are compelled by their own limitations into being their slaves. But this attitude comes into constant conflict with the laws of life, with objective reality. No one is our property, nothing belongs to us, not even our life itself. The more we resist this truth, the more we are tormented by the resistance created in us. The power of the soul, which floods us before surging outwards to achieve a task, whatever that task may be, is withheld within ourselves. The body, however, cannot tolerate this withholding, causing pain, constriction and illness.

The energies of the soul have to be externalised by all means supplied by human nature. We must live in balance with our whole self, letting our mind work, our heart beat, our body experience physical love and our senses uniting us with the world surrounding us. All these are manifestations of the soul, they are the various forms of its energies, as they penetrate the body and scatter within it. But the soul cannot possibly express itself when humans are overwhelmed with obsessions, when they want to 'have' something which at that time does not exist. Then they simply lose what is being offered to them, because something is always being offered to all of us, even if we do not see it as an offering. Even a deprivation is an offering, because through it we learn to live without what we desire. We learn, that is, to live self-sufficiently, over and above external conditions.

During the time that I have been serving my discipleship with the Master, my observations from my personal experiences and from those of the people around me, have proved to me that only those who equally accept everything that life gives them can freely express the powers of their soul. That is, to let the energy penetrating them function on each occasion as and when it should. If need calls upon them to carry out manual labor, for example, they should perform it without regretting not having time for reading. If, again, they have a friend that needs support, they should not think about the fun they might be missing out on. If an action is not performed with a positive disposition, the energies of the soul will not find a way out to express themselves, thus creating forms of resistance, and illness often follows; an illness which starts out by inhibitions, preferences and repressions regarding a reality which surrounds us as is, whether we want it or not. Is it not simpler to accept the need, to respond to it, and then perhaps to find the freedom to do what we desire? Then the gratification is double, as we will not be tormented by the idea of having left something unaccounted for.

The inhibition of the soul's energy flow has as its basis human self-centeredness. Behind all resistance lies the individual 'I want' which presents itself as fear, rage, hurt pride, sorrow, weakness and as a thousand other patterns and forms. But always hidden deep down inside is the human need to hold on to something for oneself, to insist on acquiring things which are impossible to have.

This withholding gives rise to overcharging, the soul grows restricted, humans become the victims of themselves, and, eventually, they fall ill.

The role of spiritual healing is the dissolution of the powers withheld within the human body. The points which have accumulated large amounts of energy must be discharged, so that a natural flow can be equally restored everywhere, invigorating the weakened parts of the organism. The spiritual healers work on this through the knowledge they have acquired on the human being's energy problems. They help their patients balance the powers within them, so as not to function only with the mind, ignoring their bodily needs, or only with their emotions, without any mental supervision of their functions. All these things can happen, and are often achieved by the healing work alone, but success is more substantial if the patients participate in it of their own free will. An illness which has as its cause a psychological problem is at once overcome when this problem ceases to exist. The more humanity advances towards this understanding, always with the help of medical science, the greater the probabilities are of reducing diseases.

The Society's healing section attempts, circumstances permitting, to have personal contact with the patients. During this contact the deeper cause of their illnesses and the way which will help them to overcome it, is suggested to them. It is not always easy to come to an understanding of the problem, particularly when patients resist the revelation of an unpleasant truth about themselves. Often, even if they understand what is happening, they lack the will to change their attitude towards something which has become a permanent way of life.

I will mention a case which illustrates the direct relation between illness and psychological state, as well as the difficulty in overcoming its deeper cause. This is the case of Ms. L, who visited us in early 1986. She was then approaching 50 years of age, and had been suffering from back pains for some 25 years. She told me that she had felt this pain for the first time when she was told by the doctor that her mother was gravely ill. She had been so scared at that moment that she felt as if she was being stabbed and her body was being 'severed' at the waist. After that, the pains periodically recurred whenever something unpleasant happened, until they eventually became permanent, progressively growing worse. In 1985, she had an operation on her vertebrae with complete success. But after only a few days, the pains returned with an accompanying effect on her legs. Apart from this problem, she also had frequent cardiac irritations as well as a dysfunctional thyroid.

Conversations with her brought out a great fear she had which preceded the episode with her mother. This fear had begun with the relationship she had with her father, who was excessively strict during her childhood. It went on to extend to all men, and to all life's activities in general. Unfortunately, when she got married, this fear actually intensified instead of diminishing with married life.

Ms. L did not dare express herself freely, but always forced herself to be correct, fearing people's criticism, and that lead to a constant constriction in the whole of her body. This is what gradually caused her permanent condition, since her powers remained restricted and could find no channel to externalise themselves. The operation had been successful, but the pains continued, because Ms. L continued to be afraid and to oppress herself, placing restrictions on her every expression.

When she came to the Society seeking help, she was in unbearable pain. She supported herself with a walking-stick, because the soles of her feet and her toes felt as though they were on fire, as if they were being 'pulled out by the roots', as she told me herself. The pain started out from the left hip, next to the point in the spinal column where she had been operated on.

I could see that she was aware of her problem, to a certain extent, while we were talking about it before the healing began. She had realised that she was afraid to express herself, but she did not suspect that it was this attitude that had caused her illness. I considered this conversation essential, as I saw that it would be difficult for a healing to help Ms. L if she did not decide on her own to change and begin to express herself more.

The healing soon began, and lasted about 20 minutes. I put my hand on her hip, where the pain was located and I told her to tell me what she felt. After a little while she felt a slight relief, as the soul's energy penetrated her like a warm radiance. This warmth gradually descended to her legs and the pain began to lessen. I realised that the healing was nearing its end when Ms. L told me that she was in no pain at all, and that her soles, her toes, as well as her hip felt perfectly fine.

I asked her to get up and try to walk. She was astonished by the result. She could move about without the walking-stick, as if she had never been ill. Soon after, she left the Society and, as I was told, remained completely well for two days. But later something happened with her husband which greatly upset her, and the pain started again. The healing section then carried out a distance healing and Ms. L again felt relief.

She visited me a second time, after two weeks. She told me that while she had been well for a short while, the pains had then started again. It was established that the times when she was well coincided with the times when she was receiving a healing. She then reverted to her familiar phobia, which caused a fresh relapse, which was related not only with her husband, but arose from any event which forced her to suppress herself, depriving her of the courage to express her will.

I treated her again, with the same spectacular results as on the previous occasion. I also showed her how to relax on her own and break down her fear. But above all I talked to her about her problem, so that a greater understanding would come about. The healing section continues to work for Ms. L, in the hope that her state of wellness will be stabilised and the cause of her pain counteracted.

This case shows that a powerful cause, such as fear, hinders a patient's healing, because it continues to create the same energy charges, constantly causing the illness. This does not mean, of course, that these conditions cannot be helped by spiritual healing. On the contrary, an improvement appears which gradually becomes stabilised, provided the healing continues. This is because with their work, the healers give the patients equilibrium and a new flow to their soul's energy. This alone can gradually bring their total healing, as the energy begins to spread in their body, evenly energising it.

This steady work can also consciously reduce the cause of the illness making the patients eventually change their attitude towards life and be delivered from their mental problem; they are relieved, that is, of their negative attitude, their hate, their anxiety and all other unpleasant emotions and regain their balance and their power, which will give them back their health, externalising their soul through their whole being, freely and dynamically.

# ILLNESS:
# A UNIVERSAL PHENOMENON

> *"... disease has its roots in the past*
> *(a group past or an individual past)*
> *and may, in the last analysis,*
> *be a beneficent way of paying off*
> *ancient debts".*
>
> **Alice A. Bailey**\*

A young girl who was a member of the Society, called me one day, deeply distressed. She told me: "Four years ago, my father died. Now my mother is ill and is in danger. I'm afraid she won't live. This is unfair, so unfair".

The girl's suffering was, of course, very natural. She was about to lose her mother as well and be left on her own in life. In her sorrow, she saw this event as an injustice and couldn't accept a reality which it wasn't in her power to alter. Her mother was in a very advanced stage of cancer and nothing could help her.

---
\*Bailey, A., 'Esoteric Healing', London: Lucis Trust 1953.

SPIRITUAL HEALING

The only consolation for this young woman was something she had noticed in her mother as she was looking after her. She saw a change in her soul which was apparent to all who talked to her. She had calmed, becoming a better person, in spite of all her pain. Our healing section regularly helped her, not so much in order to cure her as to provide her with an inner peace. This happened daily, with the patient showing an incredible spiritual development.

As I talked to the daughter, I reminded her of this fact and tried to help calm her. It is, of course, no easy matter to accept the death of a loved one. It isn't easy to accept pain and illness, especially when they attack someone whose sufferings don't seem to be in any way one's own fault.

At the beginning of my discipleship, I remember studying illnesses and their psychological causes, and seeing that these causes often did not exist, or, at least, did not seem to exist. At the time I too felt the same sense of injustice as the girl with the sick mother. Isn't it unjust that a baby should be born sick and die within a few hours? Isn't it also unjust that there should be an epidemic which sweeps away a whole host of humanity, the good and bad alike, the strong and the weak? These thoughts arise in all human beings at one time or another. Faced with this injustice, as they describe it, they feel completely helpless, as if there is nothing they can do.

We might accept that a person should suffer the consequences of one's mistakes, but we cannot say the same of someone who falls ill without being in any way at fault. What do those suffering from a hereditary condition actually gain? The question of 'why?' arises in the human mind when faced with these inexplicable phenomena, often going to such extremes as to hate life and the One who created it, God himself.

The Master teaches union with God, not separateness. He teaches the acceptance of events, of situations – even of pain. He says that it is only when this acceptance comes that humans will be able to act appropriately in order to improve their negative conditions, within, of course, the limits of their capabilities. I have heard these words numerous times, in a variety of ways and with specific examples. It was a while, however, before I was able to reconcile myself with this reality, not, of course, in a passive way, but by working dynamically.

One day, a speaker made a significant remark during a lecture, which I believe explains to a large degree the existence of illness and pain, as well as their opposite states, health and joy. He was interpreting and justifying the causes of an illness which had not been caused by the patient's resistance or weakness of soul. His words were very brief and to the point. He said: "It is time we realised that there is no 'human', only humankind". Perhaps these words did not have the same effect on the rest of the audience as they did on me. Maybe the time had come for me to accept their meaning and delve into it, comparing it to the teachings I had already received.

By seeing humanity as a whole, we are able to discern the place of each person within it. Each individual, we could say, is a cell within humanity, just like the body's cells within the human organism. If we study humankind from the time it made its first appearance on earth up until now, we shall see the correlation of the past with the present, and, naturally, the future can to some extent be foreseen. There is a direct dependence between all human beings and the time-space which they live in. No one is separated from anyone else, because everything that has previously happened has left its traces on the present-day human.

Science has concerned itself with the human race throughout its known progress as Earth's inhabitant. Historians, sociologists, psychologists, biologists, doctors, all study the human existence from every scope. Their studies frequently show a collective evolution with the respective positive and negative aspects. They tell us of periods of physical well-being and, at other times, of outbreaks of illnesses. They note periods of intellectual progress, but also of decline, involving large groups of people, or even the whole of humanity. All this shows a shared path in the evolution of the species, with the exception, of course, of rare cases concerning small social groups, cut off from the whole.

It is through such collective progression that each person is subject to the influence of others, sharing in the positive and negative stimuli. One is subject to the group way of life and functioning, not only as a social being, but also as a biological one. Each of us carries within our cells what previous generations have deposited there, as proven by scientific studies of DNA. All of us also carry along experiences and memories of the past in our consciousness, even if we are not aware of it.

We could further elaborate on the quest for the causes of an illness. To be more accurate, we should include in our study the whole of our planet's evolution and see that the conditions on our planet have also undergone changes. The morphology of the terrain, the climate, the species of animals and plants, all differentiate through the ages. It all shows a gradual, ongoing change in the globe as a whole, which affects all of its inhabitants, including, of course, human beings.

Within such an overall framework, the illness of one person can be explained as the result of various currents which leave their traces upon oneself. This is, naturally, how one's good health is explained, since it is again the function of all phenomena of our planet and of humankind as a species. This global approach helps somewhat in the acceptance of unpleasant situations, even though it does nothing to reduce the pain of the sufferer and of his or her relatives. No matter how much we want to believe that 'what there is, is only humankind', it is not easy staying apathetic and indifferent when illness comes knocking at our door.

Reality, however, does not change. Resistance and the denial of truth is pointless. On the contrary, they only intensify the problem, aggravating the pain and giving rise to new psychosomatic illnesses. Instead of this approach, the human intellect needs to be further developed. Each of us, as part of the whole that is still paying for its mistakes, must work on reducing all negative situations.

Years ago I met a lady who had a child suffering from cerebral palsy. Her attitude was admirable. She had completely accepted it and had given her soul to helping her child. She behaved towards him with complete calm, just as she did to her other children; she made no distinctions, nor did she appear to feel sorry for him or to regard him as an unbearable burden. She had resolved to do whatever she could to reduce his disability. She studied, she consulted doctors and paid particular attention to the child's physiotherapy. But her prime concern was her child's good psychological health. Her approach brought substantial results, as the child grew up learning to be self-mobile, to do his school work, to care for himself. He became an independent person, above all psychologically, and this he owed to his mother's positive attitude. Unfortunately, this example is not the rule. Similar cases are faced with anguish and sorrow which, naturally, have a negative impact, not only on the patients, but on their whole family environment.

The more humans accept the fact that they are not only separate individuals, but form an infinitesimal part of a greater whole, the more they will accept the consequences of the mistakes of the past. I do not believe that there is anyone who can say that they have not suffered pain in their life. Some have known illness, others abandonment, others poverty. But all of us have likewise experienced pleasant situations, with the possible exception, of a very few, particularly burdened, cases. When we learn to accept the good and the bad alike, then the bad will be lessened and our course will change. As long as we insist on desiring only what we like, then the things which we thrust away will only come back to us with even more menace. We are not reducing the unpleasant situation, we are intensifying it, thus also intensifying the pain which it causes.

This approach to life, as members of humanity down the ages, interprets the shared problem of illnesses beyond their individual causes. But what are the causes which make humanity suffer? These are none other than the individual ones as described in the previous chapter.

People as a whole function like each individual for oneself. They have the same selfish needs and demands. The way these are expressed depends upon the period and the particular society; differently, of course, to a certain degree, but alike as to their common nature. Whether we speak at times of an outburst in criminality, at other times about periods of orgies, and of today as a consumer society, it is the same thing. Everything points to human passions, to hate, to selfishness. The mistakes were and still are shared by all. People are in the habit of saying that everything is society's fault, forgetting that they themselves are members of this society. So, as its members, we are subject to the consequences of its mistakes. Mistakes passed on from generation to generation, setting their mark on the new descendants.

An illness is inherited from grandfather to father to son. A passion leaves its consequences on the ensuing generations. When the quarrelling between man and woman, with its associated negative manifestations, first made its appearance, it did not quickly subside. It extended from generation to generation, because it was not only a matter of two people, it was a harsh war between the two sexes, spreading to all of society's individuals. This war, together with its moments of truce, was handed down from parents to children and still exists within the majority of couples, even if it is not always fierce or conscious.

The evaluation of humans depending on financial status or social position has not ceased to exist, even if great efforts are made today in this direction. The appropriation of wealth by those who possess it still continues as it once did. In the past, physical strength and intelligence were means for the exploitation and oppression of others. But doesn't the very same thing happen frequently even today?

Past generations have left their traces with their actions. They formed children with passions and weaknesses which were often manifested through illnesses. And they in turn did the same thing to their own children. Let each of us search within our self to see whether perhaps we are continuing this mistaken tradition, giving exactly the same features to our descendants.

We pay for the mistakes of the past as its collective and panhuman continuation. This is inevitable, and, if there is something that each of us can do, it is to see how we can stop this reverse flow. How to make sure that the coming generations will have a better fate for the common good, not only for our own children and grandchildren, but for the whole. Because a healthy society will take care of every family as well as each separate individual within it. For as long as this change does not come, conditions will remain unpleasant, or will only fractionally improve. There are people who say: "My family and I are fine..." They ignore the others around them, who are probably also doing the same. When this indifference is common, then it will eventually vent, with someone suffering the consequences. And this 'someone' might be any member of humanity, which was and still is on the wrong road, a road of egoism and selfishness. It seems that knowledge comes through suffering, and love is developed through conflict.

Spiritual healers work on all cases of illness, whether these have arisen through an individual dysfunction or are consequences of the general state of humankind on a patient. When I studied Harry Edwards' book\*\*, I saw a huge variety in his healings. His healing power was great and his work continued for many years. In his healings' files, there are cases of almost every pathological condition. Three of these have to do with the content of this chapter, and in all three Harry Edwards' help was significant.

In the first case, he tells of a baby that had been considered incurable by the doctors, who could not find any hereditary factors in its illness, nor could they find any method of therapy, stating that death was soon to follow. At this point Harry Edwards was summoned, who proceeded to cure the child with spiritual healing, thus saving it from death. The second case involves the healing of a hereditary illness which was passed on to the

---

\*\*Edwards, H., "Spirit Healing", The Harry Edwards Spiritual Healing Sanctuary Trust, Surrey: Burrows Lea 1960.

patient by his ancestors. Medicine was also unable to do anything in this case as well.

The third case mentioned in his book concerns an influenza epidemic with many fatalities. A school principal sought the healer's help in preventing the children from contracting influenza. Harry Edwards worked to protect the school's children, resulting in very few cases, compared to other schools which were heavily afflicted by the epidemic.

The intervention of spiritual healing is confined not only to those who have an individual difficulty or a psychological resistance. It helps all those who are sick, if, of course, it is God's will. It redeems them from the pain and the illness which is the consequence of humankind's past errors. It relieves them from the effects of the errors – both individual and collective. And so the person healed is given a fresh opportunity to live creatively and to avoid the same mistakes that caused the illness. These mistakes are based on ignorance, fear and the lack of faith in God and in the union with His will. When people see the abilities of healing and recognise the power that has healed them, then they acquire a new knowledge, their fear is diminished, and they feel united with the Divine. They can then continue their life in good health, not only physically, but, above all, mentally.

Illness is not an injustice, as it is frequently labeled. Life and death, health and sickness are simply the opposite sides of a reality. One comes and the other one goes, in a constant cycle of alternations. The existence of all Creation as we know it, is based on the dissolution of certain forms and the synthesis of others. If there is illness within this progression, it is unavoidable, at least in the present state of our development. A calmer and more comprehensive approach to things will bring improvement, will reduce illness and will bestow better health. Spiritual healers work for this, in the faith that humankind will gradually move forward, giving expression to a more dynamic and healthier aspect of itself. If the power of the soul is expressed more with love and knowledge, then resistances will be abated and a new world, a better society, with fewer diseases, will be created.

# THE HUMAN BEING AND ITS BODY

I had for many years ceased paying particular attention to my body. I obviously took care of it, as much as was necessary, but I did not feel as if it was anything special, important, or annoying. I seemed to be indifferent about it, about its beauty or its ugliness. I had already completed a large cycle of life, I had been married and had given birth three times. My purpose in one field had been fulfilled. I certainly always enjoyed the sun and the sea and I always resented having any kind of pain, but that was where my dealings with my material form ended.

When I began serving my discipleship, this indifferent part of my self was suddenly invigorated, while several of my adolescent thoughts were also revived. I remembered again certain features of my physical form that were not beautiful, whereas others met the criteria of beauty to a greater degree. I discovered, moreover, that I restrained from making movements which would have revealed my less attractive areas. I was surprised by this fact, because I had not imagined that the attractiveness or not of any part of my body or any of my face's features would still be important to me.

This was one of the innumerable realisations which occurred to me in the six years of my discipleship. The aim of such a discipleship is to shape individuals that are as consciously aware as they possibly can; to see and to observe themselves, and, in doing so, getting to know themselves better. This knowledge covers all aspects of their existence, starting out from the body itself and going on to the emotions, to the thoughts and to their entire behaviour in general. Self-knowledge comes with constant self-observation in every manifestation. It helps in the revelation of the hidden features of human existence; it is only if these are revealed that the improvement of humans and the evolution of the soul can come about.

While observing myself, I began in parallel to observe others around me. I made comparisons and, through having first learnt to study my own personal forms of expression, I was able to study their manifestations with greater ease. A moment came when self-observation revealed to me that the inhibitions I had concerning my body greatly influenced the externalisation of my feelings and ideas. In this way I was restricting my freedom and my movements were losing their harmony. I wrote on 22.7.80:

> *"Yesterday I noticed the movements of a disciple. Her ease and the suppleness of her body seemed to fill the room with harmony. My own stance was entirely different. I was rigid, ungainly. I find it impossible to imagine myself moving even a hand in a way as harmonious as she moves the whole of her body..."*

Her ease came from her reconciliation with her figure, whereas I was still in conflict with the parts of my body that were not beautiful. From these observations I realised that my entire life had been affected by my appearance. This is in fact true of most people. Generally speaking, all of us attach a certain importance to our body, even if we think it is indifferent to us. I validated this on numerous occasions, when I later began passing on the teachings at the self-study groups. These people, while observing their behaviour, discovered repressed ideas about their bodily configuration and realised how much they had been influenced by the parts of their form that displeased them.

Sometimes the difficulty in accepting the body reaches extreme forms of expression. I can remember the case of Ms. X, who was of a very short stature. She told me that she did not wish to concern herself with her body at all, because she considered it inferior to other things which she described as superior and spiritual. She reached the point of not wanting to eat properly, or to sleep well, or even to make love. She felt repulsion for all bodily functions, as well as for all tasks which required manual work, such as her household chores. This attitude had, naturally, given rise to an acute problem within her family. Contact with her husband caused her displeasure, and so did her household tasks, which were performed with complaints and annoyance.

The state of Ms. X had brought about unwelcome effects on her health. She suffered from colitis and had troubles with her heart and her spleen. Nothing could persuade her to change her attitude towards her body. Her constant suffering eventually forced her to deal with her health, as it was leaving her no time to do the things that she desired. If she had functioned differently, her body would have found its equilibrium and she could have had free time for other matters which interested her. This repulsion for her bodily form concealed a deep unconscious desire. People who want something which doesn't exist on their form often fabricate a false indifference towards it, thinking that they do not desire anything. Naturally, this hidden desire causes major inhibitions, forcing the individual to lose the simple flow in the needs and enjoyments of life.

Other people adopt a completely different attitude towards their body when they don't like it. They try to correct it by having plastic surgeries, doing special gymnastic exercises, or following strict diets. All these things again conceal an excessive reaction and show that these people are slaves to their external appearance. I remember one gentleman telling me about his wife's problem. She had undergone plastic surgery on her nose, but afterwards, as the result did not please her, she was seized with melancholy, often getting emotional. The truth was that her nose was not ugly, neither before the surgery nor after it. But she was obsessed with it and suffered needlessly, simply because of placing such emphasis on her body.

What is the body after all? It certainly isn't the sole part of our self. It is, however, inseparable from us; it is the tool for expressing ourselves and for communicating with others. If humans repel their bodily form, it is because they know its needs, its corruptibility and the pain which it often causes. They are in opposition to the physical part of their being, since they obtain no security from it. So they demand that their body should supply them with at least the satisfaction of beauty. But this is not always possible. There are things which cannot change, such as the colour of the skin, for example, or the size of the eyes or the shape of the mouth (with the exception, of course, of rare cases of jaw surgery).

Through internally studying my body with the meditation techniques which I had been taught, I saw that it is a superb organism, regardless of its external appearance. Although I had little knowledge of the human body, nevertheless my own discoveries on its functions astonished me. I acquired a complete image of this mechanical and electro-biochemical masterpiece, as I delved into myself and into others, in order to get to know it better. This acquaintance reduced my reservations as to my appearance, which I increasingly accepted, thus gaining a greater ease in all my activities.

The human form is certainly not perfect. It has many weaknesses, is subject to deterioration, falls ill, and, ultimately, dies. Neither is its external appearance faultless, if, of course, we consider only what is beautiful to be perfect. But perfection is something relative, and in the whole of Creation nothing is perfect, according to human conceptions and desires. Around us there is ugliness, death, decay, illness. Could it be that in the end perfection should be looked for elsewhere? Could it be that only with the existence of these contradictions can the whole perfect creation be constructed?

The Master says that nothing is a matter of chance. He teaches us to recognise a purpose in everything; to look for the deeper cause of things and not to restrict ourselves only to their external appearance. Humans are bound by their appearance and forget to utilise it for their life. Ugly people have lived and died in pain over their ugliness. But others have transcended it; they have evolved spiritually, and their ugliness has been forgotten not only by themselves but also by their friends, because their spiritual evolution has been much more substantial than their physical form. Even physically disabled people have managed to overcome their problem and become sociable individuals, active and creative.

The reason why some people are born short in stature while others are tall, why some have a big nose, an ugly mouth or superb skin is relative to the whole course of their soul. Through their particular form they undergo a learning process which sometimes teaches them something, while other times it becomes an obstacle. But what is this learning process? Naturally, none other than the acceptance of reality and the dynamic expression through everything. Because whatever we are, whatever our physical condition is, we must not forget that this is the will of God. Only when people unite themselves with the Divine Will, will they discover true beauty and expresses it through their body, however it may be fashioned.

The Master says that no body is perfect. Even evolved beings – saints and adepts – had imperfect bodies which at some stage followed the laws of corruptibility. But for them there was no difference between perfection and imperfection, and for that reason their actions were miraculous. The miracle is expressed through equal acceptance of everything. When people arrive at this point of evolution, they feel free within their body because they are sanctified, becoming one with God.

Often in our contact with people the problem of rejection of their physical form becomes apparent: rejection and a strong desire to be in some way different. We work with such people in two ways. First, we help them with spiritual healing, in order to eliminate the symptoms of their illness, while, at the same time, we attempt to show them their errors regarding their body. The results are, of course, much more positive when there is a response in both these areas of work.

Spiritual healing of the illness is what a spiritual healer does for the patient. But the healing of the soul is an inner changing of people. This is of primary importance and it is the only constant for the evolution of the individual and of humanity. If patients recover from their condition and change their approach to life, it is most likely that another illness will not make its appearance. The reason, as we have said, is that illnesses arise from the suppression of the soul's life within the body, suppression which is caused when there is resistance, ignorance or fear.

There are also certain physical imperfections which are confined not only to the external appearance, to beauty or to ugliness. They are genuine disabilities, which are sometimes congenital or sometimes make their appearance later, during the course of human life. These disabilities, such as, for example, deafness or blindness, have their basis yet again in a certain error, individual or collective, as we have explained in the preceding chapters.

This error is the resistance which is put up against a general acceptance of the material world's difficulties. It is, in other words, the difficulty in uniting the human soul with the physical form. The energies of the human soul seem to resist seeing the world in its full range, to listen to it, to taste it. Thus, the soul is isolated from the world and a person is born with a disability which relieves the soul of unwelcome images, sounds, and the like. It is then limited to an inner vision or hearing, which does not oblige it to accept the world of matter, with its gross reverberations. This attitude of the soul is, of course, a negative one, in spite of the fact that its deep desire is isolation within the spirit's serenity. The world is the Creation as we see it around us. We cannot reject it because we find it tiring. We are called upon to accept it and to work on its improvement.

When spiritual healers realise that an illness arises from the disposition of the individual's soul itself, they can work to a certain degree in changing this mistaken attitude. But this intervention is as much as the soul agrees to receive. They cannot go beyond these bounds and intervene with the other person's free will. They work for the patient, but they know that the decision is a matter of the soul, and only with its help can the disability be healed. With its help and, of course, by the will of God, which the healer invokes for the patient.

## SOUL AND BODY

"I don't know what suddenly happened to me. Without my realising it, my eyes closed on their own and it seemed to me that they turned inwards into my body, looking at my organs. I clearly saw my spinal column and, in particular, the area that had been causing me pain and you were healing at the time."

These words were spoken to me by an astonished Ms. B on the first day that she came to the Society seeking help. I asked her to tell me exactly what she had felt and what she had perceived on her spinal column. "To begin with, I did not see, I merely felt a power passing through me as you were holding my hand. This power flooded me, entering the whole of my body. Then, involuntarily, I began observing what was happening and feeling that this power was also my own. When it stopped at the coccyx, which had been causing me great pain, I began seeing its every detail. You, I and the point which was in pain became as one. I know, I am certain that I have been made well".

Ms. B is one of those individuals who have a great facility for union. Without knowing what is happening or wishing in any way to understand why they can see inside their body, they are united to such a degree with it that they break through the barrier of form and acquire an awareness of its interior.

Her case was one of the most difficult, but also one of the most effective, regarding the healing provided to her. On the day when she visited me, she had pains in her coccyx and in her left leg. In order for her to walk, she was supported by two relatives holding her by her arms. She had been diagnosed with Hodgkin's disease for about a year before coming to the Society. She was at an advanced stage in which the swellings of the lymph glands had spread to numerous areas (spinal column, abdomen, groin). She had been operated upon twice and had been undergoing regular chemotherapy treatments, but the pains persisted, with the most recent located in the coccyx, where a new swelling was beginning to form.

Before I began the healing, we talked a little, in order to reveal the psychological cause of her illness. It was apparent from this conversation that Ms. B was a very dynamic person who always wanted things to turn out as they should and as she had planned them. But in order to achieve this, she constantly pressured herself and others and so lived in a continuous state of tension. This need for perfection was so binding upon her that her body became weary, eventually rebelling and falling ill. I told her that if she wanted to get well, she would have to alter her attitude towards life, to work without tension, and to simplify the everyday issues which caused her constant frictions.

Ms. B understood the problem and, most importantly, showed that she wanted by all means to be healed, believing in her power to achieve this. Indeed, as soon as I began the healing, she responded immediately, feeling the energy of the soul passing through her and uniting herself with it. The result was instantaneous. With the severe pains disappearing, she stood up and walked on her own as soon as we finished. A few days later, a blood test revealed that her white blood cell count had reached normal levels. Since then she has made excellent progress, with self-healing, as I had showed her, and with the healing section working on her behalf.

I mention this example mainly in order to show the potential existing within each of us to go beyond the external form of the body and to see its interior. This happens frequently at the Society's teaching groups, during the lessons on the physical body. Many people actually manage to see their internal organs without the slightest difficulty.

At the beginning of my discipleship, I was like Ms. B. I simply worked within forms, without concerning myself with how this unfamiliar work was taking place. Only later did I begin to deal on a more intellectual level with the issue. I began wondering what happens for humans to acquire this potential – or, rather, to 'become aware' of its existence. Because they do not acquire something new, but rather the moment comes when it is revealed to them.

I began studying this issue, because I wanted to grasp what happens, how it happens, and how the phenomenon is explained. A considerable length of time passed before I was convinced that certain things cannot be completely explained with a straightforward intellectual approach. The human mind has a need to interpret everything with concrete evidence, but there are other, wider powers over and beyond the familiar specific items of knowledge. Inner vision is one of these powers. It can be theoretically interpreted only up to a certain degree. We can say, for example, that the human mind, like a force, penetrates the body and takes a picture of it which is imprinted on the brain. But this is not enough, because beyond the mental function, a much more substantial realisation takes place. There is a 'conscious union' of the soul's energies which are within the body with the body itself. It is understood, therefore, that soul and form are unified, and the human brain, which is the mind's organ, acquires awareness of the body; awareness not only of its external configuration, which is perceived by the senses, but also of its inner parts. The soul's energies are manifested not only through the senses as we know them. They are much more complex and have a range much greater than that employed by humans.

Humans gain knowledge of themselves by observing not only their body but also the powers permeating it. Knowledge means awareness and awareness is a kind of vision. I see, that is, I know my self at all its points, both the physical and those of the soul. To the extent that I know something, I become one with it, and, consequently, I am not in ignorance of what I am. I am equally the whole of my body at all of its points, even those which are not apparent and are deep within my entrails. Once, a man appearing on a television program was asked how he could lift objects without raising them with his hands. He possessed the ability to overcome gravity, to move things without the usual known means. His reply was: "To lift a glass, I become one with the glass. How can I explain to you what that means? Only someone who is conscious of this unification can move objects, as he moves himself". I think that these words show that union is simply union and not merely an intellectual concept.

Some people are alarmed when they first discover inner vision and, they do not in fact want to work in further developing it. One of the Society's senior members had been taught meditation on the body by the Master. He had acquired many experiences in connection with it, but he later left us to deal with other things. Nevertheless, this knowledge had remained somewhere in his memory, even though he no longer utilised it.

One day he called to say that something strange was happening and he wanted to see the Master immediately, because he was afraid that he wasn't well. I was present at the meeting that took place and I heard the facts. He told us that one day when he was with friends, he suddenly stopped seeing their forms and saw only their internal organs. The skeleton, the muscular system, the intestines, the blood: everything was clearly visible in front of him. This frightened him as he thought that he was hallucinating. When the phenomenon was repeated several times, he remembered that the Master would be able to help him.

Indeed, the Master immediately calmed him down. He told him that what was happening to him was the result of the meditation which he had been previously taught. Although he had not continued his discipleship, nevertheless the knowledge was still within him and at some point it was revealed to him again. He also told him that this faculty, which had been manifested so clearly, showed that he possessed what was required to become a spiritual healer whenever he wished. The young man was reassured, accepted what was happening to him and saw it in a calmer manner. He continued seeing the interiors of bodies at times, but he no longer let the issue charge him as he now understood why it happened.

The obstacles to the development of inner vision are purely intellectual. The human reason interferes and interrupts this awareness, because reason is based on the specific field of existence. It is difficult to accept the corresponding energy field, which nevertheless exists and is in fact life and its flow. In any event, it has been demonstrated that even an object of the densest matter is a form of energy. The only difference between things and life's phenomena is their density. Energies such as heat, light, electricity, or even human emotions and thoughts have very widely-spaced molecules of energy. By way of contrast, the molecules in material objects are much denser. However, they are all fundamentally the same: an energy with a material nature which is either sparser or denser. Since they are the same thing, they are in essence united, and someone who can see the interior of objects can be aware of this union.

SPIRITUAL HEALING

Spiritual healers must possess this knowledge in order to help their patients. A union develops between the two before they can work successfully. They perceive where the patients are unwell and channel the energy of the soul to them, healing them and breaking down their illness. Healing is based on a proper functioning of the energies in the body and on the dissipation of the retentions which are perceived by the healers' inner vision. Energy and body are one, just as every form is one with the energy permeating it.

Before concluding this chapter, I wish to point out one more ability which does not only concern the body but extends to all objects. At the beginning of my discipleship I was told that people can see any object, can get to know its internal molecular structure simply by uniting themselves with it. This seemed a little strange to me, until I, too, had a personal experience which validated this truth to me.

On the previous day, the Master had been telling me about the diffusion of the soul's energies outside the body, in the world around us. He had said that humans must spread their energies, must unite themselves with others, sharing their love, thoughts and interests. This lesson was among the first which I received and took place before I had even completed the first month of my discipleship. It seems that it made an impression on me, because I woke up early and began meditating on this subject. When I finished the meditation, I was very peaceful, as I write in my journal on 23.7.80:

> *"I woke up very early and got up to drink my coffee in the kitchen. The others were still asleep and there was absolute quiet in the house. I had just finished my meditation and felt very serene. On the table where I was resting my hand were the coffee-cup and a sugar-bowl. Suddenly, as I was looking at them, without paying any particular attention, something remarkable happened. I clearly saw the molecules of matter under my skin... I gazed in astonishment when the cup also disappeared, to become molecules. Then the same thing happened with the sugar-bowl, the table, the wall. Everything lost its form and became molecules, spreading and uniting in their different, separate forms. I couldn't believe my eyes! It was as though part of me, the molecules of my hand, had entered the other objects, while molecules of theirs had entered my body. Thus everything was united, everything constituted part of a whole. I felt a companionship, the disappearance of all loneliness. Since everything is within me and I am within everything, there is no separateness, no*

*isolation. This expansion enables me to know everything as I know myself. I can feel my fears fading. What should I be afraid of, if we are all one?"*

The realisation of oneness is gradually stabilised. In the everyday activities of life, humans are once again restricted, seemingly forgetting certain essential experiences. Even if healers have not yet reached a permanent level of this awareness, they are still united with their patients, while working for them, through the energy of the soul. This union alone provides the knowledge needed on the method of healing and transferring to the patients the power which they lack.

# THE ENERGY CENTRES

A few days after my first lesson in meditation, something strange happened to me. I felt as though an extraordinary force was entering my head, as if it wanted to shake me, to wake me out of some stupor. It was so noticeable and continuous that I was forced to observe it and to study its results on my brain. I wrote on 29.6.80:

> *"While I was meditating, I felt an unknown force penetrating my skull and working intensively within it. It forcefully surges deep into my brain, and appears to be changing something within. I have the feeling that an expansion is taking*

*place, such as would happen if a drill were working on a hard object. This has continued all day, and not only while I am in meditation. I wonder what is changing in my brain, what this expansion is and what it is needed for."*

I told the Master about this unprecedented experience and he said that it shouldn't worry me. It was simply a matter of certain processes taking place in the intellect centre, facilitating my awareness of the knowledge I was acquiring. As this process lasted for a number of days, I began feeling positively about this force, which I saw was helping me in a number of things.

A note I made on 2.7.80 shows something which changed perceptibly at that time:

*"I notice an enrichment of my vocabulary. It has at least doubled in size. Words which were known to me but buried long ago spring up now, finding their place in my discourse – particularly its written form".*

At the beginning of my discipleship, as I said in the previous chapter, I observed various phenomena without being able to immediately explain them. They called forth in me a magic, a surprise, as if I were faced with a new world, a world of energies and forces, previously unknown to me. An appreciable length of time passed before I managed to understand what was happening to me and what happened to people in general, even if they weren't noticing or paying any attention.

As to the force inside the brain, the explanation is simple. I had been working hard intellectually, as I was making a considerable effort to delve deeper into the new concepts which I was hearing about. The result was that I felt the energy in my head shaking the cells and energising them. Words which were seldom used and forgotten, now reappeared when I needed them, enabling me to express what I was learning. Many individuals in the Society have reported similar experiences, concerning an augmentation of their vocabulary, as they began to meditate.

Naturally, my observations were not confined only to myself and to what was going on in my brain. I soon noticed that the energy in my body displayed tensions at various points. I began looking into the subject of the human energy field, studying the relevant books which provided detailed facts. I will refer to a few of them here, as a necessary form of knowledge which is employed by spiritual healers.

The energy which flows through the human body descends from the head along the spinal column and branches off in every direction. In this way it structures a body identical to the physical one, called the energy or ethereal body. It creates a network of energies which could be compared to the nervous system. This network gives life to all the points as it activates them.

There are seven principal energy centres, which function from the top of the head down to the coccyx. Surrounding these are other, secondary centres, which branch off the energy in the body. As the energy of the soul passes through each centre, it causes its rotation. The purpose of this movement is to serve as a centrifugal force which will spread the vital energy everywhere. Although humans may not frequently be aware of its flow in the body, they nevertheless know what this causes in the various organs. They feel the skip of the heart, the sexual impulse in the genitals, a lump in the throat, and so on. No part of the organism will function if it is not activated by this vital force.

This brief description illustrates the importance of the energy centres. Through these centres, humans spread the energy of the soul within their body, thus remaining living beings with all their senses and instincts in operation. They develop their mind, experience emotions and learn how to love. A reduced supply of energy to any centre brings with it an imbalance to the organism, causing a weakness. Overcharging a centre, on the other hand, results in illness, while, naturally, the complete withdrawal of the power of the soul from the body leads to death.

# THE ENERGY CENTRES (CHAKRAS)

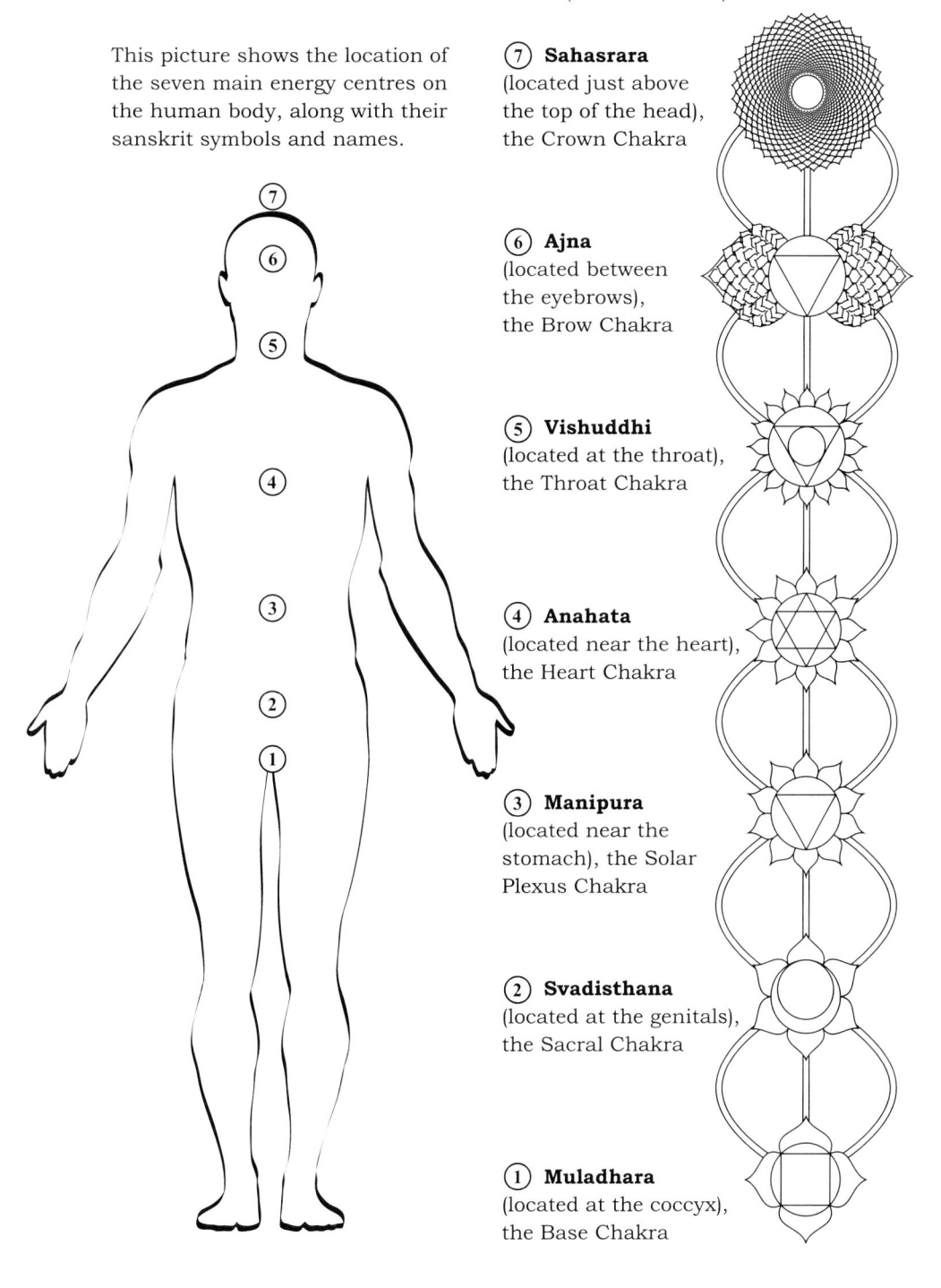

This picture shows the location of the seven main energy centres on the human body, along with their sanskrit symbols and names.

⑦ **Sahasrara** (located just above the top of the head), the Crown Chakra

⑥ **Ajna** (located between the eyebrows), the Brow Chakra

⑤ **Vishuddhi** (located at the throat), the Throat Chakra

④ **Anahata** (located near the heart), the Heart Chakra

③ **Manipura** (located near the stomach), the Solar Plexus Chakra

② **Svadisthana** (located at the genitals), the Sacral Chakra

① **Muladhara** (located at the coccyx), the Base Chakra

SPIRITUAL HEALING

The books that deal with the human energy body provide a large number of details. I do not consider it necessary for them to be mentioned here, as this is not the subject of this book. Nor is this knowledge all that essential in the recovery of balance and health. For example, if someone knows that one's illness is the result of hatred, he or she will not get well by attempting to activate the heart centre, in order to learn how to love. Love is developed by those who want to love and to sacrifice themselves for others, not by individuals who simply know about the functioning of their centres. Knowledge is a supplement to the decision and the position which is adopted towards life. It comes gradually as humans express themselves and implement their will for a dynamic life.

The Master does not place a strong emphasis on the knowledge of the centres. He mentions them when disciples need to understand what is happening to them and how they must work to overcome a difficulty. Instructions are only given in special cases, and always under his guidance. This is because it is dangerous for individuals to want to activate one of the seven centres on their own, particularly if they do not know how to use the power received from this work; a power which is not controlled by knowledge and love is often destructive for the person expressing it, as well as for all those to whom it is addressed.

## THE ENERGY CENTRES

Spiritual healers have to know how the centres function, because their work is carried out within their patients' energy body. Their knowledge, naturally, starts out from themselves, as they experience the flows of energy in their body. As they perform a healing and unite themselves with the patients, they come to understand their energy problem. They may work to give strength to their weak points or to dissipate the charge of others. There is no need for them to convey what they do as knowledge to the patients, unless they are individuals initiated into this matter.

What they can do, if given the opportunity, is to point out the result of the malfunctioning, according to the effects which it gives rise to. A constriction of the heart or a pain in the uterus can easily indicate a woman who is not expressing affection to her husband and is not gladly providing him with physical love. This explanation is much more helpful than any knowledge of her energy problem.

There is a frequently heard opinion about present-day humanity. It is said that there are now more psychological problems, more psychosomatic illnesses, greater tension and anxiety, greater demands for satisfaction. Observations and findings on this subject confirm that there is in fact a general upheaval which, like a powerful current, is flooding the world. Every current, of course, has its source; it starts out from humans themselves and spreads around them. Consequently, what is happening today must have a direct connection with the people's energies of the soul. It would seem that these should be channeled differently in order to achieve something which has not happened yet, and this is the reason for this tension.

There are two purposes served by the existence of the energy of the human soul. The first is the life which it gives to the body for it to develop and to be sustained. Its task is not confined only to the human organism, but it also develops human emotions, love and knowledge. When these are sufficiently developed, the second goal of the soul's energy comes into play: an expansion into the environment, the diffusion of the individual energy field in space.

If we wished to make a parallel between this function and the development of a child, we would see great similarities. The child needs to be well nourished for several years in every area of its being. It must receive the necessary food, knowledge, love and intellectual guidance from adults. It is called upon to give very little of what it receives, until the moment of a certain maturity arrives. Then the environment changes its attitude towards the young person and requires him or her to play an active part in life. This cusp is a difficult point, and there is often resistance on the part of adolescents, who still wish to be treated as if they are children.

Today, humankind in its entirety is at a similar turning point. Its development has reached a level where it must begin to externalise itself more and extend outwards towards others. We are referring to the spreading of the energies of the soul. The minor functions which have up to now met the needs are sufficient no more. The human-unit has spent enough time on his or her egoistic development as a personality and is called upon to move on to the function of the soul. This means that one can and must channel his or her energies into the surrounding space, and not keep them back for selfish reasons. Only when functioning in a giving manner, will the individual be relieved of illness and pain which are caused by the overcharging of the centres. The constant need to receive must also be accompanied by the expression of the need to give.

If illnesses have multiplied, if the problems have intensified, this is owing to the fact that the turning point has not yet been overtaken. To all appearances, things today are worse than in the past. In essence, however, they are at a more developed stage. We, as humankind, are engaged in a quest for a profound change. We have the restlessness of the adolescent and pre-adolescent age. We are called upon to reduce egocentrism, and this we find difficult. Naturally, there are always exceptions.

There are individuals who sacrifice themselves for the whole, who give their soul for an improvement of life's conditions. But these are rare instances and do not involve the majority, who still continue to appropriate life itself.

Gradually, through pain and problems, humans are being taught to lessen individual need and to function for the group, whichever one it is. Integration into a group effort dissolves retentions, and human centres begin to express the second purpose of their existence. They spread energy around them and in doing so dissolve all difficulties. The 'expansion of the human soul' takes place, which involves the individual's conscious union with others.

There is a dangerous point for those who are involved in a group effort when they are not sufficiently matured. It sometimes happens that egoistic characteristics are enhanced within a group; vast needs for self-promotion, quarrels, even what we call 'group spiritual egoism', are created. All these things, instead of helping humans, make life difficult for them, and often make them feel strong, as they receive the energy of the crowd surrounding them. Naturally, they do not then spread their souls' energy for the good of the whole, but, on the contrary, project a powerful personality, which imposes and oppresses. Classic examples of such cases are leaders of organisations or even of states who have succeeded in leading people astray into negative projects, precisely because they reversed their powers and those of their supporters and used them for personal ends – glory, wealth, selfishness.

At this point, I would like to mention those individuals who are endowed with some sort of special gift, a talent, if you want; artists, scholars, writers, poets, rulers of states, as well as those who have undertaken some public service. They all have in their hands power, a capacity for shaping the world. A teacher, a priest, a singer can, by a correct stance towards life, make an enormous contribution to humankind. They can, if they so wish, give themselves to it, extending their heart, working mentally for all those who consider them in some way their guides or inspirers. A work of art should uplift humans, should broaden them, should help them – and, why not? – should heal them. The same applies to everything I have said so far. Education in humankind is provided by certain individuals who have a special position. The more advanced they are spiritually, the more their task will be one of the soul's, helping others in need.

People undertaking a responsibility are called upon to forget their selves and to dedicate themselves to the world, which seeks their illumination. If they are indeed at such a level, then they will perform a task of the soul, a task which will also contribute to humankind's soul maturity, through the circle of people surrounding them and the particular matter which they deal with, through the field in which they have been trained. The greater the circle of responsibility, the greater the function of the soul must be. Leaders of a state, with the right aides around them, can work wonders for their country if they are devoted without self-centredness to the task which they have undertaken.

The expression of the soul in humans is rendered whole when they understand that all energies permeating them are in essence only one; the soul itself, the power of life which activates their centres, so that it can be spread throughout them in equal measure to the whole of their body and then around it. This power is renewed and increased only by its diffusion in the environment and not by holding it back in the individual ego. Because people who love others with their soul become united with them, in a way doubling their potential. And one who loves humanity, becomes ontologically vast, a conscious part of the group soul of all humans.

It could be said that today the majority of people are on the cusp of change. There is the individual 'I want' which insists on seeking satisfaction, on keeping the energies of the soul for the individual self. But there is also a collective awareness urging humans to acquire a group will and action. These two states give rise to major friction within the organism, since the energy centres are subject to two opposing wills. This is the reason why today so many psychosomatic symptoms have made their appearance.

There are the exceptions of people who, as we have said, have overcome the problem of this inner conflict and are at another stage of awareness maturity. For them, the matter of energy retention has closed. They function with the soul and, by virtue of their mental stance, vent their powers simply and dynamically wherever needed.

Finally, there are certain individuals still at a previous stage of evolution. For them, individual development is necessary. They do not have tensions and frequent illnesses, because, quite simply, they have not yet arrived at that point where their consciousness prompts them to expand. People describe them as insensitive or indifferent and often consider them fortunate in their serenity. In essence, these people are on another level of awareness which they express through their actions.

The seven energy centres and the secondary centres which surround them, the whole of the energy body, structure the soul; they are the soul itself. A soul which is small and limited is shut in its individual shell. A soul which is expanded is available to others. Its energies spread around the body forming a powerful radiance. Its purpose is to give love, knowledge and resolution to its surroundings. It does, however, have a second purpose, which operates autonomously. It constructs a kind of energy shield around humans, prohibiting negative currents from invading them and disturbing their balance. Thus their centres continue operating harmoniously without being easily susceptible to illnesses.

In order for individuals to serve as healers and for their healings to bring results, they must cultivate their love for others and, naturally, for the sick. The more this happens, the more successful their will work be. They will willingly integrate into the current of life, conveying it from their person to the world, without appropriating the soul's energy for themselves. Naturally, spiritual healing also has levels of evolution. The more united with the Spirit the healers become, the more united they will be with the miracle, giving expression to it, healing, diminishing illness, and providing balance and health around them.

## THE SPIRITUAL HEALER

Each and every individual can become a spiritual healer, this potential is within all of us. One day a lady, who was a disciple of the Master said: "I don't believe that I can manage it. I feel too small for such a great task". This opinion that she had of herself was preventing her from giving expression to a greater power. She had been limiting herself to only a small number of things in life and did not dare express other, 'greater', things, as she put it. The Master told her that 'small' and 'great' are merely ideas of the mind. If she considered herself united with the Power of God, then she would express this power, she would perform healings and she would help people. A person who ceases to look only at his or her small human self can become united with the great ontological Existence and perform miracles. This lady is now working successfully with the Society's healing section.

As I observed the Master performing healings, I studied the characteristics that a healer must have. Characteristics which, although exist as potentialities within us all, nevertheless do not manifest themselves without the proper will for it. The Master worked with power, love and faith in his task. He did not set time limits; he was in no hurry to finish the healing; he did not wish the sick person to get better – come what may. He was united with the Spiritual Power and it was this that he transferred to the patient, in the knowledge that what must happen will happen. He was totally dedicated to his work, while remaining detached from the result. Sometimes the healing took place immediately and sometimes it took a long time. Sometimes he had the patient's positive participation, whereas in other cases he was met with negative reactions. But none of this stopped his work, nor did it tire him, since his actions concealed no self-centredness.

It is the Master's example that those of us who have trained with him follow. This is not a discipleship primarily concerned with specific techniques. It is much more a teaching about the union which must be built up between healer and patient. A union which is fully achieved only when personal resistances have dissipated. The Master's healings sometimes left me astonished with their immediacy, whereas at other times they wearied me, as they seemed time-consuming. At the beginning of my discipleship, it bothered me that certain patients raised a thousand forms of resistance which had to be patiently worn down if there was to be any positive result. Nevertheless, he always remained the same and continued his work unflustered, no matter how many difficulties presented themselves.

One day he asked me to attend the healing of G, a young girl on whose breast some small lumps had appeared. Her doctor had told her that she had to be examined and that she would possibly have to undergo surgery. Naturally, this had frightened G; for her the thought of cancer and a possible mastectomy was unbearable. She sought the help of the Master, trusting and hoping that the lumps would be dissolved. Before the healing began, I placed my hand on her breast and confirmed their presence.

The Master began the spiritual healing by irradiating the area with his hand. He was deeply absorbed, and I would say that at that moment there was nothing else for him but the lumps which had to be dissolved. The girl sat motionless, receiving his help. Around half an hour had passed when she told us that she could feel a difference in her breast. After palpating it again I observed that the lumps really did feel softer and smaller.

The healing was continued the next day. This time it lasted longer, and when it was completed, the breast had no trace of lumps, appearing completely healthy! G, deeply moved, thanked the Master for his immediate help and the incredible result. He told her to visit her doctor and to establish that she was completely healed. He also advised her to continue preventive self-healing by practicing meditation every day. The girl did as he told her and brought us the good news of the doctor's reassurance that she was completely healthy and no operation would be necessary.

Cancer had always seemed a very difficult matter to me. At the start of my discipleship, I did not dare deal with such illnesses. Little by little, however, I became convinced that, according to human criteria, spiritual healing has no limitations. It can heal everything equally, if this is what is meant to be, if the patients are receptive to the radiance and the healers have faith and love in their work. It is then that they work freely, surrendering themselves to the union with the sick, conveying to them the power of the healing.

Alice Bailey, who wrote two volumes on 'Esoteric Healing'*, tells us that healers must work above all with love. They should not project any individual will, but should be united with the Will of the Being, of God. This Will is

---
*Bailey, A., 'Esoteric Healing', London: Lucis Trust 1953.

what brings about the healing, as the sick person is surrounded by love.

When I first began healing, I was in a hurry to see results, to hear that such-and-such patient had become well. This concealed a certain element of need for validation that often became an obstacle to healing. The power which comes to make someone well does not require any validation. When the healer understands this truth and functions in union with the healing Power, the positive results will come much more easily. No personal need will intervene in the carrying out of his or her work.

I can remember how much I was fatigued by the case of Mr. X. I had not dealt with him myself as I was still in the first stages of my discipleship. The Master had taken him on exclusively, while I simply attended his healings. Mr. X had a major stomach disorder, dizziness, dysphoria, and was in a very poor psychological disposition. His stomach troubles were so severe that he had to eat specially prepared food, which he was not even then able to digest. He received medications and was from time to time hospitalised for a few days, but without ever finding any lasting solution to his problem.

The discussion which the Master had with him made clear that the cause of his illness was a great dependence on his mother and a lack of communication with his wife. The healing he received was accompanied by the relevant analyses, which helped him to overcome his attachment

SPIRITUAL HEALING

to the one woman, improving his relations with the other. He was always well every time he left from the meetings, but each time the same symptoms quickly reappeared, and he would indeed often call to fearfully tell us that he felt terrible, as if he was suffocating or dying. The Master would then talk to him on the phone, in an effort to restore his equilibrium.

The healings lasted a long time, so long that I had become tired of hearing the same story over and over again. I was impatient to see other cases and not spend so much time on Mr. X. The Master seemed to have no sense of time or of the difficulties. He continued his work undaunted, for as long as he had to and whenever it was needed. Naturally, the obstacles came both from the patient's weakness as well as from his family environment, which was ignorant of how to support him. Improvement came little by little and some three months passed before he was finally healed. Eventually Mr. X was completely relieved of his problems and returned to his normal activities in his job, and as a husband and father. His health was restored because the Master did not regard the obstacles as insuperable, and steadily continued the healing.

The spiritual healers who operate in union with the healing Power do not fall ill or become exhausted as a result of contact with their patients. On the contrary, this

Power invigorates them, too. Naturally, a small degree of fatigue sometimes occurs, but only for a brief period of time. If they consider, however, that the task they are performing is their personal achievement, then exhaustion will overcome them and they will not be directly rejuvenated by their work. Such thoughts and personal interpolations always exist when human egoism continues to dominate, or even when it is not sufficiently curbed.

During a healing, the healers might happen to unite themselves so much with their patients' problems that they actually feel a disturbance within their own bodies, similar to that of the patients'. This lasts for a very short time and is quickly dissipated by the same energy of the soul which passes through them and is conveyed to the other person. What is important is this union to take place, the diagnosis to be achieved and the correct flow dissipating the retentions to be conveyed. Healing takes place in accordance with the healers' mentality and their development in this field. Some can clearly 'see' the patients' bodies, others can sense their energy problems, while others simply convey the power intuitively. It is not the method which is important, but the intention of the healers, for help to come, together with the faith that this healing power will be conveyed to the patients.

Healers are not special beings with heavenly powers. They are ordinary people who have come to understand certain things about the energies and powers of the soul, always in reference to God. They have accepted the spiritual power as real, and this acceptance has transformed them into channels of healing energy. It is said that in the course of humankind's evolution, illnesses will gradually diminish. Human beings will have become by then aware of things of which they are still ignorant and will be able to correctly handle the energies within their bodies. This will reduce humankind's debt, a debt of ignorance and fear. We all have the same potentialities within ourselves, and they are remarkable and considerably powerful. We can all become healers if we acknowledge our true essential nature. The apostles of Jesus performed miracles every day. Their presence next to sick people was sufficient for them to become completely well. Although we are still at some distance from that level, all of us can have it as an aspiration – to simply want to give expression to our divine nature, to the Power of the God who created us.

# METHODS AND TECHNIQUES OF SPIRITUAL HEALING

*"Experience has taught us that most illnesses start out, directly or indirectly, from the thinking or the inner state of the sick person. Thus, more important than any technique is the inner contact which we have with him."*

***Maria Charlet*** [*]

"How is it possible to carry out a healing on someone who isn't there with you, whom you can't see or touch?" This is a question I frequently get from people who seek help for someone who is ill, or who simply wish to find out how spiritual healing takes place. The question is entirely understandable. All other known methods of therapy always require contact between patient and healer. Even if, in rare instances, the patients cannot visit the doctor themselves, they still receive instructions through some intermediary as to their treatment or medications.

---

[*] Charlet, M., 'Shiatsu Philosophy and Practice', Athens: Pyrinos Kosmos 1980

## SPIRITUAL HEALING

Spiritual healing is not tied down to personal contact because it is not based exclusively on specific work which will be carried out on the patients in a certain way. It is carried out primarily through the energy body of the healers, who are united with the patients, thus channeling into their own energy body the powers of the soul. But because the soul's energy is not governed by the laws of form – it is not, that is to say, static and shaped into a particular pattern – the healers do not need to be with the patients. They can be united with them in terms of energy however far away they may be, at any time of the day. The energy of the soul is not confined within the body alone, but spreads out all around it.

The healers who know of the soul's potentialities allow by their will the soul's energies to flow towards the patients, uniting with them, wherever they are, and exerting their healing power. Just as a mother has her child in her soul and remains close to it even when it is travelling far from home, so the healers also follow their patients. The difference is that they have knowledge of this function and for this reason the union which they make with the patients is conscious and always has their healing as its purpose.

Strange as it may seem, it is a simple function of union. The energy body of the healer emerges from the physical body, sometimes entirely and sometimes in part, and goes to unite itself with the patient. Edgar Cayce, talking about his well known intuitive capacities, 'travels', as he tells us, to meet the patient, to make the diagnosis of his or her illness and to recommend the treatment with the necessary pharmaceuticals.

This method is called 'distance healing' and is frequently practiced, as it is not always easy for the patient to visit the healer. There is no qualitative difference between this method and 'contact healing'. The only difference is that if the patient is present, his or her participation in the healing may be sought, which means staying relaxed and receptive to the energy which is transferred from the healer. Nevertheless, the union's directness does not alter with distance, as has been proven on numerous occasions by the Society's group of healers.

One lady, for example, who was suffering from back pains, was always aware of the exact time we were healing her, because it was precisely at that time that the pains subsided. Other patients are not able to precisely determine what is happening to their body, because their illnesses might not cause any perceptible discomforts. But they tell us that at some specific moment (which again coincides with the time of the healing) they feel a certain wellness and well-being, which continues for many hours afterwards. Other patients wish to know exactly when our healing section works, so that they can participate and coordinate their soul with our work. They tell us that they have a better sense of the aid provided to them this way. Healers who have developed their inner vision can envisage their patients, perceiving exactly where they are and what they are doing when they unite themselves with them.

I place emphasis on the explanation of this phenomenon because I consider it necessary to understand that it too follows certain laws; laws that may not be based on material objects and facts, but 'laws' involving the world of the soul's energies. There is no mystery in this function. Its basis is the conscious guidance of the energies aiming to improve the patient's energy flow. When this initial union takes place, the healer works on the patient's energy body, exactly as he or she would do if they were standing next to each other.

One of the first patients whom we undertook to help was an elderly gentleman who had a chronic bronchial disorder. We never saw him, because it was difficult for him to leave his home, especially in winter. We began working daily on his case, as he was suffering considerably and could find no means of relief. After a week, his grandson, who had mediated on his behalf, told us that his grandfather was completely well and no longer in need of pharmaceutical help, according to his doctor. This was one of our first distance healings and, naturally, its success gave us great pleasure.

'Contact healing', as has been explained above, is easily understood. What happens in 'distance' healing happens here too. The union of the souls is again built up and the healers work to dissipate the illness and to restore the power of the affected points. They work with their hands, resting them on the patients, or keeping them at a small distance. Their work is carried out in the energy body of the patients, whose well-being is then conveyed to their physical body. Sometimes this happens immediately, in a matter of minutes, while other times a short period is required for the energy to pass to the point that is ill. I shall now mention two examples of contact healing.

The first concerns Ms. S, a member of the Society, who regularly attended a self-study group. She came one afternoon as usual to take part in the discussion, but appeared to have great difficulty in walking, while limping on her left leg. I asked her what was wrong and she told me that her knee had begun troubling her the previous day, so she went to the doctor, were she found out that fluid had accumulated in it. She had to stay in bed and see what the outcome of this issue would be.

As I saw that she was suffering, I thought of performing a contact healing, hoping that this would bring some relief. Our healing section had only recently been established and not many such cases had presented themselves. We mainly helped from a distance when people asked for our support. But Ms. S's pain prompted me to try out this method, as I had seen the Master so often do.

I sat down next to her, placing my hand on the knee which hurt, and began conveying the radiance to it. After a few minutes, Ms. S said that a quivering was passing through her leg from the knee down to the sole of her foot. I continued working and the feeling persisted, giving her the impression that the pain was disappearing into the floor, as if it was being earthed. At some point, I sensed that the fluid was no longer under my hand and so I asked Ms. S to walk, moving her knee. As soon as she got up, she realised that the pain was gone, she was no longer limping, and no discomfort remained. The next day, the doctor confirmed that the fluid was completely gone.

The second example was not so immediate. When I completed the contact healing, the patient felt no change in the state of her problem and it wasn't until the next morning that the positive results became apparent. In this case, the transfer of the healing force from the energy body to the physical body needed a few hours, as often happens in spiritual healing. This was the case of B, a chronic one. She had advanced gingivitis, and had constantly put off doing anything about it. When she went to the dentist, she had to undergo various painful procedures before seeing any significant improvement. In spite of this, the swelling in her gums was so bad that certain parts could not be cured, making their surgical removal unavoidable. The very thought of this greatly disturbed B, who had already been tormented for a number of months. Despite being an old member of the Society, she had not thought of seeking its help on her own. A friend of hers, who described to us the pain she had been going through every day, suggested it to her.

This girl proved to be an excellent receptor. When I placed my hand in front of her mouth, she immediately felt the energy penetrating her inflamed gums. I internally followed what was happening, and saw them 'shrinking' and returning to their normal state. As we were finishing, B said that she was impressed by what she had felt, but she was a little hesitant, because the swelling had not fully gone away. I advised her to continue the healing on her own, as she had been taught at the meditation group. The next day she was very excited when she came to see me. The inflammation was completely gone, and her gums were in their normal state, as they had been years before. The doctor, whom she soon visited, told her that there was no longer any reason for an operation. She was perfectly well!

I have provided these two examples to illustrate how a similar healing method brings results in a different way, depending on the condition, the patient and each problem's particular circumstances. The healing result is, however, always the same, regardless of the procedures, or even of the methods which are used for it.

Spiritual healers, notably those who are still at an initial stage, repeatedly look towards the Master for instructions and techniques. They seek to find out the way in which the work will be done, whether they should say certain words or imagine specialised formations which will help in the healing. The Master provides certain instructions and helps the learners with the necessary techniques. Beyond that, though, he says that what is important is that the union between healers and patients takes place, for the spiritual power to be conveyed. Within illness, the healers transfer its opposite, health, thus uniting the two opposites and breaking down the illness. All methods, such as 'contact' or 'distance' healings, are simply regimens, which are not all that important, when union has been achieved

Naturally, much can happen in the course of a healing. The healers might imagine, for example, that they are encompassing the patients with a light or a pleasing colour. They might also speak to them inwardly, telling them that they have no problems, that all will be well. These techniques change and adapt to the various cases, but in order for any result to be achieved, they must always take place through a stable energy linkage of the souls.

METHODS AND TECHNIQUES OF SPIRITUAL HEALING

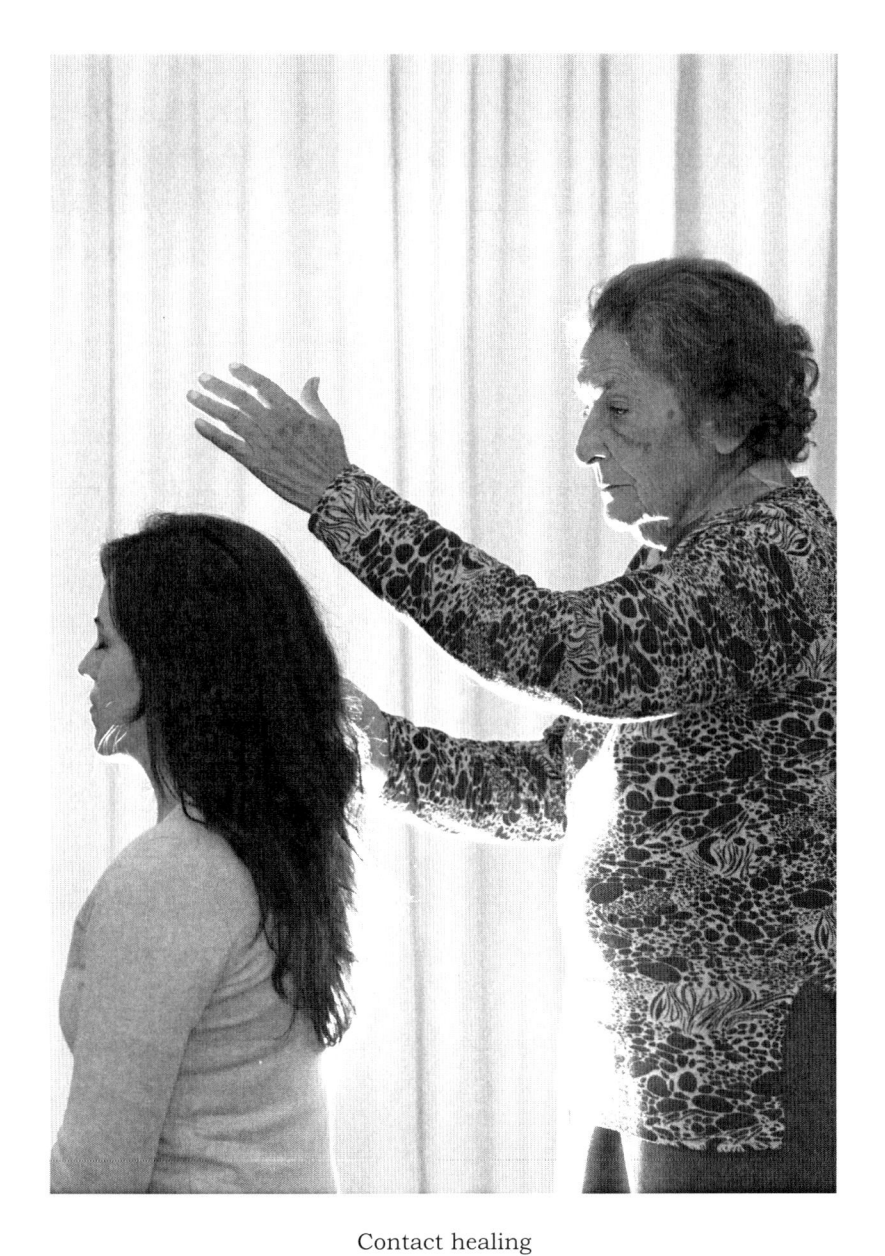

Contact healing

SPIRITUAL HEALING

The Master always recommends that we should cross-check what he tells us with teachings of other Masters or specialists in the various related subjects he teaches us. Three years ago, a Tibetan Lama, a healer, who had studied in a school for healers in his home country, visited Greece. Those who met him called him 'doctor', because of the many healings he had performed in Greece. He also used certain herbs which we, at present, do not possess the knowledge to employ. The Master suggested that I should visit him, if I wished, and obtain information on spiritual healing. I liked the idea, because I believe a comparison of information and knowledge is always helpful.

At our meeting, I told him about the Society's healing section, what it does and the level that our healings were at. I then asked him if he could pass on to me certain techniques so that we could work more systematically. His reply was as follows: "Since you pray and feel that you receive the healing power, then you can function freely, as you wish and as you feel. Union with the will and the love of God is enough. It will guide your actions, and will make you channels of the health which the patients need."

After this meeting, the fact that spiritual healing means UNION was validated within me. Methods and techniques can be used with ease if this union has been strengthened. The healers' intuition, their love and will to assist, guide them through the course that they follow. Healing comes as a result of the flow of the energies of the soul, directed by the power of the Spirit.

# THE HEALER
# AND THE SPIRITUAL FIELDS

In order for spiritual healing to take place, it is necessary for a pure power to pass through the patient and break down the illness. This power comes from a field where there is no illness, because there is no material form there to be subjected to it. It is a level of consciousness which is spiritual, amorphous, powerful. This power, this essence of life, is within every human being, even if it is not easily recognised, precisely because it does not have a specific shape. The spiritual healer, while working, becomes a channel of the spiritual power and conveys it to the patient, utilising the energies of the soul.

SPIRITUAL HEALING

The way in which healers achieve their union with the spiritual power is quite simple. They turn their own soul towards the Spirit and draw from It the power which they must give to the patient. The energies which exist within every form, every body, are given to it by the single source of life, the Spirit. When an illness makes its appearance, as a result of erroneous use of the soul's energies, the healers, having united themselves with the spiritual field, channel its power to the patients, thus restoring the correct flow of energy within their bodies.

Humans live and exist in the natural world by using its various sources of energy for their preservation. They breathe oxygen, are nourished by material food, receive stimuli through their senses. All these renew their organism and keep it alive. They all, however, have a common source, the Spirit itself, which shapes them and maintains their existence. It is not always necessary for a healing to be carried out by medicine, that is, by a source of energy from the material world, if there is an opportunity, and knowledge, for it to be achieved with the help of the energy source of all medicines, the pure spiritual power. Christ gave this power to the sick when He performed His miracles because He was at all times united with the Spirit of God. This is what healers also do, in a lesser field, as they consciously unite with their spiritual nature at the time of the healing.

## THE HEALER AND THE SPIRITUAL FIELDS

In order to facilitate the connection of spirit, body and soul, the spiritual healer invokes certain spiritual beings, requesting their help. This point must be clarified to the fullest, since the existence of certain 'unseen' entities often causes mixed reactions. Some people call them fantasies, others consider them non-existent, while some believe they are dangerous and are very much afraid of them. I remember one day, during my first year as a healer, I was trying to explain to a cousin of mine how I receive directions from spiritual guides in order to help the patients. While I was talking, I saw her expression change from upset to saddened. I asked her what was wrong and she replied: "I'm very worried about you; I'm afraid you may be harmed. Aren't you afraid that these things you see will harm you?" This reaction shows how deeply rooted in the human mind is anxiety over anything which extends beyond the limits of this world, as we have defined it.

Recently a gentleman came to the Society to meet two acquaintances of his, who were attending a self-study group. He asked to go into the room, since the discussion was reaching its end. As he entered, those present where giving an account of their experiences from the meditation they had just completed. The gentleman listened in silence and, after everyone had left, approached me and said: "The sights and experiences they were describing are totally incomprehensible to anyone coming here for the first time. It's as if you are talking about another world". His two acquaintances and I tried to explain the matter to him as best we could.

I mention these examples because I believe that the function of spiritual healing has been misinterpreted by many people. Fear, distrust and new, hitherto unknown, facts produce an opposition which, as long as it persists, does not allow the significance of this healing method to be understood, nor its help spread to the world. Indeed, when some people say that they heal with the assistance of the Virgin Mary or of a saint who guides them, they are often met with sarcasm. On other occasions, when someone happens to get well, they say it was merely a coincidence and he or she would have been cured in any case. Only the few who see the miracle in themselves or in those related to them are convinced of it. But here lies the danger of a personality cult developing around the healers, something which is unnecessary, as they simply consider themselves conduits of the spiritual power.

The existence of spiritual beings more developed than healers can be easily explained. As the world of matter which we live in holds many forms and many people of differing spiritual development, so does the world of the Spirit hold various spiritual beings. They are beings who have completed a life cycle in the material world and are now in a non-material spiritual nature. Individuals who dedicated themselves to the healing vocation, such as doctors, spiritual healers, and the like, continue their work as spirits, assisting humanity. Just as the totality of forms makes up the visible world which we all know, so does the totality of spiritual beings make up the one Spirit. Since humans are a spirit, just as much as they are a body, they can be aware of the existence of other spirits who no longer possess a physical body. This awareness comes when a person turns towards the inner self and recognises the spiritual essence within oneself.

The spiritual healers, at the time of the healing, are linked with entities in the spiritual field who are dedicated to the healing of humankind's illnesses. Union may take any form. Sometimes it simply comes as a force delegated from the healers to the patients. At other times, it is heard like a voice of conscience, guiding the healers' actions. And at other times, it comes as a figure which the healers envision, in order to better understand what must be done. This vision is not a fantasy, as is often thought. The spiritual beings which are helping the healers take on an ethereal form, lowering their vibrations, so that the healers can 'see' them and be assisted in their function.

The guides from the spiritual fields give the power to the healers, who then convey it to the patients. Whether it is necessary for them to either project a form or to give instructions in the healers' brains through specific words, is not important. It depends on how evolved the healers are, on the patients' individual case, and the need arising in each particular moment. At the Society's healing section, after the end of a healing, its members describe the way in which they worked. Some say they had a guide talking to them, others that they saw the guide actually performing the healing, and others simply irradiated the patient with power and love. Despite all of these different patterns, there is a common diagnosis to the illnesses and all are aware of it, as it was demonstrated in practice from the result, whether it was positive, or if there were difficulties. It seems from this evidence that what is important, as has been pointed out several times already, is the union with the Spirit and the delegation of its power to the patient.

In the first year of my healing work, I always sought help from spiritual guides, whom I saw in the form of visions supporting me during the healing. For a long period, a figure unknown to me, a slim man with very sensitive hands would come. I saw him healing the patients himself and I learnt from him what I should do. At other times, I saw Jesus, the Virgin Mary, a saint whom I sometimes recognised or other times did not. All these beings gave me power and guidance; I shall cite two examples below.

*28.7.80 "These days I am trying to carry out a healing on M, but I am always unsuccessful. I know that there is an unpleasant emotional relation between us which prevents me from uniting myself with her at the spiritual level. Today I woke up determined to help her deal with the pains she has in her uterus and in her heart.*

*In order to overcome my problem, I made an invocation, seeking the support of a higher spiritual healer. I waited for a little while, until Jesus appeared before me. He stood motionless, as if giving His blessing, and was radiant from head to toe. Under His guidance, I united myself with M and began to work on her energy centres. A considerable length of time passed before I felt her finally relax and feel better. I realised that the healing had ended for today, and I thought that I should thank Jesus. As I looked at Him, He began to spread outwards, disappearing into space. I finished my work and returned to my own little world".*

*1.1.81 "During the night I carried out a healing on D. I stepped through to her house with my energy body and found her asleep. I encompassed her with a radiance of love, while next to me a guide, unknown to me, stood in silence. We worked together to help her find respite from the nervous attacks that frequently torment her. It seems that D became aware of our presence in her sleep: she opened her eyes, sat up, and then slept peacefully. The healing had ended."*

When the Society's healing section was first set up, we held regular meetings with the Master, until we could assimilate enough information to become autonomous. At that time, many examples of contact with spiritual guides were reported. He listened to all of them in the same way, attaching importance only to the work which was being done and to the learners' aptitude in steadily advancing their healing. Questions were, of course, raised as to whether the guides were imaginings or mental projections. But the Master accepted them all, as he explained that a voice, a form or a specific instruction are expressions of the Spiritual Essence. If a healing is carried out with faith, then whatever form appears is helpful.

This view is now understood by all of us and there is an acceptance of what comes or does not come in healing meditation. The conscious union of the healer with the spiritual fields can be achieved through a form, just like it can be achieved through a formless field of the Spirit. It suffices that the linkage is structured and that the healing power is delegated. This is a power which is inherent in all human beings; and when we become aware of it, it can be a steady beacon of radiance.

The spiritual entities that help healers work sometimes individually and sometimes in teams, uniting their powers. Just as a healing coming from a group of healers channels greater power to the patient, so does a group of spiritual beings do the same. For this reason, it is preferable for healers to invoke the help of multiple guides, since these too are at some stage of evolution, depending on their previous work as human beings. They do not have the entire knowledge and healing power which exists only in a hyper-evolved field of consciousness. This is possessed by very few spiritual entities, such as Christ, Buddha, or other beings who are very distant from the human level and whom humans address, depending on their religious faith. Although the distance between humans and these spiritual entities is immense, they are linked with them as they become united with just a small part of their larger consciousness. This part is more approachable by humans and they are aware of it because it has already been expressed by a saint, a spiritual healer or a doctor.

A field of consciousness occupied by the great ontological powers does not concern only psychosomatic illness. It meets much broader needs relating to humanity. It liberates from every kind of pain, of the soul or of the body, and it reduces fear and ignorance, by developing the patient's power and will. It has been observed that patients undergoing healing who receive the spiritual power through both a healer and a spiritual guide do not only feel healthier. They feel stronger and more optimistic and gain a more energetic attitude towards life. The power which they receive from the spiritual field renews them in every area of their being. As has been explained in the chapter on the causes of illnesses, sickness is not only a bodily weakness. It is any negative state, any passion and restriction which oppresses humanity. All these are dispersed by the pure spiritual power which is channeled by the healing work to the human consciousness. Humans become strengthened in the soul and can freely develop its powers and potentialities without withholding them within and thus bringing about illnesses onto themselves.

# MEDICAL SCIENCE AND SPIRITUAL HEALING

*"The art of the creation and formation of souls has been lost and will only be rediscovered when science and religion, re-fashioned together into a living force, will work together in concord for the good and the salvation of humanity."*

**Edouard Schuré\***

Allow me to use the words of this great writer, adapting them to the subject of this book. I would like to say how essential I find his views and the lucidity of his mind, when he foresaw the necessity of a re-emergent 'living force' which must be structured from the two ostensibly opposite positions represented by science and religion. The same could be said of many opposing forces which constantly come into conflict, thus perpetuating the disorder caused by every conflict. If our ultimate aim is the evolution and, consequently, the constant "formation of

---

\*Schuré, E., 'Les grands initiés', Paris: L.A.P. 1960.

SPIRITUAL HEALING

souls", then a unification must occur in every area of our life. I believe that when "medical science and spiritual healers work together in concord for the good and the salvation of humanity", the results will work miracles. Their united forces will then help humans to perceive the co-existence of body and spirit and to dynamically express the powers of their souls.

In the previous chapters sufficient information has been given for an understanding of the significance of spiritual healing and the way in which healers work. Before we go into greater detail and individual issues, I find it necessary to state a position regarding spiritual healing and medical science. I shall deal with present-day reality as I have come to know it from personal experiences, and with a future reality, which, in my opinion, should be our common objective for the good of humanity.

There is a divisiveness between spiritual healers and doctors. I have often faced negative reactions from one branch towards the other as it was trying to prove that only its own way was the right one. I do not think that the motive for this reaction is simply egoistic, since both branches work to assist the human being. It arises mainly from the fact that nothing has been completely validated within us. Spiritual healing may work miracles, but not always, and, when it does, its process cannot be explained by science and its typical, specific data. Medicine, on the other hand, despite its major successes, is not always able to conquer illness. So, depending on personal experiences, each individual aligns oneself with the practice which best serves him or her, while often rejecting the other method of therapy.

Humanity is still at an early level of evolution, both in the development of science and of spirituality. Sometimes a transition takes place in one field, sometimes in the other and both methods of healing advance correspondingly. Although the achievements of medicine are enormous, nevertheless the view is often expressed that they are still at their beginning. According to Alice Bailey, spiritual healers have not evolved greatly either, apart of course, for a few exceptions. Since we are therefore taking our first steps in a common path towards deliverance from pain, there should be a substantial collaboration between the two practices. Hence, patients would be able to receive a greater and more comprehensive care.

One day an unknown gentleman called me, seeking the help of the healing section. Before even explaining his problem to me, he said: "I am receiving a large number of medications which I wish to discontinue. Can you help me?" I wasn't surprised by his words, as I often get similar requests. Patients who have grown tired of a long-term pharmaceutical treatment wish to escape from it and ask us to intervene. Naturally, this is not possible. Spiritual healers do not have the right, nor the wish, to intervene in the course of a medical treatment. They might work for

SPIRITUAL HEALING

the restoration of health, but no one but the attending physician can change a treatment or stop it altogether.

The Master does not teach divisiveness but, instead, advocates union everywhere. This includes the union of medicine with spiritual healing. He says that today, when science has advanced so far and has shown its potential, spiritual healers must choose to collaborate with it. Thus, when a member of the Society falls ill, he sometimes advises one method of treatment, while at other times the other. The disciple has to learn how to see the possibility of improvement everywhere, whether it is provided by medicine or by a healing meditation.

The Master also says that human development is achieved comprehensively. Through science, technology, knowledge of the soul's energies and awareness of their spiritual nature, humans evolve with the goal of developing a capacity for synthesis; for working through everything that they are provided with today, while recognising the expression of God's power everywhere. They should reject nothing, but attempt to integrate everything into the entire existence of things and into the general progress of humankind.

Medical science has a skeptical approach to spiritual healing, which is to some extent justified, since specific data on its function cannot be given. The inadequate explanations which are provided and the veil of mystery often shrouding the healers' work have contributed to the medical profession's general opinion of it. An example of this are the visions mentioned in the previous chapter, which were simply described without providing any further explanation. Nevertheless, the power of spiritual healing and its possibilities are vast, even if it is still disputed, usually due to semi-ignorance or a limited capacity to analyse the phenomenon. Its wonderful results have been demonstrated, with doctors free to ascertain them for themselves.

In Britain, Harry Edwards managed, after great difficulty, to establish his collaboration with the medical profession. Today, members of his foundation are invited to help hospitalised patients. Medical treatment remains in the doctors' jurisdiction, while healers work in their own way on the improvement of the patients' health. It would be a blessing if the same could happen wherever healers have proven their healing abilities and have begun working effectively.

Apart from doctors and healers, the patients themselves often have a fixation and deal with the issue of their healing one-sidedly. People who seek our help are often heard saying that they feel very bad about their health's dependence on pharmaceuticals. As to that, the Master says that pharmaceuticals are merely the botanological expression of the radiance of life itself. In essence, they are a part of the nourishment which nature itself provides. Humans are nourished by nature, thus recycling their material aspect. Drugs, then, should not be considered negative or detrimental since they too have their basis in nature. Even synthetic medicines are in some way based on it. Most pharmaceuticals are derived from herbs, have been known since ancient times, and have been popularly used for consumption even in salads. Consequently, if a herb has undergone certain processes at the hands of science, it should not for that reason be looked upon with disfavour, nor should the patients consider themselves 'condemned' when they need to use it. On the contrary, certain of the organism's deficiencies are covered with its use, which would otherwise require vast quantities of food for their replenishment. It is therefore advisable for patients to always follow the pharmaceutical treatment prescribed by their doctors when this is deemed necessary.

The same attitude should be adopted towards everything that science has to offer us (examinations, analyses, surgery, etc.). Today, laboratories are able to provide substantial aid both in diagnosis and treatment, as well as in research directed towards the fight against illness. Someone who believes in spiritual healing should definitely not ignore medicine. When a young man once suggested to the Master that we should deal with the search for a cure for cancer, he told him that his approach was wrong, concealing a superficial enthusiasm and egoism. Scientists have been working for years on the issue of cancer; it is not necessary for someone who began to meditate only a few months ago to want to find a cure for it.

Many mistakes are made with similar approaches. There are people who completely reject spiritual healing, even though they know it can help them. They don't accept it because they don't believe, or don't understand how it functions. In serving my discipleship with the Master, I have learnt to accept any help which can be given to humans for the improvement of their health. If we accept the achievements of science in other areas, why shouldn't we accept them in medicine? And if we accept the existence of the energies of the soul, why shouldn't we make use of them in healing?

I have witnessed cases of patients who have sought help from the Master and he has advised them to consult a doctor. Even when the matter was purely psychological – when the patient had only symptoms of a psychological imbalance – the Master still recommended a visit to a psychiatrist or a neurologist. There are members of the Society who have followed his advice and have been greatly aided by the pharmaceuticals prescribed to them by psychiatrists. The effect of these drugs, together with the help of spiritual healing and the dialectical method used in the Society, reduced the time required for the healing and contributed to the restoration of their health. People with serious psychological problems should seek any possible assistance which can be provided today by psychiatry. When this help is enhanced with personal work for an understanding and solution to the problem, then full recovery comes much more quickly. The patients regain their strength and can go ahead with their lives without any more drugs – when this, of course, is permitted by the attending neurologists.

I believe that psychiatry and psychology, as they increasingly evolve into exact sciences, draw closer – from a different angle, of course – to spiritual healing. When, some years ago, I attended a seminar on psychology at the University of London on the subject of 'experimental psychology', I learnt of the possibility of measuring and recording the energies of the soul. Very sensitive instruments were used to measure a person's energies through the sensory organs (eyes, hands, etc.). The percentage of the energy was always related to the individual's psychological state at the moment of the examination, as well as the side of the body which was used for this measurement – the left or the right. Psychiatry today works for the psychological balance of the human being, using psycho-analysis, drugs, and the dialectic. It works possibly in a different way than spiritual healing, but with the same purpose: the human being's harmonisation with life. If this can be achieved through medication, then it is best for us to accept the pharmaceuticals which can have a catalytic effect on our tensions and an invigorating effect on our weaknesses.

Two years ago, something happened which gave me the opportunity to combine these two methods of therapy, spiritual healing and treatment with psychiatric drugs. At that time, my father, aged 76, suffered from a severe illness. His problem had begun the previous year and was gradually getting worse. He was showing symptoms of Parkinson's disease, he had a profound melancholy and showed constant weight loss. His regular medications were not helping him in the least. His mental processes were in a situation so strange, that we decided to take him to a neurological clinic. The diagnosis was not encouraging and the doctor treating him stated that even if his health eventually improved, we should still expect a new crisis. Patients such as my father are considered extremely sensitive and vulnerable to the slightest external stimulation.

That summer was a very difficult one for all of us. On many days we didn't know how things would turn out for him, whether he was going to be able to care for himself again and recover both mentally and physically. The doctors helped him as much as possible, without promising anything. I began performing spiritual healing on him every day, whenever I was at the clinic with him, as well as at the healing section's meetings. Progress was very slow. He came out of the neurological clinic and was sent to a pathological clinic for various other examinations, but also to gain some strength. Throughout that period we worked regularly, pleading God to turn him back into a normal man of his age.

After four months, my father was back home with us. He continued taking certain drugs, but did not have any of the previous symptoms. He put on weight, the Parkinson's disease did not appear to be present, and his mental processes went back to being completely normal. He began to involve himself with various tasks, he went for a walk regularly, and went on to live a normal life. No new crisis showed itself as we had feared it would. Indeed, he now felt so well that he took up his old hobby again. He bought paints and, little by little, went on to paint the entire house.

I am not in a position to say what exactly it was that cured my father – whether it was the medical treatment or the spiritual healing. I believe that it was the two of them together that helped, each doing what had to be done in its own field. In any event, the result is what matters. I think that the fact that a suitable neurologist was found to help him, and that I knew how to carry out healings, were both the same thing: an intervention of the divine will in order to help a human being. We have no wish to prove a superiority in one function while disparaging another. They all give expression to the same thing. It is the will of God which lies hidden in the hand of the surgeon, in the drug which the patient takes, in the forces which are conveyed by a healer. They are all opportunities which are given to us for equal use, with faith that they exist for the improvement of the bodily and psychological health of all humankind.

# SELF-HEALING

> *"The more deeply conscious our life is, the more we are able to feel the depths of the soul of those who come to us. And it is in these depths that everything is created, both health and sickness."*
>
> **Maria Charlet***

The spiritual development of humans, just like their physical development, follows its own course. Maturity does not come immediately; it passes through many stages, often long-lasting and laborious. The expansion of the consciousness is something which is acquired on a day to day basis, through experience and through friction. This does not mean that will and decision cannot speed up the journey and bring about a liberating result. But until this happens, humans must pass through various levels of understanding and realisation. Depending on their own level, they can convey to others what they have

---
*Charlet, M., 'Shiatsu Philosophy and Practice', Athens: Pyrinos Kosmos 1980.

individually gained. Individual and group development inevitably go hand-in-hand, and for this reason everyone must work towards both, until a state of personal completeness transpires. Then they can now devote themselves to the evolution of others, as their own course has advanced to a higher level of consciousness.

In observing the Master, I have noticed how much more than his disciples he gives expression to power and love, which he teaches to all of us, in a variety of ways. Self-healing provides great knowledge, as it reveals to humans the hidden unconscious features of their being, giving them the will to transcend them. The healing of other patients spreads this knowledge even further, since it is employed in a creative manner. Through these two tasks, humans advance in their spiritual evolution. The Master always urges his disciples to also work in a healing way on themselves, intervening only when they cannot manage this on their own.

One of the incidents which had made an impression on me was the case of K, a young girl who for years had been bothered by a verruca on her heel. She had been given specific instructions on to how to work with meditation in order to dissipate it. K would work on the treatment of her foot for a little while, but would then neglect it as she got distracted by other matters. She asked for the help of the healing section when the pains grew stronger and she began having difficulties in walking. We started the healing, but with the same results; sometimes she would get slightly better and at other times she would get worse.

Things reached an impasse in 1985, with a new outbreak of warts on her calf and knee. K. went to a surgeon, who told her that a large part of her heel would have to be removed and she would have to undergo plastic surgery, which would immobilise her for a long period of time. Faced with this unpleasant prospect, K. once again turned to the Master, who had been leaving the situation to develop on its own all this time, in order to make K express a comprehensive self-healing on her own. Seeing the dead end that had been reached, he decided to intervene. He began a healing on her foot, while at the same time he urged her to renew her own individual efforts. He explained to her that her condition was due to an accumulation of energy in her foot, which is the base of the body. This accumulation indicated that she was still largely attached to various material gratifications and was not spreading the energy to her body, her heart and her mind.

The healing only lasted a few days, and K's heel, as well as the rest her leg, completely cleared up, as if there had never been anything wrong with it. What cured her was the power given to her by the Master, from his own stance and faith; a stance which we are all being trained to acquire some day. K's individual work did not bring a positive result because she had not yet overcome certain personal limitations. She had not, in other words, become consciously aware of her inner power and so she was not able to express it. Self-healing is successful only to the extent that the power develops and is expressed through the will for liberation from pain.

I could write of many self-healing examples carried out by patients which have been completely successful. A success which is due mainly to the faith in the task performed with the help of God and the need of relief from pain. A while ago, I was informed of Ms. A's case, who had asked the Society's healing section for help. She had visited us five years ago because of pains in her waist vertebrae as well as headaches that had been bothering her. We had then undertaken her case and helped her for a while. At the same time, however, I also showed her how to perform the relaxation exercise on her own, working on the dispersal of her illness. Her daughter, who was a member of the healing section, frequently helped her with this exercise at home. For the past few years, Ms. A has been perfectly well. She explained to us that from the time we helped her up to the present, she had never stopped practicing self-healing. She is completely convinced that her good health is due to this, and at the same time she says that relaxation greatly helps her good state of mind. Her problem was not a simple one: she received medication on a permanent basis for the pains and was always feeling listless. If she is in good health today, this is owed to the steady work which she does for her own self.

My personal experience on self-healing has passed through various stages. I will mention a few examples. I remember when I first went to the Society, I met a young girl, E, who had been an earlier disciple of the Master. One day E said to me: "I have a pain in my uterine tubes and I am going to lie down for a little while in order to deal with it". At the time, her words struck me as odd, because I had not yet been taught what a person can do about physical pain. But E. had learnt to heal herself and she did this whenever it was needed, as if it were something quite simple.

When I too first began to discern this potential, I tended to not really believe what was happening to me. I considered these things random, coincidental or rather insignificant. I kept expecting something spectacular to happen in order for me to accept the power of self-healing. Two of these first instances, which happened directly and simply, concerned the dissolution of certain pains.

One day I had a very intense migraine which began at the nape of my neck and spread to my head. I then thought of using my own hands as a means of healing to make the pain go away. I applied my palms to the nape

SPIRITUAL HEALING

and felt an energy flowing through them towards the point which was troubling me; an energy which actually seemed to spring from my own body. Within a few seconds the pain was no longer there, my head had found complete relief.

On another occasion, I had been experiencing discomfort in my uterus, because, as it seems, I had caught a chill in the sea. I remembered the Master's teaching, to visualise the interior of my body, and, wherever there was an illness, to think that all is well and healthy. As the contractions grew stronger, I focused on my womb, visualising it as radiant, healed and serene. The contractions diminished, the pains left and shortly after I got up and continued my work without any further discomforts.

It appears that these first examples had not completely satisfied me, as I did not consider the breaking down of a pain so significant. It was then that the third event occurred, and this convinced me completely, thoroughly proving to me the miracle of spiritual healing. Below is a copy of my words as they were noted down on 29.7.80, a month after meeting the Master.

> *"This morning my left sinus hurt badly. I had one of the usual relapses of my sinus infection, which has been tormenting me for years. I have grown sick of taking drugs which temporarily*

*relieve me, only for the pains to begin again shortly after. The discomfort today was so bad that I thought of meditating in order to stop this new paroxysm.*

*I let myself relax and I felt myself increasingly unite with the spiritual power. Without thinking about anything else, I remained wholly focused on my sinus, which began to receive the energy of the soul. In the first few moments the pain grew worse, as happens with a wound when it is cleaned with a medicinal lotion. In spite of that, I went on with the healing, and, little by little, the discomfort was further reduced.*

*I remained in the same position for about half an hour, until I was finally convinced that the pain had disappeared. I then stopped, opened my eyes and waited to see what would happen. The sinus gave me no pain, but it was still sensitive, as if it were convalescing. I got up and began to do my housework. But then something amazing happened! Every so often, mucus came down through my mouth and throat, as if the sinus was emptying itself of whatever had caused the illness. This cleansing carried on for more than an hour. When it was completed, I was sure that I had been permanently healed. This is the first time that self-healing*

SPIRITUAL HEALING

> *has convinced me without any doubt of the potential that we all carry within us."*

I have to say I that since then I have not been troubled by any other sinusitis attacks. Thus, I was completely convinced of the self-healing's capabilities, which similarly extend to any of the patient's ailments. I did not keep my personal experiences as knowledge or as help given simply to myself, but began applying them to other patients with similar problems.

The following year, when my younger grandson suffered from a sinus infection, I remembered my experience with self-healing and worked on him in a similar way. I focused again on the sick area, until I felt the pain going away and the cleansing taking place. The child was quickly healed and has not been troubled by this issue since.

The same happened with a friend of mine who called me to say that she had severe pains in her uterus. Since we could not immediately meet, I began a distance healing on her. I write about this on 28.7.80:

> *"I let the energy of my soul unite itself with my friend's and penetrate her uterus, which was in pain. I felt the spasms which were occurring constantly, as if it couldn't find relief any-*

*where. I began to speak inwardly to the sick woman, telling her that the pain had gone and that she could rest now. I sent her my love, until the womb's resistance diminished, the spasms stopped and a harmonious functioning returned. I had the impression that everything was following a smooth rhythm: the heart, the veins the arteries. I then began to work on the whole of her body, her legs, her back, her chest, until there were moments when I thought that my friend and I were one, one form, one human being. When I felt sure that her body was relaxed, without any pain, only then did I stop the healing. Later she called me to say that she felt well and the pains had stopped."*

There are times when self-healing takes place of its own accord, without the patient consciously working for it. It is enough for the person to relax, the energy to form a normal flow within the body, for a relief to come. This mainly applies to minor indispositions such as headaches, stomach aches, etc. Many say, in surprise, that, without doing anything special, they were automatically relieved of a bodily discomfort as they were in meditation. Such phenomena frequently make their appearance at the Society, particularly during group meditations when the energy field in the room is enhanced. People who are

SPIRITUAL HEALING

receptive can unite themselves with the energies existing around them and can be cured of indispositions. On one occasion, a girl, who had a bad cold when we began the meditation, realised that it had gone by the time we had finished.

All these examples prompt individuals to work more and more consciously on their health; to delve deeper into themselves, to discover the causes of their illnesses and to advance towards liberation from them and from the effects which they have on their body. Thus, progressively, the inner power is revealed to them and they then learn how to channel it to those who are still in need of it

# ILLNESS:
# AN INCENTIVE FOR EVOLUTION

"Only someone who has been ill understands the value of health", say many of those who have experienced both states, deeply delving into their effects, their causes, and into the ways of avoiding illness.

The same is true of everything in life. Money, beauty, friendship – we appreciate these things more when we have been deprived of them. These alternations from one state to its opposite keep us constantly alert. They provide us with the stimuli needed by our human nature, thus keeping us from falling into complacency, keeping us from living in a utopian world which is very distant from reality.

SPIRITUAL HEALING

Illness, an unpleasant and often painful state, conceals in itself a potential to teach us many lessons. It comes as a consequence of certain mistakes which we would not have seen if not for their negative effects. Thus the mind would be 'asleep' and no other awareness of life would arise. Perhaps illness seems a heavy price to pay, since it brings with it a psychosomatic weakness which causes pain and despair. But the consequence of every mistake is a teaching, which we are called upon to recognise and study.

The same is also true of illnesses, which are the results of certain mistakes. Just as indigestion indicates that we should eat less, so do all the other conditions teach us something about our attitude towards life. The more we understand why we become ill, the more easily we can avoid the causes of illness and remain healthy.

One lady, a senior member of the Society, had undergone a mastectomy many years before we met her. When she came to us, the problem had been overcome, with the exception of a certain discomfort in her arm on the side of the operated breast. This would swell up and feel hot, as if she was running a fever, many times during the year. In fact, she would often need to stay in bed, because the fever would eventually spread to the rest of her body. When we met her and she became a member of the healing section, the Master gave her instructions on how to avoid these fevers, which would disrupt her life for one or two days at a time. Little by little she learnt how to deal with the flare-ups on her own, making the fever quickly pass.

But what she was taught by her actual problem was not only the way of combating it. It was mainly the observations she made concerning its causes each time. She told us that by studying the instances of her arm's inflammations, she discovered that it occurred whenever she was in some sort of conflict. When she had negative thoughts, when she resisted responding to some need, when she simply did not partake in the flow of life as it presented itself. She learnt to regard the swelling of her arm as a 'safety valve' which drew her attention to the fact that she was on the wrong track. It urged her to look for the cause, which was usually subconscious, to recognise it and to overcome it. Then her arm would immediately heal, as long as she had changed her attitude and had consented to express what was being asked of her. Today these attacks seldom occur, as she has realised by now, after so many years of discipleship, how she must generally behave.

This example shows us how an illness can become an incentive for greater consciousness and knowledge. Naturally, to begin using it as an incentive, the illness must not be treated in a hostile manner, as an injustice, punishment or useless hardship. The individual must try to see it in a calmer manner, in order to understand its cause. Then it is likely that understanding, which is the beginning of any evolution, will come.

Something similar happened to N. She was only recently telling me that she had been experiencing a sensitivity in one of her teeth, something akin to neuralgia, which appeared not only with cold or heat, but also unexpectedly, without any obvious reason. She began taking note of when the pain started and how severe it was. She then noticed that its intensity and duration always bore a relation to a psychological cause. If she was angry, aggressive, annoyed with life itself, then the pain began and continued until her reactions had passed.

We talked about this matter and I asked her if the toothache was actually helping in the evolution of her soul. She told me that it certainly was an incentive for her, because she naturally did not want to be in pain, but she also wanted to understand why she was hurting. She added that the pain diminished as soon as she established its cause. It became even less when she accepted her mistake and ceased to react against the pain itself. She also said that when she confided the psychological cause of her pain to somebody else, it left her quicker. She added that, before she started noticing these things, she would not have imagined how many times a day she was in such a state of reaction which was due to an egoistical attitude. As she studied the beginning of every new discomfort her tooth caused her, she saw that it arose from a 'tightening', a difficulty she had in functioning simply and freely. This understanding reduced the tightening and the pain it had been causing her.

Perhaps this example will seem somewhat odd, as pains in the teeth from neuralgias are not all that common. But each one of us can make similar observations in other, much more common things, such as stomach disorders and headaches. These arise from similar resistances, which usually conceal a certain fear, an insecurity, a lack of acceptance and of expression. As an individual learns to observe oneself, the reactions diminish and so do the illnesses, since the soul's energy is allowed to flow freely within the body.

What is it, in essence, that humans are called upon to do? The Master says that they are called upon to simply unite themselves with life. To accept its every manifestation, even the most negative, and to counter it with its opposite, the positive. In this way a balance will be achieved and problems will be eliminated. Since all things are aspects of opposing forces, this union must take place everywhere. Hate must be embraced with love, fear with fearlessness; weakness must be strengthened with power. Man and woman must become a true 'couple', every need must be met and every illness must be 'united' with health, with everything, that is, which restores a patient's health.

## SPIRITUAL HEALING

Our entire discipleship speaks precisely of this union, which leads to the offset of deficiencies. I shall describe a personal example of self-healing which I regard as more important than those which I have cited because it occurred precisely with a conscious uniting of opposites, of pain with non-pain, that is, the state in which there is no illness.

A year before I went to the Society I had undergone an operation on my right foot. My anklebone had been removed and a replacement had been fitted. The operation was successful, but the orthopedic surgeon who operated on me had also examined my left foot and had predicted that it would soon need a similar intervention. I was already experiencing a slight pain in 1980, but not troublesome enough for me to start thinking of having an operation.

In early 1982, entirely unexpectedly, I began having severe pains in my left foot, exactly as had happened with the foot which had been operated on. I realised that the doctor's prediction was proven correct. I began to limp noticeably, I was unable to put on my shoe easily, and I felt the pain ascending to my back, exactly as it had happened the previous time.

I then had a conversation with the Master, during which I told him about the prospect of a new operation. However, he told me that I could get well without experiencing the same troubles. He gave me instructions for self-healing and recommended that I should immediately start working systematically. I followed his instructions and for the next four days my meditation mainly concerned my healing. What I attempted to do was to unite my health with the pain so that the latter would be dissolved. Below I have copied extracts from the notes I took on the course of my healing:

> *6.2.82 "I meditated and saw the inside of my foot. I united myself with the cells, molecules, atoms. A diagonal shadow on the toes which were in pain. I began illuminating them. I could see the cells vibrating, moving in a circular motion and the pain being dispersed. I united the pain with the health, as the positive is united with the negative everywhere in nature..."*
>
> *7.2.82 "Firstly, I consciously allowed my body to be flooded with the energies of the soul. Then I brought my will and my faith to the foot's bones for the healing. It was as if the pain had been dissolved. I got up and stepped on the floor with my ill foot. There is still pain but it is minimal... I thought of various everyday problems. They seemed simple to me because, as I learn to unite health with illness, I can now do the same everywhere, I can unite the problem with my will for its solution. I think that with*

> *this healing I am being primarily trained in the union of the opposites..."*
>
> 8.2.82 *"I am continuing the healing. I use various mental regimens. I work deep inside the ailing bone, always with the purpose of breaking down the pain, and uniting with health. It is as if what had gathered there is melting. As if the bones are straightening. The deforming arthritis is being healed. I can step on my foot with a very slight discomfort. The sole burns, the healing advances..."*
>
> 9.2.82 *"Today the healing has finished. It seemed to me like a miracle! All the sick cells have been healed, or have been replaced by other, sound ones. I walked completely free. I am no longer in pain!"*

During the days when I was working on my foot's healing, I became aware of how important the union of opposite forces is. Illness is a force, an unpleasant idea. Health is another, positive force. By bringing the power of health to the area where there was pain using my will and my constant work, I became completely well. I was taught by my own illness what union means, what the counterpoising of life's opposing forces is. After this self-healing, I tried to apply what I had understood to all other aspects of my life.

The examples which have been given in this chapter provide an image of the lessons which an individual learns from illnesses, if, of course, he or she wants to make use of them as incentives for evolution. Ms. K, who learnt to control the inflammation of her hand, N, who was able to reduce her toothache, and myself, who cured deforming arthritis – all of us were in essence taught much more. We saw the causes of the illnesses, the importance of accepting them, the value of union. Through the pain, which we tried to overcome by power and understanding, we discovered the hidden possibilities of human nature. Our mind broadened and acceptance brought a current of love, even for the most unpleasant states of our illnesses.

I consider the knowledge which is acquired by a healing as significant as the healing itself. Indeed, perhaps the knowledge is more important, because through it, many sufferings can be avoided – not only bodily sufferings, but also others which involve various aspects of our life. Because a person who learns to accept the unwelcome states of an illness can also easily accept any negative situation which he or she encounters in one's progress as a human being. And a person who learns to apply health to pain, automatically learns to also apply health to all other sicknesses of humankind, which are all its negative manifestations.

There is no use setting ourselves against whatever comes to cause us pain and unhappiness. Nor is it enough to accept these things in a fatalistic and powerless manner. What is important is to accept them dynamically, so that we can then deal with them and regain our balance. We should get to know them in depth and by that knowledge utilise them all as life's own teachings. This is what will bestow upon us health of the soul and the body.

# POSITIVE AND NEGATIVE ATTITUDE OF PATIENTS

One of the Master's most impressive healings occurred in the case of a stroke. The patient was in the hospital's intensive care unit, when his wife came to seek our help. The doctors had said that he was 'clinically dead', with slim chances of survival, and that even if he did pull through, he would probably remain in a vegetative state. The healing section began helping him immediately, and I visited him at the hospital accompanied by another girl. The problem, however, was so serious and urgent that I asked the Master to also partake in the healing.

And so he did. He went to see the patient, who was still plunged into unconsciousness, with no awareness of his surroundings. His case was considered a lost cause and everyone said that it was only a matter of time before he succumbed. The presence of the Master brought about the change. At once something began happening to the patient; the oscilloscopes started giving different readings... Within a week he was out of danger, and his attending doctors admittedly could not explain how this miracle had happened. An initial communication was established with the patient and he began conveying his wishes using sign language. The Master continued to carry out distance healing on him until he was able to return home after a considerable length of time.

Up to this point, things had gone very smoothly; the patient had shown a great will to live and had responded to the healing. The next step remained: to achieve a full recovery and overcome any speech or movement impediments. But this was something he had to accomplish on his own. The Master, who had known him for a long time, told him that if he wished to be completely healed, he would have to change his general attitude towards life. He should stop being in a constant state of anxiety over everything, and particularly over his family and his marital relationship. But the patient was unable to make the desired progress. He wanted to live, of course, as had been demonstrated by his extraordinary healing, but he also wanted to continue his life in the manner which he had long ago adopted. Luckily, during my last telephone conversation with him, I noticed a substantial change. In the period which elapsed since he was released from the hospital, he began to acquire greater calm and his faith in God strengthened. His improvement has been progressing and his problems had been diminishing, albeit at a slow pace.

This example illustrates the Master's dynamic function, by healing a person who was 'clinically dead'. But it also shows that no power can complete a healing when the personality resists. This is a very common phenomenon: people wanting to get well when they are in danger, but soon forgetting this danger and persisting in their old ways of life – even if it was the cause of their illness. Thus, while they can avoid deterioration or death, they cannot, nonetheless, mentally change, and so their health continues to remain in a precarious state. They maintain their negative attitudes towards life, despite the ordeals they have gone through.

A typical example of a patient's negative attitude occurred during the first year of our healing section's operation. Mr. P came to seek our help and his state was truly pitiful. He suffered from cancer of the genitals which caused him excruciating pain. He walked literally doubled up and could find relief nowhere. The various medications and pain-killers which he took could not help him at this stage. We undertook his case with

SPIRITUAL HEALING

the Master's help, and each afternoon Mr. P came to the Society for contact healing. From the very first day he felt the pains decreasing and within a week he had only a very slight discomfort. Our intention was to continue for as long as necessary, until he was completely healed, since his condition was in a very advanced state.

One day, quite unexpectedly, he did not show up for his usual healing and we were puzzled by his absence. He did not come the next day either, without giving us any notice. We were starting to get worried, when a friend of his, who had recommended us to him, explained what had happened. Mr. P had stated that he did not wish to continue with the spiritual healing because he did not believe that it was reducing his pains. He could not understand – as he said – what this healing was, he could not accept it, and so, he would not be coming to see us again. Mr. P's attitude shows how difficult it is for some people to accept a miracle, even if they see it in their own body. How much they resist accepting the existence of a power which cannot be measured with normal human standards. We never saw Mr. P again, nor did we ever find out how the matter of his illness ended.

At that time, I was distressed by his unreasonable attitude. I did, in fact, feel anger towards this person, who of his own accord had driven himself to pain and, probably, death. Today, after many such negative instances, I have learnt to accept denial as a part of life. I can see that when someone is in this position, perhaps he or she should undergo its consequences and be taught something previously unknown. How could a healer go against such a personal wish? By dealing with the individual's illness comprehensively, as a necessary part of the overall human progression, comes the acceptance not only of its existence, but even of the refusal to its healing.

There is a lady in the Society who has been in a self-study group for the past three years. Ever since I first met her, her problem has been that she starts every contact, every conversation or action by projecting a 'no'. Even when she is forced to accept something which has been fully proven to her, she manages to raise another factor as an objection. She accepts, out of necessity, what is perfectly obvious, but attempts to belittle it by saying that it is a special case, that there is much to be said to the contrary, and so on.

The result of this total negation is that her body constantly forms certain growths or cysts, which, fortunately, are not malignant. She has, naturally, started to soften somewhat of late, after a new cyst made its appearance in her ovary, but the final change has not yet taken place. I do not know what the eventual outcome of her health will be, or whether she will decide to look at life from a different perspective. Whether she will stop saying that she has an abhorrence for her womb, that she can't stand the male sex, that she is wearied by the responsibility of her children and that she wants to withdraw from society. She must fundamentally reconsider all these things, in order for her organism to regain its normal functioning as a consequence of her soul's proper externalisation.

These negative examples are, naturally, only part of the cases of sick people who visit us. Many respond positively and their healing results are immediate. When X – also a long-time member of the Society – spoke to the Master about a staphylococcus problem she had, he explained to her that the problem was an outbreak of a retention she had been inducing. X understood the matter completely, accepted it and requested from the Master to heal a newly appeared 'pimple' on her cheek. As soon as he touched her with his finger, she felt a current passing through her and at once the spot dissolved. Her acceptance, which indicated her soul's inclination towards evolution, is what contributed to the healing. From then on, she does not concern the Master with this matter, but self-heals any new outbreak, with the knowledge of its cause and the healing methods which she has been taught as a member of the healing section.

Four years ago I was visited at the Society by Ms. S. She was with her husband and they appeared to be one of those exceptional couples who are united by a true love and understanding. She had read the interview I had recently given to a newspaper on spiritual healing, and so decided to enquire about a health problem that had been bothering her. As I looked at her, I wondered what she could be suffering from. She was young, calm, seemed in the best of health, and, as she said, she had a very harmonious life as a wife and a mother. She showed no anxiety and her appearance seemed completely in balance.

In the conversation that followed, she told me that she had in fact been as she seemed for the greater part of her life. Every so often, however, everything changes with a terrible headache that appears without any known reason, lasting several days and confining her to bed. These attacks had begun twelve years ago and had continued up until that time, despite repeated medical efforts and pharmaceutical treatments. Not even a visit to specialists in Britain had changed anything. When an attack began, it had to go through its usual cycle and leave her as it had come, without giving her any clue as to what had caused it or what had made it go away.

I searched internally for the cause and perceived that she was very responsive to the spiritual union which had been built up between us. And so, what had happened and had continued to manifest itself up until then was revealed to me at once. Ms. S was a calm and responsible individual, without difficulties in adjusting to the social framework in which she lived. But she still had a childishness, a spiritual immaturity, which materialised as a complaint when she felt that she was not offered something by others, or if she had no time to spare from her many responsibilities as a mother and a wife. She would then, entirely unconsciously, attempt to gain the attention and care which she thought she was lacking. She would fall ill, become weak and take to her bed, where others were forced to look after her like a child. But since she also had a certain maturity, this 'nannying' was soon no longer needed. The headache would then leave her of its own accord and the mature side of herself once again took over the responsibilities of life, without difficulty.

When I explained the problem to her, she was surprised, because she had never suspected anything of the sort. But she accepted it and, moreover, agreed to join a self-study group in order to overcome it. I began to carry out a healing on her; she had some minor attacks, which eventually disappeared. Ms. S is now well, her childish weakness has left her and the headaches have not troubled her again. The important factor in this case was her unusual receptiveness, both to the healing which she underwent as well as towards dealing with the cause of her condition.

Refusal and will for life are essential factors in healing. They usually manifest themselves from the very first contact with the patient. One young man who had attempted suicide listened to me talking to him for two full hours and in the end said: "What you tell me is all well and good, but I still don't see why I should go on living". His refusal towards life arose from his difficulty in dynamically integrating into it, because, as he said, it had caused him considerable pain and distress. It took a great deal of effort on the part of the members of the Society to get him to accept their support, mostly in the form of friendship and understanding.

An entirely opposite case was a lady, a cancer-patient, who, as soon as she met me, said: "I shall get well. I want to get well. I have strength and faith in my ability to overcome cancer". And, naturally, she did. She was healed with the help she received, because she believed in the power of God, in the miracle of life. Her will-power was accompanied by an obedience in doing regular relaxation exercises in parallel to the medical treatments which she had been undergoing. All these conditions help the work of the healers. They do not come into conflict with obstinate reactions which reverse the soul's energy. When, on one occasion, for example, a gentleman was cured of bronchitis and then insisted on returning to a place which was damp and unfit for his health, it was only natural that he would become ill again. If illness is not an incentive for change, both in internal matters and in external actions, then good health is not stabilised. The refusal to change brings new negative manifestations.

The patients are not always aware of their own attitude. When we work at a distance for people who do not know when they are about to undergo a healing, we can sense whether they are responding to the radiance they are receiving. The personality is positive or negative to the power of healing, even if the individuals are not aware of it. They receive the help which is given to them and react to it as if they were present. And here, of course, the same difficulties or favourable conditions, which have been previously described, apply. The healer continues to work steadily, even if everything appears to be negative, because there is always a factor which must not be forgotten. This is the power of God, which is conveyed from healer to patient, dissolving the resistances and changing the flows in the patient, if this is what must be done.

# PARENTS, CHILDREN AND ILLNESSES

It is an undeniable fact that parents influence their children, leaving their traces upon them and, in doing so, continue their own existence through them. It could be said that every child is an extension of its father and mother and, naturally, of earlier generations, who have, in their turn, also left their imprints on their descendants.

This is apparent from the inherited features which manifest as a resemblance of the children towards their parents. It is also obvious from the habits which children adopt, imitating their parents' example. Matters of good and bad health are often carried forward to descendants, both within their cells and through the way each family lives regarding their eating and resting habits as well as their general interests.

All of this has been studied by scientists, sociologists and doctors who give advice on the improvement of health – something which must be our objective. Parents are urged to reduce in every possible way their negative influences on their children, so that a healthier younger generation will emerge. Particular care is provided to children so that they develop in a better way, both physically and intellectually. These efforts have brought about certain positive results both in their physique and in their mental development. Despite all this, we cannot say that their health is always good and that there is not a great deal yet to be done. In any event, things could not be any other way, as flaws continue to be present in parents and children as separate individuals.

The pursuit of this subject could fill entire volumes if we wished to elaborate on all factors. These are biological, social, economic and psychological and cannot isolatedly apply or encompass any one child and its family. They have to be approached in a much more comprehensive manner, within the space-time framework of a social structure, and the individual conditions of each separate case. However, this is not the exact purpose of this book. Here we shall confine ourselves to only one of the many human aspects which affect our descendants, most of the time unconsciously.

The correlation of a child's health with the mental state of its parents will be the subject of this chapter. It is striking how few of the parents who visit us seeking help for their children have realised the role which they themselves have played in their illness. They have no suspicion, in most cases, that a child's problematic attitude is directly related to its parents' attitude. Perhaps they would easily see this dependence if it concerned a friend's child, but they rarely acknowledge it when it comes to their own child.

Something which I usually hear is this: "I don't understand why my son is disobedient. From who has he learnt this kind of behaviour? Everything is civilised in our family; when I have a disagreement with my husband, we never discuss the problem in front of the child". At other times, again, parents come to complain about their daughter's laziness, about her inexplicable melancholy, which may have effects on her health, such as stomach pains, fainting fits, etc. And again the same question presents itself – how can a girl who lives in a socially normal environment manifest such phenomena.

If the problem is limited to a few tensions and mood swings, then it usually just causes anger and a certain bitterness about the 'badly behaved' child that was born to such good parents. But when it is a matter of the child's physical health, anxiety takes the primary place in its parents' attitude. They worry for their little one with anorexia that is not developing properly, and they fear that things may get worse and something even more serious may develop.

A mother once said to me: "I can't understand what's wrong with my daughter. I look after her as best I can, I give her whatever she needs, but she is still constantly weak. She wakes up in a state of anxiety, she has stomach pains and the doctors can't find any disease". When the problem was studied in depth, what emerged was the fact that the mother was not satisfied with her marital life. Externally there was no problem, but in reality she had never been able to entirely accept her husband and experience a genuine union with him. The little girl, who was at an age of dependence from her mother, received all these emotional reactions. There had never been any mention of a problem, the parents had never shown that they were unsatisfied with one another, but this was not enough to reduce the negative current which the mother emitted around her.

The daughter absorbed every one of her mother's unmet needs, and fell ill. The mother's spiritual 'sickness' materialised through the child's physical body.

In order to better understand the mother-child relationship, we must look at what connects them, apart, of course, from their natural physical continuity. The body of each child is united with the body of its mother by the umbilical cord, which enables it to develop for as long as resides inside the womb. This cord is cut at birth and the new-born becomes an independent individual regarding this specific relationship. It is for this reason that a child can still grow up, even in the absence of its own mother, who is replaced by someone else.

However, apart from this dependence, which involves the child's body, there is another significantly substantial one. This is the emotional dependence which symbolically builds another cord which is very strong and often so powerful that the child grows up without being able to detach itself from the emotional influence of its mother. This 'cord' is the energy emitted from mother to child and back again. As this energy penetrates the child's energy body, it affects its centres to such a degree that it often causes a psychosomatic disorder, as the child is vulnerable to all currents surrounding it. It directly receives them but does not know how to alter them or deal with them, since it has not yet developed defensive powers of its own soul.

Thus, it is natural that any energy outflow of the mother mostly, as it is her that the child is most dependent on up to a certain age, directly resonates the child's centres. Of course, the same thing happens with the father, since he too emits his own emotions to the child, but we shall not refer to him as much, because the mother-child relationship is usually the closest in the early years. This dependence can continue for a whole lifetime, particularly if the mother does not emotionally release her child, or if the child does not release itself from her, frequently emitting negative currents to her.

This emotional bonding is one of the most serious problems assailing human beings. It exists between man and wife, between siblings, between friends, between associates – even between mere acquaintances – and is particularly strong between parents and their children. This happens because children, due to their physical weakness, are utterly dependent on their parents and, as we have said, especially on their mother. But the parents are also dependent on their children, though this may sound like a paradox. Nevertheless, they invest in them, they seek to obtain from them certain features which they lack, and often wish to express through them something which they themselves have not succeeded in expressing. Thus the child expects something from the parents – and this is entirely natural – but the parents also expect something from it. This demand, conscious or unconscious, becomes an intolerable burden for the little ones. They are often asked to take upon themselves their parents' problems, despite the fact that to all appearances they seem to have whatever they need and no one seems to be asking anything of them.

One of our society's most basic problem – with certain exceptions, of course – is a defective relationship between man and woman. This happens so frequently that most children live in a family atmosphere of unsatisfied spiritual needs. There is no sense of fulfilment neither in the man nor the woman, and, naturally, the couple which they form cannot be complete, self-sufficient and ontologically satisfied. This lack is conveyed as energy to the children, affecting their inner world and often manifests as a physical illness.

Years ago I read a psychiatric study regarding ten young girls who suffered from schizophrenia without any hereditary cause, which showed that all of them had a common environment in their way of life. That is to say, these families, whose daughters ended up in a neurological clinic, had very strict taboos concerning relations with the opposite sex, they were intensely religious, with particular emphasis on the formal part of religion, and presented a perfect façade of respectability to society. All this placed immense pressure on the young girls, who were forced to follow an austere family life, without genuine love and union between its members, until they eventually sank into paranoia, in order to escape what they could no longer bear.

Events such as these gradually lead to the confirmation of the saying that 'the children are punished for the sins of their parents'. But it would be best to study this saying against a broader background and not as yet another source of guilt which must burden the parents for the negative effects of their actions on their children, whom, deep down, they love and want to help. A sense of guilt does not lead to the problem's solution, it only magnifies and increases it. In the final analysis, we have to look at the meaning of 'sin' and how it causes illnesses not only to the perpetrators, but also to their descendants.

When analysing the word 'sin', we see that it describes a situation, an act, or thought which is not sound, in other words an imperfect expression of something. No one is perfect, at least in the context of the present-day facts of human existence. There is no perfection of consciousness, the integration of the soul has not yet occurred. We are all aware of this and it is for this reason that we continue to consciously and unconsciously work for our evolution. And as we do so, we inevitably make mistakes. When Jesus called upon 'those without sin' to 'cast the first stone' at the prostitute, no one came forward, because they all knew that they were a very long way from such perfection. We continue to express the same thing today: an absence of perfection, a life full of mistakes and limitations. Consequently, all of us who are parents transfer to our children our own deficiencies, our erroneous mental functions and all our defects, together, of course, with our positive aspects.

## PARENTS, CHILDREN AND ILLNESSES

For example, a woman who has not found satisfaction from her husband, looks to her son to give her what she has been deprived of. She seeks, in most cases without knowing it, to keep her child close to her, so that he can fulfil the needs of her soul. He is her last resort after the previous failures of her father, her husband, or all the other men she has known. She strives despairingly for fulfilment, requiring of this young creature to give her something she hasn't found in her life, but which her son also lacks, since he hasn't received from his mother care and love to its fullest. The result, naturally, is the opposite of expectations. The child becomes weak, disappointing its parents and a state of imperfection is handed on to it by them. This is usually how a young person is trained to commit the same 'sins' onto his or hers own children.

When we turn to study the word 'punished' in the same saying, we can see that it has a double meaning. It does not only refer to a pain, a difficulty, tormenting the children. It refers at the same time to an education, a training which is given to them through the negative lessons which they are taught by their parents. It teaches them to mature, even if for this purpose they are punished. Naturally, this view must not be used to put a stop to the parents' efforts or to give them an excuse for remaining their children's negative educators. An education has much more substantial results when it is provided with love and when it comes from someone who is strong and autonomous.

A father used to say to me about his sons: "When I speak to them teasingly of sexual matters, I convey to them a shame and then I see that they too are shy". This gentleman was himself ashamed of freely expressing himself on sexual matters. His sexual desires seemed 'dirty' to him, despicable, improper. Thus, any conversation which he had with his adolescent sons, who sought some guidance on their contact with the opposite sex, was blemished by his own limited perception.

How were these young men to unite themselves with a woman when their union was presented as a vulgar function, merely because it involved bodily contact? Instead of being taught of the body's sanctity, they were mistakenly taught that it was dirty. This they would later hand on to their partners, and in all probability would end up as part of another problematic couple, with the corresponding negative psychosomatic manifestations in their children, too.

In studying through meditation the problem of a nine-year-old girl, I discovered a sexuality, an inexplicable desire, which was expressing itself through her genital centre. The child, naturally, did not know what was happening to her, since at that age there is no such impulse, particularly if the body is still that of a child, as was hers. She translated this desire into the demand for many other things of her parents, things which were often unreasonable and unattainable. At the same time she had pains in her spinal column, which were related to the charge occurring in its various centres.

An inner observation of the problem in relation to the mother showed that the charge in the sex organs came from a constant emission from her. The mother-daughter bond, through the various desires and emotions, was so strong that the child was taking into herself her mother's currents, charging herself with energy and becoming ill. Healing was carried out on this girl, but only if the mother understood her problem would the definitive solution come. Only then would she would be able to control her own powers and would cease to unconsciously transpose on to the child the currents which were overwhelming her.

Spiritual integration is a task that takes many years of conscious inner work which must be continued with firm resolution. This gradually brings about a reduction of the individual's egoism and personal demands. If the parents are not today the perfect beings who can devote themselves wholeheartedly to the upbringing of their children, this does not mean that they should be disappointed or find an excuse for not trying to become so one day. The more they learn to master their own childish needs, the more the father becomes a true 'father' and the mother expresses a fulfilled motherhood.

SPIRITUAL HEALING

When our first daughter was born, my husband, moved by the idea of fatherhood, wrote me a few words about the child and our responsibility towards it. I remember that what he said to me seemed very difficult, because it spoke of a sacrifice, an offering which I could not express. This daughter, like our other two children, did not have the good fortune to be brought up by parents without problems. They too experienced the consequences of our imperfections, which, naturally, affected them in a variety of ways. We were lacking in experience, knowledge, and the resolution to always function as true parents. I will quote an extract here from my husband's letter, because I think that it provides a very clear meaning of the parents' responsibility, and particularly the mother's. Perhaps some of those who read it will be helped and will in turn help their own children, by giving them a better, more complete love, a love which heals weaknesses and bestows psychosomatic balance.

> *1.7.56 "... Today we await the arrival of our offspring, our child. You on the bed of pain, sweet little mother, and I, filled with anxiety mixed with pride, sit and think how much our life changes from today.*
> *All the past remains behind me like a dull memory. In the eye of my imagination, you stand alone, my beautiful girl. You and the great Mo-*

*ment. Every pain you have, I feel it too, every thrill you feel in your entrails, I feel it with you. Will this tiny life arriving today in our world, appreciate all this later? Who knows? And why should we care, anyway? Towards this life we have only obligations. Do not forget, my little wife, that love is descendant, and thus we cannot expect our child to love us as we shall love it..."*

This letter was a message of love and sacrifice; an appeal to the mother, as well as to the father, to be true parents, to show unselfishness, unconditional offer, without any expectations. I believe that when such a service is expressed by the parents, then the children will become strong, firm, autonomous, social individuals.

# ILLNESSES AND THE COUPLE

Man, Woman! The two great forces of humanity. The two opposite forms that attract one another. Without these, humankind would not exist. Without this powerful attraction and their union, the human species could not exist on our planet.

A man and a woman meet, somewhere in the midst of humanity and something magnetises them. They feel the need to be united with one another, to interact in all aspects of their expression. The game of love begins, a multi-faceted, magical game. They love, they desire, they exchange views. The two forces of human existence enter the pulsation of the reverberations they produce between them, as the energies of their souls interact.

In this current of union, resistances suddenly present themselves. Two different wills make their appearance, which, instead of completing one another, cause opposition, pain, friction. Attraction diminishes and repulsion takes its place. At other times, attraction once again flares up, but it is soon reversed, as opposing desires and needs remain unmet.

For centuries now, humankind has presented the same pattern of contact between man and woman; a pattern of attraction and repulsion; an attempt at union and a reaction against it. The result is disillusioning. Endless friction leads to a breach, to despair, to loneliness, to illness. Sometimes the couple chooses separation as their solution while other times they continue to cohabit, in a climate of compromise and forced adaptation. On the subject of relations between a couple, I have given a great deal of detailed data in my books dealing with the role of Woman, Man, and the Couple in Today's Society. These relate to the present chapter, but are more extensive.

If present-day couples were asked how they feel about their relationship, perhaps they would say that all is well. Perhaps they believe that they really have no problems. Some small disagreements, some indispositions or poor psychological states are considered natural occurrences. They are not exceptions, they in no way differ from the majority of other couples. Disagreements, conflicts, indifference are all integral parts of life. The psychosomatic problems resulting from such an attitude make no difference, in most cases, to the manner of contact between them. Thus illness attacks humans, finding them weakened by their own resistances.

Before meeting the Master, I could never have imagined the extent of the problem relations had between the two sexes. I thought the existence of certain difficulties was only natural, but I suspected neither their frequency nor their immeasurable effects on human health. The Master told me, when I began taking on certain responsibilities in the Society, that most problems and illnesses are due to the poor relations between the couple. Little by little, I began to realise the truth of his words. My personal contact with those who visit us have been revealing. A variety of emotions are expressed both by the husband and the wife about their respective partner; negative thoughts, complaints, vindictiveness, endless opposition. Although, to begin with, most people usually say that they have no problems, nevertheless as the conversation progresses, a very different state of affairs becomes apparent.

A whole book could be written on this subject. The cases that have presented themselves during my six years of work at the Society are astonishing at times. I do not regard them as exceptions, because the experience which I have gained in this matter allows me to discern similar problems in most couples; problems whose existence has either been realised, or which neither of the two suspects; illnesses which have occurred as a consequence of a defective relationship.

I will select just a few examples for this chapter, in order to show the connection between illness and the constant friction between man and woman – friction which spreads its effects to the whole family, to the social surroundings, to the work environment. I believe that there are certainly exceptions, that some couples have overcome their problems, or, at least, work together harmoniously in order to achieve a better life together. In this chapter, I am refer to the majority of couples, who, whether they know the truth or not, are in conflict with one another.

The problem of a partners' repulsion towards the other is a very common one. One lady used to say to me of her husband: "I can't stand him anymore; he bothers me all the time". By the word 'bothers', she was referring to his attempts to have sexual contact with her. But she considered this an annoyance and a temptation. She was angry that he would not leave her in peace, urging her to function through her genitals, which she thought of as humiliating and dirty. Her refusal, the great repulsion she felt for him, caused her such retentions that she constantly suffered from pains in her uterus, and in other parts of her body. Her husband, on his part, unable to win her through physical contact, became more and more demanding in other areas. He unconsciously took revenge on her for her resistance and attempted to impose his views on her in all other matters of everyday life. His unsatisfied need led him to bulimia and he soon gained weight to the point of obesity. The atmosphere at home was fraught with tensions and reactions, as the dominant feature in the couple's relations was the wife's continuous rejection of her husband and his own vengefulness over this rejection. Soon their two daughters also began having psychological problems, particularly as they entered puberty.

Naturally, the culpability for such a situation must also be sought in the husband's attitude. He certainly did not know how to behave towards his wife, nor did he show her the proper loving care or the appropriate interest in her wishes. The relationship between two people is a matter for the one and the other. If even one of them is aware of the problem, it can greatly help in its improvement. But when they are both blinded by their own 'I want', then the conflict of the two opposing wills arises. The spiritual energy which should be recycled between them collides with the resistances of the personality, causing great pain. This is retained within the person, who then becomes ill, or manifests as hostility and aggression towards the other.

Another lady, a member of one of the Society's self-study groups, had a problem with her husband, who occasionally sought other women as mistresses. Her reaction to this problem was to be oppressed, to shut herself out, to not to want to give anything to her husband. While investigating her energy centres through meditation, I discovered a great accumulation in her genitals which was not allowing them to function freely. I told her to pay attention to this matter, because it could lead to very unpleasant results. Unfortunately, the need to take revenge on her cheating husband was so great that she continued shutting herself out, even leaving the Society's group. Eventually, she developed cancer, underwent surgery, and had her uterus removed.

With this example I do not mean to say that the husband was right or that he didn't play his own part in their marital problem. As was previously mentioned, every relationship is a matter between both individuals living it, developing it, or destroying it. But when one of the two seeks companionship and satisfaction elsewhere, the other should then look inside oneself to see whether he or she is to blame for the state of his or her partner. If, again, one of them refuses to respond to any form of communication, then the other should have a look at what is going on. Perhaps his or her own approach is so annoying and demanding as to cause reactions?

Man and woman are called upon to unite, to become one body, one soul; to surrender themselves simply and freely to the exchange of currents permeating them. To pulsate with the spiritual energy as it flows from the one to the other, and to feel their interaction at every level of their existence. One lady was telling me that, although she and her husband understood one another completely and she felt love for him, she had, nevertheless, remained a virgin after all these years of marriage. Her excuse was that she feared the pain of the hymen's rupture. But what she was really afraid of was to surrender herself to the other sex, to fully give herself to it. Her personality put up great resistance to the union, using the possibility of a slight pain as a pretext.

Behind every resistance is the fear of losing the personal ego, the fear that the other will exploit his or her partner's willingness to give and use it egoistically. This fear is so great that it often expresses itself as oppression and as a need to dominate. When a certain young man ended his relationship with a girl, he fell ill, with stomach pains and frequent vomiting. He couldn't bear the idea that he had lost her, in other words that she had escaped his dominance. For as long as they were together, he tried to keep her with him by playing an emotional game, which she eventually grew tired of and decided to leave him. A woman needs love, as does a man, in order to feel free next to her partner. She does not need someone hovering over her, stifling her with his demands and his needs. This is not love and it does not lead to union.

SPIRITUAL HEALING

Love liberates, it allows the other to express oneself; it does not oppress one's expressions.

The problem concerns both sexes alike, even though it is expressed differently in each. During these times there are men who have a strong sexual as well as emotional problem. A visit to some brothel does not meet their emotional needs. A number of young women, having acquired an increasing amount of freedom these days, refuse to emotionally provide for a man. Hence they believe that they are avoiding certain mistakes of the past, but they are only making new mistakes, of a new form. They limit themselves to partial functioning, such as, for example, sexual contact, and are thus not fulfilled as persons. Any lack of fulfilment means retention and every retention means illness. If at present there is an outbreak of illnesses, it is due to the crucial transitional period from an old way of life to a new, which has not yet found its proper expression. Both sexes are making desperate attempts to discover their new role in a better relationship. The tensions which arise are due to ignorance which still persists concerning the pattern of this relationship and the strong personal needs of man and woman.

When patients seek the Society's help on health issues concerning inharmonious relations with the other sex, the task carried out to overcome the illness is double. The cause of the illness is explained to the patients, if they are receptive. The discussion might then bring about a substantial change, they may change their attitude and their health may improve. At the same time, spiritual healing takes place, providing an energy balance, strengthening the patients. There are many cases where the healing is quick and completely effective.

Ms. A was a member of the Society and had been a disciple of the Master for only a few months. She showed great responsiveness to the lessons she was receiving, particularly healing meditations. She had a health problem herself before coming to the Society. She had very irregular menstrual cycles, with frequent haemorrhages. When she began meditation, she received specific instructions on self-healing. It was also explained to her that she had been functioning excessively through her genitals and not expressing a similar diffusion from the heart. Ms. A systematically worked on bringing about a balance in her centres and giving greater love to her husband. But it is not easy for change to come about when a way of functioning is a habit formed through the years. Her ailing condition persisted, with a large cyst in her ovary, measuring 11x11 cm, making its appearance. Ms. A was so worried that she asked the Master to carry out a spiritual healing on her himself.

The Master, seeing that a more dynamic intervention was needed if an operation was to be avoided, spent a great amount of time with her. One day, for example, he performed a healing on her for more than an hour. Ms. A took part in this work using the healing meditation she had been taught. She said that while the healing was going on, she felt a certainty and had faith that the Master would heal her.

Improvement began the next day with her menstrual cycle returning to normal limits. Today, as this chapter is being written, Ms. A feels very well. A medical examination has shown that the cyst has shrunk in size and its dimensions are only 7x7 cm. The doctor has told her that an operation will not be necessary and has in fact recommended that she continues spiritual healing. He stated that he considers her healing a true miracle. Ms. A is now completely calm and works systematically on her self-healing, while, at the same time, all of us in the healing section help her. She is also learning how to function in an increasingly better way with her husband.

The healing carried out by the Master leads to the breaking down of the retentions, which brings about a correct flow of energy within the body; retentions, which start out from a personality reaction and gradually lead to psychosomatic illnesses. When young S complained of cellulitis in her hips and thighs, the Master explained to her that it was the result of her fear to give herself to her partner without any resistance. Her sexual relations had always been incomplete, she was not adequately satisfied, and her body was tense, which resulted in the accumulations under her skin. S understood the problem, but it was difficult for her to overcome her emotional insecurities. The Master then carried out a very impressive healing on her. The cellulitis was rapidly broken down and her body recovered its youthful, smooth appearance. S believed in the Master's healing power, understood his words even more, and changed her attitude towards her partner. She was liberated from inhibitions and fears and felt love-making with him in a more fulfilled way, together with love, experiences previously unknown to her.

There is something else which often complicates relations between the two sexes: ignorance of the deeper motive which binds them together. Many believe that they are devoted and give everything to their partner, while in reality they are always seeking to take from him or her. They require a response to even the tiniest token of their interest or offering. They are dependent on their partner's every word, action or reaction. They become, as they say, a sacrifice to him or her, whereas in essence they do it because they cannot live without receiving support or some other gesture of care. They believe that they are giving their soul, but they are in fact giving nothing. They are not recycling the energy within themselves. Any offering which conceals the expectation of compensation is not a true offering. It is a demand, which causes greater inhibitions and accumulations in the human energy body. Love does not expect, it does not envy, it does not demand and it does not depend on anything. It simply gives, embracing others with all of their defects and delivers them from those defects.

There are moments when the endless difficulties between man and woman make me believe that there is nothing more serious than these. They are so composite, complicated, and often deeply hidden that they do not even appear to be a problem. They take on various forms of dependence, jealousy, desire, demand and expectation, so that they seem like ordinary human situations. Since humans have grown accustomed to living surrounded by such feelings, it is only natural that they should not attach particular importance to similar symptoms. Thus they find ground to develop, taking on vast proportions, and eventually overwhelming them with oppression. Who can say they have never experienced any of all these unpleasant emotions? And who could say that they have not felt bad about their condition, have not lost their vitality and their powers?

As human beings, we often live through pain. But pain is reduced when we decide to stop constantly making demands of others. Then we are able to turn to our own self and find true strength there. Our soul, the whole of our spiritual energy wants to spread around us, to unite itself with our partner, without reservations and fears. When this happens, a profound serenity is achieved. The mind and the heart expand, while the body experiences its needs in a simple manner. A balance comes as a consequence and the flow of energy is liberated within the body. Our illnesses are substantially diminished and a new pattern of life is prepared for our descendants.

A sense of responsibility towards our partner and love for him or her are necessary for a proper contact, an effective union. Through this union, better psychosomatically equipped children will be born, an improvement in society will emerge. What human beings lack, is knowledge of the problem and the love for it. If we know and accept the problem itself, we can assist in its solution, we can rid ourselves and others of its effects.

Perhaps it would be very important to take a step towards self-knowledge, along the lines of the question which the Master often asked of me during the first year of my discipleship. The cause of illness must be looked for calmly and objectively. Everyone should ask of themselves: "Why am I ill? Why is my partner ill?" This can bring about a revelation, an answer to the problem; it can expand consciousness and help in the improvement of health and in all other problems which couples so frequently encounter, which ruin the harmony of their common life.

# NEGATIVE THOUGHTS
# AND EMOTIONS

"I am afraid, I am terrified for the future of my son", Ms. K said when she came to the Society for the first time. In the conversation which followed, her fear expressed itself constantly. She used words which showed her anxiety. She said that she was worried, had doubts and many questions and did not know what to do, felt diffident and insecure.

All this had to do with her son, who had recently been showing symptoms of isolation and had begun distancing himself from his parents. Her worry was so great that she was unable to understand what I was trying to say to her. She had magnified the child's problem with her thoughts, she had blown it up out of proportion, making it impossible for her to look at it calmly.

With considerable difficulty I managed to bring to light a few details about the issue concerning her but, mainly, about its causes. It seemed that the parents' over-protection had led the young man to escapism. This escape did not bring about the appropriate change, nor did it raise their awareness of the problem, which originated from themselves and not from their son. He was on the defensive, he wanted to be delivered from the constant anxiety infecting him with their words and their attitude.

I used all means at my disposal to alter Ms. M's attitude. Several months passed and each time we repeated the same conversation. It seems that she was 'stuck' with the agonising question concerning her son's future and was unable to do anything about it, to change her attitude or to relieve him of the insecurity which she was constantly transmitting to him.

There are many children who grow up in a similar environment of fear and anxiety. It might not be as obvious as with Ms. M's case, but it does not cease to have a negative effect on them. The anxiety which is manifested, even if nothing is said about it, overwhelms the child with an unpleasant wave, which burdens and weakens it. When emotions have dominated over a person, then the soul's energies are not positive. They are emitted in a negative form, invading the receiver's emotional body, causing similar negative manifestations in him or her. Thus, a young child surrounded by anxiety currents loses its strength, wastes away and becomes ill. Even if the parents make no mention of their fears, even if no action on their part expresses them, nevertheless, the vibrations they emit reflect their feelings and thoughts; negative vibrations, which, naturally, disturb their surroundings and create an atmosphere of insecurity and endless fears. How can a healthy physical state possibly develop amid anxiety? Both the receiver of the negative current and its transmitter suffer from it.

Human beings are both transmitters and receivers at the same time, because we live in a space filled with energies which flow between us and influence us. This can be observed in mass gatherings when a member of the group expresses a negative thought. This thought invades the others like a force, giving them its own qualitative substance, and soon all of them might share the same attitude, the same negative manifestation. As a result of such a negative emission, this force is transformed into hostility, panic, or whatever else has started out from a single person. For this reason a crowd is easily led astray and follows the current projected by a powerful leader, a demagogue. These facts indicate that, if the leader is a transmitter of positive thoughts and emotions, he or she may use this power to bring about a positive group current, helping to carry out a certain task, or, on the other hand, to cause disasters by emitting negative currents.

The Master always tells his disciples not to indulge in evil thoughts or thought-forms. The word 'thought-form' suggests the emission of a mental energy which produces a mental image, an idea. This idea, as an energy of the mind, is transmitted to others, affecting them with its appearance. The Master encourages all of us to have positive thought-forms on all matters, problems and people. If, for example, someone is suffering from a psychosomatic symptom, the emission of a positive idea about him or her passes through one's energy body and begins to break down the negative state. The same happens with all undesirable problems which besiege us each day. These too are balanced out by a positive approach, not only by the specific work needed to deal with them, but also by simultaneous faith that all will be well, that everything will improve.

Human beings have knowledge of the soul's energies and speak of them as a source of power which helps or destroys, depending on their use. Children seek their parents' blessing, thus invoking, in essence, love, positive spiritual energy, which will strengthen them and protect them through their life. The simple saying 'keep wishing and it will happen' brings to light an unconscious knowledge of positive energies which can promote an agreeable solution to a certain issue. On the other hand, fear is often expressed about curses and the 'evil eye'.

The concept of the evil eye is not accepted by everyone, even though it has shown many proven examples. The reason why many people do not accept it is that they have not sufficiently understood the power of the soul's energy, transmitted through the mind from one person to the other. But over and above this, the evil eye has another point which is not easily understood. Most of the time, people 'casting the evil eye' upon others do so in an unconscious manner. They do not send out negative thoughts or feelings of envy or hate with their words. On the contrary, they seem to admire the others' beauty, their health or their clothes. But in spite of these apparently kind words, the receivers become 'ill-wished', starting to feel unwell, having headaches, vomiting and so on.

While studying the issue of ill-wishing, through personal experiences as well as through the observation of various events around me, I have noticed that the evil eye is usually cast as a positive form of energy. This happens because the transmitters do not know that, concealed underneath their admiration for something fine, is hidden a desire for that thing. Thus, whereas consciously they are praising it, unconsciously they wish to have it for themselves. This need for appropriation is so deeply hidden that it is not recognised, unless a systematic self-observation is undertaken, with great objectivity and without reactions against its revelations. In other words, when someone says "What beautiful clothes you are wearing" or "how well-behaved your child is", they should delve deep within themselves and see whether they would like these 'nice' things for their own. If this is the case, they are then covering up with positive words a negative stance – a need to have something, to accumulate within their selves something which they lack. This need results in ill-wishing, the transmission of negative energies to others and the retention of their own positive aspects.

Before I met the Master, I too, was one of those people casting the evil eye. Once in a while, something happened which took me by surprise and troubled me. Often, when I said something nice about somebody, he or she would become ill, have an accident, or feel bad. This situation reached a point when I began feeling guilty and was afraid to express myself. I could not understand what was happening to me, nor did I know of the force emerging from me and influencing others in a negative way. The Master, whom I told of my problem from our very first meetings, explained the phenomenon of ill-wishing to me and helped me to gradually transform my negative emissions into positive. He taught me to develop my love for others and to consciously think well of everybody. Thus, the force which up until then had been a cause of unpleasant results became, with the knowledge and the help he provided me, a positive healing power. This event helped me understand that every force has two expressions, depending on the way we use it. The human mind can be a transmitter of good or bad thoughts and the power of the soul can convey what he or she wishes. Of course, in order to achieve a positive function, work and resolution is needed. Then the forces of the soul become a blessing for our surroundings and the people around us.

Apart from ill-wishing, which frequently shows the peculiarity of an unconscious function, the rest of the negative currents are many and varied. Their sole source is desire which is so strong as to show itself as a negative thought-form or emotion. Many people openly show their dislike for someone, they get angry, curse, and wish for his or her ruin. Others do not have such obvious reactions and emit their negative energies silently, often without being aware of it. Their acts may be ostensibly positive, they may show interest and care for others, but their so-called 'inward' acts, the state of their emotional and mental functions, might be the complete opposite. Then the recipient of their interest simultaneously receives their negative currents and cannot be helped by their external 'care' because the energy of the soul which is channeled through the body is much more powerful than a simple action. Only if this action is accompanied by the pure current of love does it become a true offering to others.

Every unpleasant emotion, just like every negative thought, can cause great disturbances. The wife, who is 'worried' about her husband who is far away, transmits a negative state to him. A person who fears that some relative will die from a certain disease reinforces this disease with his or her own phobia, bringing about a deterioration or creating the conditions for something bad. This may be so powerful as to bring about certain psychosomatic symptoms in the recipient of these emotions, particularly if contact between them is constant, if there is a personal relationship.

We are not solely bodies, forms which move in space. We are powers and energies which spread around us and affect this space. They likewise affect our own self, which feels the reverberation, the reflection of our own energies. If we emit sorrow, insecurity, outbursts of enthusiasm, these spread around us, forming a corresponding energy field. Within this energy field are those who surround us, as are we. Thus our currents return to us, often much more intense and disturbing, because the recipients of the soul's energies may adopt them and double them with their own negative radiance. On the other hand, when the vibrations which we cause in space are positive, then their positive reflections will be returned to us.

Perhaps there will be many objections to the aforementioned, because it is considered natural for human beings to have needs, fears, doubts. It is not always pos-

## NEGATIVE THOUGHTS AND EMOTIONS

sible to be well, or to only have positive thoughts. I often hear people saying things like: "But wasn't I right to be angry with his attitude?" or "It is impossible for me not to fear for his health, not to worry about his progress." All these things are human characteristics. We all worry, we all desire or fear something. I would say that it is through these states that we acquire the necessary experience in life. At some point an understanding comes that no negative function can help in the solution of a problem. Fear does not exist to overwhelm and weaken us. It exists, on the contrary, to mobilise us into doing something about it. To see it as an incentive for a change in our attitude which will prompt us to find a solution to its cause. If fear makes us 'go weak at the knees', it is because we have let it become exaggerated within our emotion centre. We are not dealing with it with our reason, directing energy to the brain. Thus begins an energy imbalance which is projected with negative vibrations around us. It causes spasms to the emotional space which frequently lead to illness. If, when an unpleasant current begins to flood into us, we find the strength to think of its exact pleasant opposite, then a balance will be achieved and the negative manifestations will be reduced.

A young man, influenced by someone who had foretold his future, believed that he would die at an early age. The result of the negative attitude towards his own life was that he developed leukemia at the age of 27. When we began spiritual healing on him, we discovered an obsession with his death charging his mind. It was very difficult to help him, because his reverse stance and his persistent thought-form had to be broken down. With considerable systematic work and simultaneous medical help, this young man is today managing to hold his own. We are still working intensively on his problem, as he seems to frequently relapse, because he does not help himself by projecting a positive power of the soul.

I will repeat here something which I consider extremely important. Humans are a source of energy, both positive and negative. Systematic work is needed to give them the knowledge to become increasingly positive transmitters. This will gradually alter the negative emissions of others, thus preparing humankind for a better future. The sooner this knowledge is acquired, the better it will be for all of us, especially for the coming generations, our own children, who have expectations of us.

# ABUSE – PASSION – POSSESSION

Human needs are innumerable. Some manifest themselves forcefully, while others are less powerful easily fading away. There are, however, certain desires which lead humans to painful impasses. They seem to completely dominate and enslave them with their intensity. The first expression of such domination of personal needs over the individuals presents itself with the abuses in which they indulge, in order to satisfy themselves. 'Abuse' is any kind of excessive use of something that causes temporary gratification within one of the energy centres. It is not only whatever provides satisfaction to the human physical body. Excessive use frequently occurs in other areas too, such as when reading excessively in order to accumulate knowledge. These are all causes of imbalance in the centres and insufficient flow of the soul's energy, which often leads to psychosomatic illnesses.

In order for gratification to take place in a centre, certain material means must usually be employed. For example, the emotional centre of the abdomen seeks large amounts of food in order to fulfill an emotional void. The genital centre leads the individual to sexual excesses or other bodily satisfactions. The same is true of every centre which functions excessively with the singular aim of personal satisfaction. But this makes humans slaves to their partial functioning. Abuse, which is an excess, leads to the uneven charging of one of the points of the energy body, resulting in pain and illness.

When abuses become a permanent way of life, then they are no longer simply excesses, but end up being genuine passions – passions which dominate humans to such an extent that they are often unable to rid themselves of them. Common examples are alcoholism, drug abuse, gambling and any sexual perversion. In most cases, these start out as temporary abuses that, with the passage of time, become permanent, increase, and take over the entire human nature. A man for, example, who feels an ever-increasing need to accompany his meal with a glass of wine may one day reach the point when this wine is necessary to him, in large quantities and at all times of day. He becomes a slave to it and the initial enjoyment it provided turns into pain and unhappiness. Numerous studies have been conducted showing the results of passions to the human being.

Behind every passion, and every abuse, lies the inability of humans to fully express themselves through the whole of their being. They insist, often unconsciously, on limiting themselves to just one of their energy centres, wishing to enjoy the unique vibration that it provides them. But this obsession carries with it an overcharging which leads to the weakening of the organism and, often, to its eventual destruction.

A typical example of a passion that leads to the individuals' annihilation is drug abuse, which is caused by their inability to find another suitable outlet for their spiritual powers. They seek the flight from reality which they find in the illusions they experience when using drugs. These give them a powerful emotional pulsation, but still restrict the rest of their functions. The body and the mind are weakened and soon the familiar negative effects take over.

The Society's healing section has frequently dealt with drug addicts. Individuals who seek help, after reaching a dead end. The hardest part of their effort is their weakened will. Even though they are aware of the danger to their health and the imminent threat of death if they continue to use drugs, nevertheless they cannot muster the strength to quit. Adding to this is the thought of having to go through the ordeal of drug withdrawal.

When the first drug-users started coming to the Society, I had no idea what to do for them. They were in such a state of unbridled need and weakness, that I thought it was impossible that they could ever be normal people again. It was when the healing section had just been established and, naturally, we had not yet validated ourselves as healers. And so we sought the Master's help, who undertook the task of treating the first drug addicts to visit us.

Since that time, I have observed many similar healings by the Master. Common to all of them has been his endless patience and the constant radiance which he conveys to the patients. The results were not slow to appear. The addicts stopped using drugs and gradually started finding themselves again. Naturally, this necessitated the patients' firm decision, which often came into conflict with the circle of other addicts. The latter wanted to drag them back into their old way of life which they themselves wished to abandon. There were cases where individuals, though leaving the Society in a good mental state, would meet an old friend who would lead them again to places where drugs were readily available. This would briefly disrupt the healing process and a fresh effort, a new battle for their deliverance would have to begin. This, in fact, happens whenever a person wishes to be rid of a negative situation. The situation re-presents itself before him or her, through somebody who is still its prisoner. It seems that a powerful friction field is always created between the two opposing forces, which, like opposite camps, wish to defeat one another.

I could describe numerous drug addict healings here, as I observed them during the first year of my discipleship. In all of them, the Master helps the patients to relax, reducing the strong reactions manifested as extreme irritability. As this happens, he begins transferring the energy of the soul to the drug addicts, until they begin to discover its power within themselves. The Master makes frequent use of the dialectical method, as it helps the individual to express oneself and to realise that a solution to the problem exists, that it is not a lost cause.

As drug addicts start to find themselves again, they need constant support. In the early stages, it is recommended that they spend as much time as possible at the Society, in order to constantly receive the healing power coming from the Master as well as from the other members of the healing section. They are also called upon to practice relaxation exercises, which reduce the pains, and to meditate as much as possible. It is also a good idea, during the initial days, for them to be escorted home by a former addict, who can help them during the difficult night-time hours. All these things contribute to the rehabilitation's success. If there is a need for sedatives, then the doctor, who will be monitoring them, will provide the necessary prescriptions.

The healings of drug addicts which the Master has carried out are true miracles. I have seen individuals nearing death, emaciated, pale, with advanced hepatitis, and pains in their bones, healed. I have watched the gradual transformation which occurs within them and which is externalised through their movements, their actions, and even their thoughts. Hands which have been shaking from the effects of heroin are steadied by the radiance which they receive. The muscle pains disappear, the mind regains its lucidity. Little by little they recover their old self, becoming once again useful members of society.

I will quote here a few words written by a drug addict during the early days of his healing. I believe that these speak far more vividly about the miraculous healing power than any description of mine. Young Dimitris had come to the Society with a friend of his, a former addict, who had himself been healed by the Master. He was then in a wretched state and it seemed unlikely that he could ever stop doing drugs, as he himself writes using the language of addicts, which had become a way of life for him. His case was one of the most difficult and it took a long time for him to begin to recover. Nevertheless, from the very first days, a great change took place within him, as can be seen in the text which follows.

ABUSE – PASSION – POSSESSION

*Dimitris's Monologue*

"I don't know how to start.
Let's start with my present condition.
A little while ago, I, Mitsos*, was (and I say 'was', because I am not now) a junkie, a drug addict. For many people, a 'devil' whom they wanted to exterminate by whatever means, and so pushing me even further into drugs.
I have a friend, Dimitris. He was a junkie as well. I was away from Athens for ten days. When I got back, I discovered that my friend Dimitris had KICKED THE HABIT. My jaw dropped! I couldn't believe my eyes! Dimitris found me later and explained to me that he'd simply given it up. I thought he was talking 'rubbish' and that he'd given it up out of 'paranoia'. He'd become paranoid, believed in higher powers and so had forgotten the 'fib'.
Later, he talked to me about a man who had helped him. I couldn't fit it into my mind. Somebody who helps you kick the stuff!... Impossible! That's what I said... But I don't say it now. Why? Because, quite simply, I understood 'what the Human is, what Power is, what Will,

---
* Mitsos is an affectionate diminutive of the name Dimitris.

*and LOVE is'. Things that I saw within myself simply with His help. Not Dimitris', but the Supreme's. And Dimitris', who had actually become a really good guy.*

*Let's leave Dimitris aside for a moment and talk about another, new, Dimitris. Mitsos who became Dimitris, who came to understand the meaning of his life on earth. Who discovered his shattered Power, Love, Will, and united them again, through a Society.*

*Little by little, my new self, because this is Dimitris, my self, has begun to feel that some people actually loved him, without asking for anything in return. And then he understood the wrong position he had previously adopted, and God, himself, Love entered him! Without expecting to receive anything, he simply has and, since he has, he gives!"*

These words show that a passion which is transmuted into power and love ceases to be a passion. Humans are liberated from their limitations and begin to spread the powers of their souls around them, 'giving', as Dimitris says. All this can happen with spiritual healing, especially when the patients respond to it. Passions are many and varied. The sufferers are aware of their problems and their manifestations, but do not usually know how to overcome them. They do not know what the unknown, negative force is which is leading them to self-destruction, nor do they know with what positive force they can fight it. So, although they are aware of their situation, they nevertheless remain under its control. The spiritual healers, with the power they receive from God, can bring balance to the patients and bestow health upon them once again.

The difficulty in healing a passion lies in the patients' resistance to the deprivation of the ephemeral pleasure it offers. Drug addicts come up with various excuses in order to refrain from doing what will help them. They claim to be tempted by friends, they say they do not believe in pharmaceutical treatments or in the work of the rehabilitation centres, and so forth. In cases such as these, spiritual healing is discontinued and begins again only when the patients express a firm decision and a continuous will to be healed. Otherwise, the energy they receive from the healing section may be improperly used, intensifying their passion and their need to satisfy it.

Apart from passions of all forms, which seize humans and which they are aware of, though they cannot be liberated from them, there are also forms of possession which dominate individuals, without them knowing why or what has caused them. These are cases of epileptics or 'possessed', as they are called by some. People who suffer from a possession differ from those who are subject to their passions, because the cause of their state seems not to have anything to do with their individual attitude or will. Without warning, they lose control of themselves and become captives of an unknown power which transforms them into beings unaware of their actions. The attack usually comes and goes abruptly, leaving the person in a wretched state. There is no awareness of the problem, no way out, not even a difficult one. No one can be held responsible for a possession or found guilty because of their inability to overcome it.

Medical science has succeeded in controlling epileptic fits, assisting the patient with pharmaceutical treatments. But forms of possession that unexpectedly manifest in people who are usually normal have no definite treatment. These attacks, which lead to convulsions, uncontrolled movements, lack of communication or to destructive acts, such as murder, cannot be dealt with. These patients are said to have a dual personality, or that an evil spirit has possessed them. Doctors call them paranoid or schizophrenic, depending on the case. There are various ways of dealing with these cases which involve religious convictions. 'Witch-doctors' are called in to drive out the demon or priests to exorcise it.

Four years ago, an occurrence of this kind took place at the Society. We were all engaged in various tasks, when we were urgently summoned to one of the rooms. As I approached, I saw young M lying on the floor, foaming at the mouth and writhing, without any control or knowledge of what was happening. The Master was immediately called to help, and he asked to remain alone with M and two or three others. The seizure was so intense that I had difficulty imagining how it could be stopped. The Master began a contact healing and the rest of us assisted by meditation. M continued convulsing and writhing for a short time, until he suddenly calmed down. When he recovered, he was unable to remember anything of what had happened nor did he have any recollection of previous attacks. The Master sent him home in the company of another member of the Society and advised him to eat well and to rest. From then on, M showed no other similar symptom of possession. He had been decisively relieved of this unknown power which takes control and robs the individual of any control of oneself. The Master's healing was comprehensive and permanent.

Possession by an unknown negative power is caused not only by an individual weakness. It involves the evolution of humankind in its entirety which struggles between positive and negative currents. Individuals who happen to have a weak point, a personal difficulty in balancing their centres, provide an exit to the negative currents that manifest through their body. The currents unexpectedly taking hold of them are not only their individual voids, but are expressed through them, as they become their conduit. Thus they suddenly lose all control, their energy centres are reversed and they seem to become possessed by an 'evil spirit'. This, in essence, is a great negative force, a destructive force which causes an imbalance, a form of paranoia or temporary loss of the ego.

When the Master healed M of this form of possession, I realised that only pure spiritual power can bring about such a result. The Master, united with the Spirit, was able to expel from M's body the powerful negative current which had overwhelmed him. Such was his healing power that M acquired a stable balance and never again did he become a conduit of opposing forces.

I was told of a similar example regarding possession by members of the Society, as I wasn't present when it occurred. It concerned young B, who was greatly attached to her boyfriend. Such was her dependence on him that her every thought, action, and emotional reaction was influenced by this need. She had literally become a captive of her own desire, to the degree of losing all individual freedom. The very thought of autonomy, or even of a reduction of her attachment, made her ill. Whenever the Master endeavoured to show her that what she felt was not love, but pain and deprivation of her individual liberty, she reacted violently, refusing to listen to any of it.

On the day the episode occurred, such a conversation had taken place. B went into an emotional reaction, lost control of herself and was overwhelmed by her obsession.

Her senses seemed to have gone dead, she couldn't see around her, she couldn't hear or feel anything. Something akin to derangement had overtaken her, like a flight from a reality which she could not accept. She had been seized by a strong current of imbalance and presented the image of a person who had passed into a state of paranoia and could stay there permanently. Her words were unclear and unintelligible, like those of a schizophrenic. Those who were with her tried to bring her round, but her communication with others seemed non-existent. At that time the Master approached her and began to speak to her and carry out a healing. He worked ceaselessly, breaking down the barrier which B had built up against her surroundings. He worked with the power of his soul, activating her centres so that they would regain their proper function. The healing lasted a long time, because there was great resistance from the negative currents. Gradually, B began to recover, recovering her senses and feeling better. She was literally saved from a great danger – that of losing her own consciousness. The Master healed her from possession and brought her back to the reality of life.

Each of us is possessed by certain fears, needs, or intense passions. These all have the common characteristic of dominance over us, refusing to let us freely express our soul. They restrict us, cause illnesses and difficulties in life as we lose the power of our true spiritual nature. Spiritual healing has the power to break down these states, even those which, as unknown powers, cause violent attacks. Because the power of the Spirit is beyond all these limiting currents: it is the first, pure manifestation of God.

# THE IMPORTANCE OF RELAXATION

Many new members of the Society want to learn how to aid the sick in getting well. They also want to learn the methods of self-healing and, particularly, the way to relieve themselves of various psychosomatic ailments. They are looking for techniques to liberate themselves, as well as to contribute to the general improvement of their relatives and friends.

As has become apparent so far, the majority of illnesses are a result of tensions and retention of the soul's energy within the body. This, whether it happens consciously or unconsciously, is to a large degree the cause of various disorders, firstly to the human energy body and then to the physical body. Consequently, a necessary condition for the recovery of health and the avoidance of tensions is inner calmness. When it is absent, the disturbance overwhelms humans, leading them to various escape routes, which gradually bring about illnesses. In the previous chapters, many facts have been provided about friction in human relations, obsession with a limited function, as well as their various negative results.

If tension, disturbance and friction are to be regarded as the causes of illnesses, as has already become apparent, then the solution to this problem can be found in peace, in that inner state of profound serenity. Peace is in essence the source of power, of dynamic free expression, of the overall externalisation of the soul's energies. In today's society, power is very frequently misunderstood. For example, people are considered 'dynamic' when they are forceful, when they impose their will on others, when they insist on being obeyed and followed. But very often, behind this seemingly dynamic expression, fear of failure and an insecurity of rejection lie hidden. Deep down, such individuals are not secure or at peace, and so express themselves through exaggerations, in order to cover up these weaknesses. This attitude cannot help them, and the tensions which exist within them can lead to various psychosomatic disorders.

An initial method of acquiring calmness are relaxation exercises. Relaxation is taught to all members of the Society in self-study groups. The results usually become apparent in a short period of time. Many report a great change in their attitude towards life, which reduces their fears and gives them a renewed strength to face their problems. This power naturally relieves them of the consequences of tensions and their effects on their psychosomatic function.

Members of the Society who are beginners are taught a simple relaxation technique which has been adapted to the conditions and habits of contemporary society. No special posture, difficult for people of the Western world, or specific time of day, are required of those who practice this exercise. Individuals can freely choose the time best suited to them. The only recommendation is to focus on the work being done for as long as the relaxation lasts.

The individuals, lying or sitting comfortably in a position in which the spinal column is straight, close their eyes and think only of the specific task they are carrying out at that moment. They think of their body and of their surroundings, allowing themselves to calmly feel the weight of their body while observing their breathing. This helps to distract them from other thoughts and emotions which may have been troubling them up to that time. The immobility of their body and their mental observation bring calmness to the mind and moderate the emotions. If, in spite of this, tension reoccurs, the exercise can be interrupted or the cause of the tension can be calmly examined.

For as long as this relaxation is progressing successfully, the individuals can imagine that their body is in the midst of an abundance of light. This visualisation is a great help in establishing the idea that there are no problems. It brings about a feeling of calm, clarity, and a reduction of resistances. This calmness passes from the physical body to the mind and an ease of greater acceptance of all matters comes about. The individuals feel increasingly stronger and renewed.

This exercise can be repeated two or three times a day, or even more frequently. It can be practiced every morning, to help in the day's work, or every evening, to obtain a quiet night's sleep. It can also be used to eliminate minor ailments which result from an accumulation of energy in one of the centres, such as headache, a stomach pain, and more. Also, when there is no time for sleep, a brief relaxation can rapidly revitalise the organism and help individuals continue their work.

The change which occurs when you learn to relax is so great that you come to see life with new eyes, as something simple and beautiful. This is due to the fact that the power of the soul, which has been withheld, finds a way to express itself as dynamic creativity. One lady in a self-study group mentioned that since she was taught how to relax, everything seems easier to her and she has learnt to handle situations in a better way. And she told me of a particular event which shows how much she had been helped. One day she had to meet with her supervisor, who always behaved in an aggressive and abrupt manner towards everyone. She felt unhappy about the prospect of this meeting, so she decided to calm herself a little before facing her. In the building where she worked there was no place for her to be on her own and so she simply shut herself in the restroom. There she managed to relax, and, as she had learnt to do at the Society, she imagined that all was well and obtained strength and courage for the unpleasant meeting. At the same time, she mentally sent her love to her supervisor. After a little while she came out from the restroom and made her way towards this difficult contact. No difficulty arose. The usual reactions were dissolved immediately as they were dealt with by her calm approach. The problem was settled and the two women reached a peaceful understanding.

It goes without saying that a calm but dynamic handling of day-to-day issues reduces the causes which often lead to tensions. It therefore also reduces the causes which may bring about illness in the human organism. It has a considerable effect on sleep, which becomes much more peaceful and provides better rest to the body. I have heard many examples of specific change from members of the Society who practice relaxation daily. Some say that when they relax for a few minutes before going to bed, they sleep without bad dreams and, naturally, wake up rested and refreshed to face a new day of work. Others report that when they perform the relaxation exercise in the morning, they are in a very good mood during work, and have a generally more creative attitude. They are not easily distracted by irrelevant thoughts and take only a short time to settle their affairs. Many also speak of an improvement to their health: their body feels stronger, filled with vitality and energy.

The Master teaches relaxation to the patients who come to seek our help. He also provides special meditations which will help dissolve the energies which are being retained. Sick people are excellent receivers of healing power when they have learnt to relax during healing. They contribute to the healing, as there are no resistances from the energies accumulated in their centres. Thus the energy of the soul passes directly from healer to patient.

In 1985 I, too, had such an experience of the positive participation of a patient who had learnt some time before how to relax and to meditate. This was Mr. S, who regularly came to the Society and had received specific instructions from the Master on the healing for his heart condition. He had tachycardia, which from time to time gave rise to tensions and made it difficult for him to lead

## THE IMPORTANCE OF RELAXATION

a normal life. Mr. S regularly carried out self-healing with the help of his wife, a senior member of the Society's healing section.

One day, Mr. S asked me to carry out contact healing on him, as he wanted to be helped more directly. When the healing began and Mr. S was completely relaxed, I sensed his great receptivity to the power which was passing to him. My hand, which was over his heart, seemed to be directing all the energy to the point which was unwell. There was no resistance on his part, to the extent that I had the feeling that we had become a united entity, within which the healing power of the Spirit was being channeled unimpeded. Mr. S was wholly participating in the proceedings, telling me from time to time how he felt. At first, warmth flooded his heart, and then, when the energy had done its healing work, he felt coolness in my hand and realised that the end of the healing was approaching. I felt the same, as I was simply transferring power to the patient.

When the healing ended, Mr. S was completely calm and felt greatly reinvigorated. He told me: "During the whole time that you were carrying out the healing, your hand had become one with my body. And little by little I felt that you didn't exist at all and that you were simply a conduit of a power which was coming from a great distance. I was completely relaxed and I let this power heal me. I thought that your hand could never be separated from my body, so great was our union. It was only when I began to feel coolness at the point of contact that I realised that the healing was ending, and then your hand was removed from my heart".

I believe that the total relaxation and receptivity of Mr. S were an important aid in the healing which continued to occur. From that time on he has not ceased to meditate daily, the temporary crisis has passed, and he continues leading a normal life. He is one of those disciples of the Master who, when he is meditating, experiences ecstasy and union with God. He always surrenders himself to the current which floods him, with faith in His power and without resistances of any kind. He has come to understand that only the union of his individual will with the Will of God can bestow health upon him. This firm conviction on his part breaks down any resistance and gives him the necessary calmness, as the Master has taught him.

The potential for relaxation exits in every human being. All that is needed is not to have negative thoughts and not to doubt its importance. When you try out relaxation, it is likely that you will not feel any particular change at first. If, however, you are convinced of your potential and continue to exercise regularly, the results will begin to show and will be positive in all aspects of your life. Because relaxation is the precondition for the breaking down of accumulations, genuinely helping the flow of the soul's energy within the body, which is essential for the individual's good health and psychological balance.

# SINGING –RITUALS – CHORODROMENA (RITUAL DANCING)

One of my first lessons as a disciple greatly surprised me and seemed at the time irrelevant to the help I was seeking. Unexpectedly, the Master asked me to sing a song – any song I wanted. I found it impossible to open my mouth and to produce the slightest sound. Then, as a true artist, he began singing while I listened on in amazement.

When he finished singing a number of old Greek songs, I could contain my curiosity no longer and asked him the meaning of this action. The Master explained to me, to the extent that I could understand at that time, the importance of sounds and vibrations. Similar lessons frequently followed, as I continued resisting to mumble even a short melody. In spite of this, he insisted and gave me specific instructions involving the matter of music.

Song and music can help humans evolve. As I have already explained, health problems are very frequently an inhibition of emotions, thoughts and, generally, of the soul's energies in the individual ego. This inhibition often also includes a refusal to externalise ourselves through any means of expression, even a simple melodic sound, a song. Concealed behind this difficulty which many people experience, are fear and resistance over a diffusion of the soul in space. It is as if they enclose everything within themselves and are shy, they fear, they refuse to dynamically express themselves. Since that time, I have attended lessons where beginners sometimes do as I did, being so uptight that no sound leaves their mouth, not even a whisper.

Song is of enormous importance, not only for the person singing, but for the whole environment. A pleasing sound produces vibrations in space that can change a state of depression into joy – or the reverse, if the melody is a sad one. The human being, even since primitive times, has used sounds and reverberations to pulsate the environment and to differentiate certain currents. It has also been proven that music has healing properties, particularly regarding people who are mentally ill. The help provided by music is a well-known fact by now and it is

## SINGING – RITUALS – CHORODROMENA (RITUAL DANCING)

widely used on many occasions. In factories, for example, where workers have to perform well, agreeable music is played, reducing fatigue and the tension of work.

Depending on the quality of the vibrations, music affects humans on various levels. There is music which vibrates the emotions, producing joy, sadness, enthusiasm. There is also music which arouses the instincts, causing upsurges of sexual needs and sexually stimulating people, who are often unaware of the reason. And there is music which elevates to spiritual levels and gives rise to a higher state of mind, to ecstasy. This category contains many classical compositions, as well as simple songs, if they are sung in the right way.

The Master has helped many patients feel better by singing for them. There have been cases where psychologically difficult situations have been altered by his singing. Because, as he sings, he does not refer to a single specific person. He does not confine his song to anyone in particular who may have an attachment to him. When singing love songs he references the love to God Himself. He recognises His Presence everywhere and so addresses a melody, a verse, exclusively to Him. This expanded approach is also communicated to others as a power which vibrates the spiritual levels. It brings a balance to their energy centres, helping them directly receive the pure spiritual energy which the Master radiates.

SPIRITUAL HEALING

One of the most impressive cases of healing by song was that of Mr. K, who was in danger of losing his eyesight. He had been suffering from this problem for years and it had affected him psychologically, as the fear of blindness overwhelmed him. When the Master was called upon to help him, the first thing he did was to sing old Greek songs to him. He also invited him to join in, and Mr. K, after a great deal of difficulty, eventually responded. With the Master's patience, a change began to occur in his soul's disposition. The circuits of his centres started working harmoniously and, as he acquired a different energy flow within himself, the Master taught him meditation and special self-healing exercises.

Mr. K began to work regularly in accordance with the instructions he received. He was very responsive to everything and soon the positive results started showing, always with the help of the Master's healings. His eyesight improved, the danger passed and he was able to return to his job without fear. More than seven years have passed since then, and he is still very well and continues to meditate without fail. What is important in his case is that the first difficulties and resistances left with the vibrations of the sounds and the appropriate melodies. After the change in his own vibrations, the correct spiritual healing work was able to follow.

At the Society's self-study groups, members are encouraged to often sing, whenever they can. Song is a means of altering an unpleasant situation and contributes to the externalisation of the soul's energies. It is, therefore, a kind of healing – not only for the individual, but also for all who hear it, particularly if it is properly sung. The Master says that every song is a hymn of praise to God when the person who sings recognises His Existence in every word. Then the simplest, most ordinary melody takes on another meaning, becomes part of the Being and is addressed to It.

The Master, except from singing familiar songs, ecclesiastical chants or melodies from various foreign countries, has also produced certain special compositions of his own, which he calls rituals. These are addressed to a higher manifestation, to a great Being, to God Himself. The words are simple and frequently repeated, because the most important part are the vibrations produced by their melody. These lead humans from a limited level of instincts and desires to an expanded spiritual field. Thus they deliver them from abuses and open up a passageway towards spirituality. It has been observed that, whenever the Master sings or performs rituals in general, and also when members do the same, a much better atmosphere develops within the Society. People gain power and serenity from the vibrations which all of their centres receive – vibrations which provide the capability for expansion and diffusion.

# SPIRITUAL HEALING

I remember at one point having great difficulties in undertaking a certain responsibility of the Society's work. The Master attempted to explain the reasons why I should do it, but the difficulty I felt would not lessen. He then stopped talking, as I was not responding intellectually, and began his ritual, as I noted on 21.1.81:

> *"I have not yet written anything about the magic of ritual. I have not described what I felt the other evening. Faced with my unreasonable refusal to follow his advice, the Master began to perform a ritual in order to help me. After the first sounds, I felt myself calming, attaining balance. The words, but mostly the melody, gradually entered all of my pores. My resistance was reduced, a new flow entered me, following the pulsations of the ritual.*
>
> *My hands began to move of their own accord, joining in the rhythm, the inner pulsation which was flooding me. I felt that in this way I was expanding, becoming part of a greater existence. I felt that I no longer had a small, limited ego, but that I existed as a great ontological field. The more I expanded and my consciousness grew, the more my personal resistances left.*
>
> *I wanted to laugh. Yes, everything was very simple. I would act as the Master said, because*

## SINGING – RITUALS – CHORODROMENA (RITUAL DANCING)

*I no longer had any resistance over the particular issue, over this need which I had to meet. I had no resistance because I had expanded, limitation had left me, it had literally melted in the vibrations of the ritual. I had been liberated from my difficulty and was free to do whatever had to be done. Completely free!"*

Many of the Master's disciples have similar experiences to report. A ritual song helps, calms, strengthens and liberates the soul from the various bonds of personal obstacles. It prepares humans for a more dynamic way of functioning, particularly if they manage to maintain the correct vibration during the whole day. This, naturally, can be achieved if all individuals separately become used to performing rituals at home, when they are away from the Society and the Master - singing the special rituals or other known songs, always elevating them to a broad ontological field. They can also improvise their own melodies and accompany them with simple words. All these things operate in a liberating way as a healing which is based on the free expression of the human being. Truly, how often has our mood not changed when we have begun humming a song?

Apart from song, the human organism needs other means of discharging energy. Ever since antiquity, there have been many important examples of dance, of harmonious movement, usually performed in groups. In our own times, dance has always been a social as well as an individual manifestation. Humans, through the movements of their body, express the powers of life itself. These vary, as does song, as they stem from their varied needs, which originate from the corresponding energy centres. There are forms of dance which project a romantic element, while others project a sexual one. Apart from these, it is a well-known fact that in various religions, group dances have been established with the purpose of thanking and praising God. Dance, and movement in general, is necessary for humans. We all know how much walking, swimming, gymnastics help. All these things contribute to the relaxation of the organism and bring greater balance and harmony.

The Master has taught special dance movements which are accompanied by the ritual songs. He calls them 'chorodromena' (literally meaning 'acting via dance'), because every movement is symbolic. All the symbolisms which are expressed by the various movements and postures of the body always speak of the union of the person with other people, with life, with God. They break down the individual limiting functions and spread out the power of the soul.

The chorodromena performed by groups of the Society's members have proven to be very important. Those who take part in them say that they feel great energy in

## SINGING – RITUALS – CHORODROMENA (RITUAL DANCING)

their body and that often any unpleasant psychological state quickly leaves them. There is nothing strange about this, since we all know how much any movement or action can help when we are in a state of depression and inertia. The chorodromena, which are specifically devised for that purpose, help much more in banishing inertia and bringing a new life, a new flow within a person and a power of expression in all directions.

I remember on one occasion, we were on an outing with the Master, when a group formed and began performing chorodromena. The rest had spread out, talking and relaxing. But something strange happened: those who were not taking part in the performance began feeling bothered by the heat, by the long duration of the outing, etc. One lady even complained of having a headache. At that point, the Master advised those who were not taking part in the chorodromena to get up and join in, in order for these unwelcome phenomena to be eliminated. Gradually, everyone began joining in, including the lady with the headache. Their mood changed rapidly, their inertia disappeared and the lady's headache was healed.

This, of course, is not the only example of the importance of the chorodromena, but it is mentioned here because it was a group phenomenon. The help they provide has been numerously proved, a help which, in the final analysis, is also healing. It heals various disharmonious states of the soul which cause inertia, transforming it into a harmonious comprehensive action.

Song and rituals have as their purpose the improvement of the human soul's disposition and the alteration of the overwhelming negative currents of the environment. When they are accompanied by the appropriate movements, they are much more effective because they provide a way out for the energies of the soul through the entire body. Anyone can test the importance of singing and dancing, even if he or she is not familiar with the special patterns taught at the Society. A few movements and a melody quickly bring about a substantial difference. A qualitative change takes place within a person who decides to willingly take action and to cast off anything negative which has been troubling him or her.

Members attending the Society's various lessons have discovered the value of the rituals and their expression through dance. They often perform rituals on their own and it always helps them overcome any difficulties. They are invigorated, they become stronger and work more easily and dynamically in every aspect of their everyday life.

# COLOURS AND HEALING

The initial teaching given to those who wish to become spiritual healers is to visualise their patients surrounded in an unbounded, all-white light which is reminiscent of the Sun's brilliance and symbolises the purity and radiance of the Spirit. This visualisation is often projected as a lively vision before the eyes of the individuals meditating. They see this light with the eyes of the soul and with their will direct it to the patients. The vision is often characterised by its blinding radiance. The healers see it in the patients' energy body as a curative power which will bring forth the healing to their physical body. It is a pure projection of spiritual power which can work its miracle on the patients.

In the course of their healing work, healers discover that the white radiance can change, taking on a specific colour which is provided for the patients' aid. This can be one of the seven colours of the rainbow, and it is usually brighter than what human eyes can see of it in the natural environment. The colour surrounding the patients during meditational healing is, of course, part of the light spectrum. It is a special colour radiance which is conveyed to them through the healers, in order to heal their particular problem.

Members of the Society's healing section often report that the person being healed was receiving a colour that was bright pink, blue, yellow, etc. If the healers have an extensive knowledge of the healing properties of colours, they can use the one which is best suited for each case. Such knowledge is not derived only from specialist studies which have been written on the subject of colours, but is also acquired empirically, as the healers' personal experiences grow. Novice healers frequently mention that they have worked for a patient using a colour which, without their having thought of it, began to surround the patient. Their union with the spiritual power during the healing is sufficient to properly guide their work.

Much has been written about the effect of colours on human beings. Specific examples are quoted where experiments have proven the positive or negative effect of a certain colour, by helping a person's equilibrium, for example, or causing an imbalance in one's energy centres. It is a known fact that today much greater attention is given to colour shades in places where people gather in large numbers, such as hospitals or factories. Bright colours are also recommended in children's rooms and in schools. We also hear that the development of plants is affected by colour shades, as relevant experiments have shown. And, lastly, the use of special colours can achieve a kind of colour-healing which contributes to a deeper relaxation and meditation.

From a psychological point of view, certain general properties have been ascribed to colours in correlation to their effect. Blue, for example, is described as calming and cold, red as stimulating, yellow is the colour of light, which has a positive effect. Pure green is considered to promote balance, whereas when it is mixed with brown or black, it gives rise to heaviness. Mauve-red is an invigorating colour. All these are, of course, general rules which, depending on a person's individual character, show certain fluctuations. There are moments when anyone could use a stimulation from one colour or another. This, in any event, also explains why people's tastes change at different times of their lives, having a particular colour preference for their clothes or their surroundings.

The Master has provided us with significant teachings on colours. There was a time when we carefully studied their symbolisms and investigated the need various members of the Society had for the use of certain colours. Usually dark colours, without any brightness, indicate heaviness and an attachment to material gratifications. Bright colours, on the other hand, symbolise a disposition of the soul towards greater expression and diffusion of its energies. The connection between this issue and spiritual healing might not be immediately obvious. There is, however, a relation, as colours are an integral part of life and have a direct influence on all of us. They are one of the various currents surrounding us that affect us positively or negatively, depending on their vibration. If advice is given to members of the Society on a change in the colours which they use, it is so that they can be helped by the correct colour shade which will positively affect their centres by bringing them to an equilibrium.

Naturally, a colour cannot be considered able to change a spiritual state all on its own. It is simply one of the means used in a healing task while attempting to comprehensively deal with the individual. I once heard that a patient was advised by someone to frequently wear a yellow dress, as this colour would heal her. I consider this approach extremely limiting, even though it might contain an element of truth. Colour makes its own contribution towards the healing of a disease, when other, internal processes are also going on at the same time, when medical advice is being followed, or spiritual healing is taking place.

Spiritual healers practice seeing the colours inside their patients' aura, in other words, in the energy field radiating around them. In a study of the human aura, Rudolf Steiner* says that it differs from person to person, but also from one moment to the next. The combination of colours changes in accordance with the disposition of the soul. This has been confirmed by those who have the ability to see auras.

Today, the existence of this colour radiance has been proved scientifically. It can be measured by aurographs and photographed by special cameras. The human energy body has been proven to be real, measured and recorded by experiments. A television programme once showed the aura of various peoples' hands and then compared them to the aura of a yogi. The difference was great. The hand of the yogi, a spiritual man who regularly meditated, was surrounded by a large bright radiance, which seemed to permeate and illuminate it. The halo of saints, as it has been described by people who were able to see their aura, could be similarly explained. The saints emitted a steady vibration around them, as they were in a state of constant union with God. This is

---

*Steiner, R., 'Das Wesen der Farben', Dornach: Rudolf Steiner Verlag 1973.

what gave them the bright golden aura which surrounded their heads.

When a healer unites with the patient, he or she can transfer the necessary vibrations by using the appropriate colour. This is because each shade of colour produces specific vibrations, as it is on a different frequency wave which is part of the colour spectrum. In the natural world, these colours are the radiance of the Sun which, with its seven main constituents, is transmitted to our planet. These are absorbed by nature, colouring it in a variety of ways, as they are analysed and re-composed into a multiplicity of combinations. In the energy field, colours also produce a corresponding variety of vibrations as they are absorbed by the human energy centres.

The healer, always working within the energy complex, conveys to the centres the appropriate radiance, which is expressed by the corresponding colour. This helps balance the soul's energy and then passes as a healing power to the particular part of the body which is suffering. There are books which contain illustrations of the seven centres with their colours, in accordance with the descriptions of those who have developed intuitive powers. When the centres have their correct colours – that is, they absorb and transmit the appropriate radiance – then they work harmoniously, transferring the necessary vibrations to the entire body.

It is not easy to give examples of healings carried out by members of the Society by the use of colour alone. As has been pointed out, colour is a formation of the energy of the Spirit. Healing is the result of the spiritual power which passes as energy to the patient, whether it is projected as a colour, sound, sensation or simply as a formless power. I should repeat here that the whole healing process is based on the union of the healer with the patient, a union of energies of the soul in the formless spiritual essence. In spite of all this, there is a special task which can be carried out by certain healers, called colour healing. Its results have been proven and are based on the healers' knowledge of the vibration differences between colours. Through colour they channel the proper energy which heals as it flows from the power of the Spirit, the original and sole power of all life.

# SERVICE

In the three previous chapters information has been given about the help which humans can provide to themselves. Relaxation, externalisation of their powers with suitable songs and dances and the right shades of colour, all have a positive effect on the disposition of the soul and reduce tensions. This results in better health, which in turn helps the whole environment.

Here, emphasis will mainly be placed on a different area of activity which has nothing to do with methods and techniques. It concerns only the attitude of humans towards their fellow-humans. Some things have already been said about relations in general, particularly between a couple, as well as between parents and children. Now, we shall carry out a more in-depth analysis of the concept of 'service' and the way in which it is put into practice. It is directly related to good health, as will become apparent in the following pages.

The work which is done by the members of the Servers' Society has two basic ways of operation. The first is meditation and the second is service. As has already become clear, meditation helps humans to find serenity of soul, to become aware of the hidden spiritual power and to then make use of this power for their own good and for the good of all. The second basic aspect of the Society's teaching is service itself, in other words the conscious work for the improvement of human living conditions, including that of the individual self.

Service is any act in response to the needs of the individual, of situations and of the environment in which people live. It has a variety of expressions, as needs are themselves varied. It equally involves material help, mental support and demonstration of affection. A prerequisite for service is the decision to sacrifice a satisfaction when it comes into conflict with a greater need. It may involve the individual who has chosen, for example, to carry out a certain task even though he or she preferred to be entertained, as well as other people who have asked from this person to offer something of him or herself.

At the Society, we frequently have conversations on the subject of giving and of service. Those who are new to a group usually put up considerable resistance. They say that if they are continually giving, there will be nothing left for themselves. They also believe that it will give others the chance to blatantly exploit them. Naturally, these reactions are only human and point to the general problem of humankind. They point to a lack of self-sufficiency and autonomy. The more the individuals fear to give, the more they accumulate powers within them for personal assurance. They want wealth, glory, sexual love and a number of other things in order to feel the security of their own existence. But instead of security, they are driven to insecurity, which originates from the fear of losing their material possessions.

Setting retention and incorrect flow of the soul's energy as the basis for illness, we can immediately see the connection between service and health. People who respond to a need diffuse power from their body. This they give to whoever is in need of it, without inhibitions in their mind or in the centre of their emotions. This diffusion of energy automatically liberates them from possible accumulations and thus rids them of their negative effects.

I remember, for example, one lady who told us how sick she was of looking after her aged mother. Every time she had to visit her, to take care of her bodily hygiene and to deal with her, she would get a headache and a terrible sense of heaviness. She would think in dread of her mother's unpleasant conversations and endless eccentricities. On one occasion, influenced by the Society's lessons, she decided to ignore the difficulties and to treat her mother only with love and acceptance. Although she had left her home in the same negative state, when she was with her mother she treated her as a person who was in great need of support, but who expressed that need with complaints and moodiness. She ignored the complaints and concerned herself only with her mother's great need for affection and care. Her positive attitude brought an immediate and crucial result that could even be called magical. The mother, who felt as if she was being overwhelmed with love and not with coercion, stopped being difficult. The lady did what she had to do for her without feeling tired in any way. On the contrary, when she returned home there was no trace of a headache, fatigue or dejection.

Even though this example is very simple, it shows the profound importance of service when it is performed with the soul. Many serve others out of compulsion and not because they see a simple human function in their action. They do something for another person, possibly offering that person a great deal, but within themselves they still resist and feel bad. They would prefer to satisfy themselves in a different way and not concern themselves with the satisfaction of others. But that is not true giving. Here the energies of the soul are not given through the heart, since other emotional and mental functions intervene. And so, at the end of the so-called giving, fatigue comes, instead of a feeling of well-being – a fatigue caused by the friction between the enforced labour and the individual desire.

The Master says that the one who serves others serves oneself. Perhaps this concept seems a little strange at the beginning of the discipleship, but, gradually, its truth is revealed. Considering the individual human being as a cell in the pan-human organism of our planet, it is only natural that everything which happens for the good of a part of humanity serves each one separately. The energies of the soul which are diffused from one to the other build a conscious psychic union. They help the one who receives them as well as the one who gives them.

The soul's energy must first flow through each individual separately, just as his or her blood flows, and then be diffused from one to another. When this flow comes into operation, then love, unselfishness and service find expression. The greater the awareness of unity between beings, a unity of the soul and of the spirit, the more direct the outpouring of the soul to all things alike will become.

It is likely that humankind in its evolution will arrive at such a level that the word 'service' will eventually cease to have its present-day meaning, or will disappear completely. When the real unity between beings is consciously realised, then any need of any individual will be met at once. At present, this unity has not been sufficiently recognised and there is frequently great divisiveness. For this reason, the practice of service opens up new pathways – liberating, healthy, powerful pathways. It protects the human beings from their great problem: the need to appropriate. It teaches them to spread themselves with their soul, to speak, to express themselves, to love. Gradually, it eliminates individualistic limitation and leads to an expanded dimension of consciousness.

Groups from the Society often give performances free of charge at institutions for children in need. When they return from such an expression of giving, they are always renewed and in a good mood, even though they often have to deal with children with various problems. The Society's healers' group also reports that they have a much better psychological disposition at the end of each healing, because the preoccupation with the health problems of patients reduces the significance of individual problems and breaks down personal needs. The same also happens to the rest of our members when they perform a service for others.

Some might think that they cannot possibly be of service to anyone as they themselves are in need of help and need others to provide them with love and strength. This is true of certain cases – mostly of the mentally ill. But even for these, a healing way out is to perform even a small service. As soon as the individuals leave aside their own personal problems – albeit for a few moments – and concern themselves with the problems of others, they immediately feel an opening of the soul, a relief. If they steadily maintain this expression, it is quite possible that their problems disappear altogether – that they 'atrophy from lack of interest', as the Master says.

Individual problems, even those which have been expressed as bodily illnesses, are inflated by our excessive preoccupation with them. When we turn our attention to something else, then problems diminish, pains lessen, illnesses can be healed. And to what else are we to turn our attention but to the people who need us? By giving them the care which they need, we help them and at the same time we are helped ourselves. We perform a service and this act automatically liberates us from our individual worries. We learn to love, not to fear, to become one with our fellow-humans.

Regarding human resistances to giving and service, the Master provides the following teaching:

> *"People who resist serving others, are in essence resisting God Himself. They are refusing to pass into the flow of life, as it appears with-*

*in them and around them every day. It is as though they deny the everyday miracle of 'Existence' which unfolds before their eyes. They do not unite their individual will with the will of God, and for that reason they suffer, are in pain, fall ill.*

*They put forward a variety of personal desires which they insist on satisfying, even if it is not possible. They fall into many traps of their mind and often refuse to take action because they say they want to understand. To understand what God, what the Being itself is. Then they begin to analyse God, to break Him into fragments, in order to know Him. They acquire certain specific pieces of knowledge, but not the one true knowledge, which is union with God and the conscious carrying out of His work, in the activities of everyday life. As they look at things in this way, they resist even the simple biological needs of their body, causing wretchedness and illness to themselves.*

*People who refuse to carry out their task when need summons them are irresponsible. They do not do their duty, which is service to the Being itself. They do not give themselves, they do not become responsible human beings. Only people who understand that every task is a task of*

*God serve God with their will. They give, they love, they respond to needs without any reaction. In this way, true knowledge, the revelation of the Essence of life comes to them.*

*Naturally, the knowledge which humans are able to acquire is only a drop in the ocean. Because what is a human being in the Universe? But people who experience unity, people who serve others, serving the Divine Existence, of which they are a part, require no other knowledge.*

*The cause of all the sufferings of humanity is precisely this resistance to involvement in the work of God. It is the constant need for individual satisfactions only and not a selfless giving. Life this way becomes so complicated that it leads to great unhappiness. On the other hand, life becomes very simple and beautiful for those who respond to its needs. Then the soul's energy flows everywhere within them, they feel themselves flooded by the Divine Existence, and all is well."*

# THE DIVINE HUMAN BODY

*"One body and one Spirit…"*
**St Paul to the Ephesians, 4.4**

The human beings see their body, their self, and call themselves 'human'. They know, as far as they are able, of their body's senses and instincts. They experience the emotions and thoughts within their being. All these things, as well as many more, together structure the human self, which they strive to maintain by any means possible. They aspire to develop the human ego into something stronger, more integral. But in this effort they make a great mistake. They see the creature in themselves, the creation of life, and forget their Creator. They see the marvelous work of art which is the human being and ignore the active power which flows within them – after first creating them. As they remain confined to this image of themselves, they start getting attached to it and demand every gratification which it is capable of giving them. But this attachment causes pain and their body weakens, falls ill. Then humans become angry over their pain, they remember God and often regard Him as the one to blame for their own painful conditions. They fight their Creator, reject Him, and sometimes cry out in despair, seeking His help. The battle continues between God and humans until knowledge progressively comes, and truth, harmony, is revealed.

But what is the truth about humans? Are they or not human? And their body – is it then their own? George Vythoulkas*, in his book on Homoeopathy, writes that humans are not a chance happening. They are a creation of the divine all-wise will. Their end and purpose is to be liberated from their bonds and to advance towards their spiritual destiny. These words serve as a reminder of the human beings' divine origin and their spiritual nature. But a precondition of such a spiritual advance is liberation from egoism, the characteristic of the human beings which leads to the identification with their form and their various desires, whatever these are.

What is, in final analysis, the human being? St Paul says that 'the body is one and the Spirit is one'. By these

---

*Vythoulkas, G.,'The science of Homeopathy', Athens: Publications of the Homeopathic Medical Center 1980.

words he lets it be understood that all human bodies are parts of one body, the body of God, and that within all of them there is the one and only Spirit, the Spirit of God. This, in any event, is the whole Cosmos, all Creation to all its boundless extent. The word 'Cosmos' is related to 'cosmetic' – the adornment of Existence. Every part of the Cosmos, from the most insignificant flower growing in a field to the entire Galaxy, is an adornment of life. It is the presence of God's essence, the physical manifestation of His Existence. Humans, as part of Creation, are themselves, in turn an adornment of the power which fashions them, preserves them, and destroys them, in accordance with its will. The more the human mind resists this truth of the entire humanity, and of the entire world, the more it projects an individual egoism, it separates itself from the entire Existence and resists the vital power which permeates it, maintains it, and abandons it in due course. The consequence of their resistances is pain and illness, which are precisely due to the fear of this abandonment, of death.

"The only thing which exists is God", the Master says. "Each body is the Body of God, and, when humans understand this, they will be set free." At first, this teaching might appear strange and difficult to comprehend. The human ego resists, wanting to exist as a separate entity. The human consciousness objects, as it desires to perpetuate its small existence. But the truth is otherwise, because who can say that he or she has overcome the decay and death of one's body? How, then, is the body our possession when we are not in charge of it, determining neither its birth, nor its development, or dissolution?

Every obstacle posed by humans, every retention of the soul's energy has as its objective the ratification of human existence. It conceals the fear of the ego's dissolution, resistance to union with God. A union which, when realised, will not deprive humans of their body or of the joys of life. It will simply bring the knowledge that even this joy and enjoyment is a part of the one Existence which is experienced in the one body, which is all bodies. Then a new receptivity towards everything and a security beyond human norms will come. When humans surrender themselves to the power which fashioned them, then they will discover that this power takes care of their body, its creation. It keeps the entire Cosmos in harmony, it grants health to bodies, providing all its beings with anything they need.

If we made a comparison with known human norms, we would see how absolute this truth is and how pointless the human fear is. When a child is born, its parents do everything in their power to properly raise it. They care for its health, its emotional and intellectual development, they sacrifice themselves for it. So why should the divine power which has created the Cosmos not have the same concern for each of its creations? A concern and a love infinitely greater than their human equivalents. The only thing asked of humans is to acknowledge the truth within themselves, to regard it as their true higher self. To follow the currents of power as they appear in everyday life and to simply integrate themselves into the realisation of this life, within their own small world. This approach will provide the way out for the powers of their soul and human beings will begin to creatively harmonise themselves within the boundless Creation which is the entire universe.

The aim of the Society's teaching is the conscious involvement of the individual with the work of God. The aim of spiritual healing within the Cosmos in general, as it is also taught by the Master, is the aid of sick people in experiencing the soul's flow within their body, leading to the restoration of their energy centres' normal function. This is the beginning of a life of wholeness, of a more fulfilled existence. It is a known fact that people dedicated to spirituality, who consciously work for the good of the whole, enjoy very good health. Their body is in harmonious operation, they accept everything with simplicity and work dynamically for the solution to problems. They accept death as an end to the cycle of a life and pass serenely into the spiritual world which they have recognised everywhere alike, either within or outside forms. For as long as they live as human beings, they do not regard their body as an obstacle nor as a means of only sensual pleasure. They use it for life, which they have accepted as a manifestation of the spiritual nature of all beings.

Masters are sometimes mentioned as having certain health problems, too. This is true, but their illness is not due to any individual problems. As they live amid humanity, which still suffers from negative currents, they receive these currents in their physical body. They work to alter them, often allowing their body to accept a permanent adverse condition, so that the illness leaves the patients and they are given health. They consent by their own free will to take the burden of others upon themselves in order to help them. They contribute by this act of theirs to a reduction of the panhuman debt, ignorance and fear, which all give rise to illnesses. The example of Jesus Christ, who sacrificed His body in order to awaken human conscience, is perhaps the most remarkable in our religious history.

As humans are taught by life itself the true nature of things, of the different forms and of their own self, at some point they arrive at the conclusion that fighting against the unwritten laws of life is futile. It is pointless to set their tiny ego up against Existence in its entirety, which follows its course within the cycle of all life. They understand at the same time that this life, which is within them, is the offspring of love and wisdom. This realisation, which derives from various events and situations, often leads to a current of devotion and faith towards the Creator of the Cosmos. It is then that humans can, by their own will, dedicate their body and the whole of their being to Creator's work. They reach, we could say, that mysticism which is known to us from earlier times – a mysticism which is strong and absolute, in which human faith in God Himself cannot be affected by anything, by any trial of pain or misfortune.

The age in which we live is bringing with it a new current. It is no longer content with mysticism without knowledge. People, together with the love which they are called upon to develop, have to be taught why resistances bring no benefit, why the realisation is needed that their body is a part of the one entire body of Being. The energy link which exists between all phenomena has now been discovered and is proven by science. Knowledge of the energy field connecting every form confirms the interaction between human beings and other forms of the microcosm, and the same applies for macrocosmic levels. For this interaction to be positive, every part of the whole, like every cell in a body, must be healthy and creatively partake in overall life. Only then will the whole be able to maintain its cells in a proper state. When the human place within the total being is understood, resistances will be broken down and life will become constant ecstasy. The body will find its health and everything will be in a simple flow, without illnesses and problems. Then true love for everybody will develop, since everybody is part of the same ontological whole. Service to others will simply become a giving to some other part of the one Self, the one Spirit, which exists within the one body, as St Paul says.

# POSSIBILITIES AND LIMITATIONS OF SPIRITUAL HEALING

There is a question often asked by patients which shows their justifiable anxiety about their illness. This question is whether spiritual healing will definitely cure them.

I can remember the case of Ms. B, whose son was showing symptoms of depression. When I told her that we could take on his case at the healing section, she showed a questioning attitude, and, at the same time, a despairing appeal for help. She repeatedly asked whether her child would get well and when the results would begin to show. She wanted us to give her a guarantee, so to speak, of the healing's success.

## SPIRITUAL HEALING

In all similar cases, we attempt to explain something very simple: healing is not a human issue, but a matter of the power of God and His will. The healers invoke this will and unite themselves with the power which heals if that is what must happen. The healers do not work any miracles, as the miracles of life, of health, and even of death, are a matter beyond their capabilities. The only thing that the spiritual healers can guarantee is their own love and steady work through the invocation of God. The results will come, but no one can know what they will be. In any event, does the same thing not happen in established medicine? Is it not frequently the case that whereas the patient's diagnosis and treatment progress normally, something unexpectedly happens, once more disturbing his or her health?

Many factors, which have been previously discussed, play a part in the success of spiritual healing carried out by healers, as well as in a patient's self-healing. These are the healers' abilities, which depend on their stage of evolution, the receptivity and responsiveness of the patient, and the positive part played by the environment. Apart from these, there is also the unknown factor – the laws which govern life above and beyond the known facts which the human mind can understand.

My personal experience regarding unexpected results in spiritual healing has convinced me of this unknown factor which intervenes in healings. My husband and son are, generally speaking, very good receivers of the spiritual radiance transmitted to them when they have a certain ailment. But it sometimes happens that a seemingly simple problem cannot be overcome, whereas other more difficult ones might swiftly be dealt with.

One night, my husband woke with a terrible toothache caused by a gumboil. It wasn't possible for him to go to a dentist or to find a strong pain-killer at that time of night. He asked me in desperation to carry out a healing on him, as the pain was growing hopelessly intense. I put my hand on his cheek and allowed the soul's energy to penetrate his gums. He did not feel anything at first, but, little by little, some relief began. He did not want me to stop the healing and so half an hour passed while I worked through contact and meditation on the gumboil's healing. Then he suddenly said to me: "The abscess has opened and something seems to be coming out. I can feel it disappearing. It doesn't hurt at all now". And, in fact, from that moment on he was entirely relieved, feeling completely well when he woke up the next morning.

This healing might seem quite difficult, but, nevertheless, it was immediate. Knowing of my husband's receptivity, I thought that he would always be able to be helped in a similar way. And yet, I was mistaken. One day he was suffering from back pains, and he was unable to feel any better, despite all our efforts. This condition was, of course, different from that of the tooth and probably had different energy causes. But my husband and I had the same will for a healing to occur, which, for unknown reasons, did not happen.

I often wonder about the possibilities and limitations of spiritual healing. The power of the Spirit has no limitations, but healing does. This shows that if the sick person is to recover, healing will perform the miracle. It will help, directly or in time, to recover balance and health. In most cases, healing succeeds, but there are times when the laws which govern it do not permit the change to come in the way we expect it to.

At this point I would like to quote an example from Harry Edwards's* book, because it is, as he says, one of the most revealing about this unknown power which intervenes in spiritual healing. A power which operates according to laws that are beyond human knowledge and whose purposes remain unknown. It seems that the outcome of any healing has more profound raisons d' être, which we need not investigate, as we are not in any case, up to the present anyway, able to do so. It is sufficient that the patient's will for improvement is expressed and that this improvement is left entirely to the power that will eventually grant it, when and as it should be.

---

*Edwards, H., 'Spirit Healing', The Harry Edwards Spiritual Healing Sanctuary Trust, Surrey: Burrows Lea 1960.

The example which Harry Edwards gives is that of a few-month-old infant that was brought by its mother for healing. It suffered from a deformity of both feet alike, which the doctors had stated would leave it crippled for the rest of its life. Its feet were bent from birth and no known method could correct them.

When the great healer saw the state of the child, he began, after having invoked the healing power, to work, holding one of the feet in his hands. Under his fingers he felt the bones straightening and in a little while the foot was completely normal. He then did the same with the baby's second foot, but in this case there was no change, no matter how much he persevered. It proved impossible to see any improvement. In the end, the mother took the child and left, not knowing what else to do.

A whole year passed. In that time there were repeated efforts to heal the other foot, which continued having the same incurable deformity. None of these brought about the desired result, until, unexpectedly, as the year was almost out, the child's other foot recovered its normal shape under Harry Edwards's hands.

He could not help but wonder why the two healings had turned out differently, when they were both carried out by the same healer, for the same condition, on the same person. He says that this case proves that there is some law, unknown to humans, which governs all matters of health. Although the specific purpose is unknown

SPIRITUAL HEALING

to us, we nevertheless know of humanity's general duty. What is required of us is faith in the healing power and acceptance that whatever the outcome may be, everything is for the best. One could say, for example, that the child's foot was not healed immediately in order to test the mother's faith and determination. This is probably the way it was, but we cannot be sure of it. In any event, it is not so important. What mainly counts is the realisation of the spiritual power's existence and the need for us to participate in its work without objections.

One day, my son had been performing an exhausting task and his arm had swollen up from the effort. It seemed twice the size of the other, since the muscle had enlarged as a result of the strength he had exerted. He showed it to me in amazement and was clearly bothered by this extreme charge. Without paying too much attention, I simply placed my hand on his arm and focused on it for a little while. Before realising what was happening, the swelling was gone and my son's arm lightened as it recovered its normal shape. What was it that helped so instantaneously? How and why did the healing come so simply, without any particular thought or effort? It is not necessary to answer this. It simply happened because that is how it had to be, and probably because both my son and I were ready to accept the healing power's intervention, which, on other occasions, might not be as clear in the human mind.

The purpose of this chapter is not to guide us to a passive or fatalistic attitude. On the contrary, its purpose is to show that patients and healers must continue their work, without doubts, even if no result occurs. It also stresses the existence of an unknown law which governs the life of all beings. This law is wiser than any human knowledge and when something that we want does not happen, it is best to equally accept any outcome. Because, as the Master says, 'the wisdom of the human is foolishness to God'. We work, we believe in the power of spiritual healing and we entrust the results to the One who knows everything and governs all things with love.

# THE HEALING SECTION OF THE SERVERS' SOCIETY

The Society's spiritual healing section started with a small team of people, who expressed this potential in practice. As the positive results of the healing section increase, so does the number of those who wish to become healers, resulting in the healing section now numbering over 40 people. Those who wish to become members of this team must perform regular individual meditation work. They must also have an aptitude for helping the sick and must have carried out some healings – albeit very simple ones – on their own. Then, they may take part in the group healing meditation, first as disciples and then as regular members of the team.

SPIRITUAL HEALING

There are instances where the healings take place through contact, when patients visit us. Healers may work individually with the patients, as we have already described in various examples, or they may ask other members of the healing team to join them, taking part in the healing through meditation.

Most of our healings are carried out at a distance, after an initial personal contact with the patient or an intermediary, in which we are given the necessary information about his or her condition. Healings start immediately and, depending on necessity, may take place repeatedly, as an intensive task. During emergencies, members of the healing section will visit patients at hospitals or at their homes.

The only obligation upon the patients who are helped by our healing section is to inform us of the development of their health, at least once a month. If they do not do this, we assume that they are no longer in need of help and we discontinue their healing. There is no financial charge for spiritual healing. Naturally, an economic contribution helps the Society's work, which is a non-profit association and is maintained by its members' subscriptions.

The Society has received numerous letters of thanks from patients who have recovered or have experienced improvements in their problems. There are also written and signed declarations from former drug addicts who have overcome their difficulties and have once again become normal members of society.

The modes and methods of spiritual healing have been explained to a large extent in the earlier chapters. They involve not only the work which is done by the meditation of the healers but also include many items of teaching. If the patients are able to be with us, they can be aided by receiving many specific instructions. These concern their self-healing, which can be achieved through relaxation, meditation and a new attitude towards life and their problems.

Spiritual healing's most immediate and enduring successes been those when patients have agreed to accept the Society's teaching and applied it regularly to their everyday life. The filing of this teaching in special folders together with the patients' written observations regarding their personal reactions and experiences, build the necessary basis for self-knowledge and the solution of problems. As I have already pointed out, the aim of the Society is not only the healing of an illness, but also the combating of the causes which have given rise to it. These causes are eliminated only by knowledge and a decision to undertake work which will remove them in a lasting way. It is only then that we can be sure that a new illness will not make its appearance.

In order for the patients to be helped as much as possible, the members of the Society who are admitted to the healing section undertake certain obligations. These do not only concern their attendance at the regular meetings. We often treat patients with very difficult problems who need everyday, intensive healing. These patients are also given individual help by the healers when they are meditating at home. Thus the work is far more frequent and the help lasts much longer. Healers never forget their patients. As they have them constantly in their mind, they sense when they are in need of healing and work on their behalf. This is essential, because, with the exception of certain cases, the evolution of each healing gradually comes and is demonstrated in practice by regular work.

Apart from spiritual healing, members of this team are also responsible for checking if the patients regularly inform us of their condition. They also talk with the patients who visit us, helping by providing them with certain necessary parts of the teaching.

Here, I will repeat something which has been previously said a number of times: healing is not just getting rid of an illness. Above all it is the return of the soul to its normal function. This comes through the individual work which each person decides to do for him or herself. Of course, it is not always possible for patients to respond to this need. The healing section works for all alike, whether they are members of the Society or not. It has been proven a multitude of times that spiritual healing overcomes problems and performs miracles.

The members of the healing section are gradually trained in the acquisition of the knowledge necessary for healing. They study books on medicine, as well as on other methods, such as homoeopathy, for example. They crosscheck this knowledge against their personal experiences on spiritual healing, thus comprehensively expanding their mind on the vital issue of human health. Under no circumstances are healers permitted to give medical advice, since they are not doctors. They can, however, advise a patient to have a medical examination in order to obtain any necessary instructions from a specialist. Healers can also turn to experts when they encounter a condition which they are unfamiliar with. Therefore, spiritual healing also includes specific knowledge with which science supplies us today. The Master places emphasis on the acquisition of this specific data and urges the healers to study illness from every aspect. It is our hope that the healing section will someday have doctors and psychologists among its permanent members. Then science and faith in the healing power will have built up an initial harmonious collaboration for the good of us all, of the whole of humanity that suffers from the affliction of illnesses and pain.

The work of the Society's healing section at the present time has many successes to show. Nevertheless, it could be said that it is still at an initial stage of its evolution. An important basis has, of course, been built, the healers are working in full consciousness and people who are ill frequently seek our help. The work is beginning to expand and may lead to a broader and more composite operation. A change of premises, for example, will help the task of spiritual healing to find greater expression, and closer collaboration with other methods of healing, as will be explained in the next chapter. This has been made possible by the existence of members trained by the Master in validated healings who may take on greater responsibilities and meet the needs of the ever increasing number of patients.

A group of healers, performing distant healing

# A HEALING CENTRE
# FOR THE FUTURE

Humanity's history is bound up with illness. From the written and the unwritten documentation, it can be seen that humans have always been slaves of pain and sickness. If we wished to form a hypothesis on the birth of illness, we could say that it made its appearance at the same time as humans and health.

In the course of human history, various efforts have been made to combat illnesses, depending on the knowledge, the faith and the scientific training possessed at the particular period. In the first stages known to us today, humans made use of their natural surroundings for the healing of pain. They knew the importance of certain plants, they discovered herbs and they noted the therapeutic value of certain foods. At the same time, individuals appeared, the so-called 'witch-doctors' of various tribes, who, by their own methods, were able to perform cures. As the sense of religion was born, these 'witch-doctors' began being replaced by the priests of the different religions and by faith in God. Humans through pain sought divine aid, which was often given to them as a miracle.

But illnesses continued to be a scourge of humanity. Science became more active. Schools of medicine sprang up and various medical specialisations began to deal with individual problems. At the same time, however, the older methods of healing never ceased to exist. Among the diverse therapeutic methods we can include acupuncture, which assists through a knowledge of the human energy centres, homoeopathy, a correct diet, yoga, and an effort to return to the natural life through gymnastics, swimming and running. Various other methods attempt, with considerable success, to also help humankind. Spiritual healing is one of the oldest methods that still continues to be used today.

If we wanted to see the current state of humans, we should realise that, in spite of all the efforts which have been made, illnesses are flaring up. Psychologists and psychiatrists have in recent years been turning to the psychological cause of illnesses. Neurologists are working particularly on the supply of suitable pharmaceuticals which will bring equilibrium to the nervous system. Methods multiply, just as illnesses themselves multiply. It sometimes happens that a patient will jump from one method to another in order to find some relief.

We could say that all these forms of knowledge have so far built up a totality of experiences regarding illness and the ways of treating it. The human mind is now more receptive to all means which can provide help. Humans are gradually beginning to accept methods, even if they are unfamiliar with them. This receptivity is preparing the ground for a new kind of healing centre – for an establishment which will gather under one roof all the methods of healing, providing individual patients with what they need and what best suits their psychosynthesis. Although there are still people who are attached to a specific method of healing, nevertheless humanity as a whole is much more comprehensively developed on this subject. Experiences of the past are today imprinted on our memory. The use of herbs, for example, has returned to many people's life, not as the sole method of healing, as it was in the past, but as an additional aid to a health problem. The same thing is happening in other areas of treatment, which are being studied again and applied by many.

We are at a stage of synthesis of the knowledge so far acquired. We are called upon to include every possible means in the work of healing patients. We do not have the right, I would say, to reject anything, as the past may prove to us that everything has had a certain success. None of the known means has been entirely successful. Because the same illness can be healed – or not – in one of the above ways depending on the person, or even on the particular moment when the same individual falls ill. Then another method may work its miracle where the previous failed to bring about the desired results. As rational beings, with plenty of experience in the matter of illnesses, we are called upon today to make use of all existing forms of knowledge. Our aim remains always a single one: the restoration of health.

It is this line of thinking that gives rise to the healing centre, an institution which will make it possible for patients to discover the kind of healing best suited to them. This healing centre must have as its basis the co-existence of all the methods in one large space. This space may have one wing of a purely hospital nature, but will include many other departments, as described in the following pages. All sections will work together with one another for the patients' swift and comprehensive healing.

If we wished to describe the arrangement and operation of the healing centre of the future, we could imagine it as follows: the patients admitted would be received by a secretary, who would take down all the particulars of their illness. From there they would proceed to a doctor or psychologist, as the case may be, who would undertake their treatment. All the methods of healing which they could follow would be explained to them – when, of course, the case is not an emergency. The one regarded as best for their condition would be suggested to them, as well as the combination of techniques that could produce the desired results.

The treatment would soon begin, and, if necessary, the patients would be provided with a room at the clinic. The premises and the individual rooms would all be built in accordance with the relevant knowledge concerning correct layout, decoration and colour schemes. Areas would also be provided for work-therapy, such as painting, clay modelling, gardening, as well as areas for meeting other patients, monitored by specialist staff. In the healing centre of the future, music, chorodromena and the various forms of exercise would be means of healing. There must also be a well-stocked library and a room for teaching about the vital issue concerning the solving of personal problems. This teaching would have as its aim the establishment of the patients' health receiving treatment and the emergence of that power of the soul which is necessary for the maintenance of a proper condition.

It goes without saying that there will be close contact between the different treatment sections, as they must work together for the overall, comprehensive assistance of each patient. Those sections which handle a case will have to co-ordinate their efforts as they follow the patient's evolution. The choice of the healing section, as we have already pointed out, will be made in the light of the patient's individual character, the special case of the illness, and the specialists' recommendation. Pressure cannot be exerted on patients who resist following a method, unless they first accept its system for themselves. Nor is it possible for something to be imposed on patients which is contrary to their beliefs and convictions. It is for precisely this reason that there must be numerous alternative solutions, with the restoration of health, without the patient's adverse psychological reactions, as their sole aim.

Perhaps what I have written up to this point will be considered a little difficult to turn into reality. It will perhaps seem very complex and distant for today's realities. It is a fact that, up to the present, humans have generally followed a one-sided manner of functioning in their lives. They devote themselves to something, work and generally progress through one, or perhaps just a few ways of operating. This is because of the factor of a partial mental development and a limited knowledge of the very complexity of their own selves. But all these things are now starting to change, as technology, science and new philosophical approaches now penetrate every family, every home. The complexity of humans is becoming apparent and their boundless potential as a species of our planet is being recognised. It is precisely their composite nature which the healing centre of the future, with its variety of methods, must provide for.

From the time when the Society's healing section was first established, the Master spoke to us about the future pattern which must be constructed. With the passage of time, I have begun to see the necessity for this to be accomplished. Today, within the very limited framework for action, we are working for a global approach to illnesses. We carry out spiritual healing, we mentally position the patients in relation to their problems and we recommend that they should join a teaching group. We encourage them to concern themselves with the problems of others and to give them their love. We make it possible for them to take part in chorodromena, meditation, and service groups. We seek the assistance of doctors when it is needed, or we advise them to visit a homoeopathist. These things are a miniature of the healing centre of the future, which should gather into one building all these functions and be subject to a very carefully coordinated organisation.

Last year I was visited by a lady of Greek origin who lives in Switzerland. She is herself a spiritual healer and she showed great interest in our work. She told me that

SPIRITUAL HEALING

she was planning, together with four other women, to set up a clinic where different methods of healing, such as yoga, homoeopathy, etc., would be provided. It is obvious that this decision shows the need of the present-day situation for a synthesis of healing methods. We are, of course, at an initial stage, but 'the beginning is half way there'. The future will show how necessary it is for expression to be given to such work – that is, a global approach to humans in the field of their illnesses.

As I was writing the title of this chapter, my husband came up to me, read it, and asked me: "How far off do you think this healing centre is? What future is it you are talking about?" My reply was immediate, because I know that the realisation of any vision is not so much a matter of time as a matter of decisiveness and will. I said that such a healing centre might take decades to become a reality. But it also might happen in a very short space of time. The problem is not as much a financial one, because financial backers can always be found to support a project which has been proven to them to be a right one. The main problem, in my personal view, is in the mind. To construct a clinic which will house different, ostensibly opposing, functions and methods, strong souls will be needed who will decide to work for it. What is needed above all is a reduction in human egoism, which looks for personal validation and economic satisfaction. What is needed is a project of dedication to 'humans', in a collective effort towards a form of help which we all wish to receive.

Yes, I believe that the vision of the healing centre of the future, as very briefly described here, is something which can soon become a reality. All that is needed is love, love for humans, and strength, with the faith that every good work for humankind as a whole can and must be realised. If there is will, the obstacles will be surmounted and the vision will become action and achievement. An achievement which opens up new horizons for all of us.

# EPILOGUE

*"God is day and night,
winter and summer,
war and peace,
satiety and need."*

**Heraclitus**

It is characteristic of humans to give colour to things, situations and events depending on their effect on them and on the conditions of their life. They approve and reject, prefer and avoid, thus dividing life's manifestations into positive and negative. They admire strength, beauty, goodness, but abhor weakness, ugliness and malice. They adopt precisely the same attitude towards matters of health.

This human reaction is due to distress caused by an ailment or pain tormenting a body which is sick. They cannot understand or accept the necessity for the existence of these negative experiences. They desire only pleasant situations and agreeable things. They are overwhelmed with fear of illness and of all the suppressed powers, because they do not know how to alter them, to absorb them into the pure manifestation of life and to transform them into health and power.

The healers who spiritually deal with all the phenomena of illness and of health are taught something of great importance as they delve into human forms and study their manifestations. They are taught to express the same acceptance of – we could even say the same wonder at – health and sickness, pain and pleasure, sadness and happiness. They begin to recognise in all things only the One, the one Presence, their Creator and God.

When the spiritual healers, through this deeper involvement, come to realise that in illness, in decay, even in death the seed of life is inherent, they cease to resist these things and can bring about positive results with their healing. A healing which sometimes occurs in parallel with the help of medical science and sometimes intervenes in a miraculous way, in cases where this science can no longer help. When the healers learn to marvel at the pain of illness, recognising in it the light, power and wisdom of God, then the pain may disappear before the powerful manifestation of their love.

A knowledge of the deeper significance of every static, impure and diseased factor leads to the revelation of the hidden truth of life, the Essence of things. A sense of awe arises in the consciousness which in effect unites the healer with the sufferer, and with the spiritual fields. This union becomes a pure manifestation of love, which dissolves any ill feelings concerning illnesses, as, even in these, the will of God is recognised.

The spiritual healers work steadily to deliver the sick from their pain. They retain their unshakeable faith in the power of the Spirit and their absolute acceptance of whatever is the outcome of their healing. They believe in, they invoke the help of God and leave the work of healing to be effected – if this is deemed expedient and right – by the higher ontological field directing them. Faith, love and their wonder at all things keep them detached from the results of their work. Their function is a clear-cut one, without personal interpolations, because they know that health will be restored only if this is how it must be. Success or failure do not concern them as a personal matter, because in their consciousness all things are One, all things are God.

The work of healing, as a part of the whole of life, is a work of Being and the spiritual healers become simply and by their will partakers in this work. The miraculous takes place every day before their eyes, they perceive it with all their senses and are taught to recognise it everywhere, in the day and the night, the cold and the heat, life and death!

# LETTERS OF THANKS
# FROM PATIENTS

Patients who have received help from the healing section of the Servers' Society send us letters of thanks which are signed with their names, but only their initials will be given here.

The letters which we quote in the following pages are typical examples of those we have received. From these the work that is done for the patients and the relationship which sometimes develops between them and the healers can be seen.

We ourselves are grateful for the patients' letters of thanks. They provide us with necessary information which for the dissemination of spiritual healing and its establishment as a substantial means of bringing help to the sick. These letters give an account of the carrying out of a task which involves people's health, in a world full of illnesses – a task which has the potential to spread on a wide scale, with the support of trained healers and with the knowledge of the technique of self-healing, as will become apparent in the pages which follow.

### Healing of generalised mastitis

*I would like to convey the warmest thanks of my sister, E.K., to the Servers' Society for the healing of her breast. E.K. had been suffering from generalised mastitis for a number of years. Her breast had filled with painful lumps. The doctor, apart from the medication (which she never took) recommended that she should avoid stress and use lukewarm compresses, which she didn't do either! She had been affected by the fear that she had something incurable.*

*At that time I was a new member of the Society and I took the initiative of bringing her case to the healing section. Within the first month, the results started appearing. Her breast was not as painful and the lumps gradually began disappearing.*

*The spiritual healing stopped only when the pains and the lumps in the breast were no longer there. In addition to this, my sister is now much calmer and she has not mentioned any fear or negative thinking.*

*We thank you for your truly selfless care and love.*

*E. and N.K.*

### Healing of an eye condition

*My mother's family suffers from an eye condition which rapidly develops and ends in almost total blindness. My grandmother and her five sisters suffered from this illness, and a few years ago, my uncle also went blind. This disease attacks the fundus of the eye, causing swellings and haemorrhages.*

*My mother suddenly began seeing with difficulty, and her condition grew worse very rapidly. She was seized with panic. She immediately went to the ophthalmologist, she began treatment with injections into the eye and wore special glasses. But I talked of her problem to the Society and explained the urgent need for spiritual healing to immediately stop the development of the disease and to achieve an improvement.*

*And so it happened. As if miraculously, my mother is much better and her morale is marvelous. She can read with her glasses, she watches television, plays cards and backgammon... She owes it all to the spiritual healing which she received from the Servers' Society.*

*I thank the healers on her behalf and have no words to express my gratitude.*

A.T.

## Healing of the thyroid

*I had been suffering from my thyroid since 1979. It bothered me so much that I began to exclude myself from social interactions. After my contact with the Servers' Society, I underwent spiritual healing by contact and at a distance. The symptoms subsided and I am now very well.*

*But apart from this, I feel a calm which was not there before. I see life, I would say, through different eyes.*

*Things and situations which troubled me before I now accept. All the tension which I constantly had has gone.*

*I would like to send a big 'thank you' to the healing section with all my heart.*

*M.K.*

### Healing and self-healing of a cyst on the coccyx

*One day, when I was already a member of the Servers' Society, a spot, full of pus, appeared on the last bone of my spinal column. I burst it, and the next day it was greatly swollen. Three small spots appeared at this point on the same base with three different points and full of pus. The condition was accompanied by pain and intense itching. I was almost limping, and I refrained from going out from fear that people would make fun of me or pity me because of the way I walked.*

*I went to the doctor and was told that it was a cyst on the coccyx. He advised me to have an operation immediately. He also gave me antibiotics and drew the pus out. I came to the Society the same day and had a contact healing. In meditation, I saw this part pulsating, bursting and ejecting useless substances and I felt as though I was on fire. I was very receptive to spiritual healing. On Monday the cyst had disappeared! On Tuesday I saw the Master, and he told me that the cause of this cyst had to do with the way I had grown up and my relations with people in my environment.*

*When I visited the doctor, he cancelled the operation and said he wished that what had happened to me would happen to all of his patients. When I visited him the first time, he also told me that I had a fungoid condition of the genitals. This time he discovered that within three days even the fungus had disappeared! From this experience I have learnt and sensed a great deal which cannot be described in words... I have learnt to channel positive energy to my body and to make it literally glow with health. I have come to believe in God, spiritual power and healing.*

*I feel great gratitude to the Master and to the members of the healing section, who have helped me considerably in the restoration of my health.*

C.P.

## Healing of a number of illnesses

*I would like to express my thanks to the healing section of the Servers' Society for the healing of various illnesses.*

*Because of the great anxiety and pessimism which had become a way of life for me, I had neurosis of the stomach and the beginnings of an ulcer. For three years I had pains and a permanent flutter in my stomach. In the first months of my discipleship this problem ceased to exist.*

*Later, I developed a problem of streptococcal precipitation of the blood and I was unable to, even momentarily, stand on my feet. I sought the help of the healing section and of the Master of the Society. At that time, I was unable to even take a step, but after coming to the Society, I received so much strength that I was able to walk normally again.*

*The precipitation was healed, leaving me, however, with a heart murmur, which hurt on a daily basis. When I asked the Master to carry out a healing on me, I didn't believe I would be totally cured, and yet with only one treatment the murmur was healed.*

*Finally, another health problem were my gynecological matters, which gradually diminished, until finally disappearing, with the treatments carried out on me by the Master and by the team of healers.*

*I would like to express a big 'thank you' to the healing section and the Master, who sets its pace.*

*P.S.*

### Help in the improvement of relations

*With this letter I would like to thank you for the valuable help which you have given to my parents. When we brought them for spiritual healing, my sister and I had almost lost hope that these two people could ever co-exist peacefully as a couple. Their quarrels were an everyday event and a part of the war which they had started 30 years ago. After a year of healing from your team, this relationship changed radically, making both of them calmer and freer. My warmest thanks.*

*Kindest regards*
*M.K.*

SPIRITUAL HEALING

### *Healing and self-healing of eczema*

*In August I developed an eczema. Ms. Lykiardopoulou was the first to bring me relief. Then, members of the healing section carried out distance healing, though there had already been an improvement on the problem.*

*When the eczema re-appeared a few days later, I had contact healing and it left me. After a while, it returned, in a milder form, and I was unable to find the healer. I tried to imitate her movements on myself, while at the same time thinking that the eczema would disappear. And so it did! I don't know whether this was a matter of chance or whether this healing occurred so that I would learn to believe in the healing power within me.*

*I greatly thank the people who helped me.*

G.T.

### *Cured of narcotics*

*As a mother I feel the need to address you and, from the bottom of my heart, to say a big 'thank you', because in the difficult times which I and my son went through, as he was a drug-user and our life was a true martyrdom, you with your spiritual support helped us to overcome them.*

*I feel boundless gratitude for your help.*

G.S.

### *Healing and self-healing of sinusitis*

*I feel the need to express my thanks to the Servers'*

*Society for the help which they have given me psychologically and physically. I am a member of the Society and a trainee spiritual healer. I will give an account of only one of the various occurrences in which they have helped me.*

*In January I had a very bad cold and, in spite of all the medications which I took, there was no improvement. One day I started to have a pain from the left flap of my nose up to my ear. I also had difficulty in breathing, the timbre of my voice changed noticeably, and I felt unwell. I consulted the doctor, who told me I had sinusitis and that it was a fairly serious condition; he recommended certain medicines, of which I have to admit I didn't take a single one. I got in touch with the Society, and particularly with Ms. Keramida, who explained to me how to perform healing on myself, while she would do the same at a distance. I did as she told me. It seemed to me incredible, and yet within a little while I was breathing normally and my voice had begun to soften. Most importantly, the pain in the left cheekbone and the dysphoria began to leave me. That same night I slept well and the following morning I felt very good.*

*In conclusion, I would like to thank all those who have helped me and who continue to help me every day. I hope their work will continue in the interests of a better life for all of us.*

*V.M.*

SPIRITUAL HEALING

### *Healing of an ovarian cyst*

*With this letter I would like to express my gratitude to the Servers' Society for all the help it has given me over my health problem and my life in general.*

*For the last two years I have suffered from back pains which came from a cyst in my left ovary. Various treatments yielded little results, so I would often fall into fits of melancholy. My doctor didn't hold out much hope for me and a surgical operation was very likely.*

*A member of the Servers' Society, spoke to me about spiritual healing. After an analysis given to me by Ms. Klairi Lykiardopoulou, in which the cause of this cyst was explained to me, the countdown began. My case was undertaken by the spiritual healer Mr. Andreas Dritsas, who began distance and contact healing on me. In parallel, I became a member of a self-study group, in order to perform inner work on myself; I was also taught how to carry out self-healing. From the beginning I believed in the spiritual power and this faith was strengthened when I began to feel the healing energy within me during the contact healing, and also increasingly when I was carrying out self-healing.*

*Very rapidly the pains diminished, I recovered my old strength and my life acquired meaning. Confirmation came six months later – when I finished the pharmaceutical treatment which had not achieved anything the previous time I had followed it – with my doctor' diagnosis that the cyst had disappeared.*

*For me, of equal importance to the help I was given by spiritual healing is the way in which I was taken in by the healers' at the Society, where, with genuine love, they provided me with every support in building up my new attitude.*

*And all this I owe to the Servers' Society.*

T.K.

**Healing of back pains**

*I spoke for about an hour with Ms. Klairi Lykiardopoulou. It was our first conversation. Direct, warm-hearted, above the ground, but at the same time involved in life. Deeply involved...*

*As we were going down the stairs, a surprise awaited me. Ms. Lykiardopoulou – just like that, without my saying anything – touched me with her hand a little above the waist on my spinal column and said: "It hurts here, doesn't it?" I had said nothing. "Yes, that is my problem. Perhaps it is from all the years of sitting down (teaching, writing books)... It's a hindrance to me when I'm writing. It hurts..."*

*It hasn't hurt again. For months now I've been sitting up late at night writing and my back is like new. How can you not believe?*

O.K.

### Healing of a skin disease

*For the past year and a half I have been troubled by certain marks which have appeared on my genitals. After visiting the Syngrou Hospital on a regular basis for at least five times, I was not able to discern any real difference. The diagnosis varied, and so did the treatment methods, at times with injections and at other times with ointments.*

*I spoke of my problem to a friend of mine, who was a member of the Servers' Society, and asked for spiritual healing. I can say today that after the help I received, and within the span of three weeks, the marks have completely disappeared, and now, two months later, I no longer have any problem. I would like to thank the Society for the benefit I have received from them.*

N.K.

### Healing of gingivitis

*In recent years, I have had a major problem with gingivitis. My gums used to swell often, I had headaches and could eat only very soft foods. The treatment given to me by the dentist would end with the removal of the areas of the gums which couldn't be restored. I knew about spiritual healing and Ms. Lykiardopoulou and sought help.*

*I may say that I didn't expect the healing to have such an immediate effect. Once or twice after the contact healing I felt my mouth being in a different, healthier state.*

*When the healing was completed, there was no need for the dentist to intervene. The most important thing is that the psychological cause of the illness was found and that I am working on that in order to eliminate it completely.*

*My thanks go to Ms. Lykiardopoulou and the healing section of the Society for this experience which has made me aware of a great many things.*

V.K.

## Treatment for chronic headaches

*As you know, for over twelve years I have been suffering from headaches, and have been dealing with them initially using classical medicine and then homoeopathy.*

*I may say that classic medicine did not do a lot for me, whereas homoeopathy brought me relief for a two-year period, after which my problem re-asserted itself.*

*In 1983, I resorted to you and received significant help from the healing section, with the result that my headaches have now stopped.*

S.M.

## Healing of spinal arthritis

*Ten years ago, a little after the birth of my third child, some discomfort began in my spinal column, and more specifically in the vertebrae of the neck and the coccyx. As time passed, the pain became intense and began causing violent and frequent headaches. And so I was driven to make frequent visits to doctors, pathologists, neurologists, etc. All of them gave me medications which did something towards temporary easing the pain but not the real healing of the spinal arthritis which I had.*

*Five years ago, I learnt from Ms. Lykiardopoulou how to practice relaxation, visualising a light in the whole of my body and particularly in my spinal column. I began to do this exercise every day and for a period of time the healing section carried out healings on me. Daily relaxation, a correct diet and a quiet life have completely healed me.*

*A.A.*

# REVIEWS

Dear Mrs Lykiardopoulou,

When your book reached my hands, I viewed it with some surprise. As a subject it was attractive, suggesting as it does a world which – for many reasons – we willingly ignore, or, at times, we pretend to ignore. Of course, this attitude comes with a 'cost': negative consequences. So, is this pretence worth it?

Your excellent book is a convincing response to this essential question - an affirmative response. With clarity, genuine simplicity, and, above all, with admirable understanding – which is one of the greatest qualities of your work – you guide us to a magical domain of energies and powers which, at long last, we ought to witness for ourselves.

It is no exaggeration to say that your work opens up a path... a path broadening horizons and perspectives...

I would like to point out one more thing: the book also succeeds in convincing because it is well written, with minimal references, careful wording, a well-thought-out layout and a clear 'course'. In this way, the readers are able to follow your thinking and your spiritual progress without exaggerations. The result is that when they reach the end, they find themselves in a position to formulate their own questions in a fruitful dialogue with your text. And for this reason alone, your contribution is invaluable.

With kind regards
**Zoi Gaitanou – MD**


**How the Spirit Heals the Body**

The potential of humans to utilize the powers of the spirit and the soul for improving their own health and that of others is the subject of the book "Spiritual Healing" (publ. Megas Seirios) by Mrs Klairi Lykiardopoulou, President of the 'Servers' Society' Spiritual Centre.

Based on the principle of controlling the mind itself, as well as the principles of meditation in general, the author analyses the method, suggesting practical ways in which every individual, if one so wishes, can use the energies and the powers which exist within and around him or her for healing purposes. As we know, an illness is not only a disorder of the body, but any disharmonious function of the soul and the spirit. That is why negative feelings and thoughts can cause harm and are in themselves a kind of illness. So, by positively programming ourselves and sending positive energy to others, we simply prevent illness, any illness, from finding fertile ground on which to strike. In the same way, positive energy can effectively combat an illness that has already appeared.

The book "Spiritual Healing" makes it possible for the uninitiated to find the spirit of development and control of powers which exist within them but which they have perhaps never had the opportunity of knowing, while, through certain examples which are described in detail, they will be able to see how far the results of spiritual healing can reach.

**"Gynaika" magazine**


**Health through the Spirit**

Anyone can help in the healing of psychosomatic disturbances if one understands their causes. This is what the author of "Spiritual Healing" asserts. The book deals particularly with the potential of employing spiritual power and the energies of the soul by humans in order to improve their health and that of others.

In addition to a theoretical analysis of the subject, the author also provides practical methods of application with specific examples, having clarified first that 'spiritual healing is in no way opposed to classic medical science'.

This is the fourth book by Klairi Lykiardopoulou, who has worked for many years as a kindergarten teacher in Athens, following her studies in the USA.

**"Epikaira" magazine**

### Energy of the Soul

Klairi Lykiardopoulou, "Spiritual Healing". At last an optimistic book! And original, though somewhat... otherworldly in regard to Greek bibliography. We are referring of course to Klairi Lykiardopoulou's latest book: "Spiritual Healing". So, we can, in fact, not only get well – from any ailment – but we can also heal others! How?

Mrs Lykiardopoulou, in a simple way, manages to admittedly explain it in a most convincing manner. There is within us a hidden power that can be trained and tamed and, above all, used on ourselves and on others.

There is evidence of this. There is proof of people who have saved themselves and others.

This energy of the soul, which we all sense and suspect of its existence, seems to have found theoretical and practical applications in our times. Something as impressive as it is real! And something to take note of.

### "Ta Nea" newspaper – Kostas Mitropoulos

I am reading Mrs Klairi Lykiardopoulou's book "Spiritual Healing". In my opinion, perhaps one of the most interesting books currently available in Modern Greek literature. 'Life is a miracle...' K.L. tells us quite simply in the Foreword of her book. Here is a thought which is simple, but which nevertheless is in keeping with what the modern 'informatics' science – to its surprise – has discovered in the advanced world of Knowledge... Science tells us today that the world – and life, naturally – is so strange that we cannot even imagine it... as Robert Oppenheimer said, father of the atomic bomb and Einstein's partner. And as we know, we as human beings, as well as the entire 'cosmos' (the Universe), of course, live and function as tiny bio-psycho-spiritual micro-units within this marvelous world of Oppenheimer's and Einstein's. Or do we?

And so the author tells us: "My aim is to clarify that healing means differentiation of the function of the soul which will firmly establish Health in human beings, a health simultaneously of the 'soul and of the body'. Because there is no benefit in patients only recovering from an illness. If they have not understood what they must do in order to maintain their health, they are at risk from a new illness which will make its appearance as a result of the same erroneous function". What is needed is for us to learn to protect ourselves from illness. With our Thought. Or with our Spirit, if you prefer.

Among the chapters of the book are: 'What Illness Is', 'Soul and Body', 'Negative Thoughts and Emotions', 'A Healing Centre for the Future'. K.L. talks to us of these matters in her excellent book "Spiritual Healing". And they are, I think, useful for all humans. Useful particularly in our troubled age of Spirit and of matter. Let us not forget that 'Life is a miracle...' and miracles need care. Because otherwise they are easily lost.

**"Ores" magazine, Volos – Stavros Vasardanis**

### *Klairi Lykiardopoulou*

*Klairi Lykiardopoulou was born in Athens. She attended the American College and completed her studies in pedagogy in the United States. She has travelled around the world and has experienced many different cultures.*

*Her life radically changed after her acquaintance with Master Dimitris Kakalidis, founder of the "Servers' Society" Spiritual Centre, in 1980. Under his guidance, she received his teaching on self-study, on the emergence of the human spiritual nature and on practicing Spiritual Healing as a way of life. For almost three decades now, she has been President of the Society.*

*She contributed to the structuring of the Servers' Society Healing Section, for which she constantly works, training new healers. Answering unselfishly to the need of the fellow-human, she has met thousands of people seeking help for health, personal, or family problems. On a daily basis she accepts patients who ask for her help through Spiritual Healing, and continues to receive letters of thanks from patients who have been healed, either through contact or distance healing. Extracts of her book "Spiritual Healing", first published in Greece in 1987, were presented in sequels in a newspaper of wide circulation, in 1989.*

*For her literary work she has received commending reviews and is widely appreciated by the country's intellectual world. Extracts of her books have been included in anthologies and literary magazines. Her trilogy about the role of man, woman and the couple was approved by the Hellenic Ministry of Education and Religious Affairs for school libraries. In interviews for the state television and radio channel she has emphasized the need for all people to know and express their true nature.*

*She has already written 19 books, conveying her personal experiences of her discipleship and developing issues concerning various aspects of life with examples of everyday life, always based on the teaching she has received. In March, 2009, an overall presentation of her literary work was held, with renowned writers speaking of her service to the intellect.*

*Mrs Lykiardopoulou continues to work for the Servers' Society vocation, which is the devel-opment of human conscience and the dissemination of spirituality.*

## "Experiences of a Spiritual Healer"
## by Kiki Keramida

"My illness became a motive to seek spirituality that lead me to devote myself in learning and practicing spiritual healing, which I was taught in the spiritual centre 'Omilos Eksipiretiton' (the Servers' Society)."

Every page of this book is teemed with the power, the will, the creativity Mrs Kiki was expressing as being a spiritual healer.

An overwhelming book, an essential help covering both a person's body and soul.

## "The Path from Fear to Fearlessness"
## by Ioanna Dimakou

In a simple and clear language, the author describes her efforts to "conquer" fear, which for three years were a daily problem in her life. This problem was greatly reduced within the first five months after the day she met Dimitris Kakalidis and received his help. It is an example that may help those who experience similar fears and phobias. The positive results she experienced led her to seek the path of spirituality and continue her progress to fearlessness.

*See also...*

☙

### "Individuality - Unity - Monad"
### by Klairi Lykiardopoulou

This book speaks of the spiritual progress of man from the unconscious to the conscious, from the individual to the Monad. It describes the processes through which the human being passes from the moment he becomes aware of his individuality. He then expresses two desires, one to preserve his individuality, and the other to become a member of a group. And by participating in other groups, he realises at some point that his nature is like that of all men...

### "The Master
### – First Concepts - First Experiences"
### by Klairi Lykiardopoulou

In this first volume of the series The Master the author speaks of her experiences as a result of her meeting the Master, Dimitris Kakalidis. She describes how he responded in such a way as to help her understand concepts that were unknown to her. She wanted to follow his teaching because she could see the spirituality that he transmitted to all his disciples...

Praise for One Last Dan

"a muscular historical thriller with credible action, strong characters, lively plotting and an unusual, finely drawn setting."

Andrew Taylor

"Slickly written, authentic-feeling and enormous fun. A highly recommended and gripping historical detective yarn!"

Angus Donald

"a twisty thriller set in the aftermath of the First World War"

Martin Edwards

"Pacy, atmospheric and steeped in intrigue, this is a thriller that truly thrills."

Peter Lovesey

"skilfully brings 1920s Shanghai alive: the teeming streets, the dodgy businessmen, the shady establishments, the drink, the women, the drugs and the murders ... More please."

Michael Ridpath

# One Last Dance Before I Die

by

Michael Jecks

Copyright © 2023 Michael Jecks All rights reserved

The characters and events portrayed in this book are fictitious. Any similarity to real persons, living or dead, is coincidental and not intended by the author.

No part of this book may be reproduced, or stored in a retrieval system, or transmitted in any form or by any means, electronic, mechanical, photocopying, recording, or otherwise, without express written permission of the publisher.

ISBN-13: 978-1-7384675-1-8
ISBN-10: 1-7384675-1-8

Cover design by: Dave Slaney

Jecks, Michael (2023). One Last Dance Before I Die (Shanghailanders) . Pink Rickord Publishing. Paperback Edition.

# Other books by Michael Jecks

*The Last Templar Series*

The Last Templar
The Merchant's Partner
A Moorland Hanging
The Crediton Killings
The Abbot's Gibbet
The Leper's Return
Squire Throwleigh's Heir
Belladonna at Belstone
The Traitor of St Giles
The Boy-Bishop's Glovemaker
The Tournament of Blood
The Sticklepath Strangler
The Devil's Acolyte
The Mad Monk of Gidleigh
The Templar's Penance
The Outlaws of Ennor
The Tolls of Death
The Chapel of Bones
The Butcher of St Peter's
A Friar's Bloodfeud
The Death Ship of Dartmouth
The Malice of Unnatural Death
The Dispensation of Death
The Templar, the Queen and her Lover
Prophecy of Death
The King of Thieves
No Law in the Land
The Bishop Must Die
The Oath
King's Gold
City of Fiends
Templar's Acre

*The Bloody Mary Series*

Rebellion's Message
A Murder Too Soon
A Missed Murder
The Dead Don't Wait
Death Comes Hot
The Moorland Murderers
The Merchant Murderers
Murdering the Messenger
Death Comes In Threes

*Vintener Trilogy*

Fields of Glory
Blood on the Sand
Blood of the Innocents

*The Art of Murder Series*

Portrait of a Murder
Landscape of Murder

Pilgrim's War

Act of Vengeance

*Collections of Short Stories*

No One Can Hear You Scream - and other stories
For the Love of Old Bones - and other stories

*Collaborations*
The Tainted Relic - with Medieval Murderers
The Sword of Shame - with Medieval Murderers
The House of Shadows - with Medieval Murderers
King Arthur's Bones - with Medieval Murderers
The Deadliest Sin - with Medieval Murderers
The Sinking Admiral - with The Detection Club
Whodunit - with the Detection Club

This book is for my wife,
Jane,
for her patience in coping
with me and the life of
a writer's wife!

# Prologue

*Wednesday 16th October 1912*

Officer 213 had found him, so to Officer 213 went the honour of fishing him from the river.

The body had not been in the water long. It bobbed up and down in the wash of a passing junk, and he had to reach out single-handed, clinging to a chain. It was obviously a fellow Chinese from his build and clothing – simple trousers and a long tunic. Like so many, he had no queue of hair. His arms were outspread, like the Christians' portrayal of their Christ figure.

'Come on, man! Get on with it!'

213 gritted his teeth. This foreign devil had no respect. The Shanghai Municipal Police had many officers, but worst were the newest. Men like this only wanted to give orders, to shout and bully with impunity. They didn't trust the Chinese. Officer 213 wouldn't fall into the river to satisfy the sergeant's urgency. He couldn't afford another washing and ironing bill.

He strained again, but the figure was tantalisingly out of reach. Eventually Sergeant Burton ordered him back, swearing. With his longer reach he clutched a leg and pulled the body to the water's edge, where the others could land it. Burton pulled off his hat and wiped his brow. A small boy was wailing at the harbour wall, held back by Officer 426, and Burton snapped, 'What the hell's his problem? Tell the brat to belt up!'

'This his father,' 213 said.

'Tell him to be quiet. A man can hardly think with that row,' he said. 'Let's see his face.'

The officers pulled the body onto his back, and Burton recoiled. 'Sweet Jesus! Who did that to him?'

# Chapter One

*Wednesday 21st July, 1920*

The first time Rod Cottey saw her, she fell out of a Kenworthy Line-O-Eight and almost out of her dress. Its strap slipped from her shoulder as she tumbled to the ground.

It was one of those nights when the heat and humidity hit a man like a club. Even without his nightmares sleep was impossible. That night, on a whim, he had crossed the Garden Bridge and stood staring at the city. The noise was deafening, beggars and hucksters crying out, and traffic thrumming over the bridge like an elephant's stomach rumbling.

She had bawled, 'Go to *hell*!' before falling out. The phaeton's driver, appalled, sprang out, but Rod was already at her side.

'Are you all right, miss?' he said.

She looked up at him like a frightened kitten. For a moment he wondered whether she had struck her head; she looked stunned, but it was the brandy and smoke he could smell on her breath, not a wound.

'She's fine,' the chauffeur said.

'Shut up, Foster!' The girl snapped. She gave Rod a lop-sided smile, a thumb hooking her dress's strap back over her shoulder. Her only injury was a grazed knee. 'My saviour,' she said, and giggled, accepting his hand to get up.

She had wide-set eyes, and rather thin lips in an oval face. Her dress gave no hint of her figure: it was a straight up and down sheath of silk in dark cream. Rod guessed there was a fashionably androgynous figure beneath.

He released her hand. 'Hardly,' he said.

'She's fine. I'll look after her.'

'Don't be silly, Foster. The gentleman helped me up, that's all.'

The driver began, 'Your father –'

She looked at Rod again, with a coquettish slant to her head, eyes coolly calculating. 'Father needn't hear about this.'

Foster locked eyes with Rod. 'I don't know who you are, but you'd best move on. Run along.'

'Friend Foster,' Rod said easily. 'If you carry on like this, we are going to fall out.'

'Stop!' The woman pushed Foster aside.

'I won't -'

'You'll do as you are told, if you know what's good for you!'

'Don't threaten *me*, Alice. You don't want to do that,' Foster said. He glared, but strode back to the Kenworthy.

'Don't mind him,' she said.

'He's your servant,' Rod said.

'And he's rude. He takes advantage,' she said with more than a trace of bitterness.

'Are you being bothered, Alice?' A tall man with the affected laziness of the rich stood tapping a cigarette on a gold cigarette case. 'This fellow troubling you?'

'No, he saved me when I fell,' the girl chuckled, facing Rod again. 'Who are you? Have we met?'

He lifted his fedora. 'I don't think so. Rodney Cottey.'

'Oh? Well, I'm Alice Winton. Thank you for helping me up.'

'My pleasure. I hope you don't fall again.'

'Oh, I will be fine when I'm on the dance floor,' she said. 'I simply *live* to dance. Come, Charles.'

Taking the man's elbow, she walked to the hotel. She turned and glanced back at Rod, laughing at some pleasantry, and was gone.

'You'd best keep away from her,' the chauffeur said. He had returned and stood behind Rod.

Rod ignored him. It was too hot to get angry.

# Chapter Two

*Saturday 7th May, 1921*

Policing Shanghai was rarely dull. In one day Rod might experience a gangland killing, a bank robbery, and rioting sailors on shore-leave. That night Rod had one of the better jobs: keeping an eye on a man with a taste for whisky and women.

The Astor catered for the wealthiest patrons. In the ballroom, Rod sipped a martini, while young women gleaming in silks, with precious stones at their throats, wrists and fingers, whirled with partners in dinner suits.

It was a huge room, the pale blue walls decorated with dancing maidens, a glass wall behind the band designed to look like a peacock's fan. As the band played, the glass was illuminated with changing coloured lights which lit the diamonds with electric sparks. Overhead a vaulted glass ceiling reflected the scene. It was beautiful, but sometimes, as that night, his head pounded to an different music. Sudden flashes reminded him of starshells dropping from a black sky; the drums of the boom of artillery; spinning dancers became men reeling from shrapnel. He gulped his drink, ordering another until the sounds of battle retreated and he could breathe more easily.

The bar was in the corner of the room, and Rod leaned against it until his heart had slowed to a canter. At times like this he was jealous. His thoughts inevitably turned to Cecily. Just occasionally he would see a shining eye, a smiling mouth, and it would bring up an image of her, green eyes laughing, auburn hair gleaming, soft lips parted ready to kiss …

At a circular table, sat the big, round-faced Chinese flanked by two striking American girls. One, a brunette, had an air of quiet sadness about her.

It was interesting that he wanted white consorts. Many Chinese would stick to courtesans who required an *amah* to chaperone them, but there was cachet in possessing a European or American woman. Rod knew little about him. He enjoyed scotch and gambling, but his property business hardly seemed adequate for his lifestyle.

'Find him interesting, do you?' It was Eric Leigh. He stood at Rod's side wearing a wolfish grin. 'Do you have anything on Billy boy?'

'Evening, Eric,' Rod said.

'Hallo. Are you on duty? And, if so, why are you watching big, bad Billy Qian?'

Qian floated about the city like an emperor, dispensing largesse. He patronised the best restaurants, circulated with the wealthy, and between times appeared at places like the Astor with young women on his arm. A man in his middle thirties, with smiling eyes and a deep laugh that made his belly move like a sea in a tsunami, Billy Qian enjoyed life.

'I'm just enjoying a drink after work,' Rod said.

'I see. Want another martini?' Eric asked innocently.

'No, I've had enough, thank you,' Rod said, affecting a disinterested yawn.

'So you *are* working,' Eric said triumphantly. 'You'd never refuse a drink. Come on: why are you watching Billy Qian?'

'Who?'

'Not convincing, Rod. Maybe I should just go and ask him why he's being followed. That would save me thinking up clever questions – and you the effort of lying.'

'Maybe I should take you to gaol for a day or two.'

'Except you wouldn't, would you, old cock?' he grinned. 'You still believe in good, old-fashioned policing, against all reason.'

Rod gave him a sour look, and Eric threw back his head, laughing. He opened his cigarette case and offered one.

It was two years since they met on board the Blue Funnel steamer, *SS Laertes*. While Rod joined the police, Eric had taken a clerical post at the Hongkong Shanghai bank. He lasted four months before the stifling atmosphere persuaded him it was a dreadful mistake. Resigning, he managed to get a job on the 'News'. Although he was a demon for women and drink, he was hard-working, and eager to report the truth. He stood hopefully now, like a spaniel watching a pheasant drop.

'Come on, spill 'em,' he grinned. 'What have you got against friend Billy?'

'Nothing,' Rod said.

But Eric's eyes had narrowed. 'He's into property, isn't he? He's said to be one of the city's richest, if you don't count the gangsters. What's he suspected of? Smuggling? Drugs? Gambling?'

'I don't know what you mean,' Rod said, and turned back to the dance floor. A couple took his eye: a young woman with blonde hair bound in a loose bun low on her neck. She was familiar. The man too ...

'Come on, Rod. Give me *something*,' Eric pleaded. 'I'm drying up. The only stories I ever get are murders or kidnaps, and the public's had enough of them! I need *variety*!' He gave a low whistle. 'Ah! That's more up my street!'

'What?'

'*Her*. You can't afford a luxury like her, Rod, old son, she's more my type.'

'Shame she already has a man.'

'Yes.' He was quiet for a moment. 'Still, she's a potential story. Where there's a looker like Alice Winton, with money too, there's always the possibility of a story!'

## Chapter Three

Eric was right. Women like her attracted reporters like flies around a honey pot. Eric followed her progress with wolfish hunger.

'Who's she dancing with? I don't recognise him.' Eric frowned, mentally crossing names from a list of eligible bachelors.

'I have no idea,' Rod said truthfully.

'Her brother died a day or two before the end of the war, poor devil. Must have been terrible for his family.'

Rod nodded. It was one reason for his lost religious faith: seeing men who had survived years of carnage only to succumb to a shell or bullet when peace was so close. To die was sad; to die moments before the guns went silent was an abomination.

The couple looked good together, whirling to the music, but without affection. She held her head averted, yet the man's hand was splayed almost indecently low on her back in an unmistakeable demonstration of ownership.

They turned and Rod saw his face clearly: the high checkbones, pointed chin and expression of surly apprehension. He piqued Rod's interest.

Just then Billy Qian rose, and the girls linked arms with him. Rod saw them exchange a glance, just briefly. The blonde wore an expression of sly greed, like a stoat spying a chicken. She expected to make a killing tonight. The sad-faced brunette looked through her with contempt, and walked like a martyr on the way to the gallows.

Eric was still staring at Alice Winton. Rod hastily collected his hat, and Eric noticed.

'You *are* after him! What's he been up to? Not that I wouldn't mind getting up to something naughty with either of *them*.'

'You couldn't afford either, let alone both,' Rod said, pulling on his hat. 'Stay here, Eric. I don't want you getting in the way.'

He left Eric disgruntled. Outside, coal smoke from the ships on the Whangpoo moved in thick, yellowish grey swirls as Rod crossed the road and leaned against a telegraph pole, lighting a cigarette. He kept his eyes fixed on the Astor House's entrance under its heavy canopy.

He was halfway through his cigarette when an American automobile purred softly to a halt outside the entrance, and Billy and his companions appeared.

A rickshaw stood a block away, and Rod waved urgently, but before the coolie noticed him, Billy's friends had climbed inside and were wafted away.

Rod shrugged. No doubt Billy was going home and would be preoccupied with the women for the next few hours.

Finishing his cigarette, Rod flicked the stub away. That was when he saw Alice Winton. She stood clutching a purse, silk scarf about her shoulders. In the entranceway she looked tiny, a fragile porcelain figure.

Following her gaze, he saw the Kenworthy approach. It halted, and the chauffeur opened the door for her. Alice Winton climbed in, and the driver returned to his seat, released the brake and, as the car began to move, Rod saw her stare at him. She was a figure carved from marble: cold and remote. Then a shiver trembled down his spine; she was not cold - she was terrified.

'Did I scare them off?' Eric said, joining him. 'Who was the man dancing with her?'

'I don't know his name.'

Which was true because Rod had forgotten Alice called him Foster.

# Chapter Four

*Tuesday 25th July, 1922.*

Alice Winton seated herself crabwise at the dining table. Mother pursed her lips disapprovingly. Alice ignored her.

When Crowther snapped his fingers, the maid hurried to Alice, carefully pouring tea. There was no need for words: the staff knew the family's preferences. Alice's father sat at the head of the table, a tyrant in pale suit and tie, glancing over the China Morning News, snorting at the gossip, eyes narrowing as he read of another company's financial predicament. He rarely spoke at breakfast, resorting instead to a series of grunts which Crowther had long since learned to interpret.

The sun dazzled Alice where it glittered on the silverware. Opposite, her brother chewed like a man who held a grudge against toast. He had a plate of kidneys, sausage and bacon, with three fried eggs, but from his expression it might have been pigswill. She knew he had worries of his own. Ever since Ian's death Maurice had assumed he would take over the business, but father rejected him. Only yesterday she heard father bellow, 'I will not pass my company to a feckless incompetent!' in a voice that could have been heard at Pootung. Poor Maurice! All he wanted was a little recognition, perhaps an occasional compliment, but that was not their father's way.

Her brother spent much of his life humiliated - but better that, than to be a bargaining chip, a commodity to be sold in return for favours, like her.

'I like your hair like that, Alice,' her father said, peering over the top of his newspaper.

She acknowledged the compliment. Her long hair was bound in a chignon again. It kept her neck cooler.

'Where were you last night, dear?' her mother asked coldly.

'Dancing, mother.'

'Where? You were late home.'

'I met the Chamberlain brothers, and they brought me back,' she lied.

'You haven't said where you were,' her mother said, her tone brittle.

Alice looked at her unblinking. 'Why? Do you care?'

Alfred gave a long, hacking cough. Then, 'Leave Alice alone! She's old enough to know her own mind.'

Alice stared at her mother coldly. It was hard to see her as a monster, but Alice knew she was. She blamed her mother.

Edith said, 'She spends too many evenings gambling and dancing.'

'Yes, mother. Dancing and gambling. Shocking, isn't it?' she said in a voice that could dissolve metal.

'People talk, Alice.'

'You shouldn't listen to gossip.'

Edith flinched as though she had been struck. 'How dare you?'

'Leave her alone!' Maurice said. 'You want her to stay here and fester until you've married her off? You want her to remain *intact*, I suppose, to increase her value?'

'Maurice, not at the breakfast table,' Edith snapped. The butler maintained a stony impassivity.

'She loves to dance. Let her enjoy herself. Don't make her waste away in this God-awful mausoleum!'

'Be silent!' Alfred roared. 'Good God! What is the matter with this family? I wish to heaven I'd –'

'What? Sent me to the War? Kept Ian back so he could run the business? Sent me to *my* death instead, keeping darling Ian safe here?'

'Don't tempt me, Maurice!'

'No, you always hated temptation!'

'If you can't be civil, leave the table!' Alfred snapped, his face white.

'Oh, I'll go. I find the company rather astringent this morning,' Maurice said. He threw his serviette onto his plate and marched out.

Alice kept her attention on her plate.

Her mother was a monster, yes, but father was worse.

Thin Bao inhaled and let the smoke trickle from his nostrils.

He leaned against the door in the shadows, frowning at the coolies working at the French concession docks. Many would have been delighted to go pacing up the gangplanks, take up a sack or bale heavy enough to crush a man, and then pad leaden-footed down, depositing the cargo in the godowns before returning for the next load. They would be glad of the handful of rice for their day's labour in the heat.

A man slipped and fell, and a western sailor in tight black jacket and peaked cap studying a clipboard swore, pointing with his pencil. The Chinese overseer sprang forward and slapped the unfortunate fellow until he had clambered to his feet, stumbling under his load. Thin Bao spat in disgust. They were donkeys: dull-witted brutes with neither honour nor self-respect. A man of honour would have fought the foreign devil.

Half the fools fetching and carrying for the foreign devils wouldn't dare raise their eyes to Thin Bao. Twenty three years old, he had climbed his way up from the quayside. He commanded respect; he was a man of honour in the Green Gang. He had grabbed the opportunities presented. These donkeys wouldn't recognise an opportunity if it punched them. He despised them.

He buttoned his jacket. His appearance pleased him: his suit and the grey fedora with the distinctive black and white chequered ribbon showed he was important. He had demanded that the brim be snapped down sharply, giving his eyes a more menacing look. He had bashed the crown himself, pinching the front tightly like a ship's prow. It looked good; it made him feel good. The jacket was strangely uncomfortable, but it hung loosely, and even buttoned, the shoulder holster was hidden.

An engine purred and he recognised the automobile. Stepping from the shadows, he took a deep pull of his cigarette and tossed the stub away as the vehicle drew to a halt.

There was no need for words. He peered inside, nodded, opened the door and took his seat in the front.

He didn't pay any attention to the *SS Tean*, which stood at the dock and now rocked sluggishly, a clot of passengers waiting at the gangway.

## Chapter Five

For Archie Lane it was like coming home.
The sun glittered from the rippling water, transforming the brown expanse into polished granite sprinkled with diamonds. River traffic all but blocked their way: junks, steamers, tiny craft of all types. It was a miracle that none was crushed by the *Tean*. There was a dull, ochre haze from the municipal power station, and through it he dimly discerned buildings as the ship rounded the bend in the river. A thrill ran through him at his first sight. It left him breathless.
*Shanghai*!
It rose on the north and western banks, a testament to Western ingenuity and Chinese labour. The Bund, glimpsed between the ships crushed together at the wharves, seemed clogged with people. Everywhere he looked there were *more*! The *colours*! Bright crimson satins, yellow silks, gleaming greens the colour of fresh grass - it was *blinding*! London was *nothing* compared to this.
His senses were bludgeoned. Even the odours were different: spices, incense, a sweet odour, another sharp and sour ... so many smells, sights, sounds ... He could not leave the deck. Instead he stood by the rail drinking it all in.
Leaving the ship was not easy. Enthusiastic passengers crowded the gangways, ship's officers holding people back until the First Class had made their way ashore, but then the way was cleared. At last Archie reached solid ground, his battered

suitcase at his feet. At the next gangway stood a man wearing a cap, clipboard in hand. Archie grabbed his suitcase.

'Sir, excuse me,' he said.

'Yes?'

His uniform had a sergeant's stripes. He peered down at Archie like a sergeant-major surveying grease on a uniform.

Archie immediately stood to attention. 'Sir, I am joining the police, but …'

'Name?'

'Archie Lane, sir.'

He peered at his clipboard and made a slow, deliberate tick with his pencil. 'Very well, Lane. Get a rickshaw to the Gordon Road Depot.'

'Sir?'

The man gave a faint smile. 'It's all right, Lane. Just remember: you're British. Tell the fellow to take you to Gordon Road Depot. He'll know. Oh, and welcome to Shanghai.'

The car halted with a squeal of brakes, the front tyre thudding into the kerbside, and Thin Bao stepped onto the running board, gazing over the crowds. He slid a fresh cigarette into his mouth.

Overhead banners moved lazily in the humid heat. Women fanned their faces, elegant foreigners strolled, pinkly damp under their sun hats, while Chinese plodded stoically. Thin Bao caught the eye of one woman, a round-faced European with straggles of weedy, pale hair showing beneath her bonnet. She looked away hurriedly, reddening, and Thin Bao felt his mouth pull into a curve of contempt. These foreigners with their money thought themselves superior. He knew better.

A sudden blaring of a motor horn caught his attention. At first nothing could be seen in amongst the hordes, but gradually he could make out the car.

He snapped his fingers.

The rear doors opened, and one man crossed the road while the other leaned negligently against a telegraph post. Thin Bao reached inside and picked up his gun, pulling back the bolt until it locked, then rested the machine-pistol on the car's roof.

He could see it clearly now. A gleaming black phaeton, roof up, but no side-screens in place. It drew closer and closer, until he couldn't miss.

'Now!' he shouted.

Archie gaped. The city was so ... so *fast*! So *loud*! At the Bund, he was assailed by the noise, but leaving the river, everything grew still more alien. Chinese women smiled covertly, half concealing their mouths behind hands or fans, moving delicately with a rolling, shuffling gait; birds sang and fluttered in cages; beggars wearily cried out; hawkers bellowed. The cacophony was deafening. It was a modern city, in which everything was familiar yet different, a place where English signs proudly advertised their wares, while Chinese banners flapped overhead. Archie was used to crowds in London, but here ... he had never seen so many people.

A tall Sikh with his carbine over his shoulder inclined his head fractionally on seeing Archie. Archie nodded back, and then saw the car appear. He knew his cars, and this was a Kenworthy: a sleek American beast.

There was a sudden rattle, and he saw the Kenworthy lurch as the driver jerked the wheel, then the metallic thuds of bullets striking the bonnet and side panels, a single loud ricochet, stars appearing in the glass as bullets punched through, and Archie threw himself from the rickshaw and scurried to the nearest cover while people screamed and fled from the hellish chatter of the guns.

Through a mist of cordite Thin Bao saw splashes of bare metal as bullets hammered the bonnet, doors, running boards, each blow distinct even over his machine-pistol's rattle. The car slammed into a shop. A wheel broke free and rolled away. As steam rose from the radiator, Thin Bau slung his Bergmann into the car and crossed the road. The cries were deafening, one woman setting up a ululation kneeling at the side of a toddler's body. A man stumbled with a bloody hand at his head, two figures lay where the Kenworthy's tyres had crushed them.

The Kenworthy was smothered in banners, and Thin Bao pulled the nearest away, glancing at the rear seats. They were empty. He opened the driver's door, pulling out his pistol. The driver was slumped, still breathing, but his throat crackling as he fought for breath.

Thin Bao fired twice, then reached in with his knife.

Archie watched as the figure in the western suit and fedora strode over the road. The two shots were deliberate, unhurried, like a Deputy Provost Marshal giving the coup de grace to a firing squad victim, and Archie found himself panting when the man reached inside. The squeals of the injured made him feel sick.

The noise, when it came, was subtle. A flick of dust near the gunman's foot, and a moment later the crack of the shot, and Archie turned to see the Sikh working the bolt on his carbine. He aimed carefully, and Archie saw the puff of burning powder.

Another bullet flew, but the murderer was striding back to his car. He stopped, lifted his pistol and fired two shots carefully, before strolling to the passenger seat and climbing in. The engine roared, and as the car moved away, the Sikh pelted up. He took aim one last time, but too late, and he snatched the gun from his shoulder with the fierce rage of failure.

# Chapter Six

Death smelled foul, Rod Cottey thought. It was cloying, and stuck in the throat. Neither whisky or brandy would wash it away, and it lined the passages ever more thickly over time. It built up and up, like effluent in a blocked sewer, until it overwhelmed a man. When he succumbed, he was lost. The police officers found late at night drinking in the mess were fighting off the last stages. They would soon put a gun to their heads, or be discovered gibbering. The horror of death defeated everyone eventually.

The trenches were at their worst in the summer, with the stench of blood and faeces and rotting flesh. Here, in the bright sunshine of Shanghai at noon, odours of petrol, sweet herbs, dyes and spices conspired with cordite in a still worse stench.

He had been at Louza Police Station when gunfire was heard, and ran from the building, forgetting even his hat.

The car sprawled like a drunk, nestling in a mess of baskets and groceries where it had ploughed into a shopfront. A banner had dangled over the shop, but the car's impact had draped it over the roof. A wheel some yards from the scene. Baskets, bags of goods - littered the sidewalks where panicked pedestrians had dropped them.

Gleaming chromium and heavy, black, lacquer-like paint caught the light, but it was wrong, out of place. Bullets had punched through the steel panels, leaving cobwebbed crackles that glittered in the sun. The driver's door was like a colander.

The bonnet's panels had buckled, the tyres shredded, the windscreen shattered.

A uniformed officer, Bert Shaw, grinned thinly. 'Hello, Rod. Come to tell us how to investigate a murder?'

'Where's the body?' Rod said.

'Under the wheel.'

Rod glanced down, and Shaw gave a dry chuckle, nodding toward at the cabin. 'No: the steering wheel, Rod.'

Archie sat on a discarded box and watched the plainclothes officer. His manner and assurance spoke of his rank, although the crumpled linen suit and lack of a hat of any sort made him look disreputable.

Reaching for a cigarette, Archie realised his hands were shaking. His match snapped when he tried to strike it, and he stared at the stub for a moment before dropping it and picking a second.

He had come here to leave war and death behind. Others were broken, their souls as mutilated by horror as the bodies dangling on the wire had by shells and bullets. He'd seen friends dismembered, decapitated, or buried under eruptions of soil. All were mates from the docks who joined the Army on the same day. They marched in his memory like a parade of wraiths. Even Stan, from his schooldays, was a blur. Archie had seen him cut in half by a shell. Perhaps he would never escape the constant reminder of death.

The smoke cooled in his chest. He was here to make a new life, and no gangster would change his determination.

Yes, the sudden violence had surprised him, but it was nothing compared with Flanders.

Rod stepped on the running board. The smell crawled out from the smashed cabin: blood and excrement. There was no need to check for a pulse. Bullets had gone straight through the door, slamming into the man sitting behind the wheel and spattering his blood over the seats and farther door. Two had distorted his face.

'Quite a slaughterhouse, eh?' Bert said.

The body lay in front of the seat, half below the dashboard, a shapeless figure clad in dark clothes with wet splashes where bullets had hit. The fellow's left arm was hooked through the spokes of the steering wheel, the other below the dashboard. He was hunched, as if trying to crawl into the footwell.

'Any idea who he is?' Rod said.

'I was waiting for a clever detective to tell me,' Bert said sarcastically.

'Thanks.'

Rod fumbled for a gasper to take away the smell. The sergeant refused his offer.

'In uniform?' he said with a grimace. 'They'd dock my pay if was seen smoking on the streets! You know that.'

Rod made a show of lighting his. There were perks to being a detective in plain clothes.

At the Bund, women would be walking in the Gardens, men and wives would be strolling along the roads peering in at shop windows, perhaps enjoying a little tiffin, or a cocktail at the Club. Rod wished he was with them.

He sighed. 'I know this car. It's a Kenworthy Line-O-Eight. It's owned by the Wintons.'

That being so, he knew the driver too.

A gaggle of locals stood pointing and chattering, the women anxious, the men impassive - apart from one elderly fellow who sat bemoaning the wreckage of his shopfront, a young woman - his daughter? - behind him. She looked more angry than distraught.

'There's a witness. Recruit called Archie Lane. He was on the way to Gordon Road, and saw pretty much all of it.'

'A new recruit?'

'Yes. I doubt he'll want to stay, having seen the downside of Shanghai,' Bert said. He jerked his head towards Archie, 'There he is.'

'God, he looks young!' Rod said.

'True enough.' Bert agreed. He glanced about him. 'What an introduction!'

'At least he's got the measure of Shanghai. I just hope he's a reliable witness.'

Archie didn't envy the three policemen pulling the body free. Soon the plainclothes man walked over. Archie watched him approach with trepidation. He took in Archie's appearance at a glance as Archie climbed to his feet.

'Archie Lane?'

'Yes, sir.' The man had the look of an officer, and possessed the same confidence that Archie had so admired in men like Major Drewett.

'Detective Constable Cottey.' His voice was calm, like a doctor's. 'Sergeant Shaw tells me you saw the whole thing.'

'Well, I suppose so.'

'What happened?'

'I was in a rickshaw, and saw the Kenworthy coming down the road, when these men started shooting at it. They all had machine pistols. There were at least two, but could have been more –'

'Take your time. At least two?'

'Yes. One was there,' he said, pointing. 'Another was on this side of the road. They held down their triggers until they ran out of bullets.'

'Can you describe them?'

Archie considered. 'The man at the car had narrow shoulders. He looked quite skinny, but dressed like a flash sort: a suit of dark blue and a grey fedora. I think he was standing on the running board, so I can't tell his height.'

'Foreign or Chinese?'

Archie looked confused. 'Foreign?'

'It's our expression for anyone who isn't Chinese. Did he look European?'

'I ... I couldn't say for certain, but I'd have thought he was Chinese from his build.'

'What then?'

'The man at the car crossed the road with the other, both pulling out pistols. One looked like a Mauser with the broom handle grip, you know? At the car, he fired twice, and then he – he reached in for something. I couldn't tell.'

Rod nodded. Lane might look young, but his evidence was clear, and given without the hesitation and obfuscation of so many who witnessed murder. 'He deliberately executed the driver?'

'It was very deliberate.' Archie shivered. 'I'd heard the streets of Shanghai were dangerous. I didn't expect to see a gun battle so soon.'

'Get used to it!'

'A Sikh officer shot at them, but missed. Then they jumped into their automobile and drove off.' He frowned. 'I forgot: there was a third man. I remember three doors slamming.'

Rod felt a pang at the sight of his face, like a fresh youngster at the Front. The first whizz-bang or howitzer shell gave them that quiet thoughtfulness. Not terror - that came later when they experienced a real stonk, or charged over the top - it was more an inward pensiveness, realising that what had just happened could easily happen to them. Rod put on a soothing tone.

'You're joining the SMP, I hear?'

'Yes, sir.'

'Don't worry, Lane. We'll soon get you trained to look after yourself. The streets aren't that bad.'

Rod watched the new recruit nod. The lad looked stunned, but not fearful. Maybe he would do.

'Do you know anyone in the Municipal Police?'

'No, I don't think so.'

'What tempted you to sign up?'

Archie shrugged. 'Well, after Flanders the thought of working at the docks didn't appeal. And I heard it was warm here. I've seen enough of mud.'

Rod smiled at that. 'Pretty much like me, then.'

A little later, Archie was installed in a fresh rickshaw trotting towards Gordon Road.

'*The streets aren't that bad,*' Rod repeated to himself cynically, watching Archie ride away.

'Rod?'

Rod sighed, shook a cigarette from his crumpled pack and lit it. 'Yes, Bert?'

'You need to see this.'

## Chapter Seven

Rod could barely recognise him as Alice Winton's dancing companion.

A bullet had torn through his cheek and eye socket, a second had entered the back of his skull, making a terrible mess. But that was not all.

'Dear God, why do this?' Rod said.

The forehead had been slashed with a knife, making three symbols. Underneath, the eyes had been stabbed.

'They wanted to make sure of him,' Bert said. Distaste twisted his features, like a matron discovering a caterpillar in her salad. 'Bullet in the head: a Chinese execution - then this!'

'Why execute a chauffeur? Can you read the symbols?'

'No. We'll need to get him cleaned up before we can try.'

'He upset the local gangs, do you think? Saw something he wasn't supposed to?'

'Perhaps. If he had insulted someone, perhaps they wanted to punish him.'

Rod could not help but think of that evening a year before, and the man who had been dancing so lightly with Alice Winton. 'Any other witnesses?'

'That lot.' Bert indicated a gaggle of Chinese. 'They thought it was firecrackers, till the car ploughed into the shop. No one admits seeing anything - do you blame them?'

'What about the gun? Lane said he thought they had machine pistols and a Mauser.'

When it came to guns, Rod and Bert had plenty of experience. Bert ran his fingers over the bullet holes. 'I'd guess these are all nine millimetre.'

'So could be a Bergmann, as Lane said.'

'Yes.'

machine pistols were appearing more and more regularly on the streets. After the Great War, there was a glut of firearms, and dealers willing to sell to the highest bidder.

Rod counted. 'There are more than thirty bullet holes in the driver's door alone.'

'A lot to kill a driver, don't you think?'

'Perhaps.'

Since the Armistice there had been a great deal of bitterness. The Chinese protested when German territories were given to the Japanese and not returned to Chinese rule. Rod agreed with them. China had entered the War supporting the Allies, and it was at best insensitive.

He peered inside the car. The seats were so well-padded, they could have been a club's. Not that they would be wanted now. The bullets had shredded the red leather, exposing horsehair and woollen stuffing by the handful.

Rod surveyed the street. Here kidnap and murder were less common. Crimes were routine: robbery, burglary, gangs demanding protection; not attacks by men with machine pistols.

But the Wintons were one of the Municipality's richest families. They were the sort of people to whom strange things happened.

The Central Police Station was a four storey red brick building with a tower that rose another storey above the roof. It loomed over the electric tram cables and the yellow-ochre roadway.

Rod took the stairs. CID was at the rear, overlooking the yard where the armoured cars were kept. Rod's desk was a scruffy teak rectangle, piled high with files he was working on. There were never enough police detectives.

'*Cottey*: in here!'

Douglas Hibbard had his own office, as befitted a Sub Inspector. Rod entered to find Hibbard glancing through a sheaf of reports. He looked up and frowned. 'Are you all right? You look like you haven't slept in a month.'

'I didn't get much sleep,' Rod said softly. 'You know how it is.'

'Oh! Oh, I'm sorry. I didn't mean ...' He looked away, embarrassed. A big man, he was the product of a school where his physique won him respect on the rugger field. Although curling, dark hair gave him a boyish look, he had killed or caught more bank-robbers in the last two years than any other officer in the SMP. His courage was never in doubt, but Rod knew he felt guilty. He hadn't joined the men on the Front, and respected the nightmares endured by those who had.

Clearing his throat, Hibbard sat at his desk, dropping the papers. 'You were at the shooting?'

'Yes, sir. With Sergeant Shaw.'

'Good. The Wintons have reported their vehicle missing, presumed stolen. You go tell them what's happened.'

'Sir? All we know is that someone took potshots at their Kenworthy and killed the driver.'

'Yes.' He began stuffing his pipe with tobacco. 'And Alfred Winton could make our lives difficult, so it behoves us to keep on his right side.' Hibbard glanced at Rod. 'Just be polite and tell him we'll do all we can to hurry things along. We'll find the murderers, but it's a hard job. He'll understand. He knows what the streets are like.'

Overhead the fan turned lazily, squeaking with each rotation. Hibbard's chair complained every time he moved, emitting a sound like a tortured donkey. The noises sandpapered Rod's nerves.

Hibbard lit his pipe and faced the fan, lifting his hands up and clasping them behind his head, feet on the desk. There were sweat stains at his armpits, and a brown smudge beneath his left. Rod's shirts had the same mark: sweat soaked their shoulder holsters and left this image.

'Sir, the chauffeur was deliberately shot in the head. Chinese characters were carved into his forehead and his eyes were stabbed. It was an assassination.'

'Oh?'

'I had a constable translate the characters. They are *er guizi* — that means, "traitor", or "collaborator".'

Hibbard had a habit of peering with a benevolent expression that was a knife-edge from patronising. When he received that look, Rod felt as much use as a tin tack on the sole of his shoe.

'Life is cheap here, Cottey,' Hibbard said, teeth clenched about his pipe. 'Likely the killer wanted to scare off witnesses. When you've fished as many bodies from the Whangpoo as I have, you learn they don't care about life. It's not the first time a man's been killed and mutilated.'

'But why Foster?,' Rod said.

'Who can tell? Maybe the gunman had been smoking opium and thought it was a dragon running down the road towards him.'

Rod didn't want to go down that route. 'There were three of them.'

'Ah, well, they shared a pipe, eh?' Hibbard chuckled.

His flippancy was disrespectful to the dead. Rod's voice was cold. 'They had machine pistols.'

'Those bloody things get everywhere. Even the coolies know where to borrow them, I daresay,' Hibbard said with a grimace.

'Yes, sir.'

'I daresay it was pure bad luck. The fellow drove past someone with a dislike of American vehicles. You'll probably find an opium-fiend in a gutter somewhere trying to remember how to load his Bergmann. Find him, but do it quickly and discreetly. I don't want Winton complaining to the Commissioner. Clear?'

It didn't seem a terrible problem. In the past year only some ten murders had taken place, and in each case the perpetrators were found swiftly. He glanced at the file on Billy Qian. Qian was involved in something - he wasn't sure what yet, but he would find out.

# Chapter Eight

Rod splashed tepid water on his face. The heat was oppressive, the humidity blanketing the city like a steaming towel. That and the dreams kept Rod awake till the early hours.

He stared at himself in the mirror over the sink: blotchy from the heat, lined and weary from lack of sleep. There were bruises under his eyes, and wrinkles at his forehead. He looked like a man in his forties, not a twenty-three year old.

Returning home after the War had felt like reprieve. To hear birdsong again, to see trees standing with branches intact, to see houses, hedges, roads, fields all unspoiled, made him want to break down. Instead, he had nervously approached the house. When his father opened the door, Rod realised he looked the older of the two.

One after another of his companions had fallen. Friends from his schooldays, officers of courage and talent. Most fell in Shrine Alley on the first of July '16, the first day of the Somme: Duncan Martin, the artist, the poet William Hodgson and many others - four hundred and sixty four casualties in a few moments. Rod had been there; somehow he survived. God alone knew why.

Afterwards, he had hoped to return to his old life, but the first time he met a woman who had lost her son in Rod's company, he knew he couldn't. It was her eyes: they stabbed like bayonets. They held a desperate, fierce yearning - and hatred. Her eyes accused him, told him that he should have died instead of her boy — or with him. Rod felt he had no right to return when others lay in their shell-holes, each a shattered mess of blood and bone. Why had *he* survived when they had not?

The widows, the girls who had lost fiancés, brothers, fathers … all possessed that same hungry look. They sucked from him the life that remained until he dare not leave his door. He might bump into one of them, or meet Cecily or Ethel. The advert to join the Shanghai Municipal Police was like salvation. There, he thought, he might escape.

But there was no escape. Even now, after three years, he could still see the faces of the men who had joined him, fought alongside him, and died. They came to him in his sleep, they appeared in the crowds as he walked the streets, they were beside him when he drank in a bar, they peered over his shoulder when he read a book.

When he was a boy, he had been called 'Smiler' by his friends. They wouldn't recognise him now - not that many were alive.

A family like the Wintons would expect a personal call. Besides, the case interested him. It was rare to see women dancing with the hired help.

He was still thinking of the two dancing when Mickey Hi called him. His eyes held a haunted look.

'What is it, Mickey?'

Mickey was a round-faced Chinese officer who greeted those who walked in off the street at Central. Although he was usually beaming, there was a slightly lunatic edge to his smile, as if he was terrified of making a mistake in front of his foreign masters. Mickey reminded Rod of the poor devils recruited and thrown into weapons drill, marching and all the other ridiculous aspects of military life which were so irrelevant to their trench existence. They too were fearful of superior beings: sergeant-majors, lieutenants, captains. And a wrong foot could easily result in punishment without defence. Mickey was fully aware of the vulnerability of his position. 'Hi' was not his surname - it was a nickname, based on his customary welcome.

'Oh, hi, Detective Constable Cottey. People here to talk to police, but no one here. One is reporter China Daily News …'

'Mr Leigh? Tell him I'm busy.'

'Yes, sir. And - one is lady, she want talk someone about robbery.'

'I understand,' Rod said, glancing at the clock. 'Bring her in.'

Soon Mickey introduced Mrs Hyland, an elegant woman dressed ten years out of date. She wore a camel-brown jacket over a high-collared white blouse, and long skirt of a colour similar to her jacket. On her head perched a tight little hat, and she held an ivory-handled fan with which she busily tried to cool herself. It must have been more effective than the slowly-turning fan overhead.

She had a sharp face, with eyes that crinkled as though smiling, but which darted about the room suspiciously. Her hair was grey, and pulled into a tight bun, her lips thin and disapproving, an impression that was confirmed by the gold pince-nez through which she peered. With her upright posture she looked like a retired school-mistress.

'I hate to be a trouble, but there have been so many matters recently. Last week a doormat was stolen from my yard, and three days ago my dog went missing. I fear I may be robbed. They do that, you know, kill a dog, so they know that they can break in with impunity,' she said, nodding seriously.

Rod didn't like to say it was more likely her dog had been cooked by one of the starving families in the city. He pulled on a sympathetic expression. 'You wish to report the loss? What sort of dog was he?'

'A yellow Labrador.' She wiped at her eye with a handkerchief. 'And since Bobby has disappeared, I have had a number of distressing occurrences: clothes stolen from the washing line, and a man loitering.'

'Chinese?'

'Of course. And plainly up to no good,' she said primly.

'Why do you think that?'

She rolled her eyes. 'Well, he is dressed like a European, with this ridiculous fashion for wide lapels and fedora hats. When I first saw him, he pulled the brim down so I might not see his face. And I have seen him speaking with an English woman.'

'Perhaps she employs him,' Rod guessed.

'Don't be ridiculous. This was private roadway. A servant would receive instruction indoors, obviously. No, this sets a worrying precedent: our position here is hard-earned. Allow the natives to take liberties, and who can tell what will happen? You mark my words, Officer,' Miss Hyland continued, 'our position is due entirely to our authority, the rule of British law.'

Cynically, Rod made the right noises. Europeans were not in Shanghai because they had a special 'authority'; they had invaded with modern weapons, subdued the people and forced them to accept Indian opium. The elites were overthrown, and the country split into warring factions ruled by warlords. That was why the Chinese hated 'foreigners'.

Rod Cottey could not blame them.

'Of course,' she added, 'we have brought them the fruits of civilisation too. We have demonstrated charity. I worked at the missionary hospital, and then the orphanage, and helped teach the children to read and write. You would be astonished by how quickly they picked up algebra.'

He was sure he would, but forbore to mention Chinese culture and civilisation. Some colonials would never accept that other cultures were as rich as their own, nor that they might be considerably older. 'I can have men patrol your street more often, if you are worried.'

She fixed him with an eye that almost pinned him to the wall. 'Detective Constable, I may look a feeble old woman, but I was born here, and it will take more than a Chinaman burglar to kill me!' So saying, she reached into a pocket and pulled out a small revolver. 'I have a pair of these. My father was a missionary, and it was my Smith and Wessons that protected us during the last rebellion. They can do so again.'

'Please, Miss Hyland, put that away,' Rod said. 'I don't appreciate having guns waved in my face. I am glad you feel safe, however, I will increase patrols near your house.'

It would, he felt, be safer for all concerned.

Thin Bao entered, bowed and walked to the wall, where he waited.

The restaurant was full. Men stood silently until called to speak. The man in the chair paid them no attention. He sipped tea, his face blank. Two spoke in hushed tones but when the man raised his hand, they were silenced. Visitors entered, crossed to the table and knelt at the side of their leader. They whispered, and he nodded or waved them to others, a lord accepting homage and dispensing justice.

When the visitors dried to a trickle, he spoke in his quiet voice, his harsh accent that of the Pootung slums where he had been raised.

'There was an attack on the car owned by a taipan today. Who was responsible?'

Thin Bao had expected this. He stepped forward. 'I was.'

'Why?'

'I was paid.'

'You did not think to warn me?'

Thin Bao heard the menace. Du Yusheng was leader of the Green Gang, and held power of life or death. 'It did not seem necessary.'

'Not necessary?' the cold eyes turned to him.

Thin Bao felt the gaze like the lick of a serpent's tongue.

'The taipan is a useful ally. Much can be achieved with such a man. If a member of the gang wishes to kill a man, that is their business, but when the man is an important friend, I *expect* to be warned!'

'It was not to hurt our friend. His driver dishonoured him and his family. I thought you would approve my helping remove his problem.'

Du Yusheng studied him. 'Very well. But in future, you will seek permission before you attempt an assassination. And now, for your foolishness, you will give me your payment.'

'Of course,' Thin Bao said, and took the money from his pocket. He walked to the table and placed it near Du Yusheng's hand.

The meeting continued, and Thin Bao did not allow his resentment to show. He remained at the wall, but inwardly he seethed.

Rod escorted her to the door and watched her walk away, studiously ignoring Mickey Hi as he bowed respectfully. She expected such acknowledgements as her birthright, and saw no need to respond.

Mickey Hi shot a look at him, ducking his head again, and Rod grinned. Mickey was rarely upset by citizens.

Rod sat again, but Eric Leigh poked his head around the door. 'So, how are your ears, then? Bleeding?'

'What do you mean?'

'Anyone who's had Miss Hyland chewing them off a strip for more than five seconds has an understandable need of strong spirits and an icepack. What was it about? Stolen pot plants? Her blessed dog? The doormat?'

'A doormat and the dog. Someone has stolen both.'

'Good God! Ah, well. That'll make a tasty roast for someone, I suppose. She's a batty old soul, but I'm sorry the dog's gone. He was a friendly fellow. Anyway, I'll be going to Dan Bailey's later. You want a drink?'

'I'll be working late.'

'The job of a policeman or reporter, eh? Who'd do it? I'll be there from about nine. I'll hope to see you then.'

On the way to the Winton house Rod glanced over the notes from his meeting with Miss Hyland.

While it was a shame her dog was missing, many accidents could befall a dog in the city. He might have been trampled by a horse, hit by an automobile, or crushed under a cart's wheels, let alone caught and eaten. However, Rod understood her need to report the disappearance. The dog was likely her only companion. She would feel his loss as keenly as any parent would feel the loss of a child. Before leaving, Rod had ensured that the officers patrolling near her house would keep an eye open for her dog.

The rickshaw took him up to the Nanking Road, past the new Town Hall, the racecourse and recreation grounds, and on along the Bubbling Well Road. He passed the Horse Bazaar Company on the right, and then the cheaper foreign houses. When they reached the Mayfair and Ewo Terraces, Rod glanced at the great building on the left, the Country Club, where Shanghailanders socialised; the club on the Bund was dedicated more to business. Soon he was passing the quieter, shaded villas of Europeans where Rod felt he could have been in England rather than Shanghai. The rickshaw turned into Gordon Road, and then right again into a quieter lane, coming to a halt outside an impressive set of iron gates.

A tall Sikh with a rifle slung over his shoulder stood guard. He saluted and opened the gates, and the rickshaw pattered up the driveway.

It was nearly five o'clock.

The paved drive led to the front of the house, with a branch to the right which Rod guessed led to garage and stables. As the gate clanged shut, it was the house that took his attention. A reddish-grey, two storey building, and servant rooms in the eaves, it could have been lifted straight from a English estate. When Rod had been demobilised, he had passed villas like this in the train. They had looked magnificent in the English countryside.

Here, this house was a piece of English eccentricity entirely out of keeping with China. However, this was Shanghai. An eclectic taste in building was one of the passions of the true Shanghailander. A property's size was important, but it was not enough merely to spend money: the expense should be conspicuous – excessive. Businessmen in Shanghai wanted extreme, even vulgar, exhibitionism. It was the outward demonstration of 'face'. They were expected to keep the imperial flag flying, even though Shanghai was a free port outside the Empire.

Before the front door there was a short flight of stairs. Three tall windows on either side were balanced symmetrically about the door. The windows of the second storey were two thirds the height of those beneath, giving the house a flattened look, as if a giant had stepped on it and crushed the upper levels. On the left was an incongruous addition: a circular tower with a conical roof like a massive candle extinguisher on top.

This was the property of a titan of Shanghai: a taipan. One of the men who owned Shanghai and all those living in it. A man who held the power of a medieval tyrant.

Squaring his shoulders, Rod knocked.

## Chapter Nine

Thin Bao entered his casino and stood gazing about him.

He was furious. The money was his, and Du Yusheng had no right to take it. Except as head of the Green Gang, he had every right. His was the word of absolute command. No one could gainsay him; all who joined the Gang were sworn to obey. Any failure resulted in immediate punishment. It was the way of the Gang, the Chinese way, but not Thin Bao's way. Thin Bao was no slave.

Moving past the tables on which the tiles had been set out neatly, past the green baize table on which the new packs of cards stood, Thin Bao continued to the bar. This room was his own design: all guests pass the tables on their way in, and again when they left. He wanted to tempt them, to take all their money. And of that money, much would be transferred to Du Yusheng. Du Yusheng took much but gave little. Thin Bao should not accept such treatment from a man who could not even read. He *would* not.

It was time for a change, and Thin Bao was the man to take over. He had the drive to replace Du Yusheng. The Gang needed fresh blood; strong blood - young blood.

He took the bourbon from the barman. The room was ready. Time to open the doors. He could plot Du Yusheng's demise later.

When the door opened, the butler was a surprise.

Most used Chinese butlers, since they were cheaper, but Alfred Winton enjoyed flaunting his wealth. This butler was imposing, a man of some forty years, clad in uniform frock coat and grey trousers that made Rod glad of his light linen suit; the man must have been boiling. A double chin and jowls framed an mournful expression of disapproval. His manner reminded Rod of a particular judge who, when Rod gave evidence against a thief, gave Rod to understand that a rabid dog was more trustworthy than a Shanghai policeman. Now, as then, Rod reminded himself he had commanded men in battle.

Now, as then, it was no help. He felt defeated in the face of such scorn.

Hearing his request to see Alfred Winton, the butler allowed a flicker of annoyance to pass over his face, but stood back and led Rod to the library, a large room on the west side of the building. The walls were full of books, although Rod doubted many had been read. They were like the house and butler: decorations to reinforce a reputation. A globe stood on a large stand in the middle of the room, and five leather club chairs were spread about.

The air was moved by a sluggish overhead fan which achieved little against the oppressive heat. Floor to ceiling French windows looked out over extensive grounds. London Plane trees stood side-by-side with monkey puzzles, beneath one of which a table and chairs were set out. Two women and a man were enjoying tea, a maid nearby, hands folded, face lowered. The man was in his early twenties, while the women could have been sisters. One Rod recognised: Alice Winton. The other must be her mother. It was a scene repeated in gardens all over England and India, and Rod felt a pang, wondering whether Cecily was enjoying tea back in England – but quashed the thought. She was lost to him.

'You keep me from my family,' a voice said quietly, and Rod turned to see Alfred Winton in the doorway. He puffed out a streamer of fragrant cigar smoke.

'I am sorry to interrupt, sir,' Rod said, introducing himself.

The Taipan stood considering Rod without speaking.

His was a face of angles, long and hard. His complexion was an unhealthy jaundice yellow. His protuberant eyes had been leached like paint to a pale gunmetal, and the street map of veins at cheeks and nose told of the colonial's gin consumption. Under his gaze, Rod felt like a beetle in a specimen jar. Taking in his scuffed shoes and crumpled suit, emanated disapproval. Taipans viewed everyone with contempt, whether Chinese, Japanese, or police officers.

'Have you found the car?'

'Yes, sir. The driver …'

'You found him?'

Winton took a long pull of the cigar held under a hooked forefinger, and nodded to himself with satisfaction. 'Good! He didn't ask to take the Kenworthy. Give him a roasting. If he's aware the police think his actions suspicious he'll be a bloody sight more careful next time.'

Recollections of Alice Winton with Foster at the Astor House slipped into Rod's mind, the hand indecently low on her back … from Alfred's tone, perhaps he suspected something.

'He is dead, sir.'

At last Rod had his full attention. Alfred Winton's smile was wiped away like chalk from a board. 'Dead? Foster? But …' He quickly recovered himself and scowled. 'What? How?'

'A gang shooting.'

'Why would someone kill a bloody chauffeur?'

'We were hoping you could tell us, sir. Perhaps he had problems? Gambling? Women?'

'He was my chauffeur: I know little about his private life.'

Winton began to cough, a long, hacking spasm that made him bend and turn away, handkerchief at his mouth. 'My apologies,' he said, embarrassed, as though such weakness was shameful.

'Was he with you for long?'

'He came to us after the War. My son, Ian, volunteered. Foster became his soldier-servant,' Winton said. He dabbed his mouth absentmindedly. When he spoke again, his voice was heavy. 'My son didn't come back. When Foster arrived, we wanted to remember his service to Ian, so we offered him a job.'

'Did you have a chauffeur already?'

'Yes. A good fellow: Dalip Singh, a Sikh. We had to let him go.'

'It must have been difficult,' Rod said, thinking of the Sikh summarily fired because of Foster's arrival.

'Yes,' he said quietly, and glanced at Rod.

Rod recognised that look. It was the same jealousy and hatred he had seen in the faces of widows and mothers back home. Alfred Winton had lost his son, but Rod Cottey had returned. And he detested Rod for that.

Maurice Winton took two cubes of sugar and dropped them into his tea. Strong Assam — he had never liked the fragrant Chinese teas. At school in England the tea had been strong, and that was how he liked it: strong and sweet. He tried to concentrate as his mother spoke, but it was difficult.

God! If only father would trust him! Ian was dead, and he regretted that as much as anyone, but it was a fact. And father had another son. Maurice had been to the same school, had been trained the same way. Father had been ruthless and aggressive; Maurice could be too. He had courage and determination to spare.

Father must recognise his abilities, and pass the business to him. Maurice would make it thrive. If father told him what he intended, Maurice would follow his instructions. He could run the bank as well as anyone. That reminded him: he still needed to speak to the property man about the godown. The paperwork was not finalised. The lawyers were taking their time. Lawyers always did.

His mother's voice broke in on his thoughts. 'Yes, mother?'

'I said, where is your father, Maurice?'

Edith Winton sat elegantly, her back straight as a pikestaff, as though entertaining royalty. She always exhibited the most perfect manners and deportment, although since Ian's death, while her face held her habitual faint smile, there was little joy in it. Hers was a face of wintry pleasure.

'He said he was coming. Send the maid to find him.' Maurice returned to considering the lawyers and his transaction. Someone else could fetch his father.

'I don't think … ah, here's Crowther. Crowther, where is Alfred?'

The butler checked the table before answering. 'A gentleman from the police is speaking with him.'

Maurice froze. There was a clutching at his belly, but didn't let anyone see his sudden anxiety. He picked up his tea cup and sipped.

'Police? No doubt they have found the car,' Edith said.

There was a giggle, and Maurice saw Alice cover her mouth. She had a mouthful of cake, and swallowed. 'It cannot have been so terribly difficult to find the Kenworthy! There aren't many! Even the local police would be capable, I'm sure.'

She grinned at him, and Maurice smiled thinly in return. Alice found amusement in any situation. She didn't have the same problems, the same fears, the same dangers.

Their mother continued, 'Perhaps so. We can only hope. What Foster was thinking of, I cannot imagine.'

'No, mother,' Alice said. She daintily stabbed another piece of cake with her fork. 'Well, Crowther? Is it about the car?'

'No, Miss Alice. I fear Foster has met with an accident.'

Maurice frowned slightly. He turned to peer towards the library. He could see his father standing with the haze of smoke over his head gradually wafted away by the feeble fans. 'Why are they taking so long?'

Another coughing fit threatened, but Alfred forced it down. He refused to display such weakness again in front of a police officer.

'Family?'

The policeman's question distracted him. 'Eh? I think he had a father.'

'It was good of you to take him on.'

Of all the *stupid* statements! Alfred kept the anger from his voice. 'Least we could do. He was with Ian all through. A loyal fellow. When Ian …'

Alfred blinked away tears. At least the officer was civilised enough to stop. He must know Foster was the last link with their boy, a compensation for their loss.

And he had rubbed their faces in it, the bastard.

'Sir, you said he had no permission to take the automobile today. Do you know what he was doing?'

'No, I've no idea.' God, he could do with a brandy.

'What of the others? Your wife, perhaps?'

'My wife was in a meeting. She supports charities: lapsed women, orphans, the poor. They keep her busy.'

He walked to the drinks table, shoving his handkerchief into his pocket, and poured a liberal measure of brandy, adding soda water. 'I never thought Ian would die. I had faith in him. He was intelligent, keen, and had the ruthlessness one needs when dealing with the fellows here. Ian would have made us rivals to Jardine, Matheson and the Hong Kong and Shanghai Bank. But …' *But suddenly Ian was gone. And God knows, I miss him every day!*

'You have another son.'

'Maurice? You haven't met him, have you?' Alfred scoffed. 'He's a feckless wastrel, interested in American girls, gambling, and little else!'

Alfred gulped brandy bleakly. 'And then there is my little princess, Alice. She is building her own road to hell. Obviously, she couldn't run the business. So it's doomed. My legacy will die with me.'

The dullness in his voice matched the emptiness he felt. He had battled to build the Liverpool and Asiatic Bank and associated businesses, but it would come to nothing. 'Without Ian the business is dead.'

'So none of the family were going to use the car today?'

'Eh? As a matter of fact, I had been going to. I meant to visit friends at the club for lunch, but I changed my mind. My liver has not quite recovered from my last bout of malaria, and I was not feeling up to snuff.'

'The man who killed your driver attacked your vehicle deliberately, I believe.'

'What do you mean, "deliberately"?'

'I mean someone shot the car to pieces and gave your chauffeur a *coup de grace* before marking him. They cut Chinese letters into his brow, and stabbed his eyes.'

'Good God!' Alfred shivered, putting a hand on a chair's back to steady himself.

'I wonder whether they intended to kill your driver, or whether they sought someone else. Someone such as you, sir.'

Alfred stared at him like a stag seeing the huntsman.

## Chapter Ten

'*Lane*!'

'Here, sir!'

Gordon Road held no terrors for Archie. He had trained under the most fearsome sergeant-majors in the army, and this man was hardly terrifying: middle thirties, a square, competent-looking fellow with a faint smile fitted to his face, sandy hair and blue eyes.

With Archie were two friends. Peter Craig had been a shepherd before the war, while John Cowan was a broad-shouldered shipyard worker from the Clyde with a gruffly incomprehensible voice when drunk. They were good company, and Archie soon gravitated towards them.

Peter pulled off his hat and ran a hand through his hair. 'Like being in the army again.'

'Up at six isn't bad,' John said.

Archie pulled a face. 'I'm not worried by that, it's the lessons what worry me.'

Their regime was: reveille at six, followed by cross country running and, after breakfast, instruction on their new duties before learning Chinese in the local Shanghai dialect until tiffin. In the afternoon there were more lessons, then training with automatic weapons or drill. Archie had never done well at school. Mathematics and algebra were a source of terror, let alone learning Chinese.

'At least they let us off from six,' John said.

'Aye,' Peter said. 'We can go and look at the sights, eh? I heard there are plenty of places to meet women. Shanghai is known for them. And gambling places. You know this place is called the capital of sin?'

Archie pulled a face. 'I don't think I –'

'Come on, Archie! You want to have some fun, don't you?'

'Yes, but I don't want to be sent home because I've been breaking the law. Besides, the streets aren't safe.'

'Who's going to give us trouble?' Peter laughed. 'We're the police!'

John glanced at Archie. 'Is it true you saw a gunfight today?'

'On the way here, yes. Some Chinese with machine pistols gunned down a car and killed the driver.'

'What did you do?'

'I ducked!'

The other two had been in the army. Both nodded.

'Still,' Peter said, 'that doesn't mean you'll get into trouble tonight. You've had your excitement for today, eh?'

Archie nodded. They had been told that they must be back at barracks by one in the morning, but that would give them time to see something of the city. And it would be good to get a feel for the place. 'So long as we get back on time,' he said.

Alfred forced a laugh. 'Me? Enemies? What do *you* think? I'm head of a bank, I have godowns all over the city. Men are jealous of me! But *kill me*? That is a high bar to leap, even here. Perhaps ...'

'Yes?'

Alfred forced his breathing to slow. This was nothing to do with the boy and his father: they were too long ago. 'There is one man: Helmut Schreier holds a grudge against me.'

'Why?'

'Before the war the Germans had a seat on the Council, but afterwards there was bad feeling and we gave their seat to the Japanese. Germans were treated fairly, I mean, we are a treaty port, not an imperial outpost, but ... well, for example, the Germans had a memorial in front of Jardine, Matheson's, in memory of a gunboat that sank off the Shandong coast in '98 or so. The *Iltis*, I think she was. Over seventy dead. In '18 French sailors tore it down. The year before, the German-Asiatic Bank was forced to close. Schreier found that hard to swallow. He couldn't get credit, his businesses collapsed, his wife left him, and — well, I suppose he has had a hard time.'

'He might blame you?'

'Perhaps,' he shrugged. 'A man doesn't make money by being charitable, and I took what I could. He would have done the same to me, if our positions were reversed. I came out here with ambition and balls, nothing else. You can see what I've achieved.' He waved his cigar to take in the house, his status and authority in one circular motion. 'When I see Schreier, it makes me think: what if the war had gone the other way, and I had lost everything? You know, it's wonderful to make your way in the world. If someone takes that away … There was a time when I thought that losing my money would be the worst that could happen.'

His gaze slid away to the photo of Ian in uniform standing on the table. Another coughing fit took him over, and he pulled his handkerchief out again, covering his mouth.

'Are you all right?'

'Yes, yes.' Winton took shallow breaths, trying not to aggravate it. 'I just have this damned cough, that's all. Can't seem to clear it.'

He stared out through the window, thinking of the meeting with the doctor, the man's apologetic, sympathetic expression as he broke the news that any man would dread. *Cancer.* The word struck fear into the strongest heart: lengthy or swift, it would be a painful ending.

The policeman was talking again, and he pulled himself back to the present.

'Would you mind if I have a look at Foster's room? I need to learn whom I should contact about his death.'

'Crowther will show you.'

Alfred Winton opened the French windows and walked out to the terrace, then down towards the group at the table. He couldn't take any more questions. Not now. He had little enough time left. He wouldn't spend it with an inquisitive policeman.

Rod watched him stalk over the grass. He spoke to the butler and pointed towards Rod.

The family was rising. Maurice stepped forward to greet his father, but Alfred ignored him and walked to his wife instead. He left his son standing forlorn, like a beaten spaniel.

Over the years Rod had met many bereaved families. Families that pulled together in mutual support, families that were shattered like dropped vases, families that tried to work through their grief... Watching Winton with his family, Rod began to wonder whether Maurice had been lost before his brother's death. He might as well have been dead, for all the attention his father paid him. Nothing he achieved could ever compare with that which his older, dead brother would not.

Crowther could not hide his distaste. The Shanghai police were little better than servants to the white community, protecting life and property, after all. This officer was not of a rank to demand entry to a gentleman's house. He should be out arresting vagrants and thieves, not bothering his betters.

In the heat, Crowther's starched collar was uncomfortable, and his face felt puffy. He could feel the prickle of sweat at groin and armpits, and longed for a cool bath. It would be some time before he could indulge in that luxury. At least Miss Alice had not broken down. Perhaps she had seen through Foster's rapacious ambition? Miss Alice was brighter than most — certainly than poor Master Maurice. Crowther sighed, as he so often did when thinking of the youngest son. The poor fellow had always been overshadowed, by his brother's pursuit of power, and by Miss Alice's beauty and intellect. Master Maurice could not compete with either.

He led the way through the hall, down the corridor beside his butler's pantry, out into the rear courtyard. 'That is where Foster lived, over the garage. It is not locked.'

'Didn't he lock it?'

Crowther cocked an eyebrow. 'Why should he? We have guards. No one would break in here.'

'What about his belongings?'

The butler permitted himself a smile. *Really!* This policeman's questioning bordered on the offensive. It was all very well for him to put on his official's voice, like an officer challenging a soldier who had failed to dig latrines, but Crowther had once served luncheon to the Prince of Wales. 'Perhaps he had few items worth worrying about.'

'You didn't like him. Why?'

His tone was so abrupt, he might have been questioning a coolie. 'I should not like you to think that. But he was ... *over-aware* of his status.'

'You mean his position with the family? In what way?'

Crowther allowed his expression to harden. 'It was nothing.'

'He has been murdered, Crowther. I expect you to tell me.'

Crowther stared toward the garage, his thoughts returning to Miss Alice, to that day a year ago, her obvious panic at being seen with Foster, her reddened face as Foster kissed her, turning to Crowther with a smile of challenge, as if daring the butler to reveal their affair. Then later: *You won't tell mother, will you, Crowther? You won't tell her?* The poor child had been so scared - obviously, he nodded and acceded to her demand.

He did not regret Foster's death. The man was a degenerate parasite who had sucked the happiness from the entire family.

What could he say that would not bring embarrassment? Then he realised what Rod had said. 'Murdered?'

'Three men gunned down the Kenworthy, and put two bullets in his head. I need to know everything about him.'

'I have worked for Mr Winton for fourteen years. A man like Foster is only ever an irritant in a close household like this. He is the piece of grit in the oyster.'

'The piece that forms a pearl, you mean?'

Crowther eyed him. 'An imperfect pearl is worthless.'

'You don't think he deserved his job here? Even after his service to Captain Winton?'

'Some might consider he took liberties on the back of his so-called "service".'

'What sort of liberties?'

Miss Alice's face intruded on his thoughts: *You won't tell them, will you?* Crowther took a deep breath. 'That is not a matter I may discuss. It is private.'

'Private to you or the family?'

Crowther ignored him.

'It is an interesting fact, Crowther, that anyone could pay an assassin. A disgruntled casino-owner, a banker – or even a butler who thought he was helping his master. So if you have any information, you will tell me. Do you understand?'

'Yes, sir.' Crowther would not speak out. It was not his place. Butlers should never divulge family secrets.

'Are you close to Maurice and Alice?' The policeman asked shrewdly.

'Of course! Master Ian was a fine young man, too. Brave, almost reckless, and universally adored. He favoured me and my judgement. He came to me for advice on his equipment when he left for the trenches. Maurice and Alice also look to me for help. Their parents are very busy.' He cast a baleful eye at the officer. 'And I advised them to have nothing to do with Foster.'

'Did he have enemies?'

'He was not the sort of man I would have allowed in the house, but –.'

'Why? What had he done to you?'

Crowther shook his head. 'Nothing. He was not cut from the right cloth. Men like him expect too much.'

'Like the affection of a daughter?'

'I don't know what you mean,' Crowther said, and walked back inside.

## Chapter Eleven

The butler looked as quick-thinking as an iceberg, but an iceberg could sink a ship. Still, Rod's last barb had struck home: by his reaction, Crowther knew Alice had been seeing Foster.

The garage was a plain building, each yellow stone cut and dressed as well as any in England. Behind trees lined a path leading, he guessed, to further gardens. On the left were stables. Any foreigner had a clutch of Chinese horses, sturdy beasts appreciated for their speed and determination. At regular hunts, the wealthy and important would ride like madmen over the countryside.

The garage door was half-glassed. Entering, he was confronted by a staircase, while on the right a door led to the garage itself. Inside was space for three vehicles. For now it held only a three-wheeled Morgan.

The workbench held the paraphernalia of a mechanic. He ran his fingers over the workbench. A mechanic's vice was bolted to the wall, while a rack of shelves held spanners, hammers, mallets, feeler gauges and other tools. All neat and tidy. A cupboard held waxes and polishes and held the fresh odour of beeswax and soap. When Rod opened a bottle he smelled the sharpness of vinegar. Chauffeurs used a mix of soap and vinegar to clean and polish paint. Foster knew his business.

Closing the door, Rod took the stairs to a small landing and another door. It was unlocked.

Foster had not been tidy in private life. His bed was made, but the sheets were untidy, as though dragged over the mattress.

The wardrobe door was ajar, and there was an empty clothes hanger dangling from it. Rod assumed it had held the clothing he wore when he died. There were two chairs at a table with folding leaves, but neither was set square, and the writing slope on top was at an angle. Two drawers were not pushed fully home. On the bedside table, papers were piled haphazardly.

On the table stood a framed photo. Rod studied it: it showed Foster, young and eager-looking, in private's khaki, standing at the side of a plant-stand, while, seated in an armchair, was a captain. It was the same man whose portrait Alfred Winton had in his library. This, then, was Ian Winton.

He had the familiar appearance of a man fresh from the Front: the thin lips, the unsmiling face. He radiated weariness and sadness. Rod felt the breath catch in his throat: Ian Winton was another who had sent boys to their death, who had walked with them over the cratered mud and seen them picked off, one after another. Like Rod he had returned to his dugout of an evening, and composed letters to widows and parents deprived of their sons. Rod recognised his look of guilty shame. It was like his own.

Foster looked younger. His eyes were bright, like those of so many boys who arrived in the trenches – before the first salvo dulled their enthusiasm.

Rod felt his hand begin to shake. It didn't happen often, but every so often something would trigger it. Sometimes a picture like this, occasionally a military trumpet or bagpipes. He had once been in the Gardens by the Souchow Creek when a military band began to play, and for absolutely no reason the tears began to flow. When that happened, it was infuriating – *humiliating*. One did not wish to be considered a weakling.

That day a child stared at him. She was too young to understand or feel embarrassed, but when her mother noticed, she shook the child's shoulder, giving Rod a glare – or a look of pity? He couldn't tell. That was the burden: of victory, of living, of surviving when so many had died.

Rod carefully replaced the picture and thrust his hand into his pocket, taking a couple of deep breaths. The craving for whisky was there, the need for oblivion. His personal demons were beckoning, and he wanted to greet them. It took an effort, but he clenched his fist in his pocket, willing his hand to stop shaking.

Gradually the desperate need to weep left him.

The table's leaves were folded. There was a drawer, and inside were needles and thread, a tin of tobacco, a churchwarden pipe and matches. The writing slope was not locked, and inside was a sheaf of good quality paper, black ink, a tin of nibs and two nib-holders. There were the usual papers: bills from cabarets and clubs, a card for a tailor in the French Concession, assorted receipts, but nothing from a member of his family. In fact, Rod could find no private correspondence. He took the papers from the bedside table and went through them. There were no letters there either, only receipts and chits for debts to various establishments. It was curious, but he knew many soldiers had deliberately hidden from family and friends after the War. They tried to insulate themselves from the past, as if by so doing they might obliterate the memories.

His hand had stopped shaking. He could breathe easily again.

At the wardrobe, he hunted through coats and jackets to no avail, then the drawers and cupboards. After an hour's searching, Rod accepted defeat. There was no correspondence. He prepared to leave, but something held him back – something missing. It niggled.

Foster had been a soldier. Yet, apart from the photograph, nothing in the room spoke of his service.

Some, as soon as they left the Army, wanted to eradicate all memory of the war. He was one such himself. Others revelled in their wartime history and kept scrapbooks and memorabilia of their time, but even those who wanted to forget the horrors would keep a memento: a cap badge, a bayonet, a spent bullet, a medal or two. It was rare for a man to discard every aspect of his service, because even those who loathed the War would not willingly forget the men alongside whom they fought. Comrades at arms were always with a man. The dead more than the living.

He was missing something.

Rod stared around. There was no obvious place of concealment, but his eye was caught by the wardrobe. A decorative wooden surround ran along the top. Externally the wardrobe was considerably taller than the interior suggested. The gap between the two was some eighteen inches.

He reached inside and felt the boards. All appeared fixed in place, but when he knocked, there was a dullness to the panels of the inner ceiling, There must be a weighty object above. He pulled one of the chairs over and climbed up to study the top. Boards above meant a concealed space above the clothes.

Climbing down, he put his hands on either side of the wardrobe and rocked and slid it away from the wall. The back of the wardrobe had a panel that was separate from the main backing boards of the wardrobe. When he pushed, it rose, sliding on rails at either side. A moment later his hand found the slim metal handle of a black deeds box. Two feet long, a foot deep and the same high, the tin box was weighty.

It was locked, and he wondered where the key may be. Reasoning it must contain valuables or secret documents, it seemed logical that Foster would have kept the key on him. Rather than force it, Rod decided to take the box to the station and test the keys in Foster's pockets, or ask an armourer to pick the lock.

Just then a voice snapped, 'Who the hell are you, and what are you doing here?'

Maurice Winton was standing in the doorway like an avenging angel.

'Well? What do you think you are doing?' Maurice demanded. The cheek of this blighter! He stood clenching his fists while the stranger set the tin box on the table, ignoring him.

'I said, who are you? What are you doing? I've a good mind to –'

'I am Detective Constable Rodney Cottey of the SMP.'

Maurice felt a little of his anger dissipate. 'You have no right to be in here.'

'Mr Winton gave his permission.'

Maurice stared at the box. 'What's that?'

'I believe it contains documents of Foster's.'

'You can't take that!'

'Your chauffeur was murdered. I am the detective assigned, so, yes, I can take it.'

'Foster is dead?' Maurice said, and then his words struck home. 'I ... *Murdered*?'

'Yes. Shot.'

'Still, that may hold private documents,' Maurice said. He licked his lips. 'Secret documents. You can't just take whatever you want from here!'

'I have to track down his family,' Rod said. 'I can see you are upset, and I am sorry, but this may hold documents that can point me to his next of kin. I'll return it to them if possible.'

'Then let's open it now and see what's inside. There could be private papers … for my family, not his.'

'There is no key.'

'Break the lock.'

'No. I can open it perfectly easily back at the police station. There is no need to damage it.'

'Look, we could pay you to –' Maurice was silenced by the look in the policeman's eyes. It sent a chill into his spine.

'I don't accept bribes.'

'That must make you unique in the Shanghai Police,' he said, only half joking.

Rod eyed him coldly, and Maurice felt the prickle of warning. He was the younger of the two, and he was quick, but there was something threatening about this cold-faced officer.

Rod said, 'I will pretend I didn't hear that, Mr Winton.'

Maurice felt his anger flare, but it burned out leaving only a resentful sourness. 'It's not right, you being here.'

'Do you know if he has living relatives?'

'How the hell should I know? He was only the chauffeur!'

'Clearly he was below you,' Rod said, his eyes hardening again. 'What can you tell me about him?'

'Oh, ask father. Or mother,' Maurice said dismissively. His questions were ridiculous. As if Maurice could give a damn. 'They know everything they needed to know about him. What would I know? I'm only their son!'

'What did you think about him?'

'Foster?' Maurice could not help himself. The pent up frustration made him lean forward and blurt, 'He was a *shit*! He came to take advantage of us, that's all! He wheedled his way into mother's affection till he knew he had a safe berth, and he made the most of it. He wrote to my parents within minutes of Ian's death, and then, up he popped! A nasty little worm sliding into the family.'

'What did he do?'

'Oh!' After so long bottling up his feelings, it was a relief to let it out, even with this stranger - or perhaps it was *because* Cottey was a stranger? 'People thought he was a loyal servant to Ian, but for God's sake! Since arriving, he inveigled his way into the family's affections. He was after more.'

'You disliked him.'

'He was a *shit*! He took advantage; tried to pull the wool over our eyes. But I saw through him.'

'It almost sounds as though you think he was the actual target of this shooting,' Rod said.

'What?' Maurice frowned. 'But you said he was murdered?'

'He was driving the Kenworthy when he was killed. Perhaps the murderer wanted to capture a passenger - but in a phaeton, how likely is that? Anybody could see it was empty.'

Maurice said, 'Who else has a Kenworthy? I'll bet someone wanted to catch my father.'

'Where would Foster have been driving?'

'How should I know? Perhaps he had someone he wanted to see.'

'A woman, you mean?'

'It has been known,' Maurice said sarcastically. 'It's surely more likely someone wanted father, to ransom him. They'd expect us to pay through the nose to free him.'

'How much would you have been prepared to pay for the release of your father? It might be convenient, for an ambitious fellow, to have his father removed.'

Maurice felt his blood run cold. 'You think I'd actually plan to have my father killed? What sort of man thinks that? You must mix with a particularly unsavoury lot!'

'No doubt I have a jaundiced soul. Your father mentioned a German who might bear a grudge.'

'Schreier? The poor devil suffered at my father's hands, it's true.'

'Is he bitter enough to hire a murderer?'

Maurice curled his lip. 'Schreier? My father destroyed him. The war damaged both: father lost his son; but Schreier lost everything. He wouldn't pay someone to murder my father.'

'He hasn't the courage for it?'

Maurice gave a short, humourless laugh. 'Schreier would pull the trigger himself.'

## Chapter Twelve

Rod left the garage with the tin box and a pocketful of documents, hoping to make sense of them back at the station. Rather than carry the box to the gates, he asked Crowther to summon a rickshaw. Then, setting the box down, he took out a cigarette. He was patting his pockets in a vain search for a match, when there was a giggle behind him.

Alice Winton had deliberately approached quietly to surprise him, and stood with her hands behind her. She was wearing a thin, sleeveless cotton dress printed with pale pink roses, and studied Rod mischievously, before holding out a slim gold lighter. Rod took it gratefully, and offered her a cigarette, lighting hers before his own.

'What's your name?' she said, tilting her head. She had a manner of facing a man very directly, which was both assertive and appealing. Rod smiled: she was attractive, but too confident: she was certain that she could seduce any man she wanted, and Rod found that off-putting.

'I'm Detective Constable Cottey from the SMP.'

She studied him. 'You don't look like a policeman.'

'How should a policeman look?'

'More seedy, I suppose, and downtrodden. Although you look perfectly careworn.'

His face shuttered, and she felt a spark of guilt. 'I am sorry. I should watch my words, I know. I didn't mean to upset you. I speak before I think.'

'I am fine.'

'Are you here about the car? Wasn't it horrid, Foster being killed like that? ' She cast him a sidelong glance. 'You picked me up once, when I fell, didn't you? Outside the Astor. I'm sure it was you.' She sucked her cigarette with lips pouting, like a child sucking a drink through a straw, her left arm wrapped about her, her right elbow resting on her left's wrist, the hand holding the cigarette cocked at the side of her head. Her green eyes considered him coolly, like a cat's.

'Yes. And I saw you dancing with him, too. I'm sorry for your loss.'

She nodded as though he had confirmed something she had suspected a long time. 'He was a wonderful dancer.' It was true. When he first arrived, she thought he was her escape from here, from the pain and treachery.

That was before his blackmail.

'Your brother thinks someone was trying to kill your father.'

She shrugged again. 'Someone must have thought he was in the car. People hate those who are cleverer, who take all the prizes in business. And father's aggressive. You have to be, in his position. He has trampled people to get to where he is. But people take offence when they are stood on.'

'Is he a hard man to love?'

'He's my father. It's easy to love your father.' She dropped the cigarette butt and extinguished it with a dainty shoe.

'You sound bitter.'

She raised an eyebrow. 'Do I? I was lucky to be born a Winton. My family has been graced with more luck than most.'

'Until your brother died.'

'That was a cruel thing to say.'

'I'm sorry.'

'Ian was a good man. He died for his country. He was brave.'

'Meaning?'

'Others were not so courageous.'

'I was in the trenches.'

'I didn't say you weren't.' She looked around as if expecting to see the automobile passing up the driveway again. 'Poor Foster.'

'You don't seem terribly distraught.'

She was surprised by that. 'Should I be?'

'You weren't planning a romantic elopement?'

'My, what a conventional mind you have! You think I would run away with him to a life of poverty and misery?' she smiled.

'Father would have cut me off without a penny. It would have been far too embarrassing. No, Foster and I were not together. Haven't been for a while.'

He found her manner confusing. 'Foster was close to your brother – wouldn't that have counted in his favour?'

'Mother thought that made him a deserving cause. She has many deserving causes, you know. From orphaned waifs and strays, to hospitals for the poor Chinese. It's her substitute for real achievement,' she said. *It was just a shame she didn't care more for her own children.*

'That sounds harsh.'

'Hmm? Oh, she cares - for the family name. She hopes father will be knighted or buy a peerage. But that doesn't mean she would willingly see her daughter married to a mechanic.'

'She must have been happy to learn you were dancing with the family's chauffeur.'

'She never knew. We kept it secret.'

Rod reflected that dancing in a public hotel was hardly secretive.

'So you think Foster died because someone sought to kill your father?'

'It makes more sense than someone choosing to murder a chauffeur, doesn't it?'

'Did Foster gamble? Drink? Have other vices?'

'My, what a dirty mind you have,' she said. 'Are you measuring him against your own standards? Commenting on his vices seems unkind.'

'It's probably his vices that will lead me to his murderer.'

'A jealous husband? A prostitute owed money? A gambling debt? How very prosaic and vulgar.'

'Murder usually is.'

When he reached the station, Rod found a note calling him to see Douglas Hibbard. Leaving the tin box behind his desk, he placed the spare papers in a drawer, then went to the Sub-Inspector's office.

'Well?' Hibbard said. He looked as if he had been dozing, tie awry, face flushed.

'The family took it well enough. They aren't happy to lose the car, but they can afford another one.'

Hibbard peered at him benevolently. 'Money is the lifeblood of this city, old fellow.' He pulled his old briar towards him and opened a wrap of tobacco, filling the bowl, talking as he tamped. 'The thing is, people like the Wintons expect a certain level of service. They're grateful, I've no doubt, that the Shanghai Municipal Police force were swift to send a representative to advise them of the demise of their chauffeur, but whether they can afford another vehicle or not is hardly our concern.'

'They want to be informed as to our progress.'

Putting the pipe to his mouth, Hibbard set a match to the bowl. The room was filled with the thick fumes of Cavendish tobacco, and Rod got the impression he was reluctant to come to the point. 'Yes. We've had a message. In future no one below Inspector rank should be sent. You made quite an impact,' he added, leaning back, his seat complaining, pipe fixed between his teeth. 'There was some comment, apparently, about being interrogated by a "pipsqueak".'

Rod coloured and felt the slow burn of anger in his belly. 'I did nothing that …'

'I'm sure you didn't. Luckily, the Commissioner doesn't believe it either. He rather likes you. Anyway, the message came down from on high, etched into tablets of stone, that you are to leave the matter alone.'

'Did they say how I had offended them?'

Hibbard pressed his thumb against the burning tobacco, tamping it more firmly. 'Would the Commissioner divulge that sort of detail?' He gazed at Rod seriously. 'Don't worry, Rod. You're working hard, and it's noticed. The Chief is on your side. The thing is, when a man like Winton makes waves, it's best to get out of the pool, if you take my meaning.'

'Yes, sir.'

'So, clear up any loose ends and get back to serious matters. What is there to go on?'

Rod bit back the sharp response. He hadn't wanted this case, but to be pulled from so soon made him bitter. 'There is a lot of ill-feeling for Foster, especially from Maurice. From what I gather, Foster was making free with Winton's daughter.'

Hibbard wafted smoke away with a hand. 'You think Maurice could have been responsible?'

Rod considered. 'Possibly. Maurice is weak, but a weak man with money can pay someone else to do his bidding. The other possibility is that someone was trying to kill Alfred Winton, not Foster.'

'And?'

'Winton himself said that there is an embarrassing number of people who would be happy to see him pay for past actions. But …'

'Yes?'

'Why would someone carve "traitor" on Foster's head if he was not the intended victim?'

'Using a chap as a notepad is a little outré,' Hibbard agreed. 'Did Winton mention anyone in particular?'

'Helmut Schreier.'

'Ah, the fellow who ran the German Asiatic Bank?'

'Yes. Apparently he blames his troubles largely on Winton.'

'Very well. Go question the Boche. It can't do any harm.'

'But Winton said —'

'He said he didn't want you visiting his house again. You don't have to in order to speak to Schreier.'

'I'm still working on the Billy Qian case.'

'It'll wait.'

'But Billy is involved in …'

'Something, probably, but we have no evidence. What we do have is an important member of the city who requires his chauffeur's murder resolved. I think that deserves our attention, don't you?'

It was nearly ten o'clock when Rod reached Bailey's Bar. An insipid quartet was playing, and two women were dancing in a lacklustre fashion, watched by a trio of young men with the hollow eyes of the already drunk. Rod ignored them. All he wanted was a drink.

The bar was owned by the flamboyant Dan Bailey, who tonight sported a bright red silk waistcoat with a bow tie of the same material. He was invariably dressed like a dandy from New Orleans. Slim, tall and elegant, his unfashionably long hair half-covered his ears. His cheekbones were enough to make a Hollywood starlet spit in jealousy, and his piercing blue eyes missed little.

'Good evening, darling,' he said in his slow drawl. It was his customary welcome. Tonight, he was smoking a thick Cuban cigar. Rod knew he ordered Churracas from Kelly and Walsh every month. Rod snuffed the fragrant smoke jealously. They were out of his league. Even for Dan Bailey they were expensive, but for him the display was what mattered. Like all Shanghailanders, he had a position to maintain, and his status was enhanced by extravagance.

This cabaret was a masculine bar, with a bevy of pretty women, Asian and American, sitting, waiting. They would entertain a man while Dan refilled glasses, charging an appalling amount per drink. The girls demanded the best champagne to talk or dance, but for all the extortionate sum Dan demanded, the girls would be served soda. Dan didn't want them getting drunk while they were working. And if a deal was struck, and the girls agreed to a more personal service, Dan would take a percentage of their takings. It was a shabby business, and a shabby bar, but Rod liked it because it didn't pretend to be anything it wasn't. It was a rip-off bar for those who had long since given up on everything except drink.

There was another reason why Rod liked it: the girls were safe from Dan. He preferred the company of men to that of women. It was ten years before that he had arrived here from San Francisco, almost penniless, but with a mind as sharp as a rat's. He had landed, taken a look about the city, and decided that this was where he would make his fortune. So far, his intuition appeared to have been accurate. It took six months to set up his bar, and from the moment he first threw open his doors, he had built a steady trade.

Rod took a stool. The bar was already busy with men who wanted to lose themselves in an alcoholic stupor and forget their wives, jobs, and miserable existence. They were weak, dissatisfied men, sad men, men who lived jealously, and who abased themselves before the altar of alcoholic oblivion in the hope of inner contentment - and all they achieved was a pain in the head.

Dan Bailey didn't mind. It was their choice, he would say, and his duty to supply. In Bailey's there was no false pretension. Clients paid for booze, a sympathetic ear and, perhaps, a companion.

As soon as Rod was seated, Dan served him a chilled Old Fashioned.

'You mix them just the way I like,' Rod said.

'In a glass within reach, darling.'

'How's it, Dan?'

The barman paused in his polishing of a glass. 'Life, sir, is generally not bad, in my considered opinion.'

Spying Eric Leigh chatting to two taxi dancers, Rod wandered over to him. 'Leave them, Eric. You're too young for them.'

One made a gesture that left little to the imagination as Eric joined Rod. 'Where have you been?'

'Have a guess.'

'There's only the one affair that matters just now,' he said. 'The attempted murder of one of our most prominent businessmen. Don't tell me you have that?'

'For my sins,' Rod nodded, sipping his drink. He rubbed the cold glass over his forehead. 'Not for long, luckily. How did you hear?'

'I was at the pistol club after work, and heard about it there. The Wintons' butler, Crowther, told me. He's a good shot.'

'Is he, indeed? What does he shoot?'

'Service Webley. And an automatic occasionally, I think. Why?'

'The car was shot up by machine pistols.'

'You can't believe Crowther would have anything to do with an attempt to kill his master, Rod!' Eric laughed.

'It wasn't his master who was killed,' Rod said.

Eric gave a fleeting frown. 'They meant to kill the driver?'

'Possibly, yes.'

'Crowther would have nothing to do with a grubby little murder.'

'Even if Foster threatened the family name?'

'Even then. Crowther would horsewhip the fellow, but he wouldn't resort to something that gruesome. Too frightful for words, he would think!'

'You think so? In any case, the killers were Chinese, not foreign.'

'Says who?'

Rod gave him a dark look. He didn't want to be splashed on the morning's front page. 'An Englishman.'

'Ah, how fortunate! Still, it's lucky Winton wasn't in the car. The city would have had kittens if he'd been killed.'

'I suppose so.'

'Not that I'd mourn the bastard. He tried to get me fired in my second month at the News. He said I'd made up a story about him and a business he had bought. If he'd chewed on a bullet, you might be investigating me!'

'Why? What was the matter with your story?'

'It was true!'

'What do you know about Schreier?'

'He used to be one of Winton's only competitors, but he lost everything. Winton orchestrated his demise. He's a vicious bastard, too. After revenge, do you think?'

'Perhaps.'

'I wouldn't blame him. After Winton tried to do for me, I swore I'd return the favour, but he's too powerful. No one wants to risk upsetting him.'

'So you've dropped it?'

'I didn't say that. I'm taking my time. I'd love to bring him down!'

It was gone eleven when Rod made his way homewards, but outside his apartment, he stopped. The door offered security of a sort, but tonight he needed something else. He pulled out his key, but didn't insert it. Instead he stood, torn between two paths. He put the key back in his pocket.

His mind was whirling: Foster's death, Alfred Winton, his son and daughter, the butler, the German, Eric's own comment about bringing the taipan down. Rod knew he would not sleep tonight: when he closed his eyes, he would see Foster's face again, the bloated, distorted features, the obscene marks on his forehead, the stabbed eyes. Foster would join the others, his comrades from the War, all enticing him to join them, as he should. His survival was unnatural - a betrayal. He should be with them.

They were right.

He could feel the sweat like a slow tide at every pore. His skin felt tight as a balloon filled with water.

It was wrong that he should live when they died. Sometimes he saw their faces in the streets, or imagined he did. In daylight they appeared like ordinary people; sleeping he'd see them as corpses, decayed and rotten. And then, his stomach would roil and he would wake needing to vomit.

Rod loathed his weakness. But when he was affected, like now, there was no peace for him: no sleep, no ease, no possibility of rest. When he closed his eyes, they would return.

He walked to the Tientsin Road, then up a tiny street that was little more than an alley. Here homeless refugees lay amid the refuse and excrement, congregating for the comfort of companionship, although he doubted many found it.

The door was closed, but at his tentative knock a panel behind a grille was drawn. A knowing eye peered at him. Soon he was following the doorman up a flight of stairs that was little more than a broad ladder, and into a wide room.

All about him was the heady, soothing odour of opium. Sweet-smelling swathes of smoke hung like morning mist over a river in autumn, and Rod was led along a corridor of drapery to a room beyond. He had already begun to tug at his tie, pulling off his jacket, as the man pulled aside a curtain. Behind it was a small chamber with a bed. Rod lay down, watching as the Chinese took a pea-sized lump of the treacly substance and rolled it on a skewer over a small lamp's flame. When he felt it was ready, he placed the opium in a bamboo pipe and held it out, holding the lamp up. Rod inhaled. He could feel the effect almost immediately – the room took on a rosy hue, his servant seemed to beam with pleasure. There was a second Chinese, a big man, but he seemed to waver, insubstantial as a will-o-the-wisp. In Rod's dreamy state, he appeared a cheerful, welcoming fellow.

And then the curtain fell and Rod drifted away to a dreamless sleep and rest at last.

# Chapter Thirteen

*Wednesday 26th July, 1922*

Next morning Rod was up before dawn. He made his way to his apartment, where he washed and changed, and at six thirty he was at Central Police Station. There, he sought out James Munson, a bluff Northumbrian. He had been a builder's mate before the War, but now commanded the Sikhs and his men adored him.

'How are you, Jim?' Rod said. Jim was no stickler for military niceties, and despised ex-public schoolboys who insisted on calling each other by their surnames.

'Run ragged as usual.' He was leaning on his fists, head bent, scowling at a roster sheet spread over his desk. 'God save me from administration!'

Rod grinned. 'The joys of your elevated position.'

'Piss off!' Jim Munson had a square face with a vivid scar on his right temple, a reminder of a piece of white-hot shrapnel. He had serious eyes, a broken nose, and a broad forehead. 'Well? What are ye after?'

Jim was always direct - one more reason why he was popular with foreign and local officers alike.

'I'm investigating the Winton chauffeur murder. The gunmen might have been trying to kill Alfred Winton. I want to find anyone with a motive. One possible is a Sikh.'

'I see.'

'He was the Wintons' chauffeur during the War. Foster's arrival meant the Wintons sacked him. He could want revenge. Can you ask your fellows if they know him? His name is Dalip Singh.'

Jim pulled a face. 'Really?'

'What?'

'You do realise "Singh" means "lion", and all Sikhs tend to use it as a matter of course? Singh can be a middle name, a surname, or even a title? Guru Nanak wanted to break down the caste system. Before that a man's caste, his class, could be easily spotted. By disposing of surnames and calling everyone the same, the caste system broke down. It's a key teaching of the Sikhs.'

Rod winced. 'I see.'

'I have a lot of time for the Guru. It's a bloody good idea to get rid of the class system. But don't tell the Commissioner – I doubt he'd approve. Leave it with me. I'll see what I can do.'

'Thanks, Jim.'

'My pleasure. Now, piss off!'

Rod left him staring with baffled consternation at his rotas.

Germans had been involved in the city since the earliest days, but now, three years after the Armistice, all German ventures had disappeared. Winton had mentioned the memorial to the *Iltis*, but that was only one example. The Deutsche Asiatische Bank, German tobacco importers, purveyors of Bockwurst and Frankfurters, salamis and bretzeln had vanished. Even German Shepherds and Dobermans had been eradicated. Those seeking reliable guard dogs resorted to English mastiffs or powerful Chinese or Japanese breeds.

Rod walked up the Bund and two more streets before a Chinese barman directed him to the Foochow Road.

It was sweltering inside. A woman was singing supported by a band of three. Round tables were haphazardly sprinkled, leaving a space before the singer where dancers circled. Red baize and drapes concealed the walls, and gilt paint had been thrown with abandon on railings and decorative plasterwork. A bar ran along the farther wall where 'taxi' girls sat looking hopeful. None looked enthusiastic to see Rod, but perhaps they could tell he was a policeman.

Seated at a table, Helmut Schreier was slowly mopping his brow with a silk handkerchief. The overhead fans achieved little, and Rod felt the perspiration break out as he sat opposite Schreier.

The German was bedraggled. His hair was badly-trimmed and yellowed from nicotine, as was his hand. Schreier was a chain-smoker, lighting a fresh cigarette from each stub. His left eye was partly closed, the eyelid drooping, but the other was dark brown and startlingly wide, giving the appearance he was wearing a monocle. His nose was bulbous as a fat plum, and the same colour. His clothing was good quality: but the three-piece linen suit was worn and discoloured. His Panama hat had yellow sweat stains, and he leaned on a Malacca cane. He had that air of geniality that is often conferred on fat men, but in his eyes Rod saw a predator: attentive, powerful, and dangerous.

'What you want?' Schreier asked. His accent was not pronounced. It was only when he grew excited that he became more definitely Germanic, but his accent was enough to make Rod's hackles rise. It reminded him of the trenches and listening to storm troopers shouting …

Rod fitted a professional mask to his face: no smile, only a bland expressionlessness that never failed to make suspects uncomfortable.

'A few moments of your time, sir. You are Helmut Schreier?'

Helmut Schreier sat back and studied him. 'Oh, so you are a policeman?

'Yes, sir. May I ask where you were last afternoon?'

Schreier set his head to one side. 'Why wish you to know?'

'There was a shooting.'

'Who?'

By now all Shanghai was talking about Foster's death, but Schreier's diminished circle of friends may not have discussed it. 'Alfred Winton's car was shot at.'

'Was he inside?' Schreier leaned forward, his good eye intent.

Rod watched him closely. If Schreier had been responsible for the shooting, he would surely have had a report - he must know that the driver was dead, but there was nothing in his expression. 'No, he was not in the car at the time.'

'Oh.' Schreier took a long drink. It looked like a navy rum. 'How fortunate for him.'

'Not for his driver. He was killed.'

Schreier shrugged. 'Unfortunate. What has this to do with me?'

'I am speaking to all who could have had a reason to want Winton injured.'

He looked at Rod with a kind of resignation. 'I am suspect?'

'You have reason to dislike him.'

'Oh yes, very good reason,' he said. He gulped more rum. 'You saw him at his mansion, yes? He was there with all his prized possessions?' A waitress was passing, and he ordered another drink, pointedly ignoring Rod. When she left to fetch it, he continued, 'You know how this man, this *taipan*,' his voice oozed poison, 'how he came by his wealth? He stole it.'

'That is a serious allegation.'

'It is the truth. You look at me and what do you see, eh? An old man who drinks away his days. You think me a drunkard. Pathetic. But once I was leader of the German community here. I created my company alone. I traded with the big hongs, and they were keen to trade with me: silks, ivory, gold, silver. Companies like Krupps invested in me, and I invested in them. Winton craved my business. But I didn't realise. I thought he was an associate. A friend.'

'What happened?'

He pulled out a battered leather case and selected a cheroot. '*Krieg*! War happened,' he said dully. 'We in the business community agreed the war was not our concern. Whatever the faults of our homelands, Shanghailanders could live together, making money. But when the war was one year old, I was thrown from the Municipal Council, and then was our seat taken by a Japanese. And my business faltered. My good friend, Alfred Winton, he offered to support me.' He bared yellow teeth in a sarcastic smile. 'In two years, he took everything.'

'You blame him?'

Schreier leaned forward, his good eye glaring, 'If a man attacks you and robs you, beats you and leaves you for dead, *who else* would you blame?'

He was lucky. Thin Bao knew that. Others would not have survived. But he was lucky.

It was all so vivid still.

His father was killed. In those days so many died on the streets, their bodies left for the dogs or pigs that wandered the alleys, that a fresh murder hardly raised a mention. A body would not last long before the scavengers came to feed.

He would always remember the day when his father was dragged from the river. The gross, red-faced sergeant, the anxious Chinese officer, and the officer's arm about him, holding him as he wailed and screamed. The body was set upon a wheelbarrow, and Thin Bao trudged beside it, a cold hand falling from beneath the blanket which was his makeshift shroud, and Thin Bao gripping it with the desperation of despair.

After that, the strange building where they took his father, not letting him inside, the tall, terrifying woman who appeared, stern and unbending, his arrival at the orphanage, the noise of so many children, the barrack-like bedchamber with wooden frames and thin, hard mattresses, and being shouted at when he tried to go home. Oh yes, he remembered it all.

And the lessons, the cane, the strap, the letters on a page so incomprehensible. He had been taught a little, for his father had been important, a man with wealth. He owned two ships, and a large godown in the Eastern District. But with his death, Thin Bao became an orphan, and not until he was saved from the orphanage did he rediscover a sense of security.

He emptied his glass, stood and studied himself in the mirror, buttoning his jacket. The holster was hidden beneath his arm. Yes, he had come a long way from that orphanage. His father would be proud of him.

It was time to work. Du Yusheng had taken the money from Foster's assassination. One day, Du Yusheng would regret that. Because one day Thin Bao would replace Du Yusheng in the Green Gang.

Helmut Schreier spoke with fierce intensity. Why should *he* feel shame, when *he* was the victim, Winton the thief? Schreier saw no need to hide his loathing.

The detective was sour-faced, as though he blamed him, Helmut, for his failure. He had no idea, this cloth-faced, weary officer. What did he know of suffering?

'So, Detective, you think: this jealous German, he must have planned to kill Winton, yes? But you don't think: how many others has Winton hurt in his years of business, hey?'

'How did he take your business?'

Schreier sipped rum. He could recall every stage, every treacherous swindle and deception. How could he have been so stupid as to trust Winton?

'He lent me money but the interest grew higher and higher. I tried to get another loan, but the Deutsche-Asiatische Bank could do nothing. The war was biting, and they had no access to funds. The Chinese demanded repatriation of all Germans, and the Bank lost staff. Gradually, I was held to ransom. I must reduce my loans or lose my company. I bought him off with stocks and shares. The war could not last forever, and the Kaiser must win. That seemed certain, when we heard of the Russians and their revolution - but I did not understand Winton. I thought him the pleasant fellow whom I had met over many business lunches, during meetings at the Council, at the Shanghai Club and the race course.'

Winton had fooled him into thinking they were friends. Helmut had trusted the man and that trust cost him everything.

'What did he do?'

'He took my stocks and shares, and cancelled the debt. But all the while he spoke to my investors and business partners. My suppliers dried up. The people with whom I had built my business deserted me. He told them that I must go bankrupt. He told them I had given him my investments, and then, when I had lost almost everything, he came to me and offered a pittance for my company. I said, "Alfred, but you are my friend," and he looked at me like I was a damned dogshit on the pavement. I had no choice. He offered less than ten per cent of its worth, and I said to him, "This is not a fair price," and he said, "You need the money." Nothing else. No compassion, no sympathy; the answer of a tyrant, of a thief. In the past, men such as he would be broken on the wheel.'

'Except he is no felon.'

'You think I am his only victim?' Schreier chuckled coldly. 'Shanghai has few enough laws, but if you dig just a little, you will find he has committed many crimes.'

'He is a businessman. There are few laws controlling business.'

'Even Shanghai has rules against smuggling and controls certain activities,' Helmut said. 'Perhaps you should watch for such activities.' He sat back, took a swig of rum and allowed the fiery liquid to burn down his throat. *There*, he thought, *have I baited the trap securely enough for you?*

'And if your roles were reversed, would you have done anything differently from him?'

Helmut smacked his hand on the table. 'I would not have treated a *dog* as he treated me! Ask others! You will find many who loathe him.'

Rod stood. 'You could return to Germany: why don't you? You could retire, rather than staying here.'

'What you mean is, I am not welcome. Yes, you are right. Although this city is a free port, not the British Empire, yet a German can never be welcome, not since the Armistice.'

Helmut raised his hand to the waitress, and when she didn't notice him, he bellowed at her for more rum. The anger was there all the time now. No matter what he drank, what he did, the impotent rage stayed with him. It was a part of him, this hatred.

'Leave here? With the ten percent he paid me? How much of this could I take? The banks are English. How much would I receive after exchange rates, interest charges and banking fees? And then what? I left Germany thirty years ago. I have no family. All those I cared for are gone. Do you have any idea what Germany is like now? Those who survive are struggling, and there are murders while the Bolsheviks foment trouble. What would I do there? And meanwhile my businesses remain here.'

'They aren't yours any longer.'

He could not help himself. His open hand slammed onto the table again. *'One day they will return to me*!' he shouted, and then slumped back in his chair as if the outburst had exhausted him. The glass had jumped over, and he stared at the spilled drink with despair. 'At least while I am here, I have the hope. With a little luck, perhaps I may rekindle my fortunes. A little *joss*, that is all I need, so I can take it back, all of it.'

'You never said where you were yesterday at noon,' Rod reminded him.

'Where was I? Here. I was here since ten o'clock,' he said. 'Ask the manager. I am here every day from ten. Where else should I go?'

Helmut took the fresh glass from the waitress. When Rod left, he did not look up. All he had said was true. He still hoped for a little good luck. But he knew Winton had too tight a grip on power at the Municipal Council, and too much influence in the banks and trading companies, for him to succeed. Not that Winton needed to work at excluding Helmut. The fact of his birth as a German guaranteed that.

Hatred kept him warm. That and the revenge he had planned. A means of destroying Alfred Winton as effectively as he could contrive. It been months in the planning, and would come to fruition shortly.

He pulled a notebook from his pocket. Scribbling a note, he beckoned the barman. 'See this is delivered to Maurice Winton at The Wheel.'

## Chapter Fourteen

Rod confirmed Schreier's alibi with the manager before leaving. After all, although witnesses said the killers were Chinese, Schreier's hatred of Alfred meant he would surely want to witness Winton's death. It was worth checking.

If Jim Munson tracked the Sikh chauffeur there might be a fresh line, but it seemed unlikely. As Winton had said, why would a man wait three years to take revenge? And he would blame Winton himself, not the new driver. Unless Jim found Dalip Singh, the investigation could stall.

It was time for someone else to take the case. Rod wanted to get back to Billy Qian.

Sitting at his desk, he noticed Foster's tin box. It would have to be opened; now was as good a time as any.

Carrying it downstairs, he knocked on the door of Wattie Brookes.

Wattie was a small, thin, mean-faced man from a long line of Durham miners, who had decided after the war never to return to digging coal. Mining at the Front, with the constant fear of counter-mining, was enough to put any man off working underground. Sallow-featured, with hair that was permanently awry, he looked as furtive as a child stealing biscuits. He had a habit of listening carefully to other people's voices rather than looking them in the eye, as if that was bad luck.

'Afternoon, Wattie,' Rod said, shouldering the door and sidling in with the trunk.

'Aye, what's that?' His voice was an evil rasp.

'It's a trunk I would like opened, but I'm not sure where the key is,' Rod said. He set it on Wattie's desk.

Wattie's eyes moved to the box. 'And what would we have inside, then, eh? Gold? Jewels?'

'Could be, Wattie. How long, do you think?'

There were many who believed that Wattie was himself escaping justice, and if he were to return home to England, he would immediately be arrested for unmentionable crimes. This rumour had the advantage that, since the crimes were unmentionable, there was no need to invent them. There was no basis for the gossip, but it satisfied many of the older officers to think that he was a criminal, because Wattie was a proficient lock breaker.

In the whole of Shanghai no cupboard, door or safe was secure from him. Other men would scowl at a lock knowing they were beaten, but Wattie would scratch his head slowly, suck hard on a Wild Woodbine, nod to himself, and suddenly spring into action. Sometimes he wielded a flat bar of a specific thickness to attack a bolt, while on other occasions he would take a curious tool with an erratically shaped blade, which he would jiggle in the lock itself, before turning it with the dramatic flair of a magician producing a rabbit from a top hat.

'What do you think?' Rod said.

Wattie was staring at the lock with eyes suddenly vacant. He leaned back and absent-mindedly lit a cigarette.

Rod left him to it.

It was past eight o'clock when Rod looked through the papers he had gathered from Foster's room. It was better to stay at his desk than go to his apartment. He had never enjoyed his own company, and given the choice of returning to his rooms or remaining, he preferred to crack on with his work. The alternative was the temptation of the door with the little sliding panel.

Mickey Hi was in the corridor, and Rod told him to make a pot of tea before pulling out the papers and starting to go through them. He made one pile of correspondence, a second of receipts and chits.

There were several from bars, mostly for drinks, and a few from establishments providing gambling or women, all legal.

He turned to the letters. Nothing from parents or siblings, but several from a woman called Eleanor White, who lived near Birmingham.

The first was a cheerful note wishing him luck, signed "With love, Eleanor". She spoke of events with her children, the daily trials of everyday life. It was dated in the August of 1917. Then there was a parade of different letters, all about the war at first, then the flu and how it ravaged her neighbours, but she and the children were fine; Henry had fallen from his horse, but only broke his collarbone; by the sixth letter, it was fully healed, and it was the troublesome William who was taxing her.

It was the ninth letter that grabbed his attention:

'Dear Thomas, do tell me when you will return. The boys miss you terribly, and so do I. Your letters are so few now, it makes me fear that you have stopped loving me.' There was a lot more, but it was the signature at the bottom that made Rod stop. It said, 'Your ever loving wife, Eleanor.'

'White?' he muttered. There were plenty of cases of men who had run away from their women after the War, but this was curious. Why should this woman have kept her maiden name, and not adopted Foster's? Or had she thought his name was 'White'?

Rod was about to reach for the next letter when there was a commotion. He hurried to the door, and saw Bert Shaw. 'What's happening?'

'A raid! Hurry up!'

Rod grabbed his gun, took two magazines, rapping them quickly on the desk to seat the cartridges, and pulled on his jacket. The police were not routinely armed, but increasing violence meant detectives were required to carry pistols. Rod checked the Colt's slide and dry fired it once before inserting the magazine and smacking it home with the heel of his hand. Holstering it, he hurried down to the courtyard.

A van stood, engine running. Rod hopped into the back, and soon they were roaring along the Nanking Road, springs protesting, heading for a lane off the Chekiang Road. Bert had heard rumours of a ground-floor cabaret where there was unlicensed gambling and illicit drugs.

Matters had taken a turn for the worse since the prohibition on drugs. Businesses in Shanghai, Hong Kong and other freeports had made fortunes importing opium. The trade funded the development of the cities, but when locals saw the money to be made from importing drugs, they smuggled their own. Now warlords up and down the country were using drug money to fund their ambitions.

The crunch came in 1912 with an international agreement banning the import and sale of drugs. In Shanghai, importing was to cease and the opium shops were to close by 1917. But foreign and Chinese groups wanted to fill their wallets first. So they set up a cartel, the Shanghai Opium Merchants' Combine, to control imports, while also contracting with the Chaozhou Clique, the *Chao Bang*. The Clique would buy only from the Opium Merchants' Combine and control distribution. And then, in '17, when the ban came into force, the Chinese government agreed to buy up all the Opium Merchants' Combine's stocks.

But those addicted still needed their supply. When the legal market closed, criminals moved in. Shanghai was at the centre of Chinese smuggling, whether exporting goods from the interior or importing from other lands. Gangs battled for mastery, using the same methods familiar to Chicago: extortion, protection rackets, prostitution and gambling. The SMP was forced to try close down drug dens whenever they appeared. Rod was just glad that his own had so far escaped notice.

On the way, Bert Shaw briefed Rod. A Chinese officer, he said, had heard of a new cabaret, the Black Swan. It was an illegal gambling den, but rumours suggested there could be drugs too. 'The idea is, we snatch everyone as quickly as we can. It's all on the ground floor, but there's a back door leading to apartments. A door leads to an alleyway behind. We've already got men out there, and we'll go in as soon as we reach it.'

'Who's in charge?'

'Your boss: Hibbard.'

Rod nodded. Hibbard despised the drug gangs. He shivered unconsciously. He could do with a pipe. Action often had this effect on him.

'How much warning did we get?'

Bert nodded towards a Chinese officer. 'CPC 721. He reported it an hour ago.'

'This constable, is he reliable?' Rod asked quietly.

Bert gave him a sharp look. 'I find the Chinese police constables are a good lot, compared with some of our English fellows.'

There was no arguing with that, and Rod nodded apologetically. In six months three Foreign officers had been sent home. It was all too common. The pay was lousy, the hours terrible, the loneliness extreme for new recruits. It was no surprise that many turned to pink gin or whisky. Others supplemented their incomes, accepting bribes or offering 'protection' money. One had been discovered running his own brothel.

Peering past the driver, Bert sighed. 'The problem is, half the time when we get leads, it's one Chinese gang peaching on another, hoping to put them out of business. We're fighting a fire with a teacup of water. There's so much illegal activity, and always the smell of corruption.'

'That's not corruption, Bert; it's the smell of money!'

'In this city the two are synonymous, aren't they?' he said sadly. 'Oh! Our stop, I think!'

The games were loud and enthusiastic. Thin Bao walked past tables of rattling tiles or dice and made his way to the bar. There were two women with Billy Qian, the big man drinking from a balloon of brandy and watching the games. Thin Bao walked past, and one of the whores stared at him as if he was a coolie. It was tempting to slap her, make her take her round eyes and tall figure out, throw her into the street, but he knew Billy Qian. He didn't want to upset him.

That was when he noticed the other woman. 'Alice?'

She shot him a look, and he understood. Billy Qian glanced at him.

Thin Bao went through the door beside the bar. Billy Qian was still watching him, but Thin Bao feared no man. He touched the butt of his Mauser like a talisman. Thin Bao closed the door quietly.

What was the point of taking offence? She was a baboon like the others, although she had a certain arrogance which he would enjoy destroying. She should know better than to insult a man of Thin Bao's standing.

He took the staircase to the next floor. Entering the room, Thin Bao cast a glance at the reels of silk. A man sat by the window watching the road, a machine pistol beside him, the electric button on the window sill. All was well. Thin Bao was about to return downstairs, when he heard vehicles. Looking out, he saw the first of a convoy of SMP lorries.

'*Quick*!' he snapped, and his palm slapped the button down.

## Chapter Fifteen

The lorry lurched to a stomach-wrenching halt, brakes squealing like a pig seeing supper. The policemen poured out, the uniforms thundering to the nearest building like a trench storming party, two at the front swinging sledgehammers to take down the door, one at each hinge, smashing the wood, three blows at each before the door gave way. Screams and shrieks from inside, and the bellowing of the police making an unholy din. Soon officers reappeared pulling girls with them; others remained inside, concentrating on binding prisoners and searching the place.

Rod lit a cigarette, leaving the uniforms to it. British or Chinese, the death or glory boys were as subtle as a cavalry charge, and quite as likely to trample a detective as a criminal. Rod would wait until the clamour had died down before strolling in to see what could be gleaned, his hands in his pockets, fedora tipped to the back of his head, like a wise guy from the movies.

The women were herded together into a narrow dead-end alley by two Chinese officers, who stood eagerly staring at the building like greyhounds at the slips. They wanted to go and prove themselves, rather than wetnurse the women.

Bert appeared in the doorway. 'You can come in now, Rod. It's safe,' he said ironically.

It was a dim chamber thick with tobacco smoke. Chairs and tables were all dark woods, with lacquer or gilt. Hangings were mostly red or golden, and at the bar a bemused man stood, hopefully rattling a cocktail shaker, peering over the top of the bottles on his bar as though the arrival of the police was an entertainment, and he would soon return to his duties. Rod looked at the tables. One was larger than the rest, and on it stood tea pots and cups. At each corner was a jade figure, each the same size. All was tidy. There was no sign of gambling, let alone a single pea of opium.

Rod murmured. 'I hope your fellow got the right address.'

Bert shrugged and walked to speak to the captured men.

There were no rickshaw men here, as would be found in cheaper gambling dens, only wealthier traders and businessmen. And then Rod saw him: Billy Qian.

He was wearing a western suit of clothes, clutching a half-filled balloon of brandy. Seeing him here, against so many shorter Chinese men, he looked huge. Even against Terry O'Toole, the beefy Liverpudlian Sergeant, he was large, with a massive belly that reminded Rod of a Schoenhut clown from his childhood: a papier mâché cone with a weighted hemi-spherical base so that, no matter how far the figure was pushed, it would always return upright. Qian's face was round, his pale skin soft and unblemished. He had never sweated in a paddy field or drawn a rickshaw. Unlike the others, he did not maintain a dignified inscrutability, but smiled. He knew he would soon be released. There were some who knew they were inviolate. He was one. He had the confidence that money alone could buy in Shanghai.

Two waiters stood obsequiously, heads lowered to avoid upsetting the police. Their manager bowed and wrung his hands, protesting wildly about the shame and his horror that his establishment could suffer such a degrading experience; could the officers not see there was nothing illegal? Surely a man filled with malice led them here, keen to impugn the reputation of an honest businessman.

There was a lot more in the same vein, and while he ran on, Rod watched the captives. One of the patrons looked anxious, and when he caught Rod's glance, he dropped his own immediately. Something made Rod keep his eye on the fellow who, when he caught sight of Rod's stare, seemed to go into a panicked lather.

This was more than the embarrassment of an innocent man confronted with a policeman. This was a guilty man trying to avoid being noticed. There was something here.

At the larger table, Rod picked up an ornament. It was a jade figure, beautifully carved, but with a scuff mark on the top. Rod set it down again, and idly picked up the nearest tea cup. It was stone cold; as was a second. Even the teapots were cool to the touch.

More officers arrived, and the clientele was gradually moved to the door. The worried Chinese was relieved to be taken away.

He glanced up at the ceiling.

Archie and John giggled as they returned from the bar.

Peter wasn't with them. Last night the three had enjoyed an evening's drinking and dancing with taxi girls in a cabaret. Peter had enjoyed himself too enthusiastically, and had been noisily unwell overnight, showing up for cross country running with a face as green as the vegetation. Sergeant Major Fairbairn noticed his anguish, and took delight in ribbing him, running at his side the whole way, forcing Peter to greater efforts until, as they returned to the Gordon Road Depot, Peter succumbed and vomited profusely beside the road.

'You'll clean that up before breakfast,' the sergeant major said.

'Yes, sir,' Peter said. Later, sitting with the others in the mess, watching them eat with remorseful envy, he swore he would never drink spirits again.

Classes were tedious. There were maps of the city to learn, instructions covering the boundaries of their responsibility, and a primer on Chinese that had Archie wondering if he had made an appalling mistake. It was only later, when they were receiving self-defence training under the watchful eye of Sergeant Major Fairbairn, that he felt more comfortable.

The police officers' first duty was to protect the public. However, policing the streets of the International Settlement was increasingly dangerous, and the officers must learn to fight aggressively.

'We are not here to play games,' Fairbairn said. ' This is not cricket. If you want to survive on the streets, you must fight to win. Fight fair, and you will be killed. Here, the rule is gutter fighting.'

That evening, Archie and John tried to persuade Peter to join them, but he held up crossed index fingers, warding off their evil spirits.

They had returned to the same cabaret. Archie danced with a Chinese woman who begged him to buy her a glass of champagne as well as pay for his dances, and she must have liked dancing with him, because she asked for another two glasses later. They were horribly expensive, but she entranced him, with her dark eyes glittering, smiling as she moved across the dance floor. She was lovely, although when he asked to meet her outside the cabaret, her eyes instantly dulled, as though a shutter was drawn down.

It had been a pleasant evening, but Archie grew worried about John. As he drank, he grew obstreperous. Archie had no desire to be discovered brawling, so he called an end to the evening. They should be back in plenty of time, he reckoned. They were not certain of their way, but if they continued along the Nanking Road, they would be fine. They were fine until they reached a roadway where there were a number of SMP vehicles.

'What's down there?' Archie said.

'God knows,' John said with a belch. 'They might need help.'

'They won't want us,' Archie said quickly.

'They might!' John pressed forward, ignoring the anchoring effect of Archie clinging to his arm. 'Come on!'

Rod saw the Chinese man's eyes rise to the ceiling – and almost laughed aloud.

The Shanghai Municipal Council were as keen to shut down illegal gambling houses as they were to close the opium dens. In response the gamblers grew more inventive. With Chinese ingenuity they could hide many of their less-legal activities.

Glancing at the ceiling, Rod saw a dim shape, as if square panelling was installed for decoration. About it were several similar decorations.

'Bert,' he said. 'Well done.'

'What do you mean?'

'Have you felt the teapots and cups?'

'Have you spent too much time in the sun?'

'Try them.'

He did. 'So?'

'Why are they all cold?'

'They had their tea a while ago.'

Rod sighed. 'Turn your eyes heavenwards.'

'Eh?'

'Look at the ceiling, Bert.'

Suddenly the manager was all effusive assistance. Giving Rod a look of pure nitro glycerine, he tried to usher them away, but it was too late. Overhead Bert had seen the patterns directly above each table. While the men were gambling merrily, their tables rested on four ornaments balanced over tea sets. At the first sign of the police, the gambling tables rose on silken wires and fitted into slots overhead. When the police entered they would find a group of Chinese businessmen sitting innocently about a table. But their tea was cold.

Bert gave a small snort of admiration. 'You want to arrest him, Rod?'

'No, you can have the paperwork,' Rod said.

'Thank you,' he said. It sounded like a curse.

Outside Rod found a crowd of gawkers. Eric Leigh was there, as usual. Rod assumed he must have an informer in the Police. Ignoring his frantically waving notepad – he could wait – Rod went to speak to the Sub-Inspector and while talking to Douglas Hibbard, he noticed them.

Shanghai was a bustling city of contradictions. A free port owned by no one, with foreigners responsible to their own extra-territorial laws, not those of China. The city attracted adventurers: Russians fleeing Bolsheviks, Canadian fraudsters, American conmen and Britons running from justice. And women seeking their fortune.

The American girls were the most popular prostitutes. Shortly they would be overtaken by a rash of young Russians, but in 1922 American girls still filled the best brothels. There were seven standing there now, held back by two Chinese officers. A tall, willowy blonde, a red head, whose expression declared her fiery temper, two brunettes, a short ash-blonde with hair that curled indecorously from a loose bun, and a pair of women standing a little apart, one with auburn locks cut in the latest fashion with long ringlets, the other a slim blonde with bobbed hair.

Those had their backs to Rod. They spoke in low voices, the auburn one glancing at the police. She had a good profile, and he recognised her. She was the girl sitting with Billy Qian at the Astor House.

She had the posture of a princess. Rod saw she was watching the police apprehensively. He was surprised: most prostitutes did not fear the police. They tended to patronize officers; this one looked scared. Perhaps she was new to the business.

On a whim, Rod walked to her. She had just lit a cigarette, and studied him through the smoke as he approached, her face averted. Her companion still had her back turned, but then she was nudged by her companion.

She stood under a streetlamp, head bowed, blonde, bobbed hair hiding her features. The haircut gave her the look of a fair-haired Louise Brookes. A cigarette was held loosely, as though she was dozing and could drop it at any time. She wore a sleeveless, dark blue silk dress that fitted her like a sheath. It gleamed in the light above her, and about her throat a necklace sparkled.

It was late and Rod was tired, his thoughts running on tramlines towards bourbon and ice. Dully, he assumed she was an American girl. They had access to the best clothes, especially the girls from Gracie Gales's establishment. Her girls sported silks, satins, French perfume, anything that might increase their allure ... But then the woman wrapped her left arm about her belly, rested her right elbow against her left wrist, looked up at him and gave that familiar shrug.

He knew that delicate throat, the slim figure, the perfect, heart-shaped face with high cheekbones. Her eyes fixed on him with a kind of bored impatience. She drew on her cigarette and flicked it away with a casual disregard, giving him a glance of such arrogant disdain that even if he did not know her, it would be obvious at once this was no American girl.

No, this was a purebred English Shanghailander. It was Alice Winton.

'You have spoiled a perfect evening, Detective.'

Her irritability was all of a piece. Her arched eyebrows gave her a look of annoyed contempt, as if he had spilled tea down her skirt. Her lips were set, but he thought she was wearing a cloak of petulance.

'We are being held here against our will,' she said.

Her auburn-haired companion fretfully glanced at her. 'You know him?' She had a heavy, eastern European accent.

'We have met,' Rod said.

'What, you are police?'

'Yes. Your name?'

She stiffened. There was more nervousness than defiance in the way she lifted her chin. 'Eva. Eva Bugayeva.'

'You are Russian?'

'Yes. When the Reds took the country, we fled.'

'We?'

'My husband and I,' she said with a deliberate toss of her head.

'Where is he?'

'At home. Where else? We have nothing – no money, no living.'

At this, Alice Winton snapped, 'What business is it of yours what he, or Eva and I are doing? Are you going to question us all night?'

'It's for your own safety.'

She snorted. 'Safety? We're safer removed from the cabaret and pushed into the street?'

'In an illegal gambling house?' Rod snapped. 'You realise even police officers are careful here? There are sailors from America, Japan, India … You could come upon a brawl, or be raped.'

'Not if I'd been *safe* inside!' she blazed.

'You could be captured – for ransom, or worse! Do you want to put your father through that? He's lost one son, you think he could bear to lose you too?'

'Lose me?' Her mouth twisted coldly. 'No, he wouldn't want to lose me.'

'So, then –'

'Officer, call me a rickshaw. I am going home.'

'Miss Winton,' he said, 'this is a police raid, and –.'

She set her head to one side and took in his appearance, from shoes to fedora. Her lip curled. 'Where is your superior officer?'

Her rudeness was no surprise. The white population considered the SMP little more than servants. A policeman might have his own servants, but Shanghailanders knew that back home in England he had been a miner, labourer or warehouseman. In Shanghai the class structure was rigidly enforced.

'Why?' Rod said.

'Just fetch him!' she snapped, lighting a fresh cigarette.

Sub-inspector Hibbard was talking to Terry O'Toole near the cabaret's entrance. Seeing Rod, Douglas Hibbard beckoned. 'Two bloody recruits, both pissed, just came and offered to help. Get rid of them. If I see them again, I'll bite their heads off!'

'Sir, a woman over there wants to talk to you.'

'I've seventeen gangsters and gamblers here. I've enough on my plate!'

'It's Alice Winton.'

'Oh, Christ in a handcart!' Hibbard saw her now. 'Look, get rid of the children while I think of something to say to her.'

Rod didn't envy him.

Reaching the recruits, Rod recognised Archie. 'What are you doing here?'

The second, a dour Scot with the build of a wrestler, glowered. 'Who're you?'

'Just now I'm the man keeping you in a job,' Rod said.

Archie put a hand on the other's arm. 'It's all right, John, this is the detective investigating the murder I saw.'

'He doesn't look like one.'

'Archie?'

'We were walking home and saw the lorries. We just wanted to help.'

'You can't. Keep out of the way. If you get noticed by Douglas, you may be up on a charge for —'

'Who's going to charge us?'

Rod glanced at John. 'You're not in Britain now. Here, you obey orders or you get thrown from the force.'

'We will, sir,' Archie said, nudging John irritably. 'I'd like to see what happens.' He was excited to see his first raid. 'Are there many gangsters in there, sir?'

'A good number. There was gambling, and I daresay drugs —'

There was a loud report, and a sudden shriek. A Chinese officer span, walked one pace and toppled to the ground. Archie and John ducked, while Rod snapped, '*Wait here*!' and ran to Douglas.

'Which window?' Douglas said.

As he spoke there was a flash from a first floor window, and a familiar rattle. A Chinese officer returning fire was thrown back and lay, squirming in pain.

'*Machine pistol*!' Douglas spat, but Rod was already running for the door, Bert Shaw just ahead of him.

## Chapter Sixteen

Rod thudded into the wall by the door, in time to see people scuttling for cover. Eric remained leaning nonchalantly against a wall. A fresh burst knocked brick chips only feet from him, and Rod heard him angrily bellowing, 'Hoi! I'm a journalist, you ruddy fool!' Bert pushed the door wide and the two ran in, two Chinese officers close behind.

The stairs before them were plain, bare boards, and Bert took them at a run, Rod was after him, racking the slide to load his Colt, the Chinese bringing up the rear, one with a pistol. At the half-way landing Bert paused, listening intently like a suspicious guard dog, before continuing more cautiously to the first floor. Bert peered round the corner. A man was entering a doorway, a Chinese with a dark suit, grey hat and chequered hat band. He did not hold a weapon.

'The shots came from the right,' Rod hissed. Bert nodded and moved into the passage. The armed officer darted past and lay on the ground, his pistol supported with both hands, while his companion remained with Bert and Rod, his truncheon grasped tightly.

Rod breathed slowly to stop his heart pounding. This was like crossing No Man's Land in the thin light of dawn, waiting for the machine guns to rattle.

A pair of feeble bulbs provided baleful illumination. Somewhere near was a loud crash, like a slamming door, and Rod span, his gun up, but it was some distance away, not in this corridor. His heart pounded. He imagined a starshell's glare, the thud of big guns, the locomotive shriek of a massive shell overhead, and instinctively flinched, waiting for the impact ...

Outside, Archie took cover as the shot rang out. He saw Rod Cottey running for the door behind a second, thickset officer, two Chinese officers with them.

Archie saw the women. Hearing the shots, they were terrified and Archie sprinted across the roadway. One of the Chinese officers made to strike him, but Archie raised both hands, 'Police!' Hearing a ricochet, the Chinese ducked, and Archie joined the women.

'Ladies, don't worry, we will soon have this under control! You're protected by the wall. The gunman is over the way, but here you're perfectly safe!'

He had to repeat himself before his words had an impact. Two of them were hysterical, but the others soothed them.

'Thank you,' Alice said. 'Their screaming was getting on my nerves. I am Alice Winton.'

'Oh? I'm Archie Lane.'

She looked surprised, as if her name should have meant something, but before he could wonder about it, there was a fusillade. Archie was just in time to see the windows of a room lit by gunshots.

Bert had noticed his momentary dislocation. He nodded at Rod, silently asking whether he was all right. Rod nodded, wiping away the sweat at his brow.

There was a clamorous rattle as the machine pistol fired again. It came from a room halfway along, and both ran, Bert fetching up on the far side of the door, the armed Chinese officer behind Rod. Bert jerked his head at Rod, then at the door. Rod took a step back and launched himself at the timbers, his right foot splintering the thin boards. With a crunch, the door gave way, and Rod threw himself to the floor, gun forward.

A man stood in the window. He held a wicked machine pistol with a drum magazine, and as he began to turn, Rod snapped off two shots, and they, together with Bert's bullets, hit him in the belly and chest. The man was flung to the ground.

Bert went to him, kicking the gun away, and checking the room was safe before helping Rod to his feet.

'You all right, Rod?'

'I'm fine,' he said. 'Both knees bruised, that's all.'

Winches, each with a fine silken rope wound, lay about the floor. Electric motors turned them and lifted the tables up to the ceiling. It was ingenious, and Rod felt a passing admiration for the man who had designed it.

The gunman on the floor was alive, but each breath was a shallow, harsh gasp with rattling deep in his throat. His body stiffened, his back arched, and he relaxed slowly with a long sigh.

His gun was instantly familiar. Wooden stock, perforated sleeve about the stubby barrel, and the snail magazine at the side; it was a Bergmann 18, such as the German army issued in the latter days of the war. Rod had met them in the trenches when the final push came. A thought struck him. 'Bert, have you seen a pistol?'

'No. Why?'

'Someone took a potshot before this was used. Perhaps someone else was here, someone who slipped out before we got here?'

'Damn, I saw a fellow in the corridor, but he didn't have a gun on him, not that I could see.'

Rod waited in the room while Bert ran to the door where he had seen the man, peering round the doorway cautiously, then hurrying through. It was already too late.

The man in grey was gone.

Rod sent a Chinese officer to tell Hibbard that the room was secured. His hand was shaking again. He clenched his fist and, to distract himself, searched the room.

Kneeling at the largest winch, he had a sharp pain in his knee: a cartridge case. There were fifty or more identical cases about the floor, all 9mm brass from the Bergmann, and Rod was suddenly struck by a thought: a pistol had fired first. The gunman must have been near the window to fire, and …

He moved to the window, searching the floor. Of course, if the pistol was a revolver, there would be no casing. If it was an automatic and fired the same 9mm cartridges as the Bergmann, it would be impossible to distinguish, but if there was a different cartridge case, it would show what type of gun to look for. There was nothing on the floor nearby. He knew that pistols like the Luger and the Mauser would throw empty cases wildly in all directions, but all these cartridges looked the same. He was just about to give up, when he saw a glint at the farther corner of the room.

It was a Mauser 7.63mm case. The length and diameter of the bottlenecked cartridge was unmistakeable. He had heard of fingerprints being taken from unfired cartridge cases, and picked it up using his handkerchief.

He felt cold and shivery. He needed a drink.

Douglas Hibbard was downstairs in the cabaret. Seeing Rod, he poured a whisky. 'Take that. Medicinal, old chap. Always a bit of a shock, being shot at.'

'Thanks,' Rod said. It warmed his throat.

Hibbard took the machine pistol and studied it. 'I'll take it to Dan Fairbairn. He's always interested in things like this.'

'The cartridge case?'

'I'll give that to Dan too. He'll know what to do with it, if anything.'

Rod nodded and passed the case, still wrapped in his handkerchief. Hibbard jerked his head over his shoulder. 'Now get that blasted Winton girl home. The last thing I need is her father giving us hell because she was here.' He gave Rod a serious frown. 'And don't try anything on.'

'Eh?'

'Keep your hands off! Take her home, and make sure she gets there safely.'

Archie thought the blonde particularly fine. She had a confidence about her that made him feel strangely secure, as though nothing bad could happen to him while she was there. 'So what were you doing up there, then?' he said. 'Dancing?'

'It wasn't a dancing hall,' she said, with a shake of her head, and ran her fingers through her hair. 'God, it's hot here!'

'Don't you like dancing? I love it. I don't feel alive unless I'm on the floor, music playing.'

'I *love* dancing. Especially jazz. It transports me.'

'To where?' he grinned.

She tapped a cigarette on her gold case and put it in her mouth, then, as an afterthought, offered it to him. He took it, red lipstick moist on the white paper, and his smile broadened as she took another and lit them both.

'What of me?' Eva asked.

'We're talking,' Alice said. 'So, where do you dance?'

'I'm new, I don't know the city yet,' he said, then added, 'Why don't I take you to a dance?'

Eva gave a snort.

'You?' Alice said.

'Yes. I could pick you up, and we could go out.'

She laughed, but not cruelly. 'What do you do, Archie?'

'I'm in the Police.'

'And you want to take me out? Well, I would be safe with an officer of the SMP, wouldn't I?' she said.

'Not necessarily,' he said, his grin widening.

'Good,' she said.

'Tomorrow?'

She peered at him through narrowed eyes. 'Yes, all right.' She opened her bag and presented him with a card. 'You can fetch me.'

'I'll be there at seven,' he said. He glanced over at John. He had fallen asleep and two Chinese officers were prodding him. 'Excuse me!'

He hurried to John, who was annoyed to be woken.

'Hey!' John shouted, and the two Chinese stepped back.

'Stop!' Archie called, and pushed between them. John clambered to his feet. 'This is a misunderstanding, officers. We are police too. Understand?'

'What man?' one officer said.

'Eh?'

'Talkee he quiet.'

'I don't know what you mean,' Archie said.

Bert Shaw strolled over. '"What man?" means *who is he*, and "Talkee he quiet" means *tell him to shut up*.'

'Oh, thank you.'

'I suggest you take your colleague home,' Bert said.

'Yes, I … thank you!' Archie called. As he spoke, he saw a figure who looked oddly familiar: a short man, narrow shouldered, wearing a grey fedora with chequerboard band. In an instant he was gone.

What was she doing there?

Thin Bao span at a noise behind him, his hand reaching for his Mauser. It was out and ready as a dog slipped from the shadows. The urge to scream to the heavens was almost overwhelming. Du Yusheng would know of the raid already, and the blame would attach to Thin Bao. Failure was not a prized trait among Green Gang members. Certainly the gambling house was lost now. The police had discovered the carefully designed chamber with the electric reels to pull the gambling tables out of sight. All that money, time and effort wasted.

By nature Thin Bao was fatalistic. The gambling house was lost. There was little point mourning, but how could the police have discovered it so quickly? Thin Bao had first opened its doors last week.

He holstered his pistol and continued on his way.

The police knew where to come. That meant someone had betrayed his business. A client, a neighbour, or someone else: a member of the Green Gang jealous of his rise, or a competitor seeking to clip the Gang's wings. If he had to bet, it most likely a competitor. There were so many.

Who would dare set his face against the Gang and Du Yusheng? He would be relentless hunting down those who threatened his interests.

Thin Bao would find the man and make him pay.

With that resolution, his mind returned to Alice Winton. What had she been doing with the fat slug Billy Qian? She was far too good for him.

A worm of jealousy squirmed in his belly.

## Chapter Seventeen

Rod led Alice and Eva away, heading back towards the Nanking Road, where he hoped to find a rickshaw, but after only a few steps he was accosted by a broadly grinning Eric Leigh.

'So, Detective, taking these maidens into custody?' he asked, holding a pencil poised over his notepad. He ran his eyes appreciatively over Eva's charms, and then took in Alice Winton's face. 'Good God, Miss Winton, oh, I'm so sorry,' he said, hastily putting his pencil away. 'I had no idea –'

Alice took Eva's elbow and barged past without speaking.

There was a two-seat rickshaw at the end of the street, a coolie slumped wearily between the shafts. While the coolie bestirred himself, Eva kissed Alice on the cheek. 'Be safe,' she said, and Alice nodded before Rod helped her up.

'What about you?' he said to Eva. 'Aren't you going home?'

'I will walk to the Astor House. I want one last drink,' she said.

'Billy Qian may be a while,' he said.

He watched her walk up Nanking Road towards the Bund, head high and swinging her handbag from its thin leather strap like a woman without a care in the world. He was reluctant to leave her on her own, but he reflected that she had endured much to reach Shanghai; she knew what she was doing. He put her from his thoughts and clambered up beside Alice. The rickshaw lurched away, the springs squeaking with every dent and pothole, the barefoot coolie padding quietly.

'Cigarette?' he asked, offering her his packet.

She selected the least crumpled, waiting while he struck a light. Inhaling deeply, she averted her head to exhale, holding his eyes as she did.

It was uncomfortable to be in such close proximity. She smelled of citrus and fresh flowers. Their thighs touched, and he could imagine the soft, smooth skin beneath her skirt. From the corner of his eye he could see the rise and fall of her breast, and it required effort to keep his eyes averted.

'You were brave,' she said. 'I saw you run inside after the gunfire. You were a soldier?'

'Yes.'

'Which regiment?'

'The Devonshires.'

'Officer?'

'Second Lieutenant. Not that it mattered much afterwards.'

'What do you mean?'

'I wasn't right,' he shrugged. He wasn't going to describe his jealousy towards those born into wealth and accepted into the Officers' Mess, while promoted fighting men like him were viewed askance. When the war ended, it was clear there was no space for men like him. He was demobilised with the rank of Corporal. No doubt someone thought they were doing him a favour.

'My brother was there. He didn't come home,' she said.

Her voice held that note of accusation he had heard in others, particularly Cecily's ... But he wouldn't reflect on her. The memory was too painful. 'How did you meet Eva?'

'Eva?' She was surprised by the question. 'At a party in the Astor House. Why?'

'She isn't the sort of woman I would expect you to know.'

'Why? Because she is destitute, or as near to it as makes little difference?'

'No.' He didn't add, *Because she looks the sort of woman who feeds off people with money. She has nothing, so she takes advantage of people like you.* Instead, he said, 'You know Billy Qian?'

'He is ... entertaining.'

'Where did you meet him?'

'At Garcia's: The Wheel.'

The Wheel - a casino. It was one of those places that kept being targeted now gambling was illegal, but the laws were confused. Extraterritoriality meant foreigners must adhere to their own countries' laws. Garcia, being Mexican, lived according to Mexican laws. Gambling for him was not illegal. 'Has she requested money from you?'

'What of it?' she suddenly turned, searching Rod's face, a frown puckering her brow. 'If she takes a little money from me, she takes something I can afford and will not miss. Yet for her it represents life. In exchange for a little money she gives me companionship. I receive her time and attention, and she receives payment. An exchange of money for services.'

There was amusement in her tone, as if she was teasing him, deliberately hinting at prostitution. Then her tone changed, as if bored with twitting him. 'Besides, we both like to dance. Do you dance? You might enjoy it.'

'Where does she live?'

She turned towards him flirtatiously. 'Are you keen on her? She lives near the Sih Chong match factory, near Ward Road.'

That was a poor part of the city, where most rooms were let to Chinese. 'They have a room or apartment?'

'Yes. And my money keeps her there, and him in Vodka,' she said lightly. 'Isn't that what you expect me to say? A nasty, spoiled rich girl, who cares only for her own satisfaction, and nothing for anyone else - that is what you expect of me, isn't it?'

'What were you doing there tonight? Gambling with the others?'

'Seeking entertainment. Life here can be so tedious. Billy invited me to the club. He provides distractions.'

Rod wondered what other form Billy Qian's 'distractions' might take.

At the Winton's house the uniformed Sikh opened the gates. The rickshaw coolie was awestruck taking in the vast grounds. Rod couldn't blame him. He hardly believed the scale of the place himself.

'Is it so dreadful, living here, that you have to pay for a woman like Eva to be your friend?' Rod said.

She eyed him closely, taking his hand to alight. 'I think it better than giving myself to a man who would marry me for my money and a seat on Daddy's board,' she said. 'Wouldn't you?'

'Wouldn't I what?'

'Wouldn't you pay for her to spend a little time with you?'

He wasn't sure he had heard her correctly at first. She watched his reaction with narrowed eyes. He said, 'You like to create a response, don't you?'

'She is attractive, isn't she?'

He nodded. 'Yes. However, I don't think …'

'I could pay her to entertain you,' she continued. 'She would be a strong lover, Detective. Her arms and legs are muscular, for all her slimness. Let me know if you would like me to arrange it.'

'You are keen to change the subject, aren't you? We were talking about you and your need for Eva's company.'

'No. You were; I wasn't,' she said with a sharp laugh. It sounded brittle, like a wine glass struck within an inch of shattering.

'What do you know about Eva?'

'I like her company. What more should I know? That she has lost everything, that she is a paid companion for men, that her husband is a drunk who lives on her income? I know that, certainly. What of it?'

'They have nothing, and you are wealthy. You could be kidnapped and held to ransom, if her husband is truly that desperate.'

She surveyed him dispassionately, and he was reminded of a scientist watching a specimen die in a jar. 'I know more about blackmail and ransom than you might think. Eva is no threat. Detective, you are very self-assured. But when it comes to judging people, I am very good too,' she said.

Turning past him, she ran lightly up the stairs. She slipped through the door, and for some reason Rod shivered. He was reminded of a half-glimpsed spider darting out of sight. A very attractive spider.

## Chapter Eighteen

Rod rode to Bailey's.

It was hot. The streets smelled of fragrant woods, Chinese spices, and sewage, the air so dense it strained his lungs, like breathing through a sodden flannel held over his mouth. Rod was fidgety with the need of a drink – or a smoke.

He sat on a tall stool. Dan Bailey was behind the bar polishing a glass.

'Hello, darling,' he said. 'Heavens, but you look terrible!'

'Give me an Old Fashioned.'

'Why do you like that drink?'

'I acquired a taste for them in Paris on leave. A gentleman from Louisiana introduced me to one on a sweltering day like this.'

Now, he hankered for an Old-Fashioned whenever the weather was hot and humid, and it was always hot and humid in Shanghai. Dan mixed them just the way he liked and Rod hoped it would distract him from thoughts of Alice Winton and Eva. He somehow doubted it.

Bailey lifted the bourbon from the shelf, scooped ice into a low tumbler, added Demerara sugar, and stirred as he dripped bitters into it. When the sugar dissolved, he poured in bourbon and stirred again, adding a thin strip of orange peel before sliding the drink over the counter.

Rod took the glass and rolled it over his brow with his eyes closed. 'It's worth the drink just for the ice.'

'Don't get too keen,' Bailey said primly. 'I might charge extra.'

Rod closed his eyes and sipped. The drink was cold, sharp and sweet, as it ought to be, while the citrus aroma made it refreshing. 'Perfection, Dan.'

'It takes years of practice to make it right, darling. So who's been chewing your sausage?'

'A new girl I haven't seen before. Do you know a Russian called Eva Bugayeva?' He described her briefly. With her height and auburn locks, it wasn't hard.

'Eva, you say. Well, if she wants a home, tell her she's always welcome here. I don't have any women with good, fiery auburn hair. With legs and boobs as well, she would be a fine addition to my stable.'

'I doubt you could afford her.'

'Well, if she's expensive, you could always ask Gracie Gale. She is always interested in new talent, isn't she?'

'Possibly,' Rod agreed.

There was something about Eva Bugayeva. He couldn't put his finger on it, but it was there. A woman like her, who had reached Shanghai when her own country had collapsed, who had arrived, by her own admission, with nothing, could be a source of danger to a young woman like Alice Winton. As Rod had said, Eva could by design or accident lead gangsters to Alice and hold her for ransom. It was not unknown. And she was friendly with Billy Qian.

In the trenches, when leading men over the top or out on patrol, Rod sometimes felt a tingle at the back of his head. When he did, he knew he must be careful. It was always the harbinger of danger. And now he could feel it, loud and clear, like a lightship's bell on a dark and foggy night.

Kiangse Road began as a civilised area on the settlement's southern boundary with the French, and ran northward parallel with the Bund to the Soochow Creek, where scores of alleys and dark streets criss-crossed it. At this time of year it was vile, with the ever-present odour of sewage and burning caramel smell of opium. There were always figures slumped in doorways, many living in drug-induced nightmares.

Few travelled as far as the Creek. On the way was Shanghai's infamous 'Line', where very specific distractions were offered, especially at number 52, which harboured, allegedly, the finest brothel in Shanghai. In a city containing hundreds of bordellos, that was quite a claim. The owner, Gracie Gale, called it the best house of pleasure in the world.

Gracie Gale's establishment was a forbidding, red brick building with no special features. A small brass plate announced the house number, like a law office. It needed nothing more. Everyone knew of Gracie Gale's American girls.

Rod walked in. He refused to be intimidated by a brothel. On leave in France, he had visited whores; their houses tended to be shabby-genteel places where older women often took pity on soldiers who were little more than boys, many of them seeking maternal comfort rather than sex.

This was different. A glance at the chandelier in the hall told him he could never afford a visit.

Removing his hat, Rod placed it upside down on a nearby table, unconsciously tugging at his suit. A young Asian girl appeared and bowed. She beckoned him to follow her into a large sitting room in which a number of men were relaxing.

Rod stopped and swallowed.

There were blondes, brunettes, red-heads, Japanese and Chinese, and the single criterion that united them was their beauty. A ravishing Roman goddess, with tumbling waves of gleaming black hair, sat on one man's lap and whispered into his ear; a redhead snuggled into the embrace of a man on a sofa; a blonde with a satin dress so tight her breasts threatened a bid for freedom, sat smoking a cheroot, playing cards with a small man who could not take his eyes from her abundant curves. An auburn beauty with a figure that would make a Pope howl, seeing Rod in the doorway, rose slowly from a stool, stroking her hands down her silk dress, dragging the material taut, and raised an eyebrow at him.

He felt trapped. There was a strange, empty excitement in his belly … but then the moment was broken. Music blared as a door opened, and Gracie appeared.

There was no doubting that this was the owner of the establishment. Gracie Gale was only some five feet five tall, but any lack of height was compensated by a figure that could stop an army. With her waist cinched in, a bust that proudly forged a path like a ship's prow cutting through water, and hair piled in a hennaed mass on top of her head, she was every bit the mistress. And in case Rod was in any doubt, her eyes were sharp as gimlets.

She sized him up. 'Good evening, and who might you be?'

Her voice was pure San Fransisco, rich and surprisingly deep, mellowed by tobacco and brandy, and although it held a playful quality, Rod discerned warning. He was relieved to see the auburn temptress turn away. 'I am just a poor Municipal Police officer: Detective Cottey. I assume you're Gracie Gale?'

She took his hand, her head tilted appraisingly, and gave a brisk nod. 'Excuse me, Detective, but I doubt you'd be able to afford my rates, unless you're independently wealthy – or have some means of making money your Commissioner wouldn't approve of. I support the police, so I wouldn't want dirty money.' She gave a significant pause. 'Or pay it.'

'I am not involved in a protection racket,' Rod said, 'but I would be grateful for a few moments of your time. It's nothing to do with this establishment, it's another girl.'

'Really?' She eyed him with suspicion only slightly leavened by curiosity. 'How interesting. Well, let's see. I'll be free in about fifteen minutes. If you want, you can have a drink while you wait.'

'I doubt I could afford it.'

She laughed. 'Not on a policeman's salary, you can't. Have one on me.' She motioned to a slim Chinese who approached, bowing. 'Just tell Qin what you want and she'll bring it.'

'Thank you, but I'll be fine.'

Gracie looked at him very directly. 'Don't be a prude, Detective Cottey. A drink ain't a bribe. Not here. It's just a welcome. Take the drink and wait here.'

He succumbed and asked for an Old Fashioned. When it arrived, he grasped the icy glass like a soldier grabbing his last rum before the whistle. The glass was frosted with condensation, and he was tempted to roll it across the back of his neck - but it would have looked ridiculous in those surroundings: indecorous. The thought made him chuckle: it was a strange reflection, bearing in mind the place was a bordello, but there it was. He felt this was foreign territory, and, like an ambassador, he should hold himself to different standards. So he sipped his drink, and felt its coolness seep into his blood. It was delicious. He could only imagine what the quality of Gracie Gale's bourbon was; it was of a higher standard than Dan Bailey's.

The drink was disappearing quickly by the time Gracie returned. There was a delightful flush to her features, and she used a fan to cool herself. 'Sorry about that. He wanted to dance, and I didn't want to upset him. He's a good client.' She looked at Rod and her voice hardened. 'So what's this about? Another girl, you said? Not one of mine?'

Billy Qian was not held long. Douglas Hibbard gave him a cold, hard stare as he walked from Louza Police Station and stood at the top of the steps, breathing in the thick air.

It was the smell of money, Billy reflected. The smell of opportunity.

He loved this city; its hunger, the greed. So many would trample others in their desperate search for money. Men would kill – many had killed – just to make a little more. Some called themselves Christians - others Confucians. Well, Billy was no fool, and he planned to make as much money as he could. He was already rich. The main thing was, learning what people wanted, and providing it. He prowled like a scavenger, picking up the tidbits that the lions had dropped after gorging themselves, and turning those scraps into an empire.

Eva would be waiting for him at the Astor House. First, he had some business. He should speak to Maurice, perhaps take him to the godown where he could view his investment? Maurice had been growing fretful. He worried that his father might learn of their arrangements. Well, that was his concern, not Billy's, but if Billy left him waiting too long, Maurice might decide to cut his losses and find another to provide him with what he needed.

It was best not to run that risk. Billy knew where Maurice would be now. He would fetch his automobile and collect him.

Rod sat in a plush red armchair. Her office was a small room, and Gracie filled it with her presence. She lit a cigar as they entered, and her brandy glass had been refilled as they walked from the sitting room. Now she sat at her desk, fixing Rod with an eye as curious and bright as a sparrow's.

'I met a Russian tonight. Her name was Eva Bugayeva. I wondered if you knew her?'

'Why, so you can buy her? Haha! Don't give me that! You look like a stuffed frog! I deal with attractive women all day, every day, and the men who lust after them. D'you want to bed her, or is this police business?'

'Let me put it like this: she has befriended a wealthy family, and I am not convinced of her reasons. She may have an ulterior motive.'

'I see.' She kept her eyes fixed on him. 'So you reckon this girl could be a threat to this family? Which family?'

'I can't say. If there is something - say a matter of blackmail - it would be better to keep names out of the public eye.'

'So you want me to take your word, but you won't trust me?' She shook her head. 'I think the interview's over, officer.'

'Surely you can see my hands are tied?'

'Why, because I'm a *madame* I can't be trusted? A secret wouldn't be safe in my hands?' she gave a snort. 'Look around you, Detective. This decanter? That's from Edinburgh. This glass? From a Bavarian glass works - and don't sniff, the Boche make the best glass in the world. The chairs in my sitting room? All made and lacquered by the best Chinese craftsmen. This place is worth a fortune, and the main reason is, whatever happens in here, you'll never hear. My girls and servants know not to tell. I never had a problem with a secret being shared, and I'm not likely to start now. My girls don't talk, and neither do I. Men come here to relax, and we see they do. You know how many of your senior officers come here, how many members of the Municipal Council? No. And you won't, either. Because in this house we lock secrets tight so clients' wives and children don't get hurt, so clients don't hear their little games bruited about in the streets. This house is based on secrets. If you speak to me, your information goes nowhere. You tell one of your colleagues in the Police, and I'll hear it within a day.'

She sat back and shook her head. 'You men! I tell you now, you know nothing of the secrets of the city. If you want my help, shoot. If you mean to keep your mouth buttoned, the door's behind you.'

Rod stood. 'I am sorry to have wasted your time.'

'Wait.' She frowned, disgruntled. 'Why'd you come here, if you weren't going to tell me anything?'

'As I say, it may be nothing. I just cannot tell whether it's a matter I should be pursuing.'

'Because this Eva has befriended some family, or someone in the family?'

'One person. A rather young person.'

'A boy who's going to be seduced?'

He hesitated. 'No, a girl.'

'Oh. Right, I see.' Gracie Gale toyed with a letter knife on her desk. 'If you're a detective, who d'you work for?'

'Sub-Inspector Hibbard.'

'Oh, Doug. Right. And you were in the War, weren't you?'

'I served, yes.'

'What rank?'

'I rose to second lieutenant.' The second time that evening he had been asked about his rank. It was irritating: his position in the police was important, not his military rank.

'Don't get arsey with me. It's obvious in your eyes, fellow. You've seen things I can't imagine.' She gave a rasping chuckle. 'But hell, I guess you could say the same about me, huh?'

She was still for some little while, considering. Then she nodded. 'I'll see what I can do. I'm not a charity, Detective Cottey. I'm a business woman. But I don't like the thought of someone taking advantage of a youngster. So, okay, leave it with me and I'll let you know if I learn anything.'

## Chapter Nineteen

Outside, Rod adjusted his hat and loosened his collar to dissipate the clamminess. The night was humid as a steam bath.

He reflected that Gracie was, by her own lights, a law-abiding woman. The city made her a non-person in polite society, yet the men who controlled the community paid for her services and kept her in the luxury she enjoyed. It was their wives who saw that Gracie was excluded. She might entertain their husbands, but that didn't mean they had to accept her into their social circles.

A little more alcohol might help him sleep. He didn't want another pipe of opium – that was a rare indulgence. If he was discovered, he would be out of the SMP; but when the faces of the dead came at night, nothing else worked. Opium banished his nightmares. Luckily, he had it under control. He wasn't addicted.

As he consoled himself with that thought, an American automobile appeared in the road ahead, driving faster than was safe. As it passed, he saw Billy Qian driving, while Maurice Winton sat, pale and anxious, in the passenger seat.

The car barrelled off up the road towards the Souchow Creek, turned left, and disappeared. Rod stood for some minutes staring after it thoughtfully.

'Usual again, darling?' Dan asked as Rod entered Bailey's.
'Yes.'

'Did you learn anything from Gracie?'

'She has better bourbon.'

Dan nodded knowingly. 'Oh, it was the *bourbon* caught your attention, was it?' he said, passing Rod his drink. 'Nothing to do with Gracie's girls?'

'You're getting bitchy, Dan,' Rod said.

'Well, the girls are stunning, I guess,' he said. He breathed on a glass and buffed it to sparkling perfection. 'I suppose a hot-blooded man like you will always be tempted by their like.'

'I saw Maurice Winton just now.'

'Oh? Was he with the bevy of beauties?'

'There were no women in the car with him. Only a Chinese.'

'Really?'

'I suppose this isn't the sort of place Maurice Winton would come,' Rod reflected.

'Why would you suppose that?'

'The quality of the bourbon?'

Giving him a glare, Dan walked to the farther side of the bar where a pair of men were slurring a request for drinks while eyeing Dan's women. They were British: clerks, maybe, in one of the banks - Hong Kong and Shanghai, perhaps, or Liverpool and Asiatic, or Jardine's. They had drunk enough for ten, and were growing noisy, so he was about to finish his drink and go home when Bert Shaw entered.

'Ready for another, old cock?'

'Oh, hello, Bert. Yes, one for the road. Thanks.'

Bert Shaw waited patiently while Dan served the two bankers, and then came to serve him. 'What will it be, Rod?' Bert asked.

Bert chose the same, signed the chit, and soon they were sipping fresh drinks. Rolling his glass between his palms, Bert said, 'It was unbearable today. The heat was appalling. I thought I would collapse.'

'It's the humidity.'

'Yes, it kills a man. I spent time in Kenya, you know. The country there, well, it's wonderful. They say that once a man has Africa in his blood, he never gets it out of his system. I can easily believe it. What I loved was the variety. Tea plantations, coffee, the uplands where the air was cool and fresh, the splendours of Naivasha and Nakuru, fresh pineapple every day - yet go to the coast, with the Indian Ocean twinkling, and the beauty was entirely overwhelmed by the *blasted* humidity! It was just like this: hot, damp, intolerable during the day, unbearable at night! If it weren't for the winters, I would leave this place like a shot.'

'I didn't know you had been to Africa.'

Bert Shaw had been in the 2nd Battalion of the Manchesters. He was good-looking, in a clean-living, English way, with fair hair of a reddish tinge, and blue eyes that held a slight anxiety, like a man who has seen much he would prefer to forget. Everyone in Shanghai came to escape something, or someone. It was good manners not to ask. Shaw was cordial, and reliable in an unfussy, calm way. He reminded Rod of a schoolmaster: he had a manner that made a man think he was being praised, but never patronised. Neither discussed their wartime experiences, but there were clues. Occasionally, when there was a gunshot or a cry, there was a look in the eyes. Veterans all had it.

'Yes, when I was young, callow, and excited by adventure. Before ... well, you know.'

'Were you there when the War started?'

'No. I'd left by then,' he said. He stared into his glass, sipped. 'I thought that the heat wouldn't do me any good. You know: malaria, or another fever. It seemed a good idea to return home - until I experienced the winter in Picardy! If ever a man regretted a decision, I was he.'

'I can imagine,' Rod said. 'How did you get to Africa? You told me your family had no money.'

'Did I, though?' he said with a slight twist of his lip. 'I left home. Ran away for adventure like a bloody little fool! Got myself to Southampton, and onto a ship. Sailed round Cape Horn, and up. Mombasa seemed as good a place as any to stop. I liked the look of Fort Jesus. And there were lovely, sandy beaches. It looked like heaven.'

'Where were your family from?'

'This is how you interrogate your suspects, is it?' he laughed. 'Hampshire. "Gentleman" farmers, which means broke.'

'I see. Whereabouts? Hampshire's a big county.'

'You'll have to buy the next round,' he said, sinking his glass and holding it up to Dan for a refill. 'What about you? I recall you said that you came from the wilds of the West country.'

'Yes, I was born and raised near Cadbury, a little village in Devon,' Rod said. 'We were farmers, too.'

He suddenly had a vision of the old house, Furnshill Manor, the soft, green pastureland, the trees, the stooks of wheat standing in the sun, rooks wheeling overhead as they mobbed a buzzard, larks singing. Cecily and Ethel, Dick and he, sitting in the meadow, drinking cider in the sunshine. The girls so pretty, Dick red-faced and playing the fool, tackling Rod and bringing him down. Love, friendship, joy: that last summer in 1913 had been idyllic.

Bert saw his expression. He said quietly, 'It doesn't do to go back, old man, does it? The past is another life. This is all we have now.

# Chapter Twenty

*Thursday 27th July, 1922*

Next morning, Rod spoke to the duty sergeant and allocated two Chinese officers to watch Billy Qian.

Qian was supposed to have made money from developing properties and selling them, but his house was on Bubbling Well Road, the most expensive area in Shanghai. How could he afford his lifestyle?

Whether Qian was selling drugs, running a protection racket, involved in gambling or prostitution - or all of them - Rod didn't know. But he was sure that, if Qian was friendly with Alice and Maurice, there was an ulterior motive which was unlikely to be good for Alfred's family.

Was Alice his target, or Maurice? Perhaps Maurice had borrowed money, and Billy was demanding payment? How was Eva Bugayeva involved?

Rod leafed through the reports on his desk. When he reached the middle of the pile he discovered a scrawled note from Jim Munson: 'Think I have him. Drop in and see me.'

Jim was sitting in his shirtsleeves staring at a city wall map. 'I'll say this: when the SMP wants to make a chap's life hell, they're inventive. It's like the bloody army. Privates moan and complain, and their officers have to take it. They don't realise the officers are getting it in the neck from above too. It's a damned filtering system, where the poor bloody Joe in the middle - *me* - is hit by shit from both directions!'

'What's happened?'

'What *hasn't* happened? One of my fellows has been lending money to SMP officers. It happens all the time, of course, but this damn fool complained that one officer hasn't kept up payments. What the hell did he expect *me* to do about it? He's made it official, so now we're an officer down, fired for taking money from subordinates; the Sikh is out, because he shouldn't have lent money, so my rotas are all to cock!'

'But you have found Dalip Singh.'

'I've found a Dalip Singh. He's a friend of one of my men, a reliable chap. He says that Dalip was badly let down by the Wintons. Hard to imagine, I know,' he said cynically, 'but there you are.'

There was a feeble breeze stirring the dust of the street. Crossing the road, a swirl of ochre enveloped him, and he was forced to stand and blink furiously to clear grit from his eyes. The noise was oppressive. Shouting traders, but also beggars displaying sores and festering wounds – a depressing parade. They came here, displaced by war, famine, or simple desperation, and fluttered helplessly, like so many moths, at the beacon of Western plenty. Before long families would sell children, mothers their bodies, and fathers take comfort in pipes of opium.

Rod had almost reached the Peking Road, when he heard the harsh crackle of gunfire, screams, the immediate clatter of broken glass and crockery.

Rod ran towards the shots, drawing his Colt.

It was the Liverpool and Asiatic bank – Alfred Winton's business. Two men gripping bags, one with a revolver, the other a machine pistol. A third stood on an automobile's running board, firing. The robbers ran towards the car, but as they did, a Sikh officer appeared, unslung his carbine and worked the bolt.

The man at the car fired; the Sikh dropped his gun, falling to his knees. But reached out for his carbine.

Seeing the man with the handgun take aim, Rod squeezed off two shots rapid. One or both struck the man, and he fell. The automobile revved, and the man with the Bergmann pelted for it. As he did, the Sikh and Rod both fired. The windows were starred with holes, and that was enough for the driver. Engine racing, the car took off, the man at the running board clinging on for dear life.

Screaming with rage, the man with the Bergmann sprayed bullets at Rod, but the Sikh had his range. He fired once more.

Alice Winton was in the Maloo Road with Eva, studying bolts of silk. One, the colour of straw, matched her hair, and she had almost decided to buy it when the angry hornet sound of a bullet ricochetted through the doorway.

Panic paralysed her. The hairs rose on the back of her neck, and she shivered like a terrified mare.

'Alice, quickly!' Eva shrieked, but she was frozen, just as she had been when, in the darkness, she heard the slow steps approaching her bed. Her eyes widened, and she began panting. She was convinced she must die, as she had been when she had been told to *keep this a secret*, that *it was nothing, only proof of love*. It didn't feel like love when she was left abandoned, sore, and yet unable to weep.

A bullet smacked into the woodwork overhead, and Eva yelped. She grabbed Alice's hand, pulling her down. Alice felt lost. It would have been a relief: one shot to the heart and the pain, the guilt, would be gone.

She had expected her end, and to be deprived of it left her empty.

The two gunmen were some yards apart. Rod took up the pistol and pushed the Bergmann away. Both men were dead. Rod checked their pockets, but in among one man's possessions one thing stood out. A calling card, which held four digits: 1396.

'What is this?' Rod wondered. 'A telephone number?'

## Chapter Twenty-One

The violence left Rod exhausted. In his office, he hung up his hat and pulled off his jacket. It was heavy: he remembered picking up the robber's revolver from outside the bank. He retrieved it now: a short barrelled .38. Swinging out the cylinder, he emptied the chambers. Only two were unfired.

His shirt clung to his back. He tugged off his shoulder holster, emptied the Colt's breech, and removed the magazine. Dully, he remembered the flashes of the machine-pistol, and he could imagine the pain as one of them hit him, the sound like a wet towel slapping a wall. He had heard it so often before. Johnnie had been chatting when the sniper got his measure, and suddenly Johnnie's head was knocked aside, his mouth still moving mid-sentence. Rod didn't understand how he had himself survived.

He was growing maudlin. Better to be busy.

Taking a box of Eley cartridges from his drawer, he reloaded, pressing the shiny brass cases into the magazine, thinking about the bank robber's card. It intrigued him: 1396; they might be from a telephone number, but which district?

Rod filled both magazines, six in each so as not to over-stress the springs, and set them down. That was when he noticed his hand shaking.

It was the nervous reaction. Gunfights took him back to the Front. Once he had lain in a shell hole for a day while Germans attacked. Heavy rain left the shell hole half full of water. A wrist with a clutching hand projected at the farther edge as though grabbing for air, for life. Rod couldn't tell whether it was British or German, only that it seemed to beckon him to death. All the while, bullets and whizz-bangs flew overhead. It was a grey and brown and red day, a day of stormy skies, of mud, of blood, and terror. When darkness fell, he escaped, crawling slowly back to the British trenches.

He was no coward, but by God, he had endured enough. He could do with a pipe. Instead, he shakily unscrewed the lid of his hip flask and gulped down its contents. In a few minutes, his hand was still. He capped the flask and dropped it into his drawer as Bert Shaw walked in.

'I heard you had an exciting morning, old fellow.'

'A pair of bank robbers, both dead.'

'Ah, unfortunate. Would have been good to question them.'

'They were reluctant to be caught!'

'Don't get hot, Rod,' he said calmly. 'I wasn't criticising. I know what it's like when the lead's flying.'

'Sorry. Bit of a short fuse.'

'Not surprising. It's natural to get miffed at daft comments. How are you?'

'I'm fine. It wasn't my first gunfight.'

'Aye. How are things, anyway?'

'I was on my way to see a Sikh,' Rod said, explaining that Dalip Singh lost his job when Foster arrived.

'You think he could have been targeting Foster, then?'

'It's possible. Schreier detests Winton for ruining him - I'm sure he would happily put a bullet in Winton's head – but whoever shot up the car took the time to put two bullets in Foster's head, and wrote "traitor" on his forehead, as well as stabbing his eyes. Why do that, if they were targeting Winton?'

Bert pulled a face. 'It sounds like a gangster's trick.'

'Yes. A hired gunman. But "traitor"?'

'An unconventional writing surface, but not unknown. Might a local gang have a dispute with Winton? He refused them a loan; rejected their demands for protection money? Or his son? Could Maurice owe money to gangsters?'

Rod pulled a face. 'Maurice is the sort of fool who could be involved in almost anything.'

'Will you talk to him?'

'Lord, no! I'm too common to talk to Shanghai nobility. I might ravish their maids.'

'They're probably more worried you'll bugger their hounds. It's your west country accent, old fellow.'

Dalip Singh was cadaverous, taller than Rod, but gave the impression of having shrivelled. At least sixty, he had grizzled hair, a pepper-and-salt beard, and haggard features in a long, mournful face with parchment-like, thin skin. Once he would have cut a fine figure, like the impressive fellows on traffic duty, but that was some time ago.

He took a cigarette and lit it with evident pleasure, coughing at the first bite of smoke and spitting a gobbet of yellow phlegm onto the ground. The spasm exhausted him.

They were sitting outside the room where he lived, in an alley the sun hardly reached. He made a thick brew of army tea, dark and sweet, and they sipped it from piallas, sitting companionably on a bench of rotten, greenish wood.

Rod respected the Sikhs, having served alongside them. After a third coughing fit, Dalip gave a slow smile when Rod enquired about his health. 'I have a cancer. I will be dead before winter.'

'I am sorry.'

He shrugged. 'If you live, you will die. And you?'

'Well enough.'

Dalip Singh looked unconvinced. 'There is a good doctor who helps with maladies.'

'Thank you, but I am well,' Rod said. It was good to see that Dalip Singh was at ease, but that was no reason for him to impute a similar prognosis for Rod. 'What was it like working for the Wintons?'

He looked at Rod with bleary eyes. 'It was hard. I must rise before dawn to wash the automobiles, check the engines, sweep the floors, keep the seats oiled and clean. I was mechanic and chauffeur, but they treated me like a houseboy. I was up late every night, and had to be ready at any moment to drive Mr Alfred - to the Club, office, or somewhere else. I must wait for him, and still I must be up early. To Mr Alfred, I was a part of the car.'

'What was Maurice like?'

'Mr Maurice was kind. He spoke to me as to another human, but his father had no feeling for him, he only cared for Mr Ian. So, Mr Maurice spoke to me and the other servants. He knew his father did not trust him.'

'How did you get the job?'

'I was with the SMP and had an interest in automobiles. Mr Winton's automobile broke down one day and I helped his driver. I could see what the problem was – the carburettor – and mended it. A little later I was told by my sergeant that Mr Winton wanted to thank me. When I went to his office, a secretary gave me twenty dollars and told me Mr Winton would be glad if I would become his chauffeur. That was that.'

'How long were you with him?'

'That was 1912, when he still had the Garford. That was a lovely car. I was still with him in 1919.'

'That was when he said you should go?'

His bloodshot eyes looked away. 'Yes. The man Foster came when Mr Ian was dead. So they gave me a few dollars, and told me to go. Mr Maurice was very sad. He gave me some money.'

'That must have been hard. Did you plan revenge on them?'

'No, never! There are many men less kind. And I wouldn't hurt Miss Alice or Mr Maurice.'

'Have you seen them since you left the family?'

'When he has wanted a driver, Mr Maurice has asked me to drive him.'

'In the Kenworthy?'

'Sometimes, yes. Sometimes, he has borrowed another car for me if Foster was busy, and Mr Maurice wanted a car to impress when he had business to attend to.'

'What sort of business?'

'Buying goods to sell, dealing in property, anything.'

'Whom did he meet?'

'Many people. There was one, a big man, Qian, I think. Others, too, but I don't know who.'

'Qian? Where did you go with him?'

He gave Rod the address. It didn't sound the sort of place Maurice would visit: a run-down factory site in the north-west of Central District.

Rod had to keep busy; not dwell on death. It was unhealthy. Damn, but his hand was shaking again. It was one thing to catch a bullet, quite another to see the slow, predictable horror of cancer slowly eating a man from the inside. In the street he lit a cigarette, sucking the strong smoke into his lungs. Gradually the shaking dissipated and he could continue. Before long, he had reached the street where Foster had died and stood watching the people.

Rod believed Dalip Singh when he said he had no desire to harm Alfred Winton. Dalip was focused on his own impending death. Of the two, Schreier was more likely to want to repay the man he blamed for his downfall. Would he be pleased to see Winton suffer? To see Winton die? In all probability, yes to both. Schreier might have money salted away to pay an assassin, but why have him carve those characters and stab Foster's eyes?

Then again, there were the letters written to Foster. Did she bear his children out of wedlock? Was that the secret he was running from? Many ex-soldiers were running from families and commitments. They settled here with new women, new children. Many wives were allowed to believe that they were widowed, from a sense of bureaucratic compassion.

A paid assassin was more likely hired by Schreier, who had local contacts. Even if he had little money, in Shanghai killers could be found for very little.

A picture sprang into his mind of Maurice and Qian in the automobile. Qian would have contacts; perhaps he could help if a young man needed help removing an embarrassing servant. Maurice certainly didn't seem to like Foster.

And Maurice could have arranged to send Foster down that road where the assassin would be waiting.

## Chapter Twenty-Two

Almost mid-day, and the humidity was so thick every breath felt like inhaling pure water. Sweat soaked his shirt, and he had to open his jacket and flap it to circulate air beneath it.

All hints of the crash had been cleared away. Chinese wheelbarrows, monstrosities with enormous wooden wheels and benches on either side for six people, trundled by; bicycles hurtled past; stolid Chinese ponies trotted; rickshaws rattled. It was a typical Chinese street. Older women hobbled on crippled feet, while men sat and watched with frank disinterest, and children darted about, miraculously avoiding instant death. Occasionally a lorry appeared, blasting horns to move the people aside, drivers waving with angry urgency to clear a path through the hordes.

Rod watched, and as he did so, his lassitude fell away. In Picardy he had occasionally made use of pinch-points against the Germans, and this was perfect for an ambush. People moved in a never-ending stream. There was no passage between the men and women on either side that a car could negotiate with ease. Vehicles must pass around pedestrians. A car like Foster's must slow to a crawl.

Seeing an old man on a stool, Rod recognised the shopkeeper whose shopfront had been destroyed by Foster's automobile. He looked up as Rod approached without recognition. When Rod tried a little pidgin, he stared uncomprehendingly. Rod was about to seek a Chinese officer to translate, when a voice said, 'He shocked after crash. I can help.'

It was the young Chinese woman who had been with the old man that day. She ducked her head respectfully now, but without subservience. In her eyes there was bitter detachment.

'What is your name?'

'You call me Zhou.'

'Thank you. I am a detective with the Shanghai Municipal Police.'

'What you want know?'

'Anything you saw or heard that day - the shooting. Anything your father saw, anything at all.'

'Why? What you do? They destroy shop, destroy our life. But Police here for rich *British*!' This last with great disdain.

'I will find the men who did this.'

'And then they come here kill us.' It wasn't a question.

'No. I will see that you are protected.'

She looked at him with weary disbelief. 'You guard us here?'

'You have to tell me what you saw.'

'Or we be punished,' she snapped. 'So we fear police *and* murderers. Which worse?'

Rod couldn't answer that. At last she shrugged. 'It was after middle of day. Lots of people in road. I hear cries, warning. Then great roaring, like dragon spitting fire, and …'

'That was the gun?'

'I think. There was loud engine, and more roaring, and car came into shop here, causing much damage.'

'What of the man who fired the gun?'

'I see men. One square face, slim, dark suit, grey hat like foreign man, with black and white band; other thin, not so old, suit and hat too. Both standing there,' she said, pointing outside her shop. 'They lean in car, then last *bang, bang*, and walk away.' Her hand fluttered vaguely towards the south. 'Car there. Both get in and drive away. Another man, he get in too.'

'So there were three of them, and all wearing foreign clothes?' Rod said.

'Yes.'

'Did you recognise them?'

'No, no. Just men. *Qing Bang* men.'

Rod felt that like a clutching in his belly. 'Green Gang? Are you sure?'

'I know them. Thin man, he come here, sell opium, demand money to protect shop. What protection?' she added indignantly.

'You are sure they are *Qing Bang?*'

'Yes. They come from French place. Bad men. Demand money, threaten father, beat him one time.'

'Why?'

'He no pay money.'

Rod went to the police box and called Central Station, asking for a translator. Before long a flustered looking translator arrived, dressed smartly in a pale suit with a straw boater. Soon he was firing rapid questions at her, and as she spoke, her father began to interrupt, more and more expressively, until he was shouting and waving his hands, indicating the damage done to his shop and goods, and asking who was going to pay.

After another half hour, Rod closed his notebook. The translator walked out with him.

'What did you think of their story?' Rod said to him.

He was embarrassed and diffident, but Rod didn't need his answer. The girl had been definite. All, she was sure, came from Frenchtown, and they were from the Green Gang.

Rod hailed a rickshaw back to Central Station. To find out more, he must enter the French Settlement, and that would need approval from his superiors as well as from the French.

'Hello, Cottey. I heard you had a little excitement yesterday.'

'Yes,' Rod said. 'And more this morning. Robbers at the Liverpool and Asiatic.'

Dan Fairbairn had arrived in the Far East in 1901 with the Royal Marines, and six years later he joined the SMP. An expert in ju-jitsu, boxing and wrestling, he was also an expert knife-fighter, and had developed his own system of pistol shooting. Now he was responsible for musketry, drill and self-defence, his training methods based on his personal experience on the streets. Although he had the look of a country vicar, with his grey eyes partly hidden behind spectacles, appearances were deceptive.

'You weren't injured?'

'No.'

'Good. Keep it that way,' he said.

'Yes, sir.' In all his experience with Dan Fairbairn, Rod had never felt patronised. Perhaps because Dan Fairbairn respected men who had been involved in 'scrapes', as he called them.

'Let me see your gun,' he said, beckoning with the fingers of his hand. Rod pulled out his Colt. Fairbairn ejected the magazine, racked the slide to empty the chamber, and began to strip the weapon.

'You didn't come here to talk about your escapades.'

'The Kenworthy shot up on Tuesday, sir. Have you had a look at it?'

Fairbairn had removed the bushing and recoil spring, and now peered down the barrel. 'This is disgusting. You haven't cleaned it since the last firing.'

'No, sir. I was wondering whether it was possible that the gunmen were aiming at the driver or a possible passenger in the back.'

'They were aiming for the driver,' Fairbairn said. 'Most of the bullets passed through or near the driver's side, even when the car was perpendicular to his line of fire. Some bullets entered the rear compartment, but they were likely accidents.'

'I see.'

'These machine pistols are concerning. There appears to be a rash of them.' He wrapped a patch of cloth about a rod and pushed it through the barrel, pulling a face at the black deposits.

'The man last night had one, and at the bank robbery today there were two. All Bergmanns.'

'That is worrying. A gangster with a revolver is trouble, but a fellow with a submachine gun is a great deal worse.'

Rod remembered staring down the muzzle of the machine pistol that morning. 'Yes, sir. Was there a case or two inside the Kenworthy? A new recruit, Lane, said that he saw the driver given a *coup de grace* from a Mauser.'

'I'll have a look.'

'And he carved a symbol into the dead man's forehead.'

'What sort of symbol?'

Rod sketched it. 'It says traitor, or something.'

'*Er guizi*.' Fairbairn frowned. 'We had a spate of bodies like that some years ago. Before your time. Their eyes were stabbed as well.'

'The eyes were stabbed on this fellow too.'

'Perhaps a gang war? Someone trying to take over the city? Ask Records. They may have something, but it was a while ago. Unsolved crimes … it may be best to talk to whoever was on the beat at the time.'

Rod nodded. 'Thank you, sir. Oh, did Douglas Hibbard bring a cartridge case for you after last night's shooting?'

'Yes. Mauser brass. You think it could be from the same gun?'

'It would be best to make sure. Oh, and I nearly forgot …'

Rod pulled the revolver from his pocket.

'Where did you get this?' Fairbairn said, swinging out the cylinder and inspecting the chambers.

Rod explained about the morning's bank robbers, while Fairbairn closed the gun and dry-fired it a couple of times. 'Not bad. You should keep this. It would make a good second gun. I'll have a look at it for you.'

'Yes, sir.'

'For now,' Fairbairn muttered, and put Rod's Colt back together again: the barrel in the slide, spring and guide on top, slipping the slide onto the rails, pushing the locking pin into place, pressing the recoil spring plug, turning the bushing to lock it in place, and then giving Rod a meaningful stare.

'I don't expect to see your gun that dirty again,' he said.

Thin Bao was at the restaurant and stood before the table with his head bowed.

'You say the house was raided.'

'Someone wanted to harm the Gang. A competitor.'

'We have no competitors,' Du Yusheng said flatly.

'If a man wished to work an area, he would tell the police of our businesses. He would harm us, and then introduce his own businesses.'

'It would avail him little. We would discover his businesses and close them.'

'A man with contacts in the police might think himself safe.'

Du Yusheng was silent for a moment. Then, 'Do you have any idea who this man might be?'

'No, but I will find him. Whoever took away my gambling house. I will find him.'

'Good. Search him out. Destroy him.'

Rod told Hibbard about his meeting with Dalip Singh and the shop owner.

'It definitely fits with them being with the Green Gang,' he said, striking a match and setting it to his pipe. 'What's your impression?'

'The Green Gang was responsible for killing Foster. He was their target. Someone told him to go down that road, knowing the car must slow to a walking pace. The gunmen had an easy target.'

'So what now?'

'I need to learn where he was going, and why. But I also need to speak to the French Police and ask for their help.'

'You'll be lucky getting those buggers to talk,' Hibbard said, frowning at his pipe. He was weary and distracted, like everyone in the heat. Nobody was immune to the humidity. 'Very well, I will ask for permission to visit Frenchtown, but don't hold your breath.'

'Thank you, sir. One other thing: Dan Fairbairn said the mark on Foster's forehead was something he'd seen before. Do you remember anything about it?'

He frowned. 'Vaguely, now you mention it. It was years ago. I'm not sure we got anywhere with it.'

'Could it be one gang's personal sign?'

'*Traitor*? Seems unlikely. Why Foster? Was he involved in one of the hongs?' He peered narrowly through the smoke. 'What will you do next?'

'Alfred Winton said he had no idea why Foster took the car, but what of the others? Maurice denied knowing where Foster was going – but Edith Winton could have sent him on an errand, and so could the butler.'

Doug pulled a face. 'I vaguely recall you weren't wanted at their house. But if you were to bump into Edith Winton, entirely by accident, that would hardly be your fault, would it? Just bear in mind,' he added, tamping hot tobacco, 'Mr Winton is a powerful man. We don't want to upset him unnecessarily.'

'You could put someone else on the case. Terry O'Toole would charm her, I'm sure.'

Doug eyed Rod balefully. 'Finbar? He has the subtlety of a mastiff. No, I prefer you keep the case for now. Billy boy can wait. Just don't embarrass me if you happen, entirely accidentally, to bump into Mrs Winton - understand?'

Alfred stood when his guest entered. The pain in his chest was back, and he had an urge to cough, but he smothered it, hand outstretched.

Billy Qian was smiling. 'Mr Winton, I am honoured.'

Alfred shook his hand and concealed his shame.

Once they were seated and had ice-cold cocktails, Alfred engaged Billy in small talk. He could not help but notice how the Chinaman gazed around. 'A magnificent restaurant, isn't it?'

Billy nodded, sipping his drink. 'Yes, although the Astor House is in rather better repair.'

'Of course,' Alfred agreed. Most places were better maintained, it was true, but there were only so many places a chap could bring a native for a bite to eat. The Club would never allow Billy Qian through the doors.

When their food arrived, Alfred had to curb his temper when the waiter took an inordinate time to serve their wine. When the waiter finally left, he leaned forward conspiratorially. 'Perhaps we should come to business?'

Billy lifted his glass and snuffed his wine. 'Of course. You wish me to help - how?'

'Short-term liquidity. We have ...'

'You have insufficient capital to cover your debts, and you fear a run on the bank.'

'We have a small difficulty for a couple of months, and I'm sure we'll ...'

'Then the stories are not true?'

'What stories?' Alfred asked. He speared a forkful of fish, but the meal had lost its savour. He put the fork down.

Billy Qian smiled. 'That you are over-extended, your bank is close to collapse, and your entire empire is threatened.'

'Nonsense! The Liverpool and Asiatic is as strong as ever!'

'Really? In that case, a little funding might be possible. But the interest will reflect the perceived risk, of course.'

'How soon could you speak to your colleagues?'

'Oh, in the next day or two.'

Alfred nodded. 'I would be grateful ...' He had been going to say *if you could speak to them today*, but that would only underline his weakness. Besides, Billy Qian knew his position - and if Billy knew, soon everyone in Shanghai would. When it came to business, in the Orient no secret lasted long.

His only comfort was the reflection that if Billy negotiated a loan, it would be in Billy's interests, and those of his backers, to ensure that the Liverpool and Asiatic did not collapse. Because if it did, they would lose all their money.

'There is more to this than I think you realise,' he said hesitantly.

123

## Chapter Twenty-Three

Rod dialled 1396, the number on the card. It rang three times, and then a man answered in the name of a company called Qiexim, a block away from the Bund, and how could he help? Rod took down the company's details. It was a firm involved in import/export. Rod felt that the number from the bank robber's pocket held some other meaning, but for now he could not imagine what it was, if not a telephone number.

He spent the rest of the afternoon in the basement, searching through records for the symbol carved into Foster's head, but there was little to go on, other than occasional references to gangs and battles to control the opium trade. There had been a rash of six bodies, all spread about the banks of the Soochow Creek, apart from one fished from the Whangpoo near the Garden Bridge. That body was assumed to have washed from the creek.

The last report had been written by Sgt. Tim Burton; the corpse was a man called Bao Xiu. Unlike the others, Bao Xiu was a businessman of some status. It was thought that he had refused to pay protection money, but that hardly explained the 'Traitor' carved into his brow.

It was late afternoon. He had spent long enough with files; his head ached. Taking the file, he returned to his desk, where he found a note to say that he had an appointment with Thomas Dubois of the French Garde Municipale at ten thirty the following morning.

The address Dalip Singh had given him, where Billy Qian had taken Maurice, was on the Kweichou Road. Glancing at the clock, he decided to go and see it.

Mickey Hi called him as he was leaving, pattering over urgently. He passed Rod an envelope, and he ripped it open, thinking it was a report on the number he had found in the bank robber's pocket. Instead, he found a note on good quality paper:

*Esteemed Detective Cottey,*

*A mutual friend has given me your name, suggesting that I should speak with you. I am a physician with experience of nervous troubles and have been able to assist many by the use of controlled medicaments. I should be delighted to discuss your situation with you.*

*Yours sincerely*
*Doctor Adil Babu*

Rod was half tempted to throw it at Mickey Hi, but a glance at his well-meaning, anxious face was enough to dispel the urge.

In the street, he studied the note again. The address was in an elegant quarter of the French Settlement, at the Rue du Weikwe, where wide roads were shaded by tall trees, and the coffee and croissants were as good as anything in sight of the Louvre.

Was this a joke? Had someone in the Force given his name to some trickster or fraud? Babu, indeed! It meant 'clerk' in Indian. If so, it was a joke in poor taste. Who could have given Rod's name to Babu? Dalip Singh had mentioned a man who could help Rod, but a doctor in the French Settlement was too expensive for an elderly Sikh. Then a fresh thought hit: had his occasional shakes been noticed by other officers? He felt a slow flush rise at the thought.

Someone may have seen, realised he was shell-shocked, and wanted him to see a doctor. He almost threw the paper away but instead, guiltily, thrust it into his pocket.

Archie gaped. 'There must be some mistake.'

The Sikh held a rifle, and Archie didn't want to test his patience, but this *couldn't* be her house. The wall was big enough for Buckingham Palace, the wrought iron gates massive. The temptation to hop back into the rickshaw was overwhelming, but when the Sikh asked if he was visiting Miss Alice, Archie swallowed his trepidation.

'Yes, I'm here to see her,' he confirmed, and the Sikh waved him on. He was soon rolling along a smooth, flat driveway.

Archie almost ran back to Gordon Road. This couldn't be Alice's home, surely? He took in the tower, the great windows, and when the door was answered, he retreated before the grim butler. There was shouting, and Archie craned his neck as Alice appeared in the doorway. She smiled and he felt his heart melt until Alice's mother appeared beside the butler, eyeing Archie with cold resentment. He helped Alice into the rickshaw, and was relieved to move into the street heading towards the city.

'Your mother didn't seem happy,' Archie said tentatively.

'They can be *so* Victorian, my parents.'

'You should have a chaperone, you mean?'

'It's more that I should not be escorted by a police officer,' she said lightly.

'Why?' Archie said.

'Never mind. Mother is just silly, sometimes.'

'What of your father?'

'Him? He is out at some meeting.'

'He's won't chase me off the grounds with a shotgun, then?'

She looked at him. 'If you were to hurt me, perhaps. He loves me. I am his princess.'

'You're his daughter,' Archie said. 'That's normal, I s'pose.'

'Yes,' she said. A cloud seemed to pass over her, but she shook it off. 'But don't let's talk about my parents. I want to dance! Let's go to the Astor. They have the best dance floor!'

The building in the Kweichou Road was down-trodden. If it had been a dog, it would have been a mongrel with three legs and no owner; it had that kicked-once-too-often look.

This was a rough area. A block north was the British Gaol, which Shanghai proudly boasted was the largest prison in the world; the gas works were north west. This was not an area visited by polite company.

Billy Qian was fond of showing off his wealth - this wouldn't impress a client. What would Billy want here, and why bring Maurice? There was no scent of burning opium, only coal and cooking fires. This was no opium den - perhaps it was devoted to gambling, or prostitution? Rod knocked, but the only response was a loud squeaking from a loose shutter overhead.

*Friday 28th July, 1922*

The French Concession bordered the International Settlement at the Yangjingbang creek. After checking his rickshaw had licences for both the International Settlement and the French Territory, Rod rode down the Khiangse Road, and crossed the border into the Petit Rue as far as the Rue du Consulat, where the functional but elegant Gendarmerie building stood.

From the first, when the International Settlement was formed, France had held herself separate. Even now the French were determined to remain independent. French Shanghai had its own *gendarmerie*, imperial administration and system of regulation. Whereas the International Settlement remained independent of China and the British Empire, the French territories were fully absorbed into France. Moving from the International Settlement zone was crossing the border. Were Rod to cross into the Chinese territories that surrounded the International Settlement, he would need paperwork, and be forced to give up his pistol. At least visiting Frenchtown there was none of that.

He paid off the rickshaw. It was muggy, and any exertion made a man break into a sweat. French officers stood chatting at the doorway, looking cool in their uniforms. Rod felt positively grubby in his linen suit and panama hat.

A helpful officer directed him, and soon he was in the office of Thomas Dubois, a whip-thin man of thirty or so. He was five feet ten, with dark hair cut smartly. His face was narrow with high cheekbones, and his wide-spaced eyes had heavy bags. From his upper lip a mournful moustache drooped like a damp flag on a windless day. Although he bore a world-weary, dejected air, he was smartly turned out and bore himself like a soldier. He had a habit of thrusting his cigarette between his lips with his hand cupping the end, the tip hidden from sight.

'You were in the trenches?' Rod said.

He nodded. 'You smoke?' he asked. Rod took one gratefully. It was short and stubby, and he inhaled the Turkish tobacco with pleasure.

'It is four years since I last tasted this,' he said.

'Picardy?'

'Yes. You?'

'Verdun.'

Dubois nodded pensively, then reached into a drawer. Pulling out two glasses, he poured generously from a bottle of Armagnac. 'To lost comrades.'

'To life,' Rod said. They saluted each other with their glasses and sipped. Neither would discuss the war. That was the curse of the men who lived through it: none wanted to remember their experiences, yet none could escape them.

At last Thomas stirred himself. 'I have been asked to assist you,' he said. 'Please, tell me how I may help.'

Rod said took a deep lungful of the fragrant smoke and let it dribble from his nostrils. It felt heavenly. 'The chauffeur of Alfred Winton has been killed.'

Dubois sniffed. 'The taipan of the Liverpool and Asiatic?'

'You know of him?'

His face grew longer. 'We keep our attention on many businessmen. During the War, he was involved in transactions we did not approve of.'

'What do you mean?'

'Winton took investments, such as shares in German companies making guns. It struck my colleagues as curious that a man would seek to give advantage to his country's enemies. But he made much money.'

Rod sat back with surprise. 'His own son died in the War.'

He recalled Schreier mentioning investments in Krupp, saying that Winton had taken everything. Suddenly Schreier's hatred for Winton seemed less extreme. Rod had faced Krupp steel often enough. How did Winton feel, knowing his own son was killed by weapons from which he had profited.

'Yes, so we have kept an eye on Monsieur Winton,' Dubois said.

Rod stubbed his cigarette in the ashtray, the base of an artillery shell case. 'The men who shot him were from the Qing Bang, I hear.'

'This is serious, if true,' Dubois said.

Rod felt convinced that Dubois would not help. He was a bureaucrat. This was not an affair to help a man's career. Rod wanted to say it was not in the interests of France to harbour murderers, when Dubois barked an order. A clerk scurried in.

'Let us see my Comprador,' he said.

He took Rod down interminable corridors, up some stairs, and into a different office.

Inside was a Chinese, about 55, dressed in a tunic with black satin cap. A comfortable-looking man, his round face was scarred by smallpox. Although his expression was amiable, his eyes were cool.

He ushered them inside, settling his guests before perching behind a broad desk. A servant brought jasmine tea, and the three engaged in the polite routine: pouring, sipping, small talk. Dubois had the military impulse to crack on and not waste time – but to do so would insult Huang Jinrong. That would affect the help they would receive. So they sat and enquired after his family, his children, and the workings of his detective organisation.

Huang Jinrong spoke in French. After Rod's time in Picardy he could understand much of what was said, although his accent was difficult. 'Since the War, with the ban on opium, smugglers work ever more diligently. We have been hard pressed, especially with manpower shortages. But we have caught many criminals. This year alone we have caught over a hundred.'

Dubois told Rod that Huang Jinrong had been promoted to Chief Superintendent of the Sûreté, and his efforts were praised throughout the city. At last they could discuss the reason for their meeting. The Chief Superintendent listened with an expression of mild curiosity, his hands in his lap, while Rod explained about Foster, frowning at the atrocity. When he heard that Green Gang members had been involved, he leaned forward earnestly.

'Three men, you say?' he mused, fixing Rod with an intense gaze.

'Yes. Armed with Bergmann machine pistols.'

Dubois made a sound of disgust. 'Those things are everywhere! I lost a Chinese officer two weeks ago to one. Chief Superintendent, do you have any idea who these men could be?'

There was a sharpness to his voice, the anger of a policeman on hearing of an atrocity apparently perpetrated from within his own territory.

Huang Jinrong stared at the wall between Dubois and Rod, perplexed.

'There are three or four who could know of such men. It is most unfortunate, but the population are mutinous and some grow restless. Since the overthrow of the Emperors, fighting has dispossessed many, and some will resort to theft or murder. Some younger fellows see men with vast wealth, and women clad in furs worth many francs, and they grow jealous.'

'We don't care what motivated them, only who was responsible,' Dubois said.

'If they are here in the French Concession, we will find them,' Jinrong said imperturbably.

'I am very grateful,' Rod said, and rose and shook his hand.

Back in his own room, Dubois graciously refused one of Rod's cigarettes. 'Since I was gassed in the War,' he explained, 'my doctor recommends that I smoke only Turkish and Syrian tobacco. The flavours are more soothing for the lungs.'

Rod lit Dubois' cigarette before holding the match to his own. 'May I ask a question?'

'But of course.'

'I felt you disliked your Chief Superintendent, but he appeared helpful.'

Dubois smiled. 'You are observant. During the War, the Gendarmerie was stripped of our young men. Many never returned. So, like you British, we recruited. There were many races whom we could have employed, but the Annanese were keen. However the recruits could not converse with the locals. We tried to teach them, but it did not work. So we learned from the businesses and employed Compradors, men who would liaise with the Chinese and translate.'

'Yes.'

'The Compradors were often corrupt. For many, it mattered little. Their businesses grew; what did it matter if their partner waxed with the business? However, with matters of law and justice, this system concerns me.'

'Why?'

'Suppose your assassins were found, but a policeman demanded money to pursue their case? If the assassins agreed, for example, to pay a hundred Taels in exchange for dropping charges, losing evidence, or finding an alibi, such a man might irreparably harm justice without ever putting himself in any danger.'

'We have the same problem.'

'I must be sure that the men he sets to finding the criminals are reliable. I would not like to think our officers accept bribes to set them free. It is one thing to help a business contract a deal, but quite another to allow a murderer to go free because he bribes a police officer.'

'Are your arrests and convictions falling?'

Dubois shook his head. 'No. Our arrests are increasing every year. Everything appears well.'

'But you feel something is amiss?'

'Yes. I have the hunch. You know this feeling, when things are not right? I have that feeling.'

## Chapter Twenty-Four

Leaving the Sûreté, Rod's feet took him along the Rue du Weikwe. It was a broad boulevard, and he smoked a casual cigarette, watching the building.

Doctor Babu was doing well. His building was clean, freshly painted, and the windows sparkled. Purple and crimson flowers abounded on the first floor balcony, and Rod watched a number of well-to-do women enter the blue front door, each leaving some twenty minutes later.

Rod stared at the note again. His initial annoyance replaced by professional interest: who had asked the doctor to write to him? And why?

He crossed the street and made his way to the blue door with its gleaming door brass knocker. A pretty maid in starched French nurse's uniform admitted him. She guided him with many a smile and duck of her head, to a room at the rear. A pair of armchairs sat at a small, round table, and she indicated that he should take his seat before bowing her way from the room.

It was fully ten minutes before a small Indian gentleman entered. He was slim, and wore round metal-framed spectacles which made his eyes look enormous. Smiling, he held out his hand.

'I am sorry to have kept you waiting,' he said, waving a hand at the seats.

'You wrote to me.'

'Yes, Detective. It seemed natural to try to help you.'

The maid returned, holding the door wide. A houseboy walked in with a silver tray, on which were teacups and saucers, two pots, and a number of dainty cakes. These were set out upon the table, and the two departed.

'Why?'

'Detective, your manner is agitated, and I can see indications of anxiety. I would not term them severe as yet, but it is clear that you underwent traumatic events while you were a soldier. And these have had an effect upon you.'

'Such as?'

He set about pouring tea, speaking briskly. 'The nervous energy of your left hand, which shakes, the left leg which is even now bobbing up and down. You are still suffering from the War.'

Tea poured, he sat back. 'Your eyes are sunken. You have the look of a man who is enormously tired, and your general demeanour is that of one who is on edge. When there is a loud noise, such as a vehicle driving past the apartment, you flinch.'

'I was in the War, yes. But I am fine.'

'I speak as a doctor: there are medications that can assist you,' he said. 'May I?'

Rod submitted to his ministrations. Compared with his experiences in military hospital, the doctor was gentle. He felt Rod's pulse, listened to his chest, and gave him a thorough examination. At last he sat back and studied the detective. 'Yes, you have been affected, but you are also in the early stages of malaria, I think. No matter, I can assist you.'

He withdrew, returning a little later with a syringe. Swabbing Rod's forearm, he tied a cord about the bicep, raised the vein, and slipped the needle in.

In no time Rod felt a luxurious happiness. Well-being and comfort filled him.

'This will help,' the doctor said, and smiled.

Rod returned to Central Station alert and confident, to find a note from Wattie Brookes. He took the stairs to the locksmith's sanctum. 'Well, Wattie?'

'Oh, it's you.'

'I only just found your note.'

'Been out in the sun, eh, while others do your dirty work for you?' Wattie said. He ungraciously accepted a cigarette, and disappeared into the storage room, returning carrying the box.

'Here you are. No idea what 'alf this stuff says,' he muttered, wafting smoke from his eyes. 'There're letters and things, and a lot of chits.'

Rod carried the trunk to his office. It seemed disrespectful to go through the man's private correspondence with Wattie watching.

At his desk once more, he opened the lid. He was confronted by an army cap, upside-down, inside which was a photo of Foster and other men. One was Ian Winton, seated in the middle. Foster sat cross-legged in front of him. The other men looked cheerful enough, officers and NCOs, some sheepish, others self-conscious. All were appallingly young.

Beneath the photograph were medals. First was a British War Medal, with the familiar face of the King on the silver front; the second an Allied Victory Medal. Both were allocated for service, not necessarily gallantry. There was also a Military Medal, so he had served under fire.

Underneath the cap were letters bound together with a blue ribbon. Under them were chits from bars and cabarets. Glancing through them, he murmured, 'You've been living well, Foster, my boy.'

Much of life in Shanghai was conducted on the system of chits. Whether a man went to a bar, to a club, a restaurant, a cobbler's or a tailor's, he would not have to provide cash. Instead he would scrawl his name on a scrap of paper, a chit, which would be added to his account. Once a month there would be a reckoning, and the bill presented. Usually, to prevent confusion, the customer would write his name after signing, but for good clients there was no need. It mattered not a whit what the purchase was, whether it was a pair of shoes, a meal, or a woman down the Line, the same system operated. The only exception tended to be the rickshaw operators, who worked for cash. They could not survive without it.

These chits showed a life high on the hog. A few of the bills were high enough to make Rod whistle. It was more than he could afford on *his* meagre salary. Perhaps Alice subsidised Foster's dancing, and these chits were for evenings where he had squired her? The chits from hotels – could he have seduced Alice? In the Astor House? It didn't seem likely. There would be too many people who would recognise her. It was one thing to dance in a ballroom where people may leave her in peace, but if they saw her taking a man to a room, that would cause a huge stink. It didn't seem likely.

And then he found the last piece of paper.

It was not a chit, but the bill for an evening's entertainment, and for an astonishing amount of money: one thousand seven hundred dollars. It suggested Rod's assumption that Alice might have helped Foster with his expenses was wide of the mark, because this was from Gracie Gale's establishment. Rod doubted that Alice would have subsidised Foster's activities in Gracie's house of pleasure.

Setting the chits aside, Gracie Gale's bill on top, Rod looked at the other items.

The letters had been neatly tied with a perfect bow. He removed the bindings and began to read.

They were written in a neat hand which had smudged in places, as though the writer had been weeping. All appeared to come from a lady called Pamela Gray, who was pleading with her man to return. But she was addressing her 'darling James'. She was 'bereft' without him, she 'longed' for his warm arms about her, and much more. She did not mention children, Rod noted. Foster had given this woman a false name, not mentioned his own wife or children ... What sort of woman would have been taken in by him?

Pamela Gray seemed well-educated, with regular, neat writing. Rod was suspicious of graphologists who claimed to be able to tell a person's character from their handwriting. Many flawed people had superb handwriting, in his experience. However, this was plainly a well-to-do women. A worker in a munitions factory would be unlikely to achieve this quality of writing.

Leaning back in his seat, he read the letters. From their dates, 'James' had enjoyed this woman's company for over two years. She commented on his dancing, which, having seen Foster dancing with Alice Winton, Rod could easily understand, but other details surprised him:

'Darling James, I so enjoyed the Savoy...' one began, while another mentioned 'Our wonderful evening at Frolics', and added 'We must return to Claridge's for cocktails', before giving a lengthy description of his better qualities. 'I know, darling, that you often feel so down since you heard about your father. You must not allow his behaviour to trouble you so.' Then, later in the same letter, 'Even if he did the things you say, you must think of your men, not the undeserving, but those who depend upon you.' Those words gave Rod pause. The man had let her believe that he was an officer when he was merely a soldier-servant.

Rod stared at the letters. Foster had married Eleanor White. With meagre leave from the Front, he had seduced another woman? How? Admittedly, some men could charm a woman into bed in moments. That had been especially true during the War, when many women sought to comfort those returning to battle. Foster must have enjoyed the favours of Pamela Gray while being married to Eleanor, from the dates.

Pamela Gray's first was dated August '16, when Foster was newly recruited. She wrote cautiously, hinting at a husband, although nothing too open. It was a polite, refined letter, a note to a friend, not a lover. Subsequent letters were equally polite – almost evasive, as though she was aware of the risk that they could be discovered. But then they changed.

In early '17 she grew more emotional. She was a 'passionate woman', she said, and despaired of life without him; she must die without him. 'If only, my darling heart, I had not married. I would be free to live with you, to love you. Sometimes I think I should be so happy, were I to hear that George were dead. Do not think badly of me. It is only my love for you. You surely feel the same for me.'

Rod felt a squirming in his belly and pushed the letters aside, disgusted. Foster was prepared to break hearts without compunction. It struck him that Alice was fortunate to have escaped his clutches. She too was educated; she too was refined. If he had set his claws into her, she might not have enjoyed a happy outcome.

Why had Foster kept these letters? Was this conquest a matter of pride? Were the letters a mark of victory, like notches in a sniper's rifle, one for every life ended?

He collected the papers and returned them to the tin, keeping only the bill from Gracie's. That exorbitant sum; he couldn't imagine how Foster could have run up such a debt.

There was only one way to find out. He folded the paper into his pocketbook and pulled on his jacket.

The bordello was warming up. Gracie was entertaining Frank in the small sitting room when she heard the knock at the door, and while she spoke, she listened with half an ear.

Gracie enjoyed this time of the evening. There was an amiable bustle everywhere, like a department store just before opening. Her girls moving about, while servants hurried hither and thither, bringing dresses, trays of drinks, sweeping the last vestiges of dust from carpets and mantlepieces, arranging flowers artfully in their vases. If the King himself was coming to visit, they couldn't have been harder at work.

It was a good life, a good business. And all her own effort. Gracie had a right to feel proud. Just now she was sipping a watered brandy, part-way through a dirty anecdote which had Frank laughing uproariously.

She looked up with annoyance to see Rod. She was with a client, and didn't want interruptions.

He had the good manners to apologise, at least. 'I am sorry, Miss Gale,' he said. 'If you don't mind, could I take a moment of your time?'

She gave him a long, cold stare before turning to her guest. 'Frank: would you mind if I was to leave you for a little, honey?'

Mild irritation passed over his features, which was good. He was not a high-rolling client, and Gracie didn't want him thinking he could monopolise her. Perhaps a little break wouldn't be such a bad thing. Frank was useful, but she didn't want him to get to thinking he was all *that* important. She picked up her glass, and walked to her office. There, she fixed Rod with a look of freezing displeasure.

'Detective, I do not appreciate being interrupted in my business.'

'Your client ...'

'Frank Dewitt is my *lawyer*. He's here to discuss business,' she lied. She was not going to give a cop a list of her clients. 'However, other clients want to feel they can come here and unwind, and a detective isn't good for business. What's this about? I said I'd tell you if I got something on the girl.'

'I know, but then I found this,' Rod said, and presented her with the bill. 'I wondered whether you'd tell me about it?'

'Where'd you get this?' she asked coolly, although she felt it should burn her hands. *Shit! If the flatfoot knew of this, so would the whole of Shanghai before long.*

'What can you tell me about it?'

'I can tell you anything I want,' she snapped. No, she had to keep her cool. 'What I will say is ...' She took a long pull of brandy. 'Sure, he ran up a big tab. And he hasn't paid for it. But he will.'

'He can't pay you now.'

'What do you mean?'

137

The flatfoot looked at her sharply, and she felt a stab of concern. 'He's dead. You must know that?'

Gracie felt her mouth fall open with shock. 'Dead? When was this?'

'Tuesday, of course.'

'But I saw him … Who're you talking about?'

'Foster, of course!'

Good God, that was a relief! She gave a chuckle, picking up her glass. 'I'm sorry, we're talking at cross purposes.'

He said, 'You mean … It wasn't Foster, then?'

Gracie felt like laughing. The poor sap was crestfallen. 'You think I'd let a servant come and enjoy that kind of service? Should I invite some coolies as well? This is a place of love, Officer, and love here is green. No dollar, no service.'

'Who did you think I meant?'

She wagged an elegant finger. 'Uh, uh, no names, Detective. What happens in Gracie's stays here, remember? But my vow of silence only holds so far. I don't like men who welch on me. This guy hosted a party, and I allowed him to have what he wanted. There were lots of his friends, and they all wanted entertaining. Where else would they go in this city? But when I gave him the bill at the end of the month, he dickered. Said they'd not spent that much, hadn't drunk that much, said the girls weren't worth it … So in the end, well …'

'You gave up on over a thousand dollars owed to you?'

'I didn't say that, now did I? I have many rich and powerful men come here, Detective. I'm not about to give you their names any more than I'd give you their sexual preferences. That's why I have a good business. If they heard I'd peached on one of them, my clients would stop coming.'

Rod replaced the note in his pocketbook. 'So will you get your money, do you think?'

She sipped brandy. That, she knew, was important, but not the real question. The serious point was, whether others heard that someone had got away with stiffing her. If she got a reputation for being easy to bilk, she might as well shut up shop. 'It's not enough to hurt me, it's just the thought that the scheming polecat tried to pull one over. Well, what the hell. He may get a surprise yet.'

## Chapter Twenty-Five

Thin Bao was furious. He had lost face before Du Yusheng, and he wanted whoever was responsible.

Last night he had spoken with the waiters and the barman, and all he had learned was that one of the waiters had an addiction to gambling. When he pressed the barman for more information, the man was slow to respond, until Thin Bao brought his hammer down on the man's thumb, then his finger. Then he became talkative.

'Yes! Yes! Yao Shihui has problems. He asked me where he could go for good gambling!'

'Who is Yao Shihui?'

'A friend, that's all,' the barman said, trying to pull his hand away. The throbbing from his smashed thumb was so intense, it felt as if his hand had been thrust into a fire. 'A friend.'

The hammer rose again. 'You told him about my cabaret?'

'I thought he would bring you money,' the man said brokenly. 'He gambles hugely, always loses.'

Thin Bao nodded. 'You cost me my cabaret.'

'I thought I was helping!'

'He went to the police, you think?'

'No! Yes! I don't know! All I know is, he asked about a cabaret where he could make good his losses, and I said yours was good because I worked there.'

'But he never came?'

'No!'

Thin Bao stared at him, unmoving. And then he brought the hammer down onto the man's hand, once, twice, a third time, and luckily before the fourth, his victim passed out.

Gracie sat still as a gecko watching a tempting fly. Her face wore the sort of poisonous expression that would make a man retreat. But then, like spray wiped from a windscreen, it passed.

'I must get back to Frank. I'll see you out, Detective.'

Rod walked behind her. She did not speak, remaining deep in thought. At the door she nodded to him, and hesitated.

'Listen, Officer. I doubt I'll get my money back, but he'll pay. If I were you, I'd get to the cathedral on Sunday. It's going to be a good service, so I've heard.'

With that, she chuckled and returned to her client. Rod took his hat from the waiting servant, and set it at a jaunty angle. He could hear the rumble of their voices, but Frank Dewitt and Gracie were speaking in such low tones that he couldn't catch their words. Besides, the Sikh at the door was giving him the sort of look his ancestors gave the redcoats at Chillianwallah. Rod took the hint and left.

It was growing late, and he headed towards the Bund. The great road that followed the side of the river was filling with night-time revellers.

There were three warships anchored, and dozens of coasters and freighters. A never-ending parade of coolies walked up gangplanks empty-handed and returned, bent almost double under the weight of bales and sacks, or striding carefully with yokes about their shoulders and unimaginable weights slung from both ends. It was a source of astonishment that such small, undernourished frames could carry so much. They looked thin and pathetic, and yet they laboured like Trojans, and all for two meagre bowls of rice a day. Rod felt a deal of sympathy for them. In some ways they reminded him of the men with whom he had served, trudging onwards, never certain what would greet them, but accepting their fate.

Trams rattled and squeaked past as he walked to the Community Gardens, where he stood smoking a cigarette. A light breeze made a pretence of cooling him. At least the sweat dried a little.

He had a memory of another day in the sun, lying with Cecily in the pasture behind Furnshill, enjoying the early April sunshine, while the birds sang and the breeze made the grass dance. They kissed, swearing eternal love for each other.

But then Dick died.

It had seemed impossible that any Germans could have survived. The barrage had gone on forever. While they prepared there was nervousness, yes, but also confidence. When the whistles blew, they sprang up, keen to get it over with, and at first there was no difficulty. The front trenches had been beasted by German artillery, and the men gathered in the communication trench behind, then formed up in the open land. It wasn't until they breasted the hill and began to scramble down the farther side that they were caught.

One of the first to fall was Captain Martin. Rod knew him slightly. The night before, when he had briefed the others about the assault, he had predicted that they would be hit right there. He had studied the land, and knew that if the artillery barrage missed that one bunker, it would be perfectly placed to cut them down. His forecast proved all too accurate. As they set off towards Mametz, that gun opened up. Captain Martin dropped like a shot rabbit, and Rod saw Dick run to him, only to collapse in his turn.

Rod wanted to go to him, but he couldn't. He was in command. The men needed him. He had to leave Captain Martin, Dick, and the others. They had objectives to reach.

Ethel never forgave him for living when Dick had died. And although Cecily tried not to blame Rod, she found it hard to reconcile his return with her brother's death.

Good God, he found it hard enough himself. He stood, watching the sluggish waters pass by the great steamers and warships, thinking of the girls and his friend. He saw Dick's face in the water, then Captain Martin's, and the faces of the men who served under him. All dead. All accusing.

Rod flung away his cigarette and went to Dan Bailey's.

After disposing of Frank Dewitt, Gracie fitted a smile to her lips and sailed around the room dispensing good will and the occasional lewd comment. She looked serene, but her mind was fixed on that debt.

Some men believed that they were immune from risk. They were so confident that they thought they could take from anyone and no one could touch them.

Well, some were right. She knew that — but Gracie had her own determination: not to be taken for a mug, not to be thought a feeble woman whom men could use and discard without danger. She'd endured enough of that back home in 'Frisco, and she would be damned if some Limey loan-shark would stiff her over a bill that size. Arriving here on the Bund, she had realised that this city offered opportunities she couldn't dream of back home. Better, she thought, to set up an exclusive establishment, hire the very best women, those with the looks and carnal inventiveness to exhaust a regiment of Casanovas, dress them in top European and American fashion, and then sit back and watch the money roll in. She had enjoyed her success. She would not allow one bloodsucker to destroy it. Rather, she would destroy him in front of his peers.

'Let's see how you enjoy that, Mr Winton,' she breathed.

Dan was as dapper as ever, wearing a green silk waistcoat and cravat, and when he greeted the policeman with a 'Good evening, darling, I'm so glad to see you,' it was almost convincing. 'Old Fashioned?'

Rod nodded. As he did, he saw Bert Shaw at a table. Dan nodded his head towards him. 'He needs someone to talk to.'

There is a posture which is rarely seen except in bars where there is steady drinking going on. Bert had both elbows on the table. His right hand held his glass, his wrist bent, the rum dangling from thumb and forefinger. Every so often, he would lower his head to the glass's rim and tilt it slightly to sip.

'What's happened?' Rod said.

'He came in like that. You know how it is.'

He did. Occasionally a policeman would have enough. The long hours, the dangerous work, the poor pay — all took their toll. Even a man like Bert, who had survived the Somme, had a limit to the additional strain he could tolerate. Rod took up his drink, the ice tinkling merrily on the glass. 'Give me one for him, Dan. I'll see what the matter is.'

'Don't get him angry,' Dan warned.

'I won't. He won't shoot up the bar,' Rod promised, but he walked cautiously nonetheless.

A man on his intake had been ejected from the Force when it was discovered that he liked nothing more, when drunk, than to hurl chairs about the Mess. As the doctor wryly noted, 'I am not convinced that a man who will fling furniture without provocation is the sort of man we should arm with a pistol.'

So many were damaged. Some, like Rod, pushed it to the back of their minds. It came out, sometimes. A chance meeting, a sharp noise, a scent, anything could grip him, and suddenly he was back in a trench or No Man's Land, cowering in a shell hole, hands over his head, while bullets rattled about him.

'How are you, old cock?' Rod said, placing the drinks on the table.

Bert looked up, eyes bleary. For an instant Rod wondered whether he had been smoking opium, but that wasn't Bert's kind of vice.

'Hello, Rod, old sport. How're things, eh?'

He was slurring, but Rod reckoned he was unlikely to get violent. Some drinkers can erupt for no apparent reason, but Rod had never seen that in Bert. He had the impression Bert was filled more with grief than rage.

'Bad day?' Rod said.

'Could say that. Remember Mark Senior? Chap with the fair hair?'

Rod nodded. 'He was on the ship with us.'

'Yes. Big man, brave as a lion. Strong. Courageous.'

Rod did remember: a tall man, six feet two or three, the sort to whom mothers would run with a coo, hoping their daughters might win him. Handsome and genial, he could charm nectar from flowers with a smile.

'He had a letter from his girl. Said she wasn't going to wait any longer. So he took his revolver and blew his brains out.'

'Oh, good God!'

'Hell of a mess. Had to deal with a similar once ... God, that was horrible. Foul little room. After the shot, anyway.' He gave a twisted grin. 'A Webley to the head redecorates most effectively.'

'Who was that?'

'Officer in my Regiment. Damn fool. A few weeks before the Armistice, he decided he couldn't cope any longer. Like Senior.' He moodily sank a half inch of rum. 'Senior left a note explaining, with an addressed envelope. Asked it be sent to her - but I don't think she'd want it. Not with half his brains on it. Think she'd want that?'

'No.'

'Nor me. Poor bastard!' he tilted his glass towards his mouth, and realised it was empty. 'Get me another, could you, old chap? Oh, you did! Capital.'

He raised it in mock salute and resumed his pose, tipping the glass at his mouth. 'Always girls who hurt the most, isn't it? A chap can see friends blown to pieces and cope, but when a woman steals your heart, that's it. They play with your affections, get you to dream of them, get you to weave them into the fabric of your soul, and then they ditch you. It's the hardest thing, losing a woman.'

'Did you?'

'Me?' he gave a harsh bark of a laugh. 'No, it was t'other way about, old man.'

'You gave her the heave-ho, then?'

'I chucked her, just as I chucked everything that was good and pure. Because when your life is a lie, there's little else to do. Unless you copy Mark. Gun to the head, *boom*!' he held two fingers of his left hand to his temple and mimed firing.

'That's no escape,' Rod said. 'It only gives others more misery.'

'What "others"? It's a way out, that's all. A way to escape the relentless reality of working all hours, getting treated like a baboon, and for what? The sort of money a waiter would sniff at in London.'

'In London I couldn't afford a decent Old Fashioned,' Rod said, trying to lighten his mood.

'They serve a perfectly acceptable one at the Ritz,' Bert said.

'I wouldn't know,' Rod said with a smile. He had never been there: the prices were officers only, not Other Ranks or recently promoted but impoverished soldiers.

'What I wouldn't do to be back in London,' Bert muttered. He sipped, but ice caught his lip, and rum was sent down his chin. 'Blast! Can't even drink straight any more!' he muttered, dabbing his face with a handkerchief.

'Come along, old cock,' Rod said. 'Let's get you home, eh?'

'Home?' he looked up with eyes full of hope, which soon faded. 'Oh, you mean the Barracks?'

Dan called a servant to help. With an arm over each of their shoulders, Rod and he half-carried, half-dragged Bert into the street. Before long Rod and he were in a rickshaw trotting towards Gordon Road. The familiar old red-brick building loomed over the complex of barracks, parade ground, armoury and administrative buildings.

Like all recruits, Rod had lived there when he first arrived. Waking up to a steaming cup of tea, finding his bed made every evening, his shirts ironed, his boots polished, was a curious pleasure. The lessons: Shanghai law, the boundaries of SMP responsibility, weapons training, Chinese, were as fresh as if they had been only last week rather than two years before. He stood gazing at the building until a retching sound reminded him why he was there. In the hallway he found a servant to help manhandle Bert to his room. It was horribly spartan: there was little beside the bed, table, wardrobe and chest of drawers, rather like a priest's cell.

'Will you be all right?' Rod said.

Bert had tumbled onto his bed and lay with an expression of disgruntled confusion.

An eye opened. 'Did you get the drinks in, old man?'

In the rickshaw again, as they turned from Gordon Road into Bubbling Well, Rod saw another rickshaw approach from the opposite direction and, seeing the passengers were foreign, Rod automatically raised his hand to his hat's brim. But when he recognised Alice and Archie, his hand fell away.

It was nothing to do with Rod. Alice and Archie were old enough to make their own mistakes; but he was struck with unease. He hoped Archie would not fall too heavily for her; he couldn't shake the idea that she was dangerous. There was something unnatural about her, something in her reserve and her callous unconcern about Foster's death.

He was still thinking about Archie and Alice when he reached his apartment.

It wasn't much. There were two rooms: a parlour, and a bedroom leading from it. He took it because it was not far from Central Station, it was moderately clean, it was cheap, and it wasn't the barracks. He poured a small whisky from his dwindling stock and took off his jacket, emptying his pockets. As he took out his notebook, he remembered he still had the reckoning from Gracie Gale. He pulled it out and spread it on his table.

It was a simple sheet of paper that listed transactions. This would have been sent to the man who had incurred the debt, and would have been collated from the chits. Each chit noted individual drinks ordered, each meal or snack, the girls whose company had been enjoyed, and had a signature confirming that the client accepted the charge. When paid it would be dated and signed. But this was not signed or stamped, and it was two months old.

Gracie had thought he was talking about another man. That was plain from her shock when he said the fellow was dead.

She wasn't thinking of a chauffeur, she was thinking of a man with money and influence. Yet Foster had acquired the man's bill.

Why?

There many possibilities, but one stood out: blackmail. Foster had taken advantage of at least two women. That did not necessarily make him a blackmailer, but it did point to a fault in his character. If he could misuse women who put their trust in him, surely demanding money from someone else wasn't much of a leap. His victim would want to silence him — paying him off or using more permanent means. In which case, the matter of to whom the chit belonged might be the key to Foster's death.

Suppose Foster had threatened to expose the man's activities - would it have worked? After all, every man and wife in Shanghai knew what went on at 52 Kiangse Road, and at 53, and all the other numbers down the Line, come to that. Rod once heard of a shipping magnate who regularly used a brothel. When a clerk was fired, for revenge he visited the magnate's wife, and told her. She said quietly, 'I know. And I sleep well, knowing how much he is worth.' Many wives felt the same. They tolerated their husbands' infidelities in the same way that they tolerated their drunkenness. With resignation.

Would a woman be surprised, were she to learn that her husband was playing fast and loose with the girls at Gracie Gale's house? Rod wondered. It would reflect badly on her in the expat community, were she to leave her husband. Better by far to pretend nothing happened. If her husband was visiting prostitutes, his wife was probably aware. Threats of exposure would carry little weight.

Another aspect struck him. Gracie Gale had not been paid, and it was plain as the nose on her face that she did not think the man responsible had died. Maybe she still hoped to be paid. If that was the case, the client must have been sure that he was safe. After all, Gracie Gale was a determined woman. She might embarrass a defaulting debtor.

He finished his whisky. It had been a long day. Whatever it was that Dr Babu had given him was wearing off. His head was hurting from all the speculation.

Rod went to bed.

# Chapter Twenty-six

*Saturday 29th July, 1922*

Rod was in the office early. His head hurt, but by six thirty he had cleared much of the dross and could concentrate on Foster's letters and the bill.

It occurred to him that there must be a reason why one set of papers had been on Foster's bedside table when others were in the tin box. Was it the most recent chits had not been filed? No: looking through them, some of the tin box chits were from the last couple of weeks before his death. Those on the table had been from a similar period. So, if the papers were not differentiated by age, what separated those which went in the tin box from those which were left out?

Rod recalled the way that drawers had been left agape. Only a little, it was true, but he would have expected a military man to be more tidy. Everything in its place, that was the soldierly way. Because Foster's room was messy, Rod assumed he was a messy person. But his garage was spotless. Leaving the papers on his bedside table seemed out of character. Rod would have expected them to be filed.

What if someone had gone to his room to search it – the drawers had been disordered, his papers rifled. Why? Whoever went through the drawers had not found the tin box where Thomas kept the things that mattered most to him. Letters from his lover, the bill from Gracie Gale and other papers. If they were held together, perhaps all were important?

Rod went through the chits again. Those loose were for cleaning, a couple of drinks, a shirt. Of those in the box, six were for hotel rooms, always for one or two nights; thirteen were for gambling, all from The Wheel, and were signed by the owner, Carlos Garcia. A couple were for St Anna's Ballroom, a place up near the Canidrome on Love Lane, a respectable cabaret, and as Rod looked through the others, he saw that these too were not cheap bars catering for sailors in rough districts like Blood Alley, but respectable places a couple might visit without impropriety. The sort of places Foster might take Alice.

Looking at the names signing the chits, Rod saw there were several versions: some had a bold hand, others were a scrawl like a drunken spider's trail. As a working hypothesis, Rod considered the chits were signed by different people: he reckoned at least seven hands - but those at The Wheel looked remarkably similar.

Rod lit a reflective cigarette. These were not chits a chauffeur could afford, and the fact that different signatures attended them was odd. What was Foster was doing with them? Three gambling chits were dated on the same night. It was unlikely that a man on a chauffeur's salary could afford to visit so many casinos in one night. In Rod's experience gamblers of moderate means would remain at one establishment, drinking and playing, and when they had lost as much as they could afford, they would stick to drinking. Only the wealthy flitted from one place to another. So, as a working hypothesis, Rod guessed that the chits in Foster's trunk were other people's. Probably at least seven.

Why? What was Foster doing with them?

His head was aching, but Rod didn't care. He felt that he was close to something. There was, he was sure, a means for Foster to make money out of these chits. Rod only had to work out how.

Rod was still sitting reflectively at his desk when Mickey Hi knocked on the door. 'Lady come see you.'

'Who is it?' he said, glancing at his wristwatch. Almost eleven.

'Tall lady, her say Winton.'

Rod was surprised to hear that. 'Old lady? Young lady?'

'Old, very old.'

He collected his jacket. As an afterthought, Rod folded the Wheel chits into his notebook. At the entrance hall he was confronted by Edith Winton.

'Detective Cottey?'

'How can I help you?' He hoped she had not arrived to ask him to berate a servant for spilling soup over a guest.

'I should like to speak with you, if you have a moment?'

'Yes, of course. But I should let you know your husband has asked that I be removed from the investigation.'

'It is about that.'

'Your husband's request?'

'No: Foster.'

He collected his hat and they walked into the sun. In this heat most people wilted like flowers thirsting for water, but Edith Winton had the figure and carriage of a duchess: tall, erect, elegant. He caught a scent of her perfume. It was like flowers in springtime, with a hint of musk; a mixture of young woman and Gracie Gale - the sort of smell a man could breathe in happily as he died.

The heat was oppressive. Rod's head began that slow metronome of pulsing that warned of an approaching headache.

It was easy to see where Alice got her looks. Edith was a similar height, and her figure that of a much younger woman. Her eyes were azure, a surprisingly bright colour here where most tended to be brown, her lips pale but full. In her respectable dress, wearing a hat and a light jacket over a white blouse, with a skirt of the same tan material as the jacket, she looked young enough to be Alice's sister rather than her mother - and far too young to be Alfred's wife.

The Bund was busy. Two steamers had docked, and coolies with wheelbarrows, carts and yokes were patiently emptying the holds. A couple of sailors kept eagle eyes on themas if they were all potential thieves, which most Captains believed with every fibre of their being. Everything that could be was lashed or nailed down, apart from the cargo.

'Foster was not pleasant, Detective.' Even speaking his name made her shudder. 'He had vices like any young man, and living here, where temptations are rather flung in one's way, must have been difficult - and yet ...'

'Which were his vices?'

She looked away. 'Gambling mostly. He built debts to Carlos Garcia, and asked me to tide him over. I remonstrated with him, telling him he should not gamble, that he should avoid casinos, just as he should avoid cabarets and opium houses, and he promised he would. But then he told me that he had debts at other establishments.'

'What did you do?'

'I told him I had taken him into our house in memory of my son, but wouldn't pay him more than he was due.'

'He was a fine dancer, so I have heard.'

She felt a sickening lurch in her belly. It took her a moment to recover her equilibrium. Did the detective know about Foster and Alice? 'I wouldn't know.'

'Was he well paid?'

'We used to pay him 200 Taels per month, and he had board and lodging, of course.' She glanced at coolies loading a ship from wagons laden with heavy bales. 'I think we were not ungenerous.'

200 Taels was a tidy sum. The Tael was Chinese currency, based on a weight of silver rather than a unit of money. It was almost double Rod's monthly income.

'What did you want to tell me?' Rod asked bluntly.

They waited at the side of the road while a parade of coolies crossed, trotting to the gangplanks in a long, unending line. A beggar at the roadside held out her hands, indicating hideous sores on the side of her face. Edith ignored her and they moved on.

This was so difficult. It was shameful to have to admit it to a policeman. She took a deep breath. 'Foster … well, he took advantage of our kindness.'

'How do you mean?'

She was uncomfortable. The heat rising from the roadway was stifling, but it was not only that which made her flush.

'I am not unobservant, Detective. I may look a foolish woman who married for money,' she said, 'but I have eyes, and I know what it is to be young. My daughter is beautiful, but in many ways she is very silly. A mere child. She likes to embarrass her parents, as do so many young people nowadays. I suppose it is natural: breaking free from her parents' control. All children must, mustn't they? But not with the *chauffeur*,' she added. She could not help the venom in her voice.

'She was intimate with Foster?'

Mrs Winton did not demean herself by glancing at him. 'Such an old-fashioned term, isn't it? *Intimate.* Yes, they were intimate.'

'When did you learn this?'

'Some months ago. A friend saw them together. At a cabaret, one of those unpleasant little dives near the French quarter, I think.'

'Did this person tell you or your husband?'

She stared at a warship rounding the bend in the river. 'She told me.'

'Who was this woman?'

'I do not see that it matters, Detective.'

He stopped. 'Someone informed you of your chauffeur's betrayal of the family's trust. Many would consider his behaviour merited punishment. Even extreme punishment.'

'You are being melodramatic. You accuse me of shooting him? I was in …'

'No. You have an alibi; however, that would not prevent your hiring someone else to kill him.'

'Are you seriously accusing me of hiring a man to assassinate Foster?' she smiled.

'Foster was killed by professionals. Someone ordered the killing. Of Foster, or …'

'My word,' she said, and her hand rose to her throat. 'You think someone tried to kill my husband?'

'Perhaps.'

'Why would someone want to hurt him?'

'Perhaps you should tell me.'

She looked at him consideringly. 'Perhaps I should.'

At the public gardens they took a park bench. Sampans and junks moved sluggishly at the mouth of the Soochow Creek and the Whangpoo river - crude, inelegant craft, she thought. They did not look as though they could survive long, they were so flimsy. She half-expected to see them disintegrate as they passed, but miraculously they continued on, tacking dangerously close to the steam launches that plied their trade from Shanghai to the coast.

How best to broach the subject? Foster and his nasty little tricks were not easy topics. It was humiliating.

'I dislike speaking ill of the dead,' she said at last. That was, at least, true. She must ensure that nothing embarrassing to the memory of the dead could surface. It must all stay beneath the waves, concealed for ever.

'You welcomed him to your home after the war.'

'Yes, because he had been with …' she paused, her mask under strain. She swallowed resolutely as she brought her emotions back under control. 'With Ian, my elder son. He died.'

'I am sorry.'

She was surprised to see sympathy in his eyes. That, she had not expected. He was only a policeman, after all. He was, she supposed, about the same age as Ian would have been. Studying him, she saw pain in his eyes. He had endured trenches too, she realised, and understood. 'I am sorry. You must feel horrible, being one of the survivors. You shouldn't, you know. It's not your fault that you lived when they died. Ian … we miss him horribly, but that is not your fault.'

'Thank you,' he said, and stared out at the ships again. It struck her that perhaps those who returned were scarred more than flesh deep.

'He was a good man, my son,' she said wistfully. 'Loyal, intelligent, and astute in business. He had an instinct for when an opponent was vulnerable. It may not sound an appealing trait, but for a taipan it's essential. No one here will give any quarter, and the man who is weak will be cut down.'

'He must have been a great loss.'

'To lose your child is tragic.' Her voice trembled, and she took a deep breath. 'My only ambition now is to keep his memory alive. On the day Foster died, I was speaking to three ladies at the orphanage. I am planning a new wing: the Ian Winton Memorial. He was proud of the men who fought under him, I know. He would like his name to be attached to a place of hope.'

'The orphanage is one of your charities?'

'Yes. There are so many Chinese children on the streets. Every so often I can give one a step up. Find a place for a promising fellow, perhaps a job. And it keeps Ian's memory alive … Ian would have copied his father,' she said, her chin lifting with pride. Even sitting her back was ramrod-straight. 'Alfred built the company from nothing. It was all his own effort, his determination and willingness to take occasional risks.'

'What sort of risks?'

'A man of business has to take risks to advance his interests. Alfred was always prepared to take a chance when it was justified. And he has built the third largest business in Shanghai.

We had expected Ian to take the business to the next ... but neither of us think Maurice can do that.'

'Why?'

Edith sighed. 'Maurice thinks only of pleasures.' She made a sad gesture, opening both hands and spreading them, gazing at her open palms. 'He has tried, but he is not capable. So, instead, he dedicates himself to wine, women and song. He seeks nothing that is not frivolous. That is all he looks for.' She glanced over at Rod, momentarily disconcerted. 'You must think me awful to talk about my son like this.'

'No. I think you have natural concerns. You fear for your son and daughter.'

'Them and the company. What would happen, were Maurice to take over the business? If Alfred were to die, and Maurice took over, my shares would collapse. What should I do without an income? What would happen to Alice? So my husband is to draft a new will – to protect the company and the family.'

'To prevent Maurice from taking over?'

'Yes.' Her face was placid, but she could not keep the panic from her voice. It was a real danger, especially with Alfred unwell. She fitted a resolute smile to her face. 'But Alfred is strong as an ox, and Maurice may develop an interest in business, rather than a constantly revolving circle of women friends.'

'Does he have no other occupation?'

'No. In many ways he is quite selfish. He has little appreciation for the feelings of others, and does not wish to expand his intellect. He has not the fascination with money and business that ... but enough.'

'Yes, we were talking about Foster.'

'Oh, yes. I believe he went to the war determined to do his best for the country. There he met Ian and became his soldier-servant. Foster was more than that, though. He was more of a valet, I suppose, and Ian confided in him. It's why it's so difficult ...'

This time a lone tear wandered down her cheek. She lifted a hand, removed it, and cleared her throat. 'It is why it is so difficult to understand how he could betray our trust so completely.'

## Chapter Twenty-Seven

Rod offered her his handkerchief, but she waved it away and pulled a small square of silk from her sleeve to dab at her eyes.

'Alice will cope, I am sure. She is rather similar to Maurice: selfish, and not the sort to allow the death of a companion to get in the way of her pleasure-seeking.'

'She has a new friend. A Russian woman called Eva.'

'Yes. I do not consider her an appropriate companion,' Mrs Winton said, her voice suddenly arctic. 'These Russians with no money, they arrive daily, and none has the faintest idea how they might earn a living. What do they expect, that we Shanghailanders should bankrupt ourselves in order to support them? I am surprised that the Police do nothing to stop these people.'

'We have little authority, Mrs Winton. They are arriving, whether we like it or not. If they cross into the city from the Chinese sector, there is little we can do to stop them.'

'Foster once said, that if he could have his way, he would set up Vickers guns at all roads and shoot any Russians as they appeared.'

'Not the Christian spirit, surely? Besides, who can tell but that some of them may not turn out to be the entrepreneurs of the future?'

'Perhaps some few might,' she said without conviction. This city used to be so fine, she reflected. It was the influx of Russians and the new generations who spoiled it. All because of the War. The good had died, like poor Ian.

'When did he arrive?'

His words broke in on her thought. 'Hmm? Oh, 1919. He came with letters and some belongings of our son. We ... well, I was touched by this last proof of his service for our boy, and I suggested that we might take him on. There would be cachet in having an English chauffeur, after all.'

'And?'

'That was it. He arrived, installed himself over the garage, and served us well for the last couple of years,' she said, staring downriver.

'May I see the letters he brought from your son?'

'No! They are private,' she snapped. Then, 'I apologise. I do not mean to be curt, but you understand, they were written at a time of great stress.'

'Of course.'

She took a deep breath. 'I believe you took the tin box that was in his room?'

'Yes.'

'It may contain ... private material. Papers that matter to my family.'

'There was nothing that should concern you. I have already searched through it all, and it was as I would expect from a man like him.'

'Really?'

'Some service medals, some photos, nothing more.'

'I see. I thought that there might be ... well, some mementos of our boy.'

She had been so sure that the letters were in that box. Where else could Foster have hidden them? Her visit to the policeman was pointless, if they weren't there. Suddenly she was keen to get away from here. If the papers weren't in the box after all, where had they gone?

Sitting at his desk, Alfred stared out over his gardens, fumbling for a match to light his cigar. The offer of a loan from Billy Qian and his friends had buoyed his spirits, but today he felt swamped by the scale of the disaster engulfing him. A rash of poor investment decisions, one disaster at sea, and the business was suddenly at risk, just at the time that his health was compromised. If only Ian had survived. Ian would have known what to do.

Edith was out – probably in town under the pretence of meeting friends to discuss the charities, while actually delighting in the city's gossip. There was always gossip of one sort or another; salacious whispers about the latest bed-hopping wife or man with a concubine. He began to chuckle, but soon a cough had him gasping for breath, his handkerchief over his mouth. When he glanced at it, there were dark flecks on the cloth, and he felt a wave of self-pity, but he wouldn't succumb to it. He must stay in control, of his body, his family and his bank.

He heard the door, and hurriedly composed himself. 'What do you want?' he snapped.

'Sorry, father.'

'Alice?' he felt his heart go to her. 'I didn't mean to …'

He could feel his heart swell at the sight of her. She was his little princess, and always had been. Nothing had been too good for her, and he had made it his duty to give her presents, little gifts to make her smile. She had appreciated them, he knew. She loved him as much as he loved her. If only she had married one of the men he had suggested, someone to protect the businesses.

'I heard you cough.' She stepped into the light by the French windows. 'Are you well?'

'Never better, child. Do not worry about me.'

'No, father,' she said. She remained on the farther side of his desk, and he felt an irrational bitterness that she didn't approach him.

'I hear you were at the Astor House yesterday.'

'Oh?'

He eyed her suspiciously. 'Who was your consort?'

'Father, I don't think it's your business.'

'Of course it is!. You are my daughter, and my responsibility. Who was he?'

'No one you know.'

'In that case, I doubt you should be in his company.'

'You'd prefer me to bring him here and entertain him in secret?'

'You know that's not what I meant!'

'I don't know what you mean. You want to marry me off, but don't want me to take a lover.'

'Child, that —'

'I am no child. You know that,' she said flatly.

He bridled. 'You are still a Winton, and I will not have you carousing with every fellow you meet.'

'What will you do to prevent me, father?'

'Who was he?' he demanded.

'It's none of your business.'

'Who?'

He had risen from his seat now. Alice let her head tilt, watching him with a calm detachment. It was infuriating, and he flung his unlit cigar across the room. '*Who the hell is he?*'

Alice flinched at his sudden bellow. 'He's called Archie. Archie Lane. I like him.'

'I remember the last man you "liked". The damned chauffeur.'

'You brought him into the house, father. Not me,' she retorted.

'What is this "Archie"? Another driver? An engineer?'

'He's a policeman.'

'Dear Christ! You will not see him again. Is that clear?'

'I am due to see him —'

'You *were* due to see him, but you will not!'

Rod was not sure what to make of Mrs Winton. She wanted to look through Foster's belongings for 'mementos' or private material that belonged to her family, but why should she think Foster had kept something of her son's? Unless she thought something else might be inside: incriminating letters from Alice? Something that could hurt the family? Items stolen by him?

It was not right to leave a European woman to walk home alone, but Rod pitied the poor Chinaman who might try to rob her. He would blunt his knife on the granite carapace of her self-assurance. He made his way back to Central Station, where Mickey Hi was waiting, agitatedly hopping from one foot to another.

'Polices from Markham Road find dead dog, sir.'

Rod looked at him blankly. 'So? Why should that matter to me?'

Mickey looked terribly hurt. 'You say, tell officers look for dog, doormat, man in suit.'

Miss Hyland. He had forgotten. 'It's dead?'

'Yes, someone shoot and throw in ditch.'

The dog went missing a week ago, so there would be little left after the rats and flies, but … 'How do they know it was shot?'

'People hear. Say man in suit shoot it.'

Rod nodded, his head heavy. At least a visit to Miss Hyland would distract him and the impending headache. 'Call me a rickshaw,' he said.

Miss Hyland's house was a bungalow some fifteen to twenty years old. A weary-looking Chinese was half-heartedly sweeping the driveway. He looked as though he would have preferred to be at home while his grandchildren served him tea or a pipe of opium. He caught Rod's eye and instantly looked away, not guiltily, but with the automatic submission of a Chinese meeting a foreigner's glance. Rod continued down the road until he reached two officers who eagerly pointed to the storm drain. He peered through the vegetation and could see a huddled mass of pale brown fur.

'It was there at least a week, maybe ten days,' a man said in pidgin.

He was tall and emaciated, with eyes that seemed dragged down by the weight of flesh on his cheeks and jaw. The dog had been there with a man in a suit, he said. The fellow had the dog on a leash and pulled him from the road to the storm drain which took the water from Markham Road to the Soochow Creek. Rod stood staring into the drain. The water from all about here would gather in what was a large, natural depression and run straight into the drain. The first big rains would wash that sad little tangle of bones and fur far out into the Creek and out to sea.

'Why did no one report this?'

He had nothing to hide, he protested, one of the Chinese officers translating while the man expostulated earnestly. 'Why would I report a dog being shot? The dog was ill, or the dog attacked someone. Perhaps it had rabies? What would I know? If every shot dog was reported to the police, you would never have time for tea! It was only a dog!'

Rod knew he was right. In Britain an unwell dog would be put it out of its misery. It was the last kindness. No one would report it. The man could tell Rod little more, save that the man with the dog had been a Chinese wearing a European suit and grey fedora.

He walked back to the bungalow. Soon he was sitting in a severe, upright armchair that was covered in some rough material. An antimacassar saved his neck from the fabric.

'May I offer you a cup of tea, Detective, or would you prefer something a little stronger? My father was a missionary, and I know that you men sometimes like to have a nip of something in the late morning.'

Rod indicated that a small whisky would be most welcome, and to his horror her manservant passed him a tumbler over half full. He was about to protest, when he saw that she had a similar tumbler for herself. Rod decided to take the line of least resistance, had a sip, and set the glass down on his side table. He reflected that, if this was the sort of drink her father would imbibe of a morning, his missionary zeal must have been inspiring. Rod would have been asleep after two glasses that size.

'Miss Hyland, I am sorry to have to tell you that we have found your dog.'

'Barney? Where?'

'My officers found him only a short distance from here. I'm afraid he is dead.' He saw no point in speaking of the dog being shot.

'Oh!' She turned away, blinking hard for a few moments. 'That is very sad. He was a good fellow, Barney. Could never be trusted with a cat, but loyal, devoted even. I shall miss him.' She sniffed, held a handkerchief to her nose for a moment or two, and then stiffened her backbone and faced Rod again. 'It is very good of you to come to let me know. I am grateful, Detective. I am sure it must have been a most unappealing mission for you.'

He took another belt of whisky. It was good, and he could feel his headache lightening.

'Officer, would it be possible to have Barney's remains brought here? I should like him buried. He was a good guard. Every time someone went along the lane behind the house, he would let me know.'

'Of course.' He stood, finishing his whisky. On the mantleshelf there were a series of photographs. He pointed. 'Your father's mission?'

'That, and that one, yes. He ran the school, teaching the children English and the Bible. These, here, were taken at the orphanage.'

'You work there?'

'Yes. Mrs Winton was good enough to endow the institution. I agreed to help.' Her eyes glowed with pride. 'I love working with the children. They are so rewarding. We are to have a party to raise more funds for an expanded wing next Wednesday. I hope you will join us?'

It was a relief to escape. With whisky fumes rising from his belly, Rod walked east towards the city, and close to the race track, he had a thought. The Wheel, Carlos Garcia's casino, where many of Foster's chits had originated, was nearby.

The building was pleasant and airy, a splendid Spanish-styled property with wisteria and jasmine growing up pillars supporting a wide verandah. Although it was shaded, there was no respite from the heat. Even the short walk from the bungalow had left him drained.

Carlos Garcia was a short, thickset Mexican with a round face who seemed always to be smiling. He was wearing a white shirt and open-fronted waistcoat with two buttons very low down over his belly. It was a dark blue, but had scarlet trim at the edges that made it look very Spanish, somehow. He had genial dark eyes, a sparse moustache, and a softly-spoken manner.

'Please, you are most welcome,' he said, shaking Rod's hand. In his left he held a huge cigar, which he waved in the air as he emphasised a point. He had the look of a successful patron of the arts, perhaps an impresario who sponsored popular operas, and Rod took an instant dislike to him. The whole of his manner was an act to persuade others to trust him. Rod considered casino managers little better than the thieves who held up pedestrians at gunpoint to rob them. They pretended to be civilised, with their smart clothes and polite manners, but they were little better than sharks, circling fresh victims into whom they could sink their teeth.

'I wanted to ask you about a customer.'

'I am sorry, I will answer what I may, Señor, but I have to be discreet, you understand?' he said apologetically.

'This is about a murder. I expect your cooperation.'

'I will answer what I may.'

'Do you have many bad debts?'

A shrug. 'Every establishment has a few such. We are not unique.'

'What of Thomas Foster?'

His eyes widened as his smile broadened. 'My establishment is for the wealthy. Not servants.'

'What can you tell me about him?'

'I barely knew him, Señor,' he said, holding his hands apart. The ash remained on his cigar even as he waved it about. 'How can I tell you of a man I do not know?'

'He has a chit from you. Did he pay it?'

Carlos Garcia's face subtly changed. 'A chit?'

Rod pulled the chits from his pocket book. Garcia took one with a slight frown. 'This is genuine, but it does not bear his name.'

'Is that his signature?'

'I should know the signatures of men I do not know?' he smiled.

'I require your help. If not, I will have a squad down here.'

'Do so,' Garcia said, and his smile broadened. 'My license comes from the Mexican government, and under the rules of "extraterritoriality", I am responsible only to the laws of Mexico, as you know. If you send men, I will be in court tomorrow, and will pay a fine.' He shrugged. 'Fines are a business expense. While they irritate, they do not affect my business. I could be fined every day of the year, and still the casino would be very profitable.' He tilted his head apologetically, waving to a Chinese waiter. 'Let me have this investigated and, I will tell you what I may. Please, avail yourself of my hospitality. A drink? Something to cool you?'

His confidence was infuriating. Rod could have happily punched his face. He detested the man and his sly, nasty business.

But Rod was not that sort of man. He was a policeman, sworn to uphold the law. So he took a seat and waited.

When Garcia's Number One Boy asked, Rod settled for a cup of Jasmine tea. His stomach was still reeling from the whisky, and he felt quite light-headed.

Carlos Garcia returned shortly after the tea. It was excellent, and Garcia rattled the ice cubes in a small glass of a greenish liquid as he sipped it. 'Tequila,' he said. 'You want some?'

'Whose chit was it?' Rod asked pointedly.

Carlos Garcia sat, spreading his hands expansively. 'Señor, I have not yet found who owed that money.'

'You expect me to believe that you would lose track of a man who owed you that much money? I think you are wasting my time!' Rod put his teacup down, and was about to rise, when Garcia held up a hand.

'Please, perhaps I can discover. This chit, it was some weeks ago. It may be that it has been settled, and I can find out, but it takes time to search through my ledgers. My book keeper is looking now, and with luck will soon find the fellow.'

At Garcia's insistence, Rod sat again, sipping the tea.

'Please, tell me what this is about?' he said. 'It is to do with the man Foster who died?'

'It may be. These chits were in his possession.'

'Perhaps it was his own, but I think it unlikely. I would not have had him here,' Garcia said.

'Because he was only a chauffeur?' Rod said, and could not keep the contempt from his voice.

Garcia smiled disarmingly. 'In my establishment I wish to have the richest men. They come in, they talk of business, which shares are rising, which will collapse, and my stock broker, he soon learns all I have heard. They play with hard cash, because they are rich. When their bills arrive, these men settle them immediately, because they wish to be able to avail themselves of my hospitality. If I have a bad debt, I will not allow the man through my doors. If that happens, he will earn a poor reputation. No one likes a man who will not pay his debts. That is why I was surprised not to recall this. It is not normal for me to forget, let alone one of this size.'

As he spoke, a bearded and bespectacled man in his thirties hurried up with a leather-bound ledger. He waited until Garcia had finished speaking, and then opened the book at a page and pointed with an ink-stained finger.

Garcia leaned forward and peered, the concentration bringing a frown to his face.

'Ah,' he said. 'It seems I was not aware of the matter; my staff took it in hand.' He considered a moment, the chit in his left hand, the cigar forgotten for a moment. 'He is of little use to me. His finances have been poor for a while, and if he is going to pay late, I do not have a need for him. He is one of your English lawyers, a man called Frank Dewitt.'

# Chapter Twenty-Eight

Rod took a rickshaw from The Wheel. Frank Dewitt had an office behind the Bund on Canton Road.

Dewitt was a name he had heard before, and he racked his brains. It was only when the rickshaw jerked to a halt that it came to him: Dewitt had been talking to Gracie Gale when Rod last visited her.

The office was in a new building with a wide entrance hall and elegant marble pillars supporting a soaring ceiling. A board on the wall listed the companies based there, and Rod soon picked out Ross and Dewitt, based on the third floor. There was an elevator, but when Rod walked to it, the operator ducked his head in apology. It was broken. An engineer had been summoned, but it would be some time before it was mended. Rod sighed and turned to the staircase.

Three flights of stairs would be nothing in London even in June, but in Shanghai's summer it was an exercise in determination and physical endurance. The heat percolated through the building, and by the time he had reached the third floor, he was streaming. He had to remove his hat and fan himself before he opened the door to the corridor.

He made his way along the passageway, glancing at the names painted on the frosted glass doors, until he reached Ross and Dewitt. He turned the handle and entered. There was a reception desk, behind which was another frosted glass door. A secretary of perhaps thirty, a thin, gaunt man with a long, face and the dull, heavily-lidded eyes of a starved bloodhound, sat pecking at a typewriter with more dedication than enthusiasm. When Rod told him he wanted to see Dewitt, he learned that Dewitt did not work on Saturdays, and was away on the company houseboat, shooting. He would return on Monday, and no doubt would be happy to see Rod then – if he made an appointment.

'I will come back on Monday,' he said.

'He is very busy,' the secretary said with the weary sigh of a bureaucrat under an intolerable burden of responsibility.

Rod leaned down, his fists on the desk, and smiled at him. The secretary looked up, and fear flared at the expression on Rod's face.

'You will make sure that he has time. I am Detective Cottey from the Criminal Investigation Department of the Shanghai Municipal Police. You will want to help me, won't you?'

The secretary nodded. His cloak of authority had been ripped from him, and he looked like a boy discovered breaking into the school's tuck shop.

Rod closed the door behind him feeling soiled. Bullying a fool was ungentlemanly. Other officers might put the fear of God into locals, or happily see a private punished for rudeness or perceived disrespect, but that didn't make him feel any better.

Walking from the building, he stood at the top of the steps leading to the pavement. The streets were full for a Saturday afternoon, and he couldn't count the Chinese and foreigners thronging the streets. Panama hats, fedoras, straw boaters, an occasional turban, all stood out amongst Chinese headgear or bald heads with long queues of hair. Rod saw faces staring, some square and flat with high cheeks, others thin and long; there was one with a round face and smiling, twinkling eyes as he served clients with chicken feet to chew, a short way away, two coolies stood with blank eyes in skull-like features, staring jealously at the food. There were so many, no matter where you were to look, and so many were hungry.

Their hungry eyes reminded Rod of a prisoner of war camp he'd glimpsed when he was resting behind the lines: the gaunt faces, the filth ingrained in every pore and crease, eyes wide and hopeless as they clung to the barbed wire, as though they were so weak their legs could not support them. His men slowed as they passed, seeing boys their own age. One of Rod's troopers commented quietly, '*Poor bastards.*' The Sergeant-Major bellowed at them to keep to the regulation pace, but Rod saw something out of the corner of his eye, and when he glanced back, he saw more items flying through the air at the German prisoners. His men, who had just suffered appalling losses, were throwing cigarettes to the Germans.

On a whim, Rod returned to the Bund. It never ceased to astonish him, the ships disgorging vast quantities of goods before loading their cargoes. All day, every day, ships arrived, were emptied by sweating coolies, refilled and were off, their places taken by fresh ships. The flow of trade was unending. He pitied the coolies working in that heat.

There were others to feel sorry for as well. At the roads' edges, on patches of grass, or sitting on a blanket or coat, were the beggars. It didn't matter where a man walked in Shanghai, there were always more, watching with infinite, weary patience. Some held out their hands, others merely sat hopefully with a small bowl to receive a gift of coin or food. The wars had deprived so many of homes and families that there was a daily influx of displaced people hoping for work, but most would never find it. The children always affected Rod the most. There was something unendurable about the thin faces, swollen bellies, the limbs deformed from malnutrition. Although many ladies, like Mrs Winton, tried to help the worst affected, their efforts were a drop in the ocean, faced with such human misery.

In the northernmost quayside, Rod recognised a face amongst the beggars.

'Hello, Tim,' he said.

Tim Burton had been an SMP officer when Rod joined. A large, bluff character, with the manner and confidence of a Sergeant-Major, he was tall and strong, with a broken nose and mouth curiously lop-sided. His brown eyes were kindly, but he had been abusive towards the Chinese officers, so Rod felt. With English officers, he was the life and soul of any party. His forceful, exuberant nature made him popular, and his cheerful attitude ensured that he was always sought out at any gathering.

But he suffered from the common defects of such a character. He gambled big, and lost big. His drinking affected his abilities, and he began to turn up late for his duties. He was forgiven much initially, because he was liked by other officers, but soon it was noticed that his breath reeked of rum. He was found drinking rum from bottles concealed in bags, and then he was accused of beating up a Chinese shopkeeper while demanding protection money.

It was the final straw. He was dismissed, and although there was a small collection for him, he squandered that on rum. Nine months ago he had lost his apartment, and took up begging on the streets. That was bad for the prestige of the Force, for the Chinese to see a white man on the streets.

Today he was at the kerbside, hopefully holding out a hand to passers-by. Most ignored him, some spat at him, others made a sign to ward off evil spirits, but a few took pity and gave him a coin or two. He was dressed in filthy pyjama trousers, with a grey shirt under a rug which he wore over his shoulders like a cloak. A cap of some material long discoloured covered his hair. With the grime in his skin, he could have passed for any race, but few would have guessed he was European.

On hearing Rod's welcome, he looked up. 'Detective Cottey. How nice to see you. Couldn't afford the price of a drink, could you?'

'How are you?'

'How d'you think?' he said. His grin was a ghastly display; he had lost the incisors on upper and lower jaws. Rod never discovered whether that was proof of the depravity of his lifestyle - perhaps alcohol had rotted them? - or whether he had been beaten. 'I've had some food today. A kind lady let me have the last noodles from her bowl, just before her husband kicked me away. He didn't want a foreign devil like me polluting his street. I expect he's smashed the bowl now. Shame. It was a pretty one.'

'Do you want to earn some money?'

'Always. I don't care how.'

Rod shook his head. 'You're not up to the rough stuff, Tim. Do you remember the body you dragged from the river? Both eyes dug out, something carved into his forehead?'

Tim's watery eyes looked over Rod's shoulder, losing focus. 'The eyes weren't dug out, they were stabbed. And the character meant "Traitor".'

'That was the only body pulled from the river like that, wasn't it?'

'Yes. The others with the eyes stabbed were found in the alleys. I remember him. His son was nearby, too.'

'What happened to him?'

'The boy? He was nine or ten, a weedy little brat. We took him to the orphanage.'

'Did you get his name?'

'Yes, but I don't remember it.'

'Did anyone find the murderer?'

'No, it was just one of a spate. Probably gang squabbles, nothing more.'

'There's been another one. An Englishman.'

'Really.'

'You don't seem bothered.'

'Look at me, Rod! No one cares whether I live or die. You expect me to worry about someone I don't know, and who would have looked down on me? You mentioned money. Do you want my life story?'

'No. I want you to watch the ships. I'll pay you a half dollar a day.'

'What am I looking for?'

'Looking for, listening out for, anything. Smuggled guns are appearing: machine pistols, mostly Bergmanns. We have no idea where they are coming from. They could be coming overland, but I suspect they are coming from the port.'

'And I'll be welcomed back into the Force with open arms?' he said. He looked down, and his hands began rifling through his clothing, hunting until he found a half bottle of rum. He up-ended it, gave a gasp of contentment, and then held it up. 'Let's drink to my reinstatement.'

'No, thanks,' Rod said, eyeing the bottle with disgust. 'If you can learn anything, it may help you. The Force won't have you back, but they might help you home.'

'And look! Up there, there's a flying pig!' he said, pointing at the sky. 'Don't patronise me, Cottey. The Force won't help - I've burned my bridges.'

'If you hear someone is bringing in guns or drugs, send a Chinese messenger to Central.'

'Oh, aye. And before you come to find me, make sure you bring a bottle with you.'

Archie knocked at the door.

Yesterday they had danced at the Astor House until past midnight, and it had been a difficult journey back. If he was out of barracks after one o'clock in the morning, he would be on a charge. The curfew for new recruits was strictly imposed, and he had only just managed to get her home and return to Gordon Road in time. It had cost him a double fare, but the coolie was happy to see the money, even as he panted after his canter from the city.

She was entrancing when she danced. Waltzing, she was so light, it was like dancing with a shadow. And when the band struck up some modern jazz, she moved with such grace and effortless precision, he could not look away. Sight for sore eyes, she was. Especially after a day being shouted at, forced to run miles, learning the finer details of Shanghai's geography, aspects of the law as it related to the various foreigners, and then Chinese. All those words … he felt his brain must explode after a day's studying. Yes, she was a real stunner, she was.

'Mr Lane.' The butler had opened the door at last, and Archie was startled. He had been too deeply engrossed in his thoughts. 'Follow me, please.'

He was taken through to a vast room lined with books. Inside, sitting in a winged seat, was a man.

'Wait there, Crowther, this won't take long,' he said, before sucking on a cigar. 'Mr Lane, I believe you have been seeing my daughter.'

'Yes.'

'Without my permission, nor seeking it. And you propose to do the same tonight.'

'If you don't mind, sir.'

'I do mind. In fact I mind very much. My daughter will marry a man of her own class and standing. You,' he said, glancing at Archie's shoes and up to his tie, 'are not from her level, young man.'

'But –'

'You will not return. You are not welcome. I trust I make myself clear?'

'She arranged to see me tonight,' Archie said, and he could not help the petulant tone of voice. He had been looking forward to seeing her all day. It was the thought of her smiling eyes, her slim body next to his, that had made the lessons and exercise bearable.

'She had no right to arrange any such thing.'

'She's a grown woman!'

'She is a minor, and before you argue further, let me remind you that she is my daughter, and I will not have a social-climbing miscreant from the slums of London chasing after her!'

Archie felt the hot blood rush to his cheeks. Alfred Winton clutched at his cigar as though wishing it were a pistol.

'Sir, I would be grateful for a word with your daughter,' Archie said stiffly.

'No, I refuse you permission to speak, write, or communicate in any fashion with my daughter, damn you! Now *go*! Crowther, see him out.'

Archie wanted to say something, but the man glared so ferociously that he dare not. Archie could hear Alfred's racking cough as he strode out, and when he reached the top step at the entrance, the door was closed behind him gently, as though the butler was expressing regret. Not that it was likely. He was as much of a snob as his master, in Archie's opinion. Archie was tempted to turn back to the door and hammer on it, but what would that achieve? Nothing. The anger was still there, heating his blood. He returned to the rickshaw, telling the coolie to take him to Gordon Road Depot. At least there he could see John and Peter. They would help him forget.

He hoped they could.

Rod walked back to Central Station discouraged. It was the sight of Burton: his wretchedness, how low he had sunk, but most of all the fact that the hearty man Rod had known could have become so defeated by circumstances that he could resort to begging on the streets. Certainly Burton had not been a model character before, but he had oozed confidence. No one could have predicted that he would founder so swiftly. Was that the fate of any officer thrown from the force? Was the line between a native, those coolies whom the British looked down upon, and English men really so narrow?

Yet his investigation was progressing. The boy from the river had been taken to the orphanage, Tim said. That would mean records that could lead him to the boy, if he was still alive. Perhaps, even after all this time, Rod might learn something from the lad. The fellow would be about Rod's age, and may want revenge for his father's murder. What would have led someone to do such a thing to Foster, though?

He stood at the corner of Honan and Foochow, his headache returning. The sight of Burton's toothless grin kept intruding. He should return to the Station, but not just yet, he told himself, and let his feet guide him. Soon, he found himself entering the French Sector.

Once more ensconced in a comfortable armchair, the good doctor sat beside him, taking his pulse. 'Your symptoms remain,' he said softly.

'My headache is back, and the shivering. I wondered whether I could have another shot of your drug.'

'It is not easy. Yes, I can inject you, but the problem is that you will need more and stronger doses to have the same effect.'

'I can pay,' Rod said. 'What is the drug called?'

'It is cocaine,' Dr Babu said. 'A most useful drug. It aids healing, and gives men a sense of well-being that is hardly equalled by any other drug, especially for those who have unpleasant memories they wish to forget.'

'Is it expensive?'

The Doctor smiled gently. 'Not for you. I don't charge police officers much.'

He rang the bell, and soon the entrancing nurse appeared bearing a silver tray on which was a vial with tabloids, a jug of water, and a syringe. Babu pulled the plunger from the syringe, dropped a tabloid into the reservoir, added water, and soon Rod was filled with that luxurious sense of happiness and certainty. All thoughts of the beggar and the murder were banished.

Yao Shihui was weary when he reached his home. He had been up at the gambling house since six the previous evening, and didn't get home until four. It was usual for him to sleep in after a long evening, and he was dead to the world when the hammering came at his door.

Lurching from his bed, he stared through the window. The shadows were not across the glass yet, so it was not midday, when he would usually make his way to one of the restaurants for a cup of rice porridge and tea. He rubbed his sparse hair and face, and when the knocking resumed, he walked to the door.

'What do you think you are –?' he began as he opened the door, but someone thrust it wide. The bottom scraped over his toe, and ripped the nail away, and he screamed, even as Thin Bao jabbed a knuckle-duster into Yao Shihui's face.

He squealed with pain, falling as Thin Bao and another man walked in. He tried to climb to his feet, but Thin Bao kicked his jaw. His head snapped back and he fell to the ground again.

'I know you did it. Tell me now, or I'll feed you to the dogs.'

'Who? What? I don't know what you mean,' Yao Shihui mumbled. A tooth had gone, and his mouth was full of blood. He cupped a hand to his face, rocking back and forth, his other hand cradling his injured foot.

'My cabaret was raided, you turd!' Thin Bao snarled. He crouched at Yao Shihui's side and glared at him. He held the knuckledusters up. 'You want more?'

'No!'

'Then tell me: who told the police to raid my place?'

'I don't ...'

His words ended in a scream of pain as Thin Bao punched him in the groin. Yao Shihui curled into a ball of agony, rolling over.

'*Tell me who*!'

# Chapter Twenty-Nine

*Sunday 30th July, 1922*

For once that Sunday there was a refreshing breeze.

Rod woke without headache or shivering and walked along the Bund glancing at the beggars, but did not see Tim Burton. He guessed Burton was curled up around an empty rum bottle. Although Rod had sympathy for Burton's present state, he could not condone those who abused their position as Burton had. Officers demanding protection from shopkeepers were an embarrassment. Europeans were trying to show the Chinese that there were better ways of living than copying gangsters.

At least Rod was not like Burton. He used drugs occasionally, it was true, but that was only because of his war experiences and the threat of malaria. It was medicinal - it didn't mean Rod was a criminal. He was a doctor's patient. Rod was no addict.

Turning up Kiukiang Road, he bent his feet towards the church.

The roads were gloomy after the bright sunlight of the Bund. The buildings here were four storeys high, cutting out the light. The narrow ways were intimidating, as though he was hurrying along a trench. Only when he saw the tall spire of the church could drive away his bleak mood.

Holy Trinity was the Cathedral Church of the Anglican Bishop of Mid-China, and filled the area between the Kiukiang and Hankow Roads. Built of brick, everyone knew it as the Red

Church. Its spire loomed over people strolling over the lawns. Rod passed under the colonnaded portico and into the interior. It was almost half past ten; the service would begin soon.

Inside it was cool, a blessed relief. The pews were already full, and Rod sat at the rearmost, idly gazing about him.

The people chattered quietly, as congregations will. He could see the Wintons: Alfred, Edith, Alice and Maurice sitting up ahead. To his left were the families of the men who ran the city: the head of Jardine, Matheson's turned and saw him and gave Rod a cold nod; the Chief of Police sat a row behind him, with other dignitaries. All those who ran the city were here for the service. At the opposite pew Rod saw a pale, bitter face: Schreier. He was staring fixedly at Winton with a gaze that could have dissolved the floor tiles.

As the Bishop began to intone, and the crowd shuffled to its feet, there was a sudden sound behind Rod, and he turned to see Gracie Gale and a magnificent woman with the flaming red hair and face from a Dante Gabriel Rosetti painting. The two strolled sedately up the aisle, Gracie's head demurely downcast, while the woman with her smiled on all sides as though this was a tremendous jest, and she was holding in her mirth with difficulty. To Rod's surprise, they took their place in the pews only five in front of him. He had somehow expected them to walk further up the church.

Gracie said something, and several heads swivelled, her sultry voice instantly recognisable. Alfred's back stiffened, and Rod was convinced that his neck coloured. His wife turned to look at him, her face frozen into a rictus of rage. Rod saw Alice aim an expression of loathing at her father when she saw Gracie. Everyone in Shanghai knew Gracie, and clearly Edith and Alice had their suspicions about Alfred.

The service went on. Standing, singing, kneeling, then the collection. Rod was surprised to see Alfred was one of the sidesmen delegated to fetch the collection. Winton walked to the front with another man, both bowing their heads, and taking the collection bags after they had been blessed. Then Winton and the other sidesman took their places at the back of the church. Winton was on Rod's side, and handed the collection bag to the rearmost member of the congregation, and stood waiting while money was dropped in. The bags were passed on, money was again added, the bags moving from one person to another along the line until it returned to the aisle once more.

Rod was in the aisle seat, so he put in a dollar and gave the bag to Alfred.

He made no comment, but Rod could not help but notice that he had gone a pale grey colour. Looking at him, it was hard not to think of Tim Burton in the throes of his DTs. Delirium Tremens made a man go grey and feverish. Alfred had none of the odour of alcohol that Rod associated with the DTs, but the symptoms were there.

He stumbled as he approached Gracie. That was when Rod realised Alfred Winton was terrified. As Rod watched, he almost dropped the collection. Gracie's companion turned and fixed on him a smile of such radiance, Rod thought he could die happy if she would give him that same look.

She said, 'Why, Alfred. How lovely to see you,' and carefully folded a small sheet of paper from her bag, dropping it into the bag. Gracie allowed some coins to tinkle in, and then the bag moved on again, Alfred moving like an automaton, taking the bag, moving to the next row, his legs moving in a curiously uncoordinated fashion, like a man under the influence of drugs or alcohol. Rod watched him with narrowly, wondering what was the cause of his sudden affliction. Then the two sidesmen collected the bags and presented them at the altar.

The rest of the service went in a blur. Rod knelt at the altar and sipped wine with the wafer, and returned to his seat, where he knelt and prayed; as usual, for Cecily and Ethel, for Dick and the men who died in the filth of the Somme, for his parents, and for his continued efforts to catch criminals and keep the people of Shanghai safe, but, may God forgive him, his mind was more fixed on Alfred and his expression of abject horror.

When the congregation was instructed to go and serve the Lord, Rod rose to speak to Alfred, but Gracie accosted him. 'Did you like the show?'

They had a small space about them. Although they stood in the middle of the aisle, those leaving the church swept about and around them, as if the three were quarantined. Shanghailander wives walked past with noses high, as though they were unable to see Gracie and her companion. None would sully her dress by actually touching the clothing of the madam.

'What was that all about?' he asked.

She chuckled. 'Didn't you realise, honey? Someone who refuses to pay my bills has to take the consequences. He'll have to pay the church now: I donated his bill. The Bishop will be pleased, I'm sure, and Alfred can console himself thinking, well, he helped towards the upkeep of the church rather than my brothel. But he won't be allowed inside again. No, sir. He's no longer welcome in my house.'

'It was an expensive revenge on your part.'

'Yeah. But worth it. He saw Nicole here, and he'll regret never seeing her again. And he can't bring clients to my place anymore. That'll hurt.'

'The hypocrite,' Rod muttered. 'He said his son was a womanising hell-raiser, but all the while he was jumping on …' he glanced at the women. Nicole was smiling but Gracie wore a prim expression of warning. 'I can easily understand why, of course. But that doesn't make him any the better.'

'No.'

'Why didn't he just pay up?' Rod wondered. 'He surely has enough money.'

'You'd think so. Some guys kick against their own bills. He never did before, though.'

'He's been a … client before?'

'Many times. This is the first time he was a problem.'

'Perhaps his bank is in trouble?'

'I hope not,' Gracie said. She pulled down the hem of her jacket. 'I have a lot of money invested there.'

After Gracie left, Rod stood considering her words.

Why would Alfred Winton risk upsetting her? Gracie could divulge secrets that any man would prefer to keep hidden from his wife, children and clients. He had been to Gracie's before, she said, and always paid on time. Why should he hold back this time?

There were several potential reasons. It could be a problem at the bank, a difficulty with his own money, or even a sudden realisation that he should not have participated in activities at the brothel. He had been acting as a sidesman - perhaps he had rediscovered his religious faith, and that prevented him from paying for the services of whores?

It didn't ring true. Rod watched the Wintons approach their new automobile, another American phaeton. Alfred held the door for his wife and daughter, but as Maurice bent to enter, Alfred caught Rod's eye. Alfred snapped a command to the turbaned driver and closed the door. His wife ignored him. She stared into the middle distance as the vehicle pulled away.

'You saw?' Alfred looked even worse than in the church.

'Yes.'

'I spoke to your Commissioner. I demanded someone else should investigate Foster's death.'

'I know. But there are not many Detectives in the Force.'

'I see.' He looked about him as though suddenly lost. 'Hell, I need a drink. Come with me.'

Alfred led the way to the Bund.

His shock at Gracie's act was dissipating. After all, the men in the congregation would be jealous of Alfred for enjoying Nicole. She had been magnificent, as good as Gracie had promised, he recalled wistfully. Edith was furious for being humiliated before the other Shanghailanders, and Alice was mortified, but all Alfred could think of was Nicole's naked body as he plunged into her, or her smiling face when she squatted over him, breasts moving with her rolling hips. Lost, and all because of trying to rescue the ruddy bank. Alfred would never be allowed back into Gracie's house on the Line. Not until he had paid for that evening, plus interest, at the very least.

At the workings for the new Hongkong Shanghai Bank building, he slowed jealously. It was taking shape after only a few months of work, and it would be immense. Piles had been driven into the marshy soil, and the first levels were installed, massive lumps of rock and stone forming the shape that would dominate the waterfront. Bamboo scaffolding grew like ivy, and workers swarmed over it.

'Hongkong Shanghai is our most powerful bank,' Alfred said quietly, his mood tinged with sadness. 'I had intended to compete with them.'

Shanghai's Club was a magnificent building in white stone, with brown marble pillars, and turrets at each corner. The hallway was like a London club's; dark wood and patterned tile floor. A visitor's book lay open on a desk, and Alfred dipped a pen in the inkpot to sign in his guest.

The Club boasted the longest counter in the world. This being Sunday, many men were escaping their families, and there was little space at the bar itself, but that suited Alfred. He didn't want the company of other taipans.

'Follow me,' he said, and took a table at a window overlooking the Bund and the moorings. Alfred had always loved this view. It reminded him of his early days, importing opium, exporting silks and teas, and gradually building his financial empire. All of which was now in jeopardy. When he died, the business would collapse. He ordered a large whisky, and Rod asked for an Old Fashioned.

'You're honoured,' Alfred said. 'This is where taipans sit. Young newcomers, the "griffins", go to the far end. Other members fit in the middle, depending on seniority. You shouldn't be here. I daresay I'll be asked why I brought you.'

'Why did you?' Rod said.

Alfred lit a cigar, waving the match to death, eyes narrowed. He coughed, a handkerchief over his mouth.

Rod waited until the coughing was done. He could see speckles of blood on the white cloth. 'I know about your debt to Gracie Gale, but I am investigating a murder. Death takes priority over your enjoyment of Gracie's favours.'

The taipan nodded, stuffing the handkerchief into his pocket as their drinks arrived. A bucket of ice was placed on the table, a crystal glass set before each of them, and the waiter disappeared as silently as he had arrived. Rod sipped his drink. It was almost as good as the one in Gracie's.

'When Ian died I went mad. I speculated wildly, and some of my investments have tumbled.'

'Yes?'

Alfred rolled whisky around his tongue. 'The bank is sound, of course, but I didn't invest wisely.' He leaned forward suddenly. 'I'm still secure, don't mistake me. But Ian's death was hard ... Edith didn't ... well, we didn't get on as we had. I needed companionship, and Gracie provided that. But the debts kept mounting. It was a terrible time.'

'So you couldn't pay Gracie.'

'No. And now I *have* to find the money, because she gave my chit to the Church. They will think it an enormously generous gift!' he spat.

'The bank is safe, though?'

'Yes. There is no problem. It's merely a temporary liquidity issue for me personally.'

'How much?'

'That's my business!'

He knocked back the remains of his whisky and beckoned the waiter. Two fresh drinks were deposited before them.

'Why are you telling me?'

'I asked you to be removed because I thought you might discover my financial ... embarrassment. I thought it might get out.'

'If the bank is safe, what does it matter?'

'You don't understand business! The men here are sharks. You see *him* at the table, there?' He indicated a tall fellow with slightly bulging eyes, an enormous paunch, and bedraggled linen suit smoking a cigarette in a holder, engaged in an affable altercation with two others. 'GH Stitt: you won't meet a more friendly, generous soul in a bar. But if he had a notion I was in trouble, he would rip my throat out. Just as I would him. He manages the Hongkong and Shanghai Bank. A man doesn't reach that position without knowing how to stab another if there's profit in it.'

'Have you thought any more about who could have shot Foster?'

Alfred looked away. 'No. He made people wary, and perhaps …'

'What of you?'

'I don't understand.' Alfred did not meet his eyes.

'Was his death because of you?'

He scoffed. 'Why would —'

'Was it your business? Had he learned something and used it against you?'

'He wouldn't have dared.'

'Did you approach less scrupulous businessmen for investment?'

'I told you —'

'The city is full of gangsters. Did you go to them? Is that what this is about: you took a loan, and they reminded you your payment is late by shooting up your car?'

Alfred knocked back his whisky, and took a long pull at his cigar, eyeing Rod with distaste. He suppressed a cough. 'Suppose I did. Suppose I had no choice. And they were clear that they expected more than the usual rates of interest.'

'Who?'

'I can't tell you! You know what these people are like!'

'You have to tell me. You know you do. We can protect you, have the gang leave you alone. Otherwise, next time your car is shot up, you may be inside.'

'I know. It was a miracle I wasn't in it that day,' Alfred said. 'All because of a weak liver. If it weren't for that, I'd be buried next to Foster.'

'Who did you borrow from?'

'Hell, you're relentless, aren't you? You want the truth?' Winton leaned forward so Rod could smell the rancid sweat, the sour, tobacco-laden breath. 'What if Foster was trying to get rich? What if he was a duplicitous, thieving bastard who'd do anything for money? What if he used his position in my family to … He wasn't a nice man, Cottey. He was a crook, and he'd use anyone to get what he wanted.'

'Was he trying to get money from you?'

'*Yes*!' Winton's eyes were cold and hard. 'By stealing my daughter.'

# Chapter Thirty

That evening Archie went to town with John and Peter, visiting a bar and cabaret. Peter had not been inside a great hotel, and although Archie knew the price would be exorbitant, they went to the Astor House. Archie reckoned that one more visit couldn't hurt. Perhaps he might see her again: Alice.

She had been intoxicating. Her smile, her deft footwork while dancing, the feel of her slim, strong body in his arms, the slightly aniseed scent of her breath, the reflection of the chandeliers in her eyes, all were thrilling to a lad from London's docks.

'You thinking of her again, Arch?' John said.

'It's hard not to.'

'You couldn't afford her. Her sort isn't for the likes of us. We're only bobbies. She wouldn't look at anyone below the owner of a bank,' John laughed.

'I know. But she was fun.'

The hotel was quiet. Most stayed at home after the Sabbath lunch, with some few wandering to the country club or some other quiet venue. Archie and his friends took a table and watched the dancers, chatting about training, examinations, and the cruelty of their superiors. Peter was anxious about passing, as was Archie, but John was confident. 'And if I don't, what of it? I'll soon get another berth here, you'll see. A man like me, with all the opportunities there are in this place, I'll make myself a millionaire if the police don't want me.'

They were onto their third drinks when John and Peter went to visit the washroom. A hand touched Archie's shoulder, and he looked up, then sprang to his feet. Alice Winton was laughing.

'Did I make you jump, Archie? What a positively horrified expression! You look too perfectly shocked for words!'

'Miss Winton, I was miles away.'

'I am sure you were. You look like a man who has been working too hard,' she said, taking a seat next to him. 'Who are your friends?'

Archie explained, and Alice giggled. 'How lovely. John looks coarse. Peter seems too gentle to be a policeman. One expects the police to look dangerous, but he looks like a mouse.'

'They are good fellows.'

'I am sure they must be,' she said. A waiter appeared and took her order. 'I am sorry about father. He gets terribly jealous, you see. He doesn't want to share me. He treats me like one of his paintings, something to be held at home so that only he can ... well!'

'I suppose all fathers feel like that,' Archie said. '*I* would, if I had a daughter like you.'

'That's sweet,' she said, and looked away. 'But I'm sure you wouldn't be like my father.'

Archie glanced up to see Peter and John gaping. 'Would you care to dance?'

'I would love to. I can always have just one more dance,' she smiled.

'Good God, Rod! You look like hell frozen over!'

'It's been a hard few days.'

At Bailey's, Rod and Eric spoke of inconsequential matters. For once Eric was not chasing a story. 'It's the Sabbath,' he said. 'Even a reporter needs an evening off.'

'Lucky you aren't a policeman.'

'Have you been working today?'

Rod nodded. 'Alfred Winton took me to the Club.'

'What have you done to deserve that?'

Rod was jittery. There was a shaking in his hand, accompanied by a tingling of pins and needles in his left arm. He clenched his fist to ease the sensation. 'I think he wanted company.'

'Taipans aren't so desperate that they invite policemen to the Club,' Eric scoffed.

'So you're working again now?'

'No, only gossiping.'

'There's nothing to gossip about. He wanted a drink, that's all.'

'So nothing was said that I could use to trash his reputation?'

'Do you think he'd tell me something like that, any more than he'd tell you?'

Eric nodded bleakly. 'True enough.'

'You once told me Winton tried to get you fired.'

'Yes. When I was investigating him and Schreier.'

'How far did you get with that?'

He looked bitter. 'I proved the bastard had German shares. Schreier had Krupp stocks, and Winton took them, but I couldn't get anywhere with the story. My editor spiked it, because Winton has shares in the paper. It's the old story.'

'Is that it?'

'*Is that it?* you ask? This was the height of the War, Rod! He was profiteering from the enemy's arms manufacturer, while their shells were being fired at our chaps at the Front!'

'It's old history now, Eric.'

'Perhaps for you, but it's all too recent to me.'

Later, Rod felt sure that Alfred Winton had only invited Rod to the Club to impress him. Perhaps because Rod made him nervous; Rod liked to think that he could provoke unease in one of the city's taipans.

Rod made his way past the municipal buildings, avoiding the people on the street. Even on a Sunday the roads were packed. Slipping inside the tobacconist's, he thought he saw a familiar, Chinese face in the street, but it was only a fleeting glimpse, and although he felt his hackles warning, he dismissed it and bought cigarettes.

He should have paid more heed.

Archie took Alice's hand. The band was playing a waltz, and the two moved together. She was as fine as a flower, he thought, or rather, like a small bird, delicate, perfect, but fragile.

'What are you thinking?' she said.

'Mainly, what will your father say! A lecherous police recruit dancing with the prettiest girl in Shanghai!'

'Prettiest, you think?' she said, looking up at him.

From that angle, she made a most appealing figure, her lips slightly parted, her slender neck, the swelling of her breasts. Archie had to avert his eyes.

'What?' she said.

'I don't want to dribble.'

She chuckled. 'Aren't we complimentary today? Is there nothing else you like about me? Or is it only my looks?'

'Aren't they enough?'

'You really aren't interested in my money, are you?'

'How could I think about money when dancing with you?'

'Flatterer! If I could, I would die dancing. I *love* to dance!'

There was a clenching in his stomach. She was so lovely, so *exciting*. 'Alice, I haven't admired any woman this much - not ever.'

'You "admire" me too?'

The music stopped. He reluctantly took his arm from her waist, but she kept hold of his hand, and patted it gently. 'You want to stop already?'

'There must be others you want to dance with.'

'No. I only want you,' she said, and as the band struck up a lively jazz tune, she laughed and pulled him back to the dance floor. She was animated, full of life and vivacity, like a kitten with a ball of wool. She span and whirled, her feet striking a staccato rhythm with the beat until she had to pause, fanning her face with a menu card.

'Why don't we go somewhere quieter?'

'Where?' he said dimly.

'I know a place.'

It was a scruffy area Archie didn't recognise, and he was surprised when Alice told the coolie to stop. 'I keep a room here,' she explained.

She took his hand and led him inside and up the bare boards of the stairs, their footsteps echoing. Archie thought the building listened to them. At the top was a door with brown bakelite numbers which read 55. Alice opened it with a key.

'Do you remember Eva? You met her when the gambling house was raided.'

'Yes,' he nodded.

'She lives in the next apartment. I have this,' Alice said. She pushed the door shut behind Archie.

Archie was awkward, but she took a pace nearer, gazing into his eyes. He could smell her scent, but over that there was another odour: an animal smell, of desire and lust. She put her arms out straight, one at either side of his neck, her fingers interlaced behind him, her mouth an inch from his. 'What do you think we should do?'

He was tingling. Pushing his head forward, he waited until their lips were touching before saying, 'Perhaps something like this?'

'Perhaps.'

Archie could not stop himself. He clutched at her, and she gave a throaty chuckle as he felt the soft moistness of her lips.

*Monday 31st July, 1922*

Archie woke with the conviction that his servant had called him too early. After shaking Archie awake, the boy stood waiting impassively, a tray with morning tea in his hands, his eyes fixed somewhere in the middle distance.

'Put it on the table. I'll pour it myself,' Archie said, and as the boy padded from the room, he threw off the sheets, yawning prodigiously.

His time with Alice had been so precious. He had not expected her to invite him into her flat, into her bed. The memory of that slim figure was branded on his memory. Her smiling face, lips parted in passion, her slender body rising and falling over him, the way her hair hung over his face as she reached her climax. And he too.

Downstairs he met John and Peter in the hallway.

'What's today? Oh, I know, let's have a cross country run, then exercises, before we're allowed somethin' to eat,' John said, 'and then learn a load of cobblers about the law and that, and some lessons in Chinese too, eh? That'd be fun.'

'You had a good evening?' Archie said.

'Him?' Peter said. 'He got into a fight with an American sailor, and two SMP Sikhs were all that stopped the pair of them slugging it out.'

'He was rude.'

'What did he say?' Archie said.

'I can't remember, but he was bloody rude,' John stated.

'What happened to you?' Peter asked. 'Your grin's big enough to cut the top of your head off!'

'I may tell you later,' Archie said. He dare not here, with other recruits within earshot.

'It was the girl, then,' Peter said. 'The girl whose father's a big noise?'

'Well, yes.'

'Archie, don't get yourself in trouble,' Peter said.

'Or her,' John added with a snigger.

'What trouble is there in seeing a girl?' Archie said. 'Anyway, I'm seeing her again.'

'When?'

'Tomorrow.'

Rod was at Ross and Dewitt's offices at eight. As he opened the door, the secretary looked up disapprovingly, but then slipped through the door behind to inform his employer that a policeman insisted on seeing him.

'He won't keep you long,' he said when he returned. He closed the door behind him and made a deliberate effort to forget Rod existed, collating carbons and fresh sheets of paper, winding them into his typewriter and starting to type.

Rod toyed with his hat. The window was open, and every so often a light wind made the curtains shiver. Rod wished he could feel the draught. If the door had been left open, there might be a cooling breeze, but the door had a self-closing spring.

He gave up and sat. Along the corridor came the thud of a door slamming. It sounded close. He heard a man's voice.

And then there was a loud crash, not a door: a gunshot. Rod dropped his hat as there was another report, pushing past the squeaking secretary, and barging the door wide. It led to a passageway, with a door at the opposite end and two doors on the right. A door on the left, he guessed, led to the building's main corridor. A man had appeared at the farther end, whiffling incomprehensibly through a thick moustache and beard, eyes popping with indignation; a second man pulled open the nearest door, expostulating furiously as though Rod was responsible for the noise. Both were silenced as he drew his gun.

The middle door stood ajar. Rod crouched low before peeping around the door's jamb. The was that familiar smell –

cordite – and a haze of gunsmoke. Rod hurtled in, fetching up against the wall, his gun roving swiftly over the room.

There was only one man inside, and from the blood, he was no threat.

# Chapter Thirty-One

Rod shouted to the secretary to call the police, yanking open the door to the main corridor. He flung himself through, hitting the wall opposite hard enough to make him grunt. The staircase was a few paces away, and he shoved the door wide, Colt at the ready. He could hear footsteps rattling below him, and rushed down as best he could, pistol in one hand, the other sliding down the wooden handrail, whirling round each corner.

A door slammed. He ran on, still half a level to go. At the ground floor, gasping, legs complaining, he pulled the door wide. There was a shout, a scream, and people ran at the sight of his gun. He saw a man at the doors, a Chinese in a dark suit, with a fedora that held a chequered band about it.

'*SMP! Stop! Police*!' he shouted, running through suddenly-crouching people. Rod saw the figure delicately pitter-patter down the steps outside, poised as a tap-dancer.

Rod thought he had him then. There was no escape, he thought, and he rushed forward, but as he did so, he saw the man turn. Short and slim, the fedora tipped to the back of his head, he had his own gun up, a Mauser, and was already firing, and Rod had to leap to avoid the bullets slamming into the wall, one ricocheting from the pavement and narrowly missing him, others following him as he darted behind a pillar. He heard someone struck by a bullet, the glass shattering, screams and cries.

There was the slam of the vehicle's door as Rod rolled to the side of the pillar, his gun ready, only to see the car with the assassin make off up the street. With all the people milling, he couldn't fire; he would miss the assassin, but he'd be certain to hit bystanders. Instead, he climbed to his feet, sore and bruised but unwounded, as a pair of Chinese officers appeared with a Sikh, who instantly shouldered his rifle when he saw Rod's pistol. Once Rod had convinced them that he was a police officer, he had them hold back the crowd, contact Central Station, and have someone search the ground with gloves for cartridge cases from which they might get fingerprints.

Then he made his way back inside.

The man with the impressive beard was Basil Ross, the business partner of Frank Dewitt. The other was an articled clerk, who sat in his office, head in his hands, moaning.

'I cannot believe this,' Ross kept repeating as he stood looking down at the body of his partner. Dewitt had been shot once in the chest, and once in the centre of his forehead. He wore a look of surprise rather than fear or anger, as if he had realised he had come to work wearing carpet slippers instead of shoes. His brains were spattered liberally over the wall behind him.

The room was not huge, perhaps fifteen by twenty feet, with the narrower side facing the street and the company's interior corridor. His desk was between two windows looking out over Canton Road. A Chubb's safe stood to the left of his desk, and a series of filing cabinets on the right, while most of the wall space was devoted to law reports and files. At the other end of the room, near the entrance, was a sofa and two chairs set about a low table. There was a tray, on which two decanters stood together with a quartet of glasses.

'Did you see the man?' Rod asked.

'No, I was in my office when I heard the shot. I reached the door just in time to see you.'

Rod nodded, walking about the room.

'What are you doing?' Ross said.

'He tried to shoot me with a Mauser. There must be two cartridge cases somewhere. We may be able to take a fingerprint from them, or … ah!'

He had found one. It had rolled behind the sofa. The second lay behind the open door. He collected both in his handkerchief and dropped them into an envelope.

'How long have you known your partner?' Rod asked.

'Frank and I have worked together these last fifteen years. He was a very clear-thinking fellow. Bright, well-versed in the law – professional. He specialised in company law, and with the number of new firms being set up, he was always in demand.'

'Did he have enemies?'

'Enemies? He was a lawyer, not a gangster! No!'

'Was he married?'

'No. I suppose that's a blessing. The thought of having to tell his wife ...' He looked devastated.

'What of his social life?'

'I don't know that he had much of one.' He saw Rod's expression and gave him an old-fashioned look. 'Yes, Detective, I do know what you mean. He enjoyed a visit to a nightclub on occasion. This is Shanghai; show me a man who doesn't. But he was reliable and hard working.'

'Was he an inveterate gambler, do you know?'

He scoffed into his beard. 'He enjoyed a day at the races, I have no doubt. We used to entertain clients and take a box at race days, but nothing more than that, I'm sure.'

'What about casinos?'

He peered at Rod like a medical student seeing a new and wonderful form of cancer. 'The poor man is hardly dead, Detective! Do you wish to sully his name?'

Rod grabbed his lapel and pointed at Frank Dewitt's body. 'Yes! He's still warm! Look at him, Mr Ross! Your partner is the victim of a premeditated *assassination*! You may find my questions distasteful, but I'm here to learn anything that might help me find his murderer. I am here because the manager of The Wheel told me your partner owed the casino money. I am prepared to ask as many questions as I need, whether you like it or not.'

'The Wheel?'

'The murderer might have been paid by a competitor of yours. This could be retaliation for something your firm has done to another, or a threat to stop you doing something. If you don't help, I won't find out. But if this *is* to do with your business, it would be better to discover that as soon as we may.'

Ross glowered, chewing at his moustache, and then nodded. 'My apologies. You are quite right, of course.' He looked down at Rod's hand on his lapel, and Rod relaxed his grip.

Ross nodded. Glancing down at the body, he shook his head.

'I'll miss you, Frank,' he said quietly.

Ross took Rod to his own office.

'I am sorry about my manner. It's been a horrible shock. I thought of Frank almost like the son I had never had. Seeing him dead ...' he trailed off.

It was clear from the room that he was the senior partner. His office was considerably larger, some five-and-twenty feet square, and there were three leather armchairs: one wingback, two captain style with padded back and arms, and a three-seater sofa. There was a table, but this one held six decanters and a humidor.

'Feel free to take a cigar, Detective. Would you care for a brandy and soda? I feel I need one after seeing ... him.'

'Thank you, but I'll stick to my cigarettes,' Rod said. He accepted a light from the lawyer's lighter, and both smoked thoughtfully. Ross poured a large brandy, and sat pensively snuffing it.

'Have you seen action, sir?' Rod asked. 'You were very cool in there.'

Ross cocked an eyebrow. 'I have lived here almost twenty years, sir. In that time I have seen many bodies on the streets. You know how violent the city can be. You mentioned debts?'

'I know that this must be distasteful, but I have found chits which appear to have been signed by Mr Dewitt. Were you aware that he was a keen gambler?'

'No, and if I had, I would have dissolved our partnership. I do not approve of gambling.'

It was natural, as Rod knew, for gambling addicts to conceal their compulsion from others. That was particularly important for a man of business like Dewitt. 'Did he handle large sums? Could he have taken money from client accounts?'

'Heavens!' Ross paled. 'He has his own clients ... Goodness, if he has defrauded them, it'll come down on my head!'

'You must look to your resources, obviously. Meanwhile, was he working with any clients who could have taken offence? Perhaps a legal matter that he lost? Did he mention clients who worried him?'

'There was no client who could have complained at his work as far as I know, no.'

'You say he commonly worked for businesses?'

'He was a commercial lawyer, yes. He handled every aspect of business law, and a little litigation when necessary, but not often.'

'Has he been working on any litigation recently?'

His gaze became unfocused, as if he was searching through a mental filing system. 'There was one, although it was hardly litigation. A man had been planning a new building in the Northern District, not far from the Silk works. Well, this chap started receiving threats from another businessman. He took little notice, but then he was kidnapped and murdered. Your fellows dragged him from the water.'

'A foreign businessman?'

'No, a local. I can find you the files, I expect. They'll be in Frank's office.'

'Good, I would be grateful. What happened after that?'

'The other businessman approached Frank to buy the building, but Frank said he couldn't until probate had been settled. It was a complicated matter, because the man held shares in a number of properties and had other investments. The fellow became quite sharp, I understand.'

'What was his name?'

'Let me ask Jenkins to search it out for you. He knows Frank's filing better than me.'

He called the clerk, who nodded and reluctantly walked to Dewitt's office. Dewitt's body had already been removed.

'Can you tell me anything more about Mr Dewitt? I know it's disagreeable, but I have to know everything I can.'

'I quite understand.' He puffed at his cigar for a moment. 'The chances of catching the murderer are remote, aren't they?'

'I will do all in my power.'

'Yes. I suppose you will,' he sighed. 'I have lived here long enough to know that the city is sham. There is gold everywhere, people believe, but it's really gilt. If there is a death, Shanghailanders will turn out to send the fellow off, but how many truly care? Justice is the same. Lots of effort goes into seeking a killer like the man who murdered Frank, but even with the most intensive efforts, what can you achieve? He will be in the French Settlement or the Chinese sector by now.'

'Yes, but something in your files may point me in the direction of the man responsible. The instigator may be living here in the International territory. Perhaps there will be justice for him, even if we don't catch the actual perpetrator.'

'I suppose so,' Ross said. 'We can only hope.'

Jenkins knocked and walked in quietly. He passed a blue folder to Ross. Without speaking he left the room, quietly shutting the door behind him.

Ross glanced at Rod. 'Jenkins was at the Dardanelles, poor fellow. Hasn't got over it yet.'

Rod nodded. He had seen many others in a similar state. 'Do you have that name, sir?'

'Yes, I thought so! A man called Qian. Billy Qian, through his company, Shanghai Qiexim.'

Rod took down the address of the contested building and hurried back to Central Station. The number he recovered from the bank robber had been Qiexim's. How was Qian connected to the robbers? Done, he went to the armoury to find Dan Fairbairn at his desk.

Fairbairn looked up as Rod held out his handkerchief.

'What's that?'

'Cartridges from another shooting. They could be connected to Foster's killing, possibly the shooting at the gambling house, too. The gunman today matched the description of the fellow who killed Foster, and was using a Mauser too,' Rod said.

'If the gun's new, proving cartridges came from the same gun is not easy.'

'I understand, sir.'

'I'll do my best. Now,' Fairbairn continued, 'I have done some work on your revolver. You should keep it as a spare, in case of jams or other problems.'

'Good God! What have you done to it!'

Fairbairn gave him a cold stare. 'As you can see, I have removed the front of the trigger guard so it's easier to get your finger positioned quickly. I've also cut away the hammer spur. In a gunfight, the spur's unnecessary, but if there, it might catch and fumble your draw.'

'I see.' Rod handled the pistol unenthusiastically. The cylinder opened easily to display six empty chambers, and when he snapped it shut and tested the trigger, it felt smooth.

'I've also filed the foresight round: again, so it won't catch on clothes.' He opened a drawer, pulling out a holster. 'Have this. It should suit. Be careful.'

Back at his desk, Rod found a note saying Dubois had called. Rod went to the telephone in the hallway and soon heard Dubois' voice crackling over the wires.

'I wanted to tell you that we have had little fortune so far,' he said. 'Huang Jinrong has sent his men to investigate, but there is no news. I was wondering, do you have any more information?'

'No, the two Chinese who witnessed the attack told us all they knew.'

'There were two witnesses?'

'Yes. When Foster was killed, his car crashed into their shop. A man and his daughter. They saw the whole thing.'

Dubois sighed. 'Well, I shall try to have Huang Jinrong work harder, but I do not have the great hope.'

Rod hung up the receiver. He believed that the same man had murdered Foster and Dewitt, and he was determined to find him and make him pay.

# Chapter Thirty-Two

Qian's palatial villa lay on Bubbling Well Road. Deliberately English, built of brick but painted a pristine white, even wealthier Shanghailanders would eye it with envy.

The rickshaw stopped, and a pair of suspicious Chinese appeared at the gates. He had to show his warrant card before they would allow him inside. They opened the gates with surly reluctance.

A stern Chinese manservant bowed at the door. The hall was vast. Rod could have fitted five apartments the size of his own inside. All white, oval, a staircase on the right sweeping upwards, following the curve of the wall. The floor was black and white marble, with a four-pointed star in the middle like a map's compass.

The servant opened a pair of doors, and Rod was led to the verandah.

Billy Qian relaxed on a couch clad in only a light silk robe. A woman sat near, peeling an orange. Rod recognised Eva Bugayeva.

'Mr Qian.'

Billy lifted a glass in which ice rang merrily. 'Detective Constable Cottey. To what do I owe this pleasure?'

Rod felt indescribably grubby, the sweat marking his jacket. 'Mr Qian, I have some questions.'

'Sit. Number One Boy will fetch you a drink. What would you like? Gin? Whisky? Bourbon? Ah, but of course, for you it's the Old-Fashioned, isn't it?' he chuckled.

'How did you know what I drink?' Rod said sharply as the servant hurried away.

'I was returning the favour,' Qian said. His eyes narrowed as he smiled, but they held no humour. 'After all, you have been following me. It seemed reasonable to learn a little about the man who was so keen to learn about me. I am glad to have an opportunity of talking to you, Detective. I think you have the wrong idea about me.'

'I am investigating murder.'

'Yes, the tragic death of poor Mr Foster.'

The Chinese servant returned, carrying a salver with a frosted glass. Rod took it. The coolness was divine. Eva stood and walked inside with the restrained economy of a dancer. When she reached the doors, she cast a glance at him, and Rod felt it like the lick of an electric cable. Then she was gone.

He said, 'What can you tell me about Foster?'

'He was servant to a family I barely know. What would I know of him?'

The question was innocent enough, but Rod had seen him with Maurice. He obviously knew at least one of the Wintons. Did he know Foster was squiring Alice?

'What of Frank Dewitt?'

'Who?'

'The lawyer who refused to sell you the building on Hanon Road.'

'Dewitt? The name is familiar,' he said vaguely, 'but then, I have many business associates. What of him?'

'He was murdered today. A gunman entered his office and shot him at point blank.'

'That is terrible! The city grows more violent daily,' Qian said. 'I hope you will capture the perpetrators quickly, Detective. It would be a poor show were a second murder to go unresolved.'

'Both are under investigation. I am confident I will find the assassin and the man who commanded him.'

'*Assassin* singular?'

'Both were killed by the same man,' Rod said. 'So possibly the same man ordered both murders. Tell me about the factory on the Honan Road.'

Qian didn't like the fact Rod knew of it. 'It was a dyeing godown with a large yard. Nothing much to look at but, as you know, there is a crisis of accommodation. If I knock down the factory and build apartments, I can sell some and rent out others. The money raised will pay for the demolition and building, and I will have a steady income from those rented.'

'But you cannot acquire the building.'

'Ah, *probate*! Lawyers can be so slow and old-fashioned,' Qian chuckled, but there was a hard glitter in his eyes. Resentment?

'I understand you hoped to buy it through your company, Qiexim. A bank robber last week had a note with your company telephone number.'

'Many people have my telephone number.'

'Many bank robbers?'

'Many people. Not that I fit in. Did you not know? I am half-caste.' Qian's voice altered, grew sharper. 'You know, in England, I was used to being stared at, but other fellows accepted me. I had an excellent education at a small public school, and then at Oxford, but here – here I am still foreign, wherever I go. In the street, the English call me *the Chinaman with the money*, while the Chinese call me *foreigner*. I sit between two races and cultures.' He gazed at his glass belligerently and called for his number one boy to replenish it. When he turned back to Rod, he was smiling once more. 'So you see, I have a perfect accent, but that doesn't make me English.'

'And that makes you bitter.'

'Bitter? No, I have always believed a man makes his own fortune. There are bigots all over Shanghai, but that gives me an opportunity. When fools look on me as an animal with slanted eyes and nothing between my ears, I see men I can beat. It's how I have built my business.'

He smiled, but his eyes were sad. For all his wealth and women, he would have preferred to have been accepted.

Rod left Billy Qian on his couch. Eva returned as Rod walked away, bending to massage Billy's back.

He could never fit in. Billy Qian was neither one race or the other, and was viewed askance by both.

Rod's head was beginning to pound, and he lit a cigarette. It helped a little. He took a rickshaw to the building on the Honan Road.

The Northern District roads were less congested. They still held hordes of pedestrians, cyclists, and wheelbarrow taxis carrying three men on each side of the huge wheel, but there was less urgency. People moved more sedately. However ochre dust rose from every footstep, creating a yellow-orange filter before his eyes.

Like most of Shanghai, the Honan building was only twenty years old, but already Billy Qian reckoned it could be profitably demolished. It seemed ridiculous, but Billy Qian was convincing.

The site was almost a half block long, about eighty yards, but building only took up half. As for the rest, Rod was reminded of Gordon Road's training depot: a large oblong space, roughly forty by eighty yards. Low sheds stood at one wall, and the rest could have functioned as a parade ground.

It was the frame that grabbed the attention. With the low buildings here, it stood out like an oak tree in a desert. An immense structure of bamboo poles lashed together, taller than a four storey house, designed to dry huge bolts of cloth up to a hundred feet long.

Gates enclosed the grounds, but they were not locked. Rod pushed them wide and strolled towards the building. In the middle there was a double doorway, while smaller doors were set into the walls on either side. There was an air of genteel dilapidation, like a spinster who knew her time for marriage was past, but nonetheless kept up appearances. Doors and window frames were painted, but it was shoddy work preparing the place for sale. Blisters had already appeared.

Peering through the windows, Rod saw a large, open chamber. Steel beams, and rails with wheeled hooks, blocks and tackles, to move heavy items. In one corner there were tanks in which materials could be left soaking in dye. At the back Rod made out packing cases.

'Hello?'

Rod found himself confronted by a tall Chinese and a companion. Three more stood watching. 'Who are you?'

'We are guarding.' The man said. He had a good command of English, although the man at his side did not, and spent his time glowering at Rod and throwing sidelong glances at the speaker.

'There is little enough to guard, isn't there?'

'Some of the equipment inside is valuable.' He was holding a cudgel. Not threateningly, but he did give the impression that there was always an option of something along those lines. 'Mr Qian asked us to guard it.'

'Billy Qian?' Rod said.

The cudgel tapped his open hand, and Rod took the hint. 'Very well, I'm leaving.'

They watched Rod walk through the gates. He noticed cart tracks in the ground at the gates. It would be a good storehouse; perhaps goods from the docks. There was plenty of space in that godown.

Rod hailed a rickshaw to the Central Station, and he was lighting a contemplative cigarette when he saw another rickshaw approach from the opposite direction. The man in it was reading a sheaf of papers. It was Maurice Winton.

Turning, Rod saw him halt at the building and enter the gates. Unlike Rod's welcome, the guards pulled the gates wide for Winton, pushing them shut after him.

Maurice was involved with Billy Qian, and Qian knew Alice too, so Qian had lied when he said he barely knew the family. There had been two murders: those of Foster and Dewitt. Dewitt had refused to sell this building to Billy. Billy did not own it, but had instructed guards.

All the way to Central Station, Rod tried to make sense of it. And where Maurice fitted in.

Rod telephoned Ross at his office, but the secretary told him brokenly that his senior partner had left for the day after a tragic attack which had left Frank Dewitt dead.

'This is Detective Constable Cottey,' Rod said. 'I was with you today when Mr Dewitt was killed. Do you remember?'

'Yes, sir.'

'Mr Ross told me that someone tried to buy a building in Honan Road before probate. Do you know if the building was sold?'

'No, sir. I do not think so.'

'Can you fetch the file?'

'I can't, sir. It is confidential.'

Rod's frustration burst into anger. 'I'm trying to find the murderer! Don't you think Mr Ross would want to let me know?'

'I don't know. I shall speak to Mr Ross in the morning.'

'Wait! Is Mr Jenkins there?'

A moment later, the nervous voice of Jenkins came on the line. 'Hello? Can I help you?'

'Mr Jenkins,' Rod said, and deliberately slowed his voice, speaking clearly and calmly. He had seen so many shell-shocked men and knew that the slightest thing could set them off. 'I am the Detective Constable who was with you today.'

'Yes.'

Rod kept his tone easy and confident. 'Mr Jenkins, Mr Ross asked you to fetch him a file from Mr Dewitt's office. Do you remember?'

'Yes.'

'There is one thing I must check, but Mr Ross is not there. Could you help me?'

'I ... I can try.'

'We spoke about the Honan Road. I must know whether the building has been sold.'

'No, I can speak confidently to that. I was sorting through the details only the other day.'

'The building is empty?'

'No. A client was most insistent that he should be permitted to use it.'

'That was Mr Qian?'

'No, sir. Mr Dewitt was adamant that Mr Qian should not acquire it until the will had passed probate. Mr Qian persisted, and Mr Dewitt permitted me to know that he would be unwilling to sell to that man for all the tea in China. He disliked being hectored, sir.'

'So what happened?'

'Another client rented it for a short period, sir.'

'I see. Mr Jenkins, could you tell me who that client is?'

'Of course, sir. Mr Maurice Winton.'

Rod nodded to himself. Another link. 'Tell me, was Mr Dewitt working on a building in the Kweichou Road?'

'Yes, he handled that for Mr Maurice too.'

'Do other members of the family have business dealings with your company?'

The voice at the other end of the line became more agitated. 'I don't know that ...'

'I quite understand. You must maintain confidentiality.'

'Yes, sir.'

'But of Mr Dewitt's clients, most were businesses, weren't they? Could you tell me whether Ross and Dewitt worked for Alfred Winton's businesses?'

'Mr Dewitt was company secretary to the bank and other businesses of Mr Winton's. That is no secret, of course.'

'I am most grateful for your help.'

Rod hung up, thinking furiously.

He had seen Maurice Winton with Billy Qian in Qian's car on their way to the building in Kweichou Road, and Maurice was involved. Qian had tried to buy the godown in Honan Road, and subsequently Maurice rented the place. The two men were collaborating, but what was their interest in a building out in the Northern District and a smaller place in a rough part of the city?

Mickey Hi had dropped a note on his desk. Gracie Gale had called and asked him to visit her.

# Chapter Thirty-Three

'I've heard,' she said flatly. She walked to a table and poured two large brandies. Passing one to Rod, she sat at her desk. When he sipped, he was grateful. It was smooth, warm and delicious.

It was early evening. Guests were arriving, and Gracie's American girls were decked out in their finest. Gracie boasted that she travelled to San Francisco twice a year, buying the latest fashions for her girls, and Rod found that easy to believe. A tall woman with darker skin smiled at him with liquid eyes as she strolled past the door, fanning herself. It was hard not to stare.

'Frank Dewitt was a good man. I don't like to think he's been slaughtered by some madman.'

He pulled his attention back to her. 'He was no madman. I was there.'

'So I heard. What happened?'

Rod told her of the morning's shooting. 'The killer was possibly the same man who killed Foster, the Wintons' chauffeur,' he finished. 'I have a description from witnesses, and I saw him myself.'

'Why would someone shoot Frank? There are plenty who come here I wouldn't mind seeing disappear, but Frank? He was harmless.'

'Someone considered him a threat. Perhaps financially, in business terms, or because he worked for a competitor. Could he have been involved in anything illegal?'

'Not knowingly. Oh, I know that as a lawyer he would have had dealings with men who were not, what, *savoury*? Not every man in the Shanghai Club earned his money in ways the Good Lord would consider wholesome! But Frank himself was whiter than white.'

'Even a good man can be saddled with a client who is not.'

'Yes; I guess Frank may have had the odd rat - but he was always the soul of discretion. He never told me about his clients.'

'Did he speak of business? Even if he did not give the names of the men involved?'

'Why, sure. Only the other day he told me about a client who died. Frank said he wasn't the kind he would usually take on, because his business was murky as mud. Those were his words: murky as mud.'

'Did he ever speak of a bar in the Kweichou Road?'

She eyed him closely. 'This to do with the same folks you were talking about before?'

'They could be associated. I don't know. I'm just trying to follow any angle I can.'

She set her head to one side, pursed her lips. Then, 'All right, Detective. I'll let you in on a secret: a lady like me can't afford to have all her money tied up in movable assets, if you understand me. My assets are asses and tits. Some while ago I started looking into properties, so my investments were spread better. Way things are, it's possible I'll be out of the whoring business in a couple of years. If the city bans all the whores, what'll happen, eh? Sailors and visitors will still want their diversions, and there'll still be girls wanting money, so the trade will carry on, but not in the open like now. It'll get hidden away in shithole apartments or alleyways, just like drugs are now they're banned. I don't want to be a part of that.'

American evangelicals determined to stamp out the trade in female flesh had organised a campaign, and the Municipal Council hit on the novel approach of banning the trade by degrees. They held a ballot each year, and those whose numbers were selected must close. So far Gracie had survived, but it must happen before long, as she said.

'So you have bought up buildings?' Rod said. 'Did you buy that one?'

'No. It would do as a godown, but that's all. A Chinaman was interested, but Frank reckoned the guy was up to no good. He said the man had his finger in too many pies, and one day someone was going to cut off his fingers.'

'Do you know who he was?'

'Maybe, but why should I tell you? You're taking but not sharing.'

'The man who tried to buy the place in the Kweichou Road may have realised Frank blocked him. He might have paid someone to kill Frank.'

'Hmm.' She gave a wry grin. 'You're not just a flatfoot with a little truncheon, are you? Okay, it was Billy Qian.'

'I see. Did Frank say anything about the business Billy was involved in?'

'He was always discreet, but he did say one thing surprised me.'

'What was that?'

'He said that the German, you know, Schreier, was hired by him. He laughed when he said that, said it took one to know one.'

'Engaged how?'

'The Chinaman took Schreier as a comprador. Frank thought it was so Billy had a contact who could advise him about business or buying properties. Schreier tried to get hold of the godown in the Honan Road, but Frank was wise to him.'

'I see.'

'Are you going to find the man who killed Frank?'

'I will try to.'

'And you still want to find out what you can about this Eva, I guess?'

'Yes. Have you learned anything?'

'Maybe. She seems a bright thing, but desperate for money. Her husband's a drunk, and she's making a living best she can but it's not easy on the street, so she's tagging along with Alice Winton.' She fixed him with an eye at once shrewd and amused. 'You didn't think I wouldn't learn who her friends are, did you? Information, here, is the currency of life.'

'I see.'

'And, now I know who you're talking about, I can help a bit. This Eva is getting real friendly with little Alice, but she's not above making a cash on the side. She worked as a dancer in The Wheel – Garcia's joint? She was working as an escort. A man comes in and wants company, he'll ask for the type he wants. She's quite popular. Russian girls are still exotic here, and I've heard she wasn't choosy. Doesn't work there now.'

'I see.'

'She lives here,' she said, passing him a slip of paper. 'Now, I have a full house of guests, so I have to go, but Detective Constable, if you have any problems finding the guy who killed Frank, let me know. You understand me? You have any problems getting him, you let me know.'

The house on Rue Wagner was less a mansion than a fortress. Thin Bao nodded to the Chinese guards, and was permitted to enter.

Du Yusheng lived in luxury. He had twin mansions, each with two courtyards, one in front of each house, one behind, the pair surrounded by a high wall with one entrance. The guards were men known for their loyalty, but Thin Bao knew that the mansions held White Russians, too. Du Yusheng went nowhere without at least four of them. One was standing now at the top of the steps leading to the house's front door. He watched impassively as Thin Bao approached.

'I was called here,' he said.

The man jerked his head to his right, and Thin Bao walked past. He felt revulsion that Du Yusheng would hire foreign mercenaries to protect him. This one stank like a hog. When Thin Bao became a great leader, he would rely on local men, honourable, trustworthy men. Not foreign scum.

A servant took him through the house, past silks and opulent drapery, carpets, seats, and out to the rear courtyard where Du Yusheng sat on a divan, watching two of his sons wrestling. Behind him stood two more Russian guards; hulking, square-faced figures. They would be easy targets for his Mauser, he thought. Neither had the speed of reaction that a natural Chinese like him possessed.

He bowed low.

'Do you have news of the traitor who had my cabaret raided?'

His voice was quiet, as usual. He knew it was better not to share matters like this.

'I have spoken to my barman. He had given news of the cabaret to a man called Yao Shihui, who paid another called Wong Tiecheng. I will find him.'

'That is good. There is another matter.'

'Yes.'

'There were witnesses to the shooting of the Winton driver. The shop that the car ran into. They are talking to the police. And the people in that road are not paying their protection.'

'I will see to it,' Thin Bao said.

The meeting was at an end. Du Yusheng leaned back, his pupils dilated. He held out his hand. A young girl held up a tray, and he took a cup of rice wine, sipping. Thin Bao walked backwards from him, until he could turn and return to the hallway, out to the front courtyard, and into the street.

One day, he would sit on a divan enjoying the fruits of his efforts. But first he had to rise to that level, and that meant establishing his reputation. He would have many jobs like this to perform. And he had yet to find Wong Tiecheng.

Central Station was quiet when Rod arrived. Hungry, he went to the mess for food. When he entered, Bert Shaw was at a table.

He grinned, 'Old chap, may I buy you dinner to repay you for seeing me home on Friday? Sorry to get so stinking drunk, but you know how it is. One starts thinking, and before you know it, you're in a bit of a funk about things.' He eyed Rod more closely. 'How are you? You look rather grey about the gills.'

Bert tried a steak, while Rod ordered a steak and kidney pudding.

Rod said, 'When you say, "About things", what do you mean? Aren't you happy in the job?'

'Oh, I am happy enough.'

'Even with the pay?'

He grinned. 'That is hard to cope with, I know, but it's better than … well, other jobs.'

'In Bailey's, you mentioned you had lost your woman.'

'Did I?'

'I know how it is,' Rod said.

'You too?'

Although Rod didn't intend to share his story, Bert was a man Rod imagined would remain a friend long after they had retired and left Shanghai. 'I had a girl, before I joined up: Cecily. Her brother Dick was my best friend, her best friend was Ethel. Everyone assumed Ethel would marry Dick, and I would win Cecily. We promised ourselves as much. And then there was the war.'

Rod could see her in his mind's eye, bright-eyed with tears she refused to let fall. Trying to be brave in front of the other men, Dick giving him a comforting nudge. Rod tried to smile, but it felt as though his heart was ripped apart when he glanced back and saw Cecily and Ethel with his mother, all waving, the Old Man behind with his hands on Rod's mother's shoulders. He stood as straight as he had in the army in his own day, before he gave up soldiering and took up farming.

'We were in the Ninth Devons. On first of July, sixteen, we went over the top; near Mametz. We couldn't muster at the advanced trench, because it had been beasted by German artillery, so Captain Martin had us form up in the support line. Which was far enough back that the Germans couldn't see us, because of a little hill. But as we carried on, a machine gun started up. I don't know how we kept going. I could hear the bullets strike, men falling on all sides. Captain Martin was one of the first. The officers always caught it first, didn't they? I hate snipers. When we captured one, we weren't gentle. And all the while the Spandaus kept up their infernal chattering. The men fell like nettles under the scythe. It's not like the films, is it?'

Rod stopped. He had said more than he had intended. 'Sorry. I don't know why I suddenly started. I didn't mean to …'

'I know what it was like. I was in the 2nd Battalion of the Manchesters, in 32nd Div. We were pretty badly mauled, too.'

'We managed to capture the place, but at huge cost. Over four hundred and sixty casualties. Nearly two hundred dead or missing. All in the space of a few minutes. The Padre had the fellows buried a couple of days later. He put up a notice: *The Devonshires held this trench; the Devonshires hold it still.* It was a kind thought, but it didn't help. When Captain Martin fell, Dick went to him. The next time I looked, he was gone.'

Rod sighed. 'That was the end of Cecily and me. You know how it is. Once she heard that her brother was dead, she devoted herself to supporting her parents and Ethel. Every time Cecily saw me, it was a reminder that she'd never see Dick again. So I saw her less and less, and when I saw an advert to come out here, I thought it would be a chance for both sisters to get over Dick, and perhaps Cecily may come to terms with things and – I don't know, perhaps to choose whether she still wanted me or not.'

'And she didn't?'

Rod gave a half-hearted shrug. 'I had a letter. She thought I would find a better life out here than she could offer me. You know, sometimes I think our women were more damaged by the war than we who fought. They saw their husbands, brothers, sons march away, and then they received the telegrams. Either their boys were dead, or they were amputees, or blinded by gas, or injured in some other way. And those whose men came back were treated like lepers, because they were happy, and why should they be happy when so many others were grieving? The widows trying to support their children, the mothers who had lost their children. They hated those who had their lives return to normal.'

'You're a good man, Rod,' Bert said.

'I just wanted you to know that you're not alone. When you feel bad, tell me, and we'll share a drink or two. It may help.'

'Yes. Perhaps later.'

They ate in companionable silence. Then, 'So, how's your case? The Winton's chauffeur?'

Rod explained, and Bert nodded thoughtfully. 'You know, I should look into this Foster more closely.'

'What do you mean?'

Bert avoided his gaze. 'The family is not distraught about his death, is it? Perhaps there's more to Foster than met your eye at first glance. What if he knew something about the son: how he died, for example?'

'Their boy Ian? He died at the Front. What could Foster know that led to his murder three years later?'

'Perhaps nothing. I don't know ... but I should look into it if I were you.'

Later, at his desk, Rod considered Bert's words. Bert had been insistent about learning more of Ian Winton's death. His persistence niggled. In the end, Rod grabbed a message note and scribbled quickly, 'Information Request stop Details death of Captain Ian Winton in action 1918 stop Late of Dorsets stop Information required in murder enquiry stop.' He called Mickey Hi, and addressed the note to CID in Scotland Yard. 'Mickey, take this to the telegraph office. There won't be a reply today.'

'Yes, Detective Cottey.'

It would take two days, possibly more, for any useful information, and by the nature of the telegraph it would be brief, but Rod hoped it might help. He couldn't imagine how police forces operated before the telegraph.

He picked up the file concerning Bao Xiu's body being fished from the river by Tim Burton. There was a note appended: the boy had been taken to an orphanage, and Rod realised that it was the one run by Edith Winton. It seemed curious that the Wintons kept appearing. First Foster, then Maurice and Alice, and now Mrs Winton.

Dan Fairbairn appeared in the doorway, a clipboard in hand. 'I have something for you.'

'What is it?'

Rod joined him in the armoury.

'Look here,' Fairbairn said, setting three envelopes on his workbench. Each was marked with a number and contained a cartridge case. He withdrew them, setting them on their respective envelopes. 'This is from Foster's shooting, this from your raid, and this last was one of the two you gave me from Ross and Dewitt's. No useful fingerprints, I'm afraid, but …' Opening a drawer he took out a magnifying glass and passed it to Rod.

Rod focused on the nearer of the cases. It was rimless, with a slight bottle-neck. Dan impatiently told him to study the back. Around the primer, Rod saw 'DWM' printed above the primer, and '403' below. On either side were the letter 'K'.

'It's authentic German ammunition,' Fairbairn said, offering a cigarette. 'The "DWM" stands for "Deutsche Waffen und Munitionsfabriken". They made machine guns and pistols in the War, and obviously cartridges too. Now, look at the percussion caps.'

Rod did. Each was hit slightly off-centre with a circular dent that had a small mark on one side, a little as though a tiny rodent had nibbled away at one edge.

'You have the dint? Look on the opposite side of the cartridge, on the rim.'

There were two scratches on the metal. 'What is that?'

'My guess is the extractor is vicious. However, what is important is that the shape of the firing pin is the same on all the cases, and the position of the pin's strike is the same relative to the marks on the case's rim. It means that those three cases were fired from the same gun.'

'You're sure?'

Fairbairn stared at Rod coldly.

'I'm sorry,' he said quickly. 'It's new to me.'

'Yes. Well, you can take it from me that the same gun fired these bullets, and if you find the gun, we can test fire it and prove the fact.'

## Chapter Thirty-Four

Rod visited the Astor House that evening. It was good to see normal people enjoying themselves. Real, ordinary people, who had nothing to do with shootings or robberies or frauds. He sat at the bar. It had been a long day, and he sipped an Old Fashioned, feeling lonely.

Confession, so Catholics said, was good for the soul. Not for him. If anything, he felt a fool. Bert had listened sympathetically, but he wore a kind of half-amused expression that was almost patronising, like being given a supportive hearing by the army padre. Bert must think Rod a complete idiot.

Rod ordered another Old Fashioned. They slipped down like iced honey. He lit a cigarette, inhaling deeply. Dancers whirled and span, the peacock background sparkling and changing colour, the band played with gusto, until the noise began to thunder in his head. He saw again the flashes of the big guns, the rattle of Spandaus, the men spinning as they were caught, Martin and Dick falling…

And then he was back in the Astor House, an Old Fashioned in his hand, shivering. In that moment he could understand how men could blow their heads off. It was a release, an escape.

When Billy Qian arrived, he smiled broadly and waved as he took his seat, and a few moments later, Eva joined him. She saw Rod, but he might as well have been formed of glass, for her glance passed through him as if he didn't exist.

She sat at Billy's side, and they ordered cocktails, him a whisky, and she something colourful that appeared bright blue under the lights. It looked like she was drinking petrol.

Rod turned away. His own loneliness felt sharper with the retelling of his broken affair with Cecily. He resented Billy. Eva's companionship may be due to Billy's money, but at least he had an attraction. He was more fortunate than a detective constable in the SMP.

A third Old Fashioned materialised.

Rod sipped this more slowly. When he glanced over, he saw Eva dancing, not with Billy, but with Maurice Winton. Billy Qian sat, his eyes fixed on the couple. Rod saw no jealousy, in fact it seemed rather the opposite, as though Billy was pleased to see Eva dancing closely with Maurice.

On a whim, Rod walked to Billy's table, pulling out a chair.

'You don't mind, do you?' Rod said as he sat down. He lit a cigarette, waving the match to extinguish it.

'I wondered whether you would visit me here,' Qian said.

'I had a look at the place on the Kweichou Road. And the godown on the Honan Road. A good sized property.'

'Yes. It should bring in a good return.'

'You have already rented it, haven't you?'

The smile remained, but his eyes seemed to freeze. 'How do you mean?'

'I understood you had rented it. Through an intermediary.'

'No.'

'How odd. The lawyers told me it was rented to Maurice. I thought you had evaded the lawyers' dislike for you and got it using a proxy.'

'I have no idea what you are talking about. He may have rented it. If so, it has nothing to do with me.'

'So if I looked around the place, it wouldn't upset you?'

'Not in the slightest. It is nothing to do with me.'

'Strange. The guards said you hired them. I admire your taste, by the way.'

'My taste?'

'Eva.'

'She is rather precious, isn't she? Elegant, beautiful, and so fragile.'

'I thought her rather hard. Like a well-polished diamond.'

Qian chuckled. 'I think I know her better.'

'Perhaps. So are you retaining her, or throwing her at your business partner?'

'I have no partner.'

'What of Maurice?'

He sighed and signalled to a waiter to replenish his glass. 'What of him?'

'He is your partner in the building.'

Qian placed both hands on the table's top and took a deep breath. 'Let me be clear, Detective, I am not involved in anything with Maurice. He is not a partner, companion or associate in my business dealings, and I am not involved in any of his. We are friends. Eva is another friend. I enjoy her company, and I am happy to pay for her time, since her finances are strained.'

'She has nothing.'

'Quite so. However it would be churlish on my part to refuse Maurice the opportunity to dance with her.'

'I see. I wonder why Maurice was at the building in Honan Street, if he is not in partnership with you?'

'Perhaps he has business of his own. I will warn him that when I take over that building his venture will cease. It would be foolish to invest in converting the place to his own uses, since I will demolished it soon.'

'*If* you gain the building.' Rod's headache was returning. It felt like it might explode into a two-day bed-rest migraine.

'No one else wants it.'

'The lawyers may decide not to sell to you.'

'That is always a possibility.'

That was when Maurice appeared at the table. 'What the hell are you doing here?' he demanded, standing over Rod.

At school and the Army Rod had met bullies who, like Maurice, believed money and aggression meant they could push others about. Maurice was petulant, like a playground tyrant who had sweets confiscated after stealing them.

Rod glanced up. 'I wanted a drink. Why, is the Astor House out of bounds for police officers?'

'Clear off! We're having a pleasant evening here.'

'Good. Tell me, what will you do with the godown on the Honan Road?'

'I don't know what you mean.'

'That's odd. You were reading a lot of paperwork as you rode to it today, so perhaps you were distracted. It is an impressive building, certainly.'

'You're talking nonsense.'

Rod sipped at his drink. 'Maybe you should tell the truth and stop pretending you're some sort of hard man.'

'Maybe you should go back to your shabby little police station and find criminals instead of bullying innocent citizens.'

Rod's head was throbbing. 'I repeat: I saw you in the Honan Road just after talking to the guards. You rented it through Ross and Dewitt.'

'All right, so I've rented the place, what business is it of yours?'

'Just casual interest. What will you do with it?'

'Storage. I'll rent out space to merchants. Why? Do you have a problem with that?'

'So long as it's legal, no,' Rod said.

Maurice was red-faced. Qian watched calmly. He had lit a cigar, and heavy blue smoke coiled. He gave no hint of unease, but seeking concern on a stone basilisk's face would be easier.

Eva looked worried.

'You dance well,' Rod said. 'It's an important skill. Shanghailanders look on dancing as a religion, almost.'

'I learned to dance at home,' she said.

'You should be careful with whom you dance,' Rod said. 'Rumours fly if you dance with the wrong man.'

'You suggest,' Qian laughed, 'that the son of Alfred Winton could be a "wrong man"?'

'I didn't mention Maurice.'

Before ten, Rod was at Dan Bailey's, nursing a bourbon and ice, rolling the glass over his forehead and thinking bleak thoughts about shallow people as the headache continued its assault. Rod often thought of his headaches as attacks. There were the unnoticed gatherings, like troops in communication trenches; the undermining of the brain's defences, like sappers tunnelling; testing random thoughts, like scouts seeking the best lines for attack. He hoped the cold glass would postpone the moment when the whistle blew and his mind was overwhelmed. So far it wasn't working.

Maurice's evasiveness was suspicious, as was Eva's anxiety – was her concern to do with Qian or Maurice? And what could they be doing that was so alarming?

Rod sipped bourbon. It slipped down smoothly, but didn't chip even one corner from his headache. It felt like the weather was turning sullen and angry. He lit a cigarette, and was just enjoying the first soothing inhalation when Bert came in. His face was ravaged, as if he had just witnessed an accident.

'I thought I'd find you here. I'm sorry, Rod. Your witnesses in the Foster killing.'

'What about them?' Rod said foolishly. One look at Bert's face told him.

'They're dead, Rod.'

The gawkers were three deep. Five smart Chinese officers stood with a pair of ferocious-looking Sikhs, ready to beat any interlopers back into line.

Rod pushed through, Bert close behind. 'Who's in charge?'

The nearer Sikh pointed to a uniform inside the shop. It was Terry O'Toole, who glanced up. 'Hello, Cottey. Not nice.'

Bound to a chair was the old man, shot in the heart and the head - just like Dewitt. His daughter lay sprawled. She had been raped before they killed her, her skirts left above her waist. Her mouth was raw and bloody, as though they had punched or smothered her to silence her cries. Rod forced himself to absorb the result of his investigations.

'They attacked her before they killed the old man,' O'Toole said. 'They made him watch.'

Rod picked up a blanket and covered her. His heart was beating like a steam hammer. 'Anything stolen?' he asked, his voice little more than a murmur. He wanted to rage, but dare not trust his voice. The anger boiled in his veins like acid.

O'Toole shook his head. 'No, this was a warning not to talk to us. The locals have all taken the hint. No one saw or heard anything.'

'Damn!' Rod looked down at her figure. Her murder was an insult – and a challenge.

'How did they know to come here?' Rod wondered.

'The assassins? They must have realised these two saw it all.'

'But how did they know these two had spoken to us? There were many witnesses, yet they came straight to these two?'

Rod saw a glint and bent to it, carefully picking it up in his handkerchief. Another 7.63mm cartridge case. He peered closely, and could see the familiar dent on the primer with his naked eye.

'Perhaps someone saw you speaking to them and made the connection?' Bert said.

'Perhaps.'

Rod was not convinced. Chinese crime gangs were intelligent. They had learned to infiltrate the police, and had willing help even among officers of the SMP, who would be happy to earn some extra money. Several Sikhs and even British officers would be glad of the cash.

'When I was last here, she told me they would kill her and her father if she spoke to me. I promised we'd protect her. It didn't occur to me that they would act so swiftly.'

'It's not your fault, Cottey,' O'Toole said. 'These fellows kill for little or no reason. Life means nothing to them. If they're told to murder, they just go and do it.'

'Who ordered this killing, then?'

'You tell me.'

'The Green Gang,' Rod spat. It must have been them.

Guilt tore at Rod, but it wouldn't drag him into a pit of remorse and self-condemnation. He'd been there before in France, and he wouldn't go there again.

Instead, he let the anger build. He could feel it in his blood, all-encompassing fury, like those moments in battle when the terror dissipated, and he was filled with blood-lust, to slaughter, to hack, to stab, until the maddened hatred was sated, and he could fall to his knees in the mud and vomit out the last of the craziness. In Flanders Rod had welcomed that sensation. Especially when Dick died. He slew many Germans that day, and would have continued if Sergeant-Major Goodwin hadn't slapped him hard about the face.

But this was different. This was righteous wrath, focused on justice. Foster's body, and Dewitt's, had not affected him as the Chinese girl's did. Her death had been demeaning and painful, and Rod was responsible. He had promised they would be safe.

Ignoring his tiredness, Rod marched to the armoury. It was late, and Dan Fairbairn had left, so Rod scribbled a note, placing the cartridge case in the same envelope.

In his office, a bottle of whisky was hidden behind manuals on the bookshelves, and he poured a large measure and lit a cigarette before writing down all that he knew about the Chinese couple: the automobile, Foster's murder, the Chinese girl and her father; their evidence about two men, both from the Green Gang; their demands for protection money.

That was the place to start, he decided: those demanding their protection money. Rod had heard that criminals often returned to the scene of their crimes. Where had he read that? From a Sherlock Holmes story? It must be even more true of a gangster returning to fleece victims who had witnessed the effect of displeasing their protector.

# Chapter Thirty-Five

*Tuesday 1st August, 1922*

Next morning found Rod back in the street. Street vendors tempted passers-by, calling to the traipsing coolies, each barely rested after their exertions the previous day, followed by a night on a bare floor.

Seeing a Chinese officer, Rod beckoned him and sent him to find reinforcements. Soon Rod had three, and told them to keep a close watch for one or two Chinese men visiting each shop, collecting for protection racketeers. They must be assumed to be armed and dangerous, he told the officers. These were those happy days before crime increased, leading to the routine arming of Chinese officers, and Rod didn't want them to put themselves in danger. If necessary, they should call for the support of armed Foreign police officers.

Only when Rod had seen them begin observing the crowds closely did he hail a rickshaw and go to Frenchtown. Soon he was at Dubois' office. He sat, taking off his hat and rubbing his brow. His headache had returned.

Dubois appeared, calling for café au lait for two. The boy brought a steaming pot, and poured. Rod took his and winced at another stab of pain behind his eyes.

'I have news,' he said, and told Dubois of the murdered witnesses. 'The description of Foster's murderer matches the man who murdered a lawyer, Dewitt. Do you know him?'

'No, I do not think so.'

'What of Qian? We know him as "Billy". He is a rich man who claims to have made his money from dealing in properties.'

'But you do not believe him?' Dubois said.

'I don't trust him. Did you have any luck finding the two men?'

'Not yet, no. My officers are searching everywhere.'

Rod nodded. 'The Green Gang is growing in influence. They have guns.'

'Mausers are popular,' Dubois agreed, refilling their cups. 'But if men smuggle drugs, it is easy to bring pistols too. Last night a boy was caught carrying a half kilo of opium. He had a pistol; he could have acquired the gun from the same source.'

'We have more and more guns too,' Rod said irritably. His head was hurting, and he was desperate to get closer to finding the murderers of Foster, Dewitt and the Chinese girl and her father.

'My friend, as soon as I have news, I will let you know,' Dubois said.

Rod finished his coffee and stood. 'I am grateful. And now, I must find out what I can about Billy Qian.'

But he had another visit to make first.

Rod took a rickshaw to Doctor Babu, and soon he was filled with the joy of energy. The cocaine banished his weariness along with his headache, and he felt invigorated as he rode back to where Foster and the witnesses had died.

The three policemen were still standing near the crash site, and Rod could have sworn aloud to see them. He had hoped that they would have caught the Green Gang members by now. Maybe the gangsters were keeping low. Perhaps it was foolish to think that they would return to the scene so quickly.

The Chinese officers were competent to catch the two if they did turn up. Rod left them and went to the offices of the North China Daily News. It was a faded, grubby-looking building, and looked down-at-heel, just like a newspaperman.

At the front desk, a young, hopeful-looking man with unkempt fair hair that had rarely seen a comb, met him. He had printer's ink on cheek and forehead, and a bewildered expression. His sleeves were held up with spring retainers that signally failed to keep his cuffs from getting as stained as his cheek.

'Eric Leigh?' he repeated.

'Yes. Where is he?'

'Is it a story?' he said hopefully. 'I can write it up, if you like?'

'Where is he?' Rod said more sharply. He didn't want to waste time.

'He'll be at Dan Bailey's, I expect, having tiffin.'

He hadn't realised it was already past noon. Rod left without thanking the man whose only interest was scooping his colleague.

'Ah, Rod, come on in! I've had a wonderful morning. Ran up to where Foster died, wrote it up on the way back, got it filed before breakfast, wrote a piece on the violence on Shanghai's streets, how the deadly arms trade is providing gangsters with weapons, and now I can enjoy a day without work! Have a drink, Rod. Dan? Can we have a ... what will it be?'

'Eric, I don't want a drink, I need to talk.'

'Oh, really?' He grimaced, but brightened and ordered himself another. 'What do you need?'

'The girl at the gambling den we raided, you remember?'

'Oh, yes,' he said, beaming. 'The lovely Alice Winton. Phew, I wouldn't climb over her to get to you, old sport. A lithe, lissom little ...'

'Shut up. Do you remember the tall girl with her?'

'Her? Oh, she's a Russian, I think. Why?'

'What do you know about her?'

Eric screwed up his face with the effort of concentration. 'Um. Eva, I think. Eva ... Poliakoff? Something like that. She turned up about four months ago. First as a taxi dancer. You know the sort: Russian girl, down on her luck, needs help, needs money. I wouldn't mind taking care of her. Nice young thing, if you ask me. These Russians, you know, they are a lot cheaper than trying to pay by the hour. Put 'em up in your apartment, and they don't ask much, from what I'm ...'

'Eric, I'm not interested. She was with Alice Winton. Do you have any idea why?'

'No. Why?'

'What can you tell me about her?'

Eric frowned into his glass. 'It's said she's Billy Qian's girl.'

'Good, now surprise me: tell me something I don't know.'

'How about this: Qian is planning to open his own bank - especially for locals.'

This was a surprise. With a bank of his own, Qian could easily conceal illegal profits. Winton must have heard of this - if he was in financial trouble, perhaps Qian could help him - or tip him over the edge?

'Qian has backers, do you think?'

Eric shrugged. 'He has friends. Many would prefer a local man rather than the unholy Trinity of Jardine Mathieson's, Hongkong and Shanghai, or the Liverpool and Asiatic.'

'You said Winton had been involved in murky deals. What did you mean?'

'Only that he holds a lot of German stocks, and they are falling in value daily. His investments must be dire.'

'So if Qian did open a bank, Winton would be hurt? Could it cause a run on his bank?'

'My word!' Eric gaped. 'I hadn't thought of that: it could send L and A to the wall!'

Now Rod knew the reason for Alfred Winton's grim attitude. It was not Gracie's actual debt; he couldn't pay her bill. His empire was collapsing.

Eric was set up for the day. He would be drinking pink gins until Dan threw him out. Rod left him there.

Gracie Gale had written Eva's address on a slip of paper: the Sih Chong building towards Ward Road.

Built of brick and pale stone, it had endured fifty years of soot. Now it was the colour of a cold sea in a storm. The faded doors lacked paint. To one side, Rod saw a clean rectangle where a brass plate had announced the building's name; it had been stolen.

Inside, Rod's nostrils were assailed by a melange of poverty: sweat, boiled cabbage, tobacco and urine. It was dark, and filth lay in all corners. A staircase led up, and he ascended, warily watching for danger. It grew dimmer. There were windows on each landing, but each was smothered by years of grime.

One hand on the rail, he kept the other on his gun, ready to draw at the first sign of danger. On the first floor a child bawled its head off; on the second a dog began barking, but suddenly stopped with a yelp; on the third he heard the regular squeaking of bedsprings - but nothing to cause him concern. At the top were six doors. The fifth was the one Gracie had given. Brown bakelite numbers proclaimed 54, but the 5 had snapped in half, and now the two halves made a left pointing chevron with an 'n' below.

He knocked, then rapped again more loudly. Inside he heard snoring. The intensity did not diminish. When he tried the handle, the door opened. The snoring was louder.

Calling, 'Hello?' he stepped into a short corridor with three doors. The snoring emanated from an open door on his right.

A large man with a hairy belly lay on a thin mattress on the floor, his vest rolled up, exposing his stomach and striped underpants. He was in his middle fifties, Rod guessed, with grizzled hair and a two-day beard on his jowls. His nose was purple, and broken veins stood out. With fleshy lips and puffy eyes, he could have passed for a successful taipan, if shaved, bathed and clothed in a suit, but from the smell he had not cleaned himself in days. Probably not since his last shave.

As he snored, Rod smelled stale liquor on his breath.

'Wake up!' Rod called. A lukewarm jug of water sat on a shelf. Rod tipped it over his belly.

The man gave a grunt that must have rasped his throat, and shot upright. Seeing Rod, he frowned blearily. 'Who you? What you do here?'

'The door was open.'

'What right you have to come and ...'

'Who are you?'

'What?'

'Who are you? I am a police officer.'

'Police?' He shrank back fearfully, a hand over his face as if wiping away water. Many Russians behaved this way when meeting policemen. It said much about the police in Russia.

'Your name?'

'My name?' he repeated dully, but then he met Rod's gaze, and his voice grew deeper. 'I am Admiral Yevgeny Bugayev, of the Imperial Russian Navy.' He continued in a bitter tone, 'Although I have no country, no navy and no ship.'

# Chapter Thirty-Six

Bugayev lumbered across the corridor, blundering like a new-born foal in the tiny apartment, to a tiny room. There was a bucket inside, and he stood emptying his bladder, as unconcerned by Rod's presence as a dog. Finished, he returned to the bedroom, and donned a cotton robe, patting his pockets in dumb show until Rod took pity and gave him a cigarette. Bugayev led the way to the last room, which served as a kitchen and parlour.

'Excuse mess,' he said thickly, inhaling deeply. He coughed, a thick, phlegmy rattle that threatened to choke him, but then indicated a glass. 'Drink?'

'No, thank you.'

He shrugged and searched through the cupboard. Rod heard empty bottles rattle, before he found one and held it up sadly. There was a bare inch of clear liquid in the bottom. Eschewing a glass, he tipped it into his mouth and closed his eyes with a contented sigh. With another cough, this time less strained, he glanced at Rod. 'What you want, policeman?' he demanded.

'Where is your wife?'

'She out. She is confidential secretary to big man, you know? Taipan.'

'Who?'

'She tell me, but I, I, *ach*, my head remember little, you know?' he mimed forgetfulness, tapping his skull.

'What does this taipan do?'

'He bring things to Shanghai, yes? On ships.'

'What sort of things?'

'I not know. It matters to me? Why? I seek job. When I find job, I work hard, bring in much money, and wife stay home, clean this mess,' he added, looking about him sombrely. 'Why you ask about wife? She working. She is good woman.'

'Does she have another job?'

'No. This takes much time. She never home. It not what I thought when we come here. I think, Shanghai: freedom! New life! We walk, many days, from Vladivostok, escape Reds, damned *Bolsheviks*! They slaughter all, women, children, all. Starve people in cities, murder them in streets. For what? What we do them? We serve our Czar, is all. But the men rise. Even my men, *good* men, and kill officers. Only we escape. Come here, think, new life, rescue. But Russians not people here. This city for English, for American, for French, for Japaners, but no place for Russian. No place for me.'

'Is your wife well paid?'

'Money? Sometime she has much. Others,' he shrugged, pulled a moue. 'We survive. We live. Until I find work.'

'Her taipan, does he own the ships which bring goods?'

'Nyet. No, he makes use of space.'

He stared at the empty bottle with the sadness of a whipped cur. Rod could smell the sickly odour of defeat. Bugayev had been important, a commander of men. All that had been left behind in the chaos of civil war. He had no interest in his wife's taipan. She brought in money which kept them in food and him in alcohol. His addled brain was barely capable of coping. The chances of his remembering ships' names, if he had ever heard them, was remote.

'Thank you for your help,' Rod said, and made to leave, but Bugayev stopped him with an ingratiating smile.

'My friend, I have need buy food, but wife is not here. I have temporary embarrassment of money. I wonder, could you make loan? I can pay, as soon as my wife here. I am admiral in Russian Imperial Fleet. You can trust my word.'

Rod was sickened – by his disintegrated pride, the failure of his dreams and his dishonesty. Both knew he would sink any money into the first bottle he could find.

Rod gave him a dollar.

At his office, Rod was called to the telephone.

'Yes?'

'This is Alice Winton. I would like to speak to you about Eva. You warned me about her, and I'm afraid you were right. I didn't realise how dangerous she was.'

They agreed to meet at the Astor House, and he grabbed his hat and jacket.

The main dining hall was huge. Square tables were set out on either side four seats at each, while a number of circular tables formed a third row in the middle. Alice Winton had taken a square table to the right.

Her usual confidence had fled. She looked pinched and anxious, her eyes bright and red as though she had been crying. She took the cigarette he offered, and held it to Rod's match, her hand holding his still, puffing quickly and then holding the cigarette high, left arm about her torso, right elbow resting on the left hand, while smoke trickled from her nostrils. 'It's about Eva,' she repeated.

A waiter appeared with tea and sandwiches. Then a tower of small cakes was wheeled to their side. Rod refused, but Alice accepted a cream cake. It was set before her on a plate with a cake fork and napkin. The Astor staff knew how to arrange a table to perfection, taking just long enough to make Rod snap at them to go.

'What about her?' he said when they were alone.

'She's been using me, just as you said.'

'What has happened?'

'She has always been so friendly and helpful, and I thought she was eager to keep me as a friend. But yesterday I found her in my room. We were going out, and I suppose I thought she was just looking at my earrings and things. So, we went out …'

'Where?'

'Does it matter?' She looked at him and somewhat grumpily admitted, 'The Wheel, if you must know. Carlos is always accommodating, don't you find?'

'I told you once, I don't gamble.'

'No, I don't suppose you do,' she said bitterly.

'What happened?'

'Eva was with me early in the evening, but at The Wheel we met Maurice and Billy Qian, and Eva left with them. I stayed, but it was dull. A tiresome man kept offering me drinks, and made lewd suggestions, so I left. When I got home, I was walking along the corridor and heard a noise. When I looked into Maurice's study, Eva was going through his writing desk. She looked like a spy.'

'Did you accost her?'

'No. I should, shouldn't I? I was going to, but then I caught sight of her face …'

'And?'

'She always looks so down-trodden, so worried. It's the money, of course. I am used to her looking like a spaniel that fears being kicked. And yet last night, she had an intensity about her, like a determined woman, I suppose like Mata Hari. It was such a shock, and really terrifying. I didn't know what to do.'

'So you thought you'd come to me.'

'Yes.'

'Where was your father?'

'Asleep. It was rather late.'

'Or early?' Rod suggested.

She lowered her eyes coyly and gave a half shrug, lifting a shoulder, tilting her head towards it, holding the pose, letting them both return to their normal position.

'Did she see you?'

'No, I'm sure she didn't.'

'Do you know whether she stole something or not?'

'I don't think so.'

'Did she put anything in her pocket so far as you could see?'

'No.'

Rod held out his hands. 'What can I arrest her for?'

'You're a policeman, can't you question her? Threaten her with gaol – or worse – unless she confesses what she was looking for?'

'You say it was Maurice's study?'

'Yes.'

'Where was he?'

'Asleep, I expect. It was late, as I said.'

'How long were you at The Wheel after the others left?'

'Does it matter?'

'Does Maurice usually fall asleep before you?'

'No, but perhaps she gave Maurice something to drink that knocked him out, so he went to sleep?'

Rod smiled. Acquiring knock-out drops was not as easy as the films suggested. 'Perhaps. But if she were looking for something valuable, surely she would have been more likely to seek it in your father's desk? If she wanted jewellery, wouldn't she have searched your mother's room? Are you sure nothing of your own is missing?'

'I don't think so.'

'What was she doing in Maurice's study, then?' he wondered.

'I don't know, but I want you to find out,' she said.

'First I need to find her. I've tried her apartment, but her husband was alone there, and his only interest lay inside a bottle.'

'Come to our house this evening and I'll make sure she's there.'

'Your father doesn't want me near your family.'

'He does what I ask,' she said.

The news came later that day. One of the Chinese officers watching for the protection racketeers called to say they had seen a man sidling from one shop to another, and they were keeping him under close observation.

Rod was in a rickshaw in moments. With the offer of double his usual fee if he was quick, the coolie flew along like a Chinese pony on race day. Rod was amazed that they didn't plough down numerous pedestrians.

Throwing the man his money, Rod ran to join the policemen.

'Where is he?' Rod said.

The officers pointed to a shop. Rod ordered one officer to join him, the other two to wait at the back of the shop in case the gangster tried to flee. Then Rod felt the pistol under his arm, making sure it moved freely, and walked inside.

The man was easy to spot. He wore the gangster's uniform of a suit with broad shoulders and wide lapels, a dark brown fedora, and gleaming black shoes. When Rod entered, he was berating the shopkeeper. Much of his shouting was beyond Rod's limited Chinese, but the inflection and threats were clear enough.

He turned as Rod entered. It was Rod's first glimpse of him. Thin, he had a scar on his left cheek that had pulled his mouth into a sneer, and he gazed at Rod with dark, expressionless eyes. Rod guessed he was in his early twenties, and the fact that he could afford such a suit spoke of his importance in his gang. He turned back to the shopkeeper, and as he did Rod marched to him. He turned again, this time his face twisted with fury.

Rod would remember every fleeting moment for months to come: the gangster, the terrified shopkeeper, and then the flutter of the gangster's eyes and the move of his hand towards his armpit.

Rod's hand went for his Colt, but it was like reaching through treacle. He would never reach his gun in time, so instead he moved forward.

The gangster had his gun free, but Fairbairn had taught him how to disarm a gunman. Rod caught the barrel, gripping it tightly, pointed it away. He pushed forward, all his body's weight behind him, and grabbed the gunman's wrist, levering. The gun twisted, and now the barrel pointed at the gangster's belly, and his finger was clear of the trigger. Then it was out of his grip and in Rod's.

The man made a mistake, trying to punch Rod. He blocked that and counter-punched in the throat.

'I'd like a word with you,' Rod said, as the man squirmed on the floor gasping for breath.

In Rod's office he was handcuffed to a sturdy chair. Two Chinese officers stood behind him while Rod toyed with the Mauser, a square, boxy gun with a grip like a broom handle. The slender barrel looked too slim for the power of the bullets. He had already emptied the magazine, and let the bolt run forward. When he snapped the trigger the hammer fell with a loud, positive *clack*.

'What is your name?' Rod said. The man gazed back with angry bitterness.

Rod tried speaking more slowly. 'Your name?'

There was no response. 'You know the punishment for people guilty of murder. You're Chinese. Under Chinese law, there's a post set into the ground. A rope passes round your neck and through holes in the post, and they tighten the rope, slowly. Then release it, so you are slowly throttled. We know three men have been murdered with a gun like this. The Chinese authorities hate these guns, don't they? And you will be handed to them, unless you can tell me that someone else killed those people.'

The gangster sneered. 'We don't care about death. We are honourable men.'

'Really? We shall see how honourable you are when the life is squeezed from you at the post. Of course you will go without the normal honours if you don't tell us your name.'

He glanced about him, licked his lips, muttered, 'Chen.'

'Thank you, Mr Chen,' Rod said, picking up the gun again. 'How did you come by this?'

'I found it in street.'

'Which street?'

'I didn't notice.'

'We have tests we can apply to this gun. If it was used in the murders, you will be charged.'

He didn't answer.

Rod smiled. 'We shall leave you to think about how helpful you would like to be. Two days in the cells will help, I have no doubt.'

'What you mean?'

Rod had guessed right. Many gangsters used drugs. 'I believe life without opium can be extraordinarily painful. You will learn how painful.'

At last doubt flickered behind his eyes. 'Take me to Chinese police.'

'Why? So you can bribe them to sell you opium – or release you?'

He started to chew his lip. 'I live Frenchtown. Take me French police.'

'Our cells are good enough,' Rod said. But Chen's words made him wonder. Did he think the French police would be more likely to accept a bribe and release him?

'Frenchtown,' Chen repeated with rising anxiety.

'Take him to the cells, and have someone keep an eye on him. Don't let him kill himself,' Rod said, and was relieved when Chen was dragged from the office, alternately shouting insults and pleading, proof he was dedicated to his drug. Only time would tell how painful his withdrawal experience would be.

That was not Rod's concern. He sent the Mauser to Fairbairn for testing. With luck it would prove to be the same gun that killed Foster, Dewitt and the two witnesses. That hope put a spring in his step as left.

He had a meeting with Eva.

His welcome was not warm. Crowther's look said Rod should jump back into the murky pool whence he came and stop troubling the family. The glance he threw at Rod's shoes was enough to make them want to run away on their own.

'Tell Miss Alice I'm here.'

'Please follow me.'

He led Rod to the room where he had met Alfred. Rod could see people laughing and chatting on the lawn. How they contrived to look so cool and comfortable, he could not comprehend. Even here, with ceiling fans revolving, he was ridiculously hot.

'Detective Constable.'

Rod turned. It was Mrs Winton. 'Hello.'

'You said there was nothing I need worry about,' she said.

'That's right. Your daughter invited me.'

'Oh!' she seemed to sag, as though the heat had got to her. 'I thought you had discovered something.'

'If I had, I would be sure to tell you.'

'Thank you. I have to hope that … has Crowther offered you tea, or something stronger?'

'I don't think he wants me to stay any longer than necessary. Like your husband.'

'Nonsense! I shall have a pot brought up immediately. Unless you want something more cooling than tea?' she asked at the door.

'No, I am fine,' Rod said. 'But may I ask: you run the orphanage trust, I understand?'

'I am involved in several charities. I am involved with the Children's Welfare. Why?'

'Do you remember a boy called Bao? His father, Bao Xiu was murdered.'

'Why, yes. He used to work here. A pleasant young fellow. Quite spirited, and the children enjoyed playing with him. You know how difficult it is for English children to find friends of their own age. Thin Bao was a good companion.'

'But he left?'

'There comes a time,' she said primly, 'when young ladies need to be protected from boys.'

'You didn't keep in touch with him?'

'How could we, Detective? You know how many children there are sleeping on the streets. If a boy decides to run away, and ignores our offers of support, we cannot force him. And there are so many deserving children.'

When Rod glanced outside, he saw Maurice, and then he saw Crowther go and whisper in his ear. Immediately Maurice marched towards the house.

Rod moved away from the window and was sitting in a comfortable wing-backed seat near the fireplace when Maurice appeared in the French windows. 'What do you want now? Why are you here?'

'You appear irritated, Mr Winton.'

'You're following me, aren't you? Well? What's the meaning of this? I could knock your block off, you know, and I'm not sure I won't!'

'If you try to punch me, you will regret it.'

'Oh, quite the bravo, aren't you? But here I have men at my beck and call, and I doubt you could fight off all of them.'

Rod pulled his Colt from its holster and placed it carefully on the table beside him. 'I am here to speak with your sister and her friend Eva. It has nothing to do with you, but if you have something to confess, please do so now rather than later. I may have less room for manoeuvre once this story gets out.'

Maurice was goggling at the pistol, like a mouse seeing a prowling cat. Rod imagined he had rarely had a barrel's eye view of a pistol, and a .45 calibre muzzle tended to hold the attention. 'What do you mean, what "story"?'

'That, I hope, is what Eva will tell me,' Rod said.

'You're mad!'

'Why?'

'She doesn't know anything.'

'About what?'

Maurice scowled. If he had been wearing short trousers, he would have been the perfect picture of a primary schoolboy seeing his prized toy confiscated during morning assembly. The thought almost made Rod laugh out loud.

'Go back to your friends, Mr Winton,' he said. 'Don't try to threaten a police officer again. It won't do.'

'You could find your job taken away, if you're not careful!' Maurice hissed, flushed with anger and resentment.

'More threats?' This was a mouse with teeth, or so he thought. 'I shall forget them, Mr Winton, but I assure you, if you try to curtail my career, there will be repercussions.'

'You think you could do *anything* that could harm me?' Maurice said with derision.

Rod stood. 'You are used to bullying coolies, Mr Winton, and some police officers perhaps, too, but I am investigating four murders. My superiors and the Commissioner are fully aware of my work. If you try to threaten or influence my enquiries, you will receive an unpleasant surprise.'

'My father …'

'Cannot stop me. But your attitude intrigues me. Why should you seek to hamper my investigation into your driver's death, unless it may lead to you?'

He flinched, as if fearing Rod would hit him. Then the tea arrived, and shortly afterwards Alice entered. She shot a look at Maurice. Rod couldn't read her expression.

'Shall I be mother?' she said.

'Please do,' Rod said.

She crouched beside the table. 'You, Maurice?'

'I think Maurice will return to his friends,' Rod said.

Maurice looked from Alice to Rod and back. His black scowl had returned, and Rod rather admired his perseverance. It must have been wearing. Rod was tempted to shoo him away with a wave of his fingers, but he didn't want a further row.

Muttering under his breath, Maurice stalked back outside.

Alice passed Rod a cup of tea. 'If you could move your metal manhood aside, I can put this down,' she said sweetly, looking at the Colt.

## Chapter Thirty-Seven

Rod holstered the pistol and sipped. The jasmine tea was perfect. 'Your brother is on edge.'

'He's upset. Poor Maurice wants to help the business, but Father is absolutely resolute. They had a blazing row last week, Maurice saying he would be damned if the business was taken by someone else, and Father saying the family would be damned if he let it fall into the hands of an incompetent fool. Or something like that. It was rather loud.'

'Before Foster died?'

'Oh, yes, two days before, I think.'

'What else did they say?'

'You are a strange one.' She set her head to one side, placing a cigarette between her lips and lighting it. She peered at Rod through narrowed eyes. 'Maurice said something about proving himself, but Father sneered. He can be mean when he wants.'

'I wonder …'

'What?'

'What it was Eva sought.'

'I've no idea! I suppose police officers are used to burglars, but I'm not … It's horrid.'

'In my area, I'd be more likely knocked on the head for my wallet than be burgled.'

'Where do you live?'

'I have an apartment on the corner of Canton and Shantung Road.'

'That sounds nice.'

'It isn't,' Rod said. 'It's rough.'
'Why don't you move?'
'It's cheap. Look, Alice, when Eva gets here, I would like you to leave us.'
'Why? I'm the one who saw her.'
'She doesn't know that. I may be able to learn more if she doesn't realise who saw her. And if she has an explanation, you may be able to keep friendly with her afterwards, if you want.'
'I suppose so.'
'Why is she here today?'
'We are going to a dance at The Wheel. I invited her to supper first.'
Just then Eva walked in.

Eva looked at Rod, a perplexed frown forming. 'Is all right?' she said, her accent suddenly very strong.
'Yes. I wanted to speak with you, and Mrs Winton said you would visit,' Rod said.
Alice was ill-at-ease, uncomfortable at the thought of Eva being questioned. 'May I help?'
'I am sure it is nothing,' Rod said. 'Mrs Bugayeva, would you like to sit? I have some questions after seeing your husband.'
Her face went very still at the mention of her husband. 'You have met my husband?'
'Yes. Earlier today.'
'I have not spoken to him. Please, what is this about?'
'Miss Winton, if you wouldn't mind leaving us?' Rod said.
'I … Of course. Eva, I …' Alice rose and stood, unsure what to do for the best, teetering slightly as she looked at Eva. Eva shook her head curtly, and Alice's face fell, as if dismissed. She turned and left.
Rod watched her go with no little surprise. If she had been acting, she had missed her vocation. Alice might have fared well on the stage.
Eva was composed, holding Rod with her magnificent eyes, hands clasped tightly.
'You're sure you won't have some tea, Mrs Bugayeva? Won't you at least take a seat?'
'I prefer to stand if I am to be interrogated.'
'That is a strong word. I merely wish to ask you some questions.'

'That is what Cheka say,' she said. Her face was very pale, and Rod feared she might faint.

'This is Shanghai, not Russia. You are in no danger here. Just tell me the truth.'

'What truth you want?' she said. 'The truth I am refugee, I have nothing, I must sell myself to maintain my husband? The truth I do not know what happened to my brother, my sister, my parents? That I believe they are all dead, murdered by Bolsheviks? Or truth Wintons saved my life? That Alice showed me kindness when I did not hope for it?'

'The other evening, dancing, you were happy – until you saw me. You were worried. Why?'

'You are policeman. Why I not be worried? You think all people see police as friends? All people see police, they think, I will be picked. They will arrest.'

'No. You do not scare easily. I could see that the first time I saw you. You had courage and certainty, like a Shanghailander. You were taken from a gambling den, but you were not fearful, yet last night you were scared to see me.'

'I don't know.'

She was reluctant to speak. It was time to drop the shell. 'Why did you go through Maurice's desk last night?'

Eva grunted as if she had been punched. 'Who says this?'

'You were seen. What were you looking for?'

'Nothing. I had dropped a brooch, and thought it was there.'

'You were looking among papers. What were you looking for?'

'I … I do not know what you …'

'You are Russian, Eva. You came here because your country has fallen, and you have no papers. You cannot leave Shanghai without a passport. You know that. But here, you are stateless. You cannot claim extraterritoriality. You know what that means? You have no rights in an English court, nor French nor American. If you're suspected of a crime you must be tried in the International Mixed Court, under Chinese law, and their justice is not charitable. You realise that, don't you?'

She stared at him with a kind of wild terror: she had been married to a powerful man, but they had lost everything, and she was now forced to accept her position as a supplicant. Her world was shattered.

'Can we walk?' she said. 'Please … outside.'

They walked in silence until they had passed beyond the house. Only then did she begin to speak, in a low, nervous tone, fearful that someone might overhear.

'Who told you?' she began, but then waved a hand. 'It doesn't matter.'

Rod offered her his cigarettes, and she took one distractedly, barely noticing when he struck a light. She sucked the smoke greedily, like a condemned prisoner.

'Yevgeny was good officer,' she said. 'Not as he is now. Now, he is pitiful, a broken man. Four years ago, he was responsible for many men, a man of honour and importance. When the army and navy rose against the Czar, he remained loyal. It was his way. He had given his oath. I don't think he believed things would come to this. No one did.'

'You escaped to Vladivostok?'

'Yes. All the fighting and killing, the starving. It was horrible. You cannot imagine. But we reached Vladivostok, and there those loyal to the Czar wanted to rally and rescue the Imperial family. But then came news - the Czar and Czarina had been murdered! The children ... Vladivostok was sombre that evening, I swear to you. Then we heard the Reds were moving. Other countries tried to help us, to save the Czar and his family, but with them dead, all who promised help ran away: the British, the Canadians, even the Japanese said they would leave us to the Reds. Admiral Kolchak was caught and murdered, and we saw that our beloved country could not be saved. Shanghai was the only place we could go. We thought we could start a new life, but we didn't think we would be treated as the meanest beggars.'

At a large London plane tree, Eva stared up into the branches. 'No one cared. I suppose the Great War, the Spanish flu, cholera, mean that people have had enough of death. You British care only for your empire. We had no value. We were convenient in the War, but now? Yevgeny tried everything. He sought work with a bank, with the Council, he applied to become a police officer, but nobody wanted him. No jobs for foreigners without papers, they said. And with that came despair. He would prefer to have died in Russia than suffer this indignity.'

'What of you?'

'I was *lucky*,' she said bitterly. 'I could work in bars and dance halls. Cabarets let me wait until a man would hire me. I would dance, and try to persuade them to buy me a drink, and drinks for themselves. I hated it. Afterwards, men tried to offer me money for other … *services*. And as our money ran out,' her voice dropped to a whisper. 'I took their offers. It kept us fed. Yevgeny understood, I think.'

'The desk. What were you looking for?'

'A paper. Something important. Maurice wants to show his father he can make money. He has a cargo in the Whampoa. I was told to find details of the cargo.'

'Who told you this?' But Rod knew who connected all these people. 'It was Billy Qian, wasn't it? He asked you to find the bill of lading.'

'Yes. He was going to pay me handsomely.'

'Did he want anything else?'

She coloured then, a hot, angry flush. 'He told me to do anything I must, to get details of the cargo.'

Qian had assumed his prostitute would happily ensnare another man, but Eva was still delicate enough to resent being instructed to seduce another. 'Why? What does Billy want from this?'

'He is an honourable man.'

'What does that mean?'

'Whatever you want,' she said wearily. 'You think honour is British. You see nothing of value in other people. All you see is, control, take their money, their land …'

Rod remembered Billy Qian's anger when he spoke of being neither Foreign nor Chinese, and the idea that he was honourable was not difficult to believe – although Rod would not have been surprised to learn Billy wanted to find out about the cargo so he could take it for himself.

'What did you find?'

'Nothing,' she said. 'Nothing in his desk. Perhaps I was looking for the wrong kind of papers? I don't know.'

'I will have to ask Billy Qian,' Rod said.

'Yes,' she said sadly. Her head rested on the tree's trunk. 'And I must find another man to support me.'

'Billy Qian paid your rent?'

'He and Alice. Without them we must lose the apartment. Without the money I bring, we cannot survive.'

'You think he'll survive by drinking all day long?'

She gave Rod a look which was so tragic, he felt guilty.

'What else is there for him?'

## Chapter Thirty-Eight

When Rod left Eva, her head hung if in despair, but it was a calculating despair, he thought. Eva was many things, but first and foremost, she was a survivor.

She was the victim of the chaos of the last decade. As she said, what future was there for her? She had no rights; all she could hope for was a man to take care of her, and pay for her husband's bottles. The two were doomed, aspiring to respectability, but forced to suffer the worst indignities life forced on them. Yevgeny would die unless he curtailed his drinking, and Eva would not cope long as a prostitute, but life had dealt them these cards. It was hard to see how she might escape the fate towards which life was driving her.

'Have you finished?'

It was Maurice. He stood in Rod's path, arms akimbo, for all the world like a policeman hearing a dodgy alibi.

'Excuse me,' Rod said, and stepped around him.

Maurice moved to block him again. 'What were you doing with her? Bullying the innocent?'

'You are in my way.'

'You didn't answer my question!'

Alice appeared at Maurice's side. She had been watching, and wanted to learn what Rod had learned. 'Maurice, stop shouting,' she said. 'The whole road can hear you.'

Maurice clenched his fist. Alice put a hand on his forearm. 'Stop!'

Rod wasn't sure whether Maurice's truculence was bravado for his friends, but he was losing patience. 'Please get out of my way.'

'I want to know what …'

Rod stepped forward, thrusting his cupped hand under Maurice's chin. His teeth clicked together as his head was slammed back, and Rod had already hooked his foot behind Maurice's leg. He fell like a cut tree. Alice gave a short squeal.

Maurice tried to rise but he was winded, and Rod crouched, a hand on his chest.

'Maurice, I know you have the brain of a drowned slug, but concentrate. Your friends have seen that I can beat you. If you try to block my way, I will arrest you. I don't care who watches. Is *that* bloody clear?'

He nodded, rubbing his neck.

'Now, before I go: what is on your bill of lading?'

'What are you on about?' There was more bluster than arrogance in him now.

'You have a warehouse, you want to fill it. With what, Mister Winton?'

'That's none of your business!'

'No. Not if it is a legal shipment. When is it due?'

'You'll have to wait and find out. No, why shouldn't you know? I am importing tobacco and spirits. Why, do you have something against good whisky and cigars?' He climbed to his feet.

'Why? To win back your father's favour?'

'Go to hell!'

'Which ship?'

Rod saw Alice shoot him a glance - why? A warning?

Maurice ignored her. 'The *Lucky Strike*. She's in the estuary now.'

'And you will be selling the goods to the highest bidder?'

'That is how business tends to be conducted.'

'How well did you get on with your brother?'

He paled. 'Ian was my best friend.'

Alice said, 'Don't be cruel, Detective. We both loved Ian.'

'Not that it's any of your business!'

'You resented him.'

'Father idolised him, doted on him. But he didn't see the other side to him. He thinks me weak, but if he had known …'

'Known what?'

'Ian had his faults, the same as any man.'

'Women?'

Maurice sneered. 'Clever guess!'

'I doubt that would shock or even surprise your father.'

'Do you?' Maurice said. 'Father looks on everything as a commodity, but he has some standards. Even women deserve better than my brother gave them.'

'In what way?'

'Ian liked women, but he wasn't the committing sort. He picked women who were available, but less risky.'

'Prostitutes, you mean?'

Alice gave a hissed intake of breath. 'I'm not listening to any more of this!'

When she had gone, Maurice stood, rubbing his chin. 'Proud of yourself? Now you've scared Alice too?'

'Which women?'

'Not whores! *Married* women! Women like Schreier's wife. Oh, Ian could be charming when he was seducing another man's wife. But it didn't make him popular.'

'Schreier's wife?'

'She left Schreier after Ian seduced her. I suppose she realised there were better pickings, and took herself off to America with their children.'

'So Schreier had cause to hate your brother as well as your father?'

'But Ian wasn't murdered. He died nobly, like the hero mother and father always knew him to be.'

Rod said nothing. In his experience those who died on the Front didn't find it noble or heroic. They struggled on until they were found by the shell or bullet that had their name on it.

'Why are you here?' Maurice said. 'Is it Alice? You want to take Foster's place? I'd be careful, Detective. She is far too fine and precious for a policeman. You should try Eva. She's more your budget. And her old man's little use. She would be glad of a few pennies a month, and some attention. No doubt Yevgeny'll soon be dead.'

'You are a cruel sort of man, aren't you?'

'I speak the truth as I see it,' he said. His face degenerated into a sulk. 'What, do you think a man with a bottle-and-a-half of vodka a day habit will live long? She'll soon be free. You'd be better off with her. She's already an outcast, just like you, *policeman*!'

It was tempting to hit him again, but there was no point. He was just a spoiled, rather foolish young man.

'Where is the ship's manifest?'

'In my office. Why, do you expect me to fetch it for you? Damn you!'

'Who sold you the tobacco and spirits?'

'It's none of your business. I am bringing in perfectly legal goods.'

'So you can persuade your father you are a safe pair of hands?'

But Maurice ignored him and walked back to his friends.

Billy Qian was not at home. The servant told Rod that Billy was at his office. Rod took a rickshaw to the Bund first, hunting for Tim Burton amid the rubbish. He eventually found the beggar sitting at a wall near the entrance to the communal gardens.

'Brought me rum?' he said with a snarl of a smile.

'I'll bring you rum if you make sure I hear when the *Lucky Strike* docks,' Rod said, and threw him a pack of cigarettes.

Billy Qian's office was in an unimpressive block that looked ready for demolition.

Qian's was a large room. It was bland. There was dark wainscoting, chipped and shabby, the woodwork was badly in need of a fresh coat of paint. Behind his desk hung pictures of Chinese scenes, while opposite were oils of English landscapes.

'You like my paintings?' he said.

'I merely wondered whether they were an indication of your feelings of statehood.'

'What, firmly set in China, you mean?'

'Allied with China, while your gaze remains fixed on Britain.'

'You are a philosopher.'

'No, a student of life.'

Billy Qian chuckled. 'Cigar?'

Rod did not refuse. There were two easy chairs and a small round table on which stood a humidor. When Billy opened it, Rod was presented with a small, tight-wrapped cheroot. It tasted like a year's salary. Both sat in easy chairs.

'So, Detective, to what do I owe this undeniable pleasure?'

'Last night, when talking to you, I noticed Eva looked unhappy.'

'Yes.'

'Why?'

He waved his hand expansively. 'Who can tell?'

'Perhaps you had told her to sleep with Maurice,' Rod thought aloud. 'Except she is not inured to her profession, maybe. Perhaps she thought you were her lover and protector? To hear that you wanted her to seduce a young man possibly distressed her, because it showed her real value to you.'

'Why should I ask her to sleep with Maurice?'

'So that she would have an excuse to visit the Wintons, and could find the bill of lading for Maurice's ship in the Whampoa.'

Qian smiled. 'So Eva has been talking? That is a shame.'

'Why, because you will punish her?' Rod said, and allowed a trace of harshness to enter his voice. 'Be assured, Qian, if anything happens to her, I will assume that it was you or your men who were responsible.'

'Wait!' he said, holding up his hands with a smile on his face. 'My men? What men?'

'Hirelings are two a penny here in Shanghai. I daresay you could find friends for a handful of dollars. What was your plan? Let Maurice off-load his goods, and then take them for yourself?'

'Detective, detective!' Qian said, shaking his head in mock offence. 'Please! You know that I found him a warehouse where he can bring goods for storage. Do you really think that I would be so poor a friend as to try to rob him?'

'This is Shanghai,' Rod said sourly. 'Even Helmut Schreier has finally learned that the best of friends can become enemies at the drop of a large profit.'

'But I am no Schreier,' Qian said. 'He dabbled in weapons. I am only interested in land and buildings. I am making a good living, as you saw at my house. I have no need to steal from friends.'

'With your money, why do you have a place like this?' Rod said, looking about the room. 'It would not impress a client to think you are hard up for money.'

'It is a hard balance. An expensive, up-market office makes clients think I must be making too much money, while a shabby office makes people think I'm not good at my job. It is the eternal question: how smart should I look?'

'While in reality you have a wonderful villa.'

'As good as any in America,' he agreed complacently. Then he leaned forward, his elbows on his thighs. 'Detective, I shall be frank, for you possibly deserve it. Let me say this: I am very fond of Eva. She has had a hard time and I want to help her.'

'She was clearly upset and worried in the Astor House the other evening.'

'Yes, I had asked her to do something with which she was not comfortable.'

'The bill of lading.'

'I will leave that to your imagination.'

'But you are trying to harm Maurice Winton, aren't you?'

He laughed. 'My dear friend, I say again, I like Maurice. I am not in competition with him. He is a transparently innocent young man, and I wish to help him. That is all.'

'Then what are you doing?'

'Protecting people. Merely protecting people.'

Archie was finished early that day. Although recruits should dress themselves in uniform when walking about the city, Archie did not intend to go dancing as a policeman. Far better to put on his lightweight suit and panama hat, and when he studied himself in the mirror, he grinned broadly.

They had spent a day apart. There were good reasons for that, the main being that he was feeling the pinch. Drinks were expensive. Then again, he was exhausted. He yawned so much yesterday that the sergeant at the blackboard hurled his wooden board duster at his head. That had at least woken him up.

But his weariness left him as he entered the Astor House. It was horribly expensive, but Alice had promised to cover the chits herself.

The hotel was busy, and he stood at the ballroom's entrance, watching young men and women dancing to a new jazz tune. The leader of the hotel band was beating time with his trumpet. Archie couldn't see Alice, and he debated fetching a cocktail, but decided against; no point getting squiffy before she appeared. Instead he went to the racks of newspapers and picked up a China Times, retreating to a comfortable chair near the reception area.

It was there that Archie saw him.

A slender figure in a dark suit wearing a grey fedora with black and white band. The man was familiar, and something sent a shiver up Archie's spine.

To distract himself, Archie shook out the newspaper and read about a bank robbery. The *News* was always full of the robberies and hostage-takings. It seemed nothing of any note happened in Shanghai except murders and shootings. About to turn the page, a glimpsed photo stopped him: a man lying dead, gun at his side, and Archie almost dropped the paper. That was where he had seen the man before: the shooting!

He had disappeared. In the lobby there was an endless procession of people, and when Archie stood, he could see panama hats, fedoras of all types, but they appeared and were gone again in a flash. He could see no grey hat with a chequerboard ribbon. There was a pillar nearby, and Archie stepped on the decorative plinth, giving himself an extra nine inches of height, to the scandalised horror of a member of the hotel staff. From there he had a clear view.

And he saw the fedora.

The man was smoking, leaning against a pillar near the entrance, his hat low over his brow. He was waiting for something or someone.

Archie sprang down and made his way to the pillar where he had seen the man, thinking to arrest him, but when Archie reached it, the man had disappeared amongst the crowds as effectively as a wraith walking through a wall. But he was no ghost. Archie swore quietly, but then he spotted the hat again. He pressed forward and, reaching a pillar, peered round it. There, he saw the Chinese man with the light grey hat and chequered band talking to a woman. The man nodded, taking something from her, then turned and was gone.

'There you are!' Alice said, seeing him.

'Who was that?' he demanded.

Alice looked frightened. 'You mustn't tell anyone you saw him with me.'

'Who is he, Alice?'

Her voice was quiet. 'He's my brother.'

# Chapter Thirty-Nine

He was 'protecting people'. That phrase ran through Rod's mind all the way back to the Station.

Qian and Eva, Alice and Maurice, Alfred and Edith – they all had secrets. Qian was 'protecting people' by asking Eva to spy out Maurice's shipment; Eva was trying to keep body and soul together by selling her body and burning her soul; Alice seemed filled with resentment, but was it the spoiled jealousy of an unfulfilled rich girl, or something else? Maurice was a bully, resorting to threats at the slightest provocation, while Alfred was teetering on the brink of financial ruin. Edith was anxious to keep a secret of her dead son and prevent it becoming public knowledge. Something linked these lives, but it evaded Rod. It was an itch he couldn't scratch.

The assassin who shot Foster and Dewitt connected the Wintons to the two witnesses to Foster's murder; Billy Qian's involvement in the properties on the Kweichou Road and Honan Road linked him to the murdered lawyer and to Maurice Winton's business; the same business had some connection to Billy Qian, although he stated he was Maurice's friend. And Eva was a go-between or spy.

Billy Qian was up to his neck in this.

Rod sat rereading his notes.

If Maurice was trying to prove his ability, recreating the wealth his father had enjoyed, the obvious merchandise for a fast profit was opium. It was easy to smuggle, and had a ready market since the prohibition. Was that Qian's interest? American gangsters hid behind a legal façade that could explain their profits from prostitution, illegal alcohol or protection rackets. They created legitimate construction companies, hotels, restaurants, and claimed the funds came from them. Perhaps a good place to conceal illegal wealth would be a property company? When building a large office or apartment block, surely there must be ways of creatively paying for work or goods?

And then he had another thought: if Qian could conceal money in property deals, how much easier would it be for him to hide money in his own bank.

The ship was in the Whangpoo, Eva had said. It was difficult to find opium on a ship, because smugglers were inventive. Opium took up little space, and could be hidden in small compartments, or trailed from a ship in watertight packages ready for a different vessel or diver to collect, and as soon as it arrived ashore, it could be broken into ever smaller parcels and distributed.

However, if an entire building was worth renting … an entire building, just for drugs? That implied a huge quantity of opium, enough to keep Shanghai and the surrounding countryside smoking for a year. It was inconceivable that Maurice could have garnered such a vast amount. He didn't have the contacts.

So who could have put him in touch with the people necessary to supply him? It had to be someone with contacts in the opium growing areas. In the Empire, that meant India.

Rod knew nothing about Maurice's connections with India, but Qian had been educated in Britain; he said he had been at Oxford. It would not be surprising, if he had studied with other aspiring businessmen, that he might have made contacts in the subcontinent.

Rod would have to check into his time at university.

His eyes were heavy, and he could feel himself begin to nod. To clear his head, he lit a cigarette. It didn't help. He was too hot, too tired, and too frustrated.

Instead, he walked to Dan Bailey's and drank three Old Fashioneds in quick succession, ate a bowl of what Dan promised was oxtail soup, and made his way back to his apartment, where he dropped into a chair cradling a glass of whisky.

It was late when he went to bed. For once he slept without difficulty.

In the trenches, artillery bombardments often lasted for hours at a time. Once, the Germans had tried to 'soften up' Rod's area by raining shells for twenty four hours without stop.

During such barrages, no conversation could be held. Concussions overwhelmed them, their ears battered into submission. Besides, all they could think of was the horror of a shell above, smothering them in the blink of an eye. That was uppermost in their minds: the perpetual proximity of death. At such times the mind could wander. One of his men, Dickie Smale, went raving mad, and had to be knocked down. He was convinced that, if he could only escape the bunker, he could run all the way home to safety.

Rod was there again. He could hear the *crump, crump, crump* of mortars slamming into the ground. Smaller detonations told of anti-personnel shells bursting over the trench sending razor-sharp steel splinters whizzing over the lines. He could hear the shards whirring and whining through the air. And shortly afterwards he heard the muffled screams of the men whose shelter had collapsed, the timber supports shattering and crushing the men beneath.

It was intolerable. Rod felt the sweat break out. He wanted to escape, like Dickie Smale, and flee, run into the open. At least in the open a man could face his terrors. If he were to die, so be it. Better to die there than in here, in the cloying darkness.

The ceiling collapsed. Tons of filth and rubble, earth and the chemical odour of burned explosives filled his mouth and nostrils, bound his legs and arms and back, and he was slowly smothering, incapable of movement. The air was burning in his lungs with the effort of trying to breathe... He couldn't breathe ...

And he was in his bed, face buried in the pillow, the sheet wound about his legs. He took a deep, shuddering breath, hardly daring to imagine it had been a dream, but as he felt the warm air in his throat, he sobbed with relief – and despair. For he knew he must live through that death a thousand times more before he died.

Rod rolled from his bed and walked to his bedside table, filling a cup with water and drinking it in one draught before refilling it.

These dreams were less common now, but when they returned they left him shaking with the memory of the horrors.

Perhaps he was beginning to go doolally, like so many in the trenches.

That was when he heard the handle turn.

He had lived here almost a year, and had not got around to oiling the door's handle. As it turned, it squeaked, low and insistent, like a nail drawn down a slate. It made the hairs on the back of his neck stand up. It was a nerve-shredding sound at the best of times, but now, in the middle of the night, it was like hearing a demon's laugh.

His Colt was on the bedside table. He could not reach it in time; he had left the revolver in his office, too. Cursing his stupidity, he froze as the door opened, a black shape appearing. Rod was behind the door. There was a sudden bark, and a flash lit the whole room. Rod snapped his eyes shut a moment too late. His vision was a blur of orange and blue, and as a second and third shot went off, he covered his eyes, hoping to retain some residual sight, and as the shooting stopped, he grabbed the pistol, yanking it quickly to break it free from the man's grasp. It roared, and leapt, the fore-sight gouging the fleshy part of his hand. He didn't let go, tried to pull it into the room, shoving his shoulder hard into the door, trying to break the man's forearm or at least wrest the gun from him, but then the door was shoved hard. A second man was there. The gun was suddenly jerked from his grasp, and the door struck as though by a sledgehammer. It threw Rod to the floor, and he looked up to see the man with the gun aim at him. Behind him was the Chinese with the fedora with the chequerboard ribbon, but Rod concentrated on the man with the pistol. He could see the man smile, a man with thin lips, undernourished features, high cheekbones, eyes as black as coal, and then he stopped and stared at his pistol.

It wasn't firing.

Rod dived over the mattress, grabbing his gun, the grip in his fist like a friend's support, and then he was blazing away, straight at the doorway, three shots rapid, then another for safety, and heard two shots in return, but they were well over his head. Then there was silence. Rod's ears sang with a high pitched tone that deadened all other noise, and he stood cautiously, still aiming at the doorway.

A man was on the floor, squirming, his hands at his throat trying to staunch the flow of blood. His mouth opened and closed without sound, like a fish in its bowl, and a spray of blood jetted between his fingers, but gradually the spurting grew more feeble, slowed to a trickle, and his eyes went blank.

His friend had already disappeared.

The bullet passed so close to his head, Thin Bao had heard the sizzle of its passage. Never before had he been so close to death and the feeling of instant, imminent destruction.

Thin Bao's vision was gone. He saw only bright green and blue where gun flashes had gone off, and then Chang started to make a bubbling noise, and another bullet hit the plaster, and Thin Bao was showered in lime, and some was in his eye, and he couldn't see, and he fled down the stairs, stopping at the bottom in case he was being pursued, but then he was out, through the window where they had entered, and into the maze of alleys that twisted and wound between the houses here, while he heard shouts and whistles.

He hid his Mauser in its holster, and kept to the shadows.

The man had been waiting. He must have been. To fight back like that, like an enraged tiger. Thin Bao should have shot him through the door, but in the darkness, with Chang in the way, he couldn't. He had helped push the door wide, to get inside, but Chang had stopped firing, and then the policeman shot back.

Those bullets had been so loud, so ...

His heart was pounding so, he thought he might vomit. He leaned against a wall, while nausea washed through his body. It was supposed to be a quick job. That was what he'd been told. Chang and he had gone to his apartment thinking they need only slip in, kill him, and get away. An easy job.

Chang was dead.

He cursed. Last week his future had seemed secure. Now, because Winton wanted to be rid of that driver, he had been forced to remove two Chinese witnesses, lost Chang, and his cabaret was gone as well. He would avenge Chang, but for now he would stick to his own business.

First, his cabaret. Du Yusheng had told him to find that out, and he must do so quickly.

Rod felt as though someone had tried to flay the skin from his hand with a blunt knife; his knees had bruises on bruises. Diving to the ground and shooting was hard on knees and elbows. Soon three SMP officers arrived and eyed him suspiciously, but he was able to reassure them that, first, he wasn't injured, and, second, he was entitled to kill the man sent to assassinate him.

There was no doubt in his mind that this was a deliberate assassination attempt. The quiet entry, and the firing without reason, were all of a piece. They had tried to murder Rod in his bed. He had no idea who had tried to shoot him, so this was not revenge for a slight, real or perceived.

While he waited for the doctor and coroner's men to arrive, he had time to study the dead man's features. He was young, with a deep scar along the right side of his face that must have come from a not-very-sharp knife of some sort. A razor would have healed more cleanly. He had no papers on him, only a wallet with a few dollars, some cigarettes and a book of matches from a restaurant called the Montmartre in the French Settlement. He threw the matches onto his table with the rest of the contents of the man's pockets.

His pistol was a .32 calibre Browning. Rod recognised the model. A French officer he had known used to carry one. He had always praised it as being faster to fire and reload than a revolver, although Rod twice saw it jam in a fight when mud got to it. He opened the breech now to find that there was a fired case inside. When Rod had been fighting to take it from the gunman and gripped it hard, when it went off, the slide couldn't move. It couldn't eject the empty case, re-cock the hammer or load a fresh cartridge, so when the man tried to pull the trigger, it couldn't fire.

But that set Rod thinking about the two shots he had heard fired at him. Since the three officers were standing about rather pointlessly, Rod suggested they might search for the brass cases from the gunshots. Three .32 cases were discovered almost immediately, but then a fourth case was found. Another 7.63mm Mauser bottleneck case.

# Chapter Forty

*Wednesday 2nd August, 1922*

Rod's head felt like someone had been dancing on it in hobnailed boots. Looking in the mirror, he saw a glowering face like a gorilla's with a bad hangover. In the station washroom he splashed cold water on his face and neck and wiped himself dry. Fleetingly, Doctor Babu sprang into his mind, but he forced it away. He would not become an addict to his mixed drugs.

At this time of day Dan Fairbairn would still be running drills with new recruits. Rod left the bullet case in a fresh, labelled envelope before making his way to his office. Mickey Hi was in the corridor, and Rod asked for a pot of tea.

He opened the drawer and took up the revolver Fairbairn had so drastically remodelled. From now on, he would carry the second gun at all times. He fixed the holster on his belt, behind his hip, and installed the pistol, practising drawing and aiming while he waited for the tea.

The attack was surely proof that his enquiries had rattled someone, but was it his questioning of Billy Qian, of Eva, or Maurice that had led to the violence? When Mickey Hi arrived with the tea, Rod sent to have the gangster brought from his cell. He should be nicely desperate, Rod reasoned, having been without drugs for a night.

Rod wrote a report on the attack last night. If he was right, the same gun had been used in all the shootings, and that meant the same man was almost certainly present at each.

It was while he was rereading the statement of the Chinese girl that he realised there was another connection: she had described one man who was wearing a dark suit and a grey fedora with a chequered band. The man last night, who had seemed so oddly familiar, had been dressed in that manner. Checking his notes, Rod had a flash of memory: a face in the crowds on Sunday while he was buying cigarettes. He was surely the same man whom Rod saw last night. Perhaps the man Rod had killed was the second of the two who had killed Foster and the Chinese?

There was a knock, and the gangster was led in by two Chinese officers. Behind them was a grinning O'Toole. 'Thought I'd best help you. My, but he's a terrible looking fellow!'

The man did indeed look terrible. His face was yellowish grey, and both hands shook. There was a fine sheen of sweat on his forehead, and he clutched at his stomach every so often. One of the officers held a metal pail in his hands. He pulled a face. 'Sick, much.'

'How are you?' Rod asked in Chinese.

'Not well. Not well. Need go, find friend.'

'You want drugs, you mean,' Rod said. 'For now, you will remain here. When you start to talk, we will see what will happen. Since you are suspected of involvement in a protection racket, we will have to consider what to do with you.'

'No, no, I need go. Back home, Frenchtown, home,' he said plaintively.

He kept repeating his demands, now insistent and demanding, now, as the belly gripes got to him again, pleading pitifully.

'Where are you from?'

'Pootung.'

That was the other bank of the Whangpoo River, the dismal gatherings of shanties and ill-constructed shacks that housed so many Chinese who crossed the river to work in the cigarette, match, silk and other factories. They earned a tiny sum for hours of unrelenting, hard work, with just enough time to return home and sleep before they must rise again.

'What did your parents do?'

'Father, he was a carpenter. My mother she died,' he said, both hands on his belly, rocking back and forth.

'You have it bad, eh? I have heard of drugs being brought here. Do you know anything about a ship in the Whangpoo with opium?'

He looked up hopefully. 'Ship with more?'

'Do you know anything about a big shipment?'

He shook his head mournfully, then winced and bent again.

'Where is your father now?'

'He dead. I came, to Frenchtown, to work. Liked gambling, earned money to go and bet. Lots of bets. Good life.'

'How did you join the Green Gang?'

'No, no, I work insurance company.'

'You work for the Green Gang. The girl and her father were murdered by the Green Gang because they witnessed the murder of the man in the car. Did you kill him?'

'No, no, I work insurance.'

'You were there. The girl told us. She described you. Then you killed her and her father.'

'No. Insurance. Try to protect shops.'

'You can afford opium on your salary?'

'Let me, Detective,' O'Toole said. He leaned his enormous fists on the desk. 'I'll beat it out of him.'

'Do you hear? He will take you downstairs and beat you if you don't tell us the truth,' Rod said. 'We know you were selling protection. You told them, if they didn't pay, the same could happen to them as happened to the girl and her father, didn't you?'

'No!'

'You want to go to Frenchtown? Why? Do you think the French will let you free?'

A fleeting deviousness passed over his face, quickly concealed, but Rod was sure of its meaning. He thought he would be safer, perhaps even get released, if he were to reach Frenchtown.

After an hour, Rod decided he had endured enough.

'Keep him here,' he said to the Chinese officers, and beckoned O'Toole outside.

'Well?' O'Toole said. 'A pathetic little scrap, isn't he?'

Rod wiped his forehead. His head was aching.

'Are you all right, Cottey? You look like you could do with a rest.'

He sounded solicitous, but Rod sensed an ulterior motive. Did he want to take over the Foster case? It wouldn't be the first time a policeman had tried to advance his own career by taking over an investigation. Rod said sharply, 'I'm fine! Yes, he's so befuddled with his need for opium, he'd confess to murdering William Rufus if we asked him.'

'Christ!' O'Toole glowered. 'Another killing?'

'William Rufus, son of the William the Conqueror. He died a long time ago.'

'Oh! What now, then?'

'We need to find out which gang he's from.'

'You'll keep him sweating a bit longer, then. I can use more forceful methods. We have ways of helping people with their memory.'

Rod disliked using force because the results were often unreliable. A man exposed to torture would confess to anything to make the pain end. 'No need. The opium will exert the strongest pressure.'

'You could threaten to send him to the Chinese to be tried.'

'I doubt I'd be allowed to. The Commissioner would take a dim view of sending a murderer to the Chinese when he committed crimes in International territory, against Shanghailanders. Someone accused here should be tried in the Municipal courts.'

'He killed two Chinese. Surely that would put him under Chinese jurisdiction?'

'No, they were killed in our territory, so he should be tried by the Mixed Court. Besides, I don't want *him*. It's the man who initiated the murders I want to catch.'

There was a call from along the corridor, and Mickey Hi pattered to a halt. 'Sir, Hi, sorry, Sarn't Major Fairbairn would like to speak, sir.'

Archie spent the morning in a daze. At exercises, he could not concentrate; at breakfast he could hardly swallow his food. Alice had explained it all so clearly.

'It all started many years ago,' she had said.

They were sitting at the bar, where they could speak quietly. The waiter served them drinks, and then they were alone.

'I don't understand.'

'How could you? It was many years ago, and Mother ... well, she didn't want anything to do with him.'

'Please, explain.'

'My father had an affair with Thin Bao's mother. I believe father paid the family to keep the boy, but then Thin Bao's mother died, and shortly afterwards, his father was murdered. The boy was brought to mother's orphanage, and he did well. So, he was allowed in our house as a servant. It wasn't unusual for mother to bring an orphan into the house. But Thin Bao was a cause of trouble. I think mother must have guessed that ... well, father was affectionate to the boy. He grew more and more – well, obsessed with him. Finally mother couldn't take it any longer.'

'They had a row?' Archie could imagine that if his father had brought his bastard into the house, his mother would have had plenty to say.

'You know how families are. She didn't raise her voice; she never would. But she made it clear. We went away with father on a houseboat for a few days, and when we came back, Thin Bao was gone.'

'Just like that?'

'He didn't know what he had done. He found it terribly hard, but he got work in a grocer's shop, and then started working with gamblers, and ... well, I have always felt sorry for him. I know what it is to be loved, and then for someone to take it away.'

'What do you mean?'

'Oh, nothing. I helped him with money whenever I could. I was paying him a little more today when you saw us. It's only a few dollars, but it's the least I can do for my brother.'

'I see,' Archie said, but he didn't. His parents didn't bottle up their feelings. When his mother was angry, she let everyone know. If his father told her he had been seeing some woman, her screeching would have been heard from Wapping. And uncle Tom would have beaten seven barrels of shit out of him ... but Alice's family were different. This was how a rich family worked: they remained calm while tensions rose, and then got rid of the problem. And if the problem was an unwanted boy, he must be sent away. Archie tried to absorb this, but he couldn't.

'Your father didn't mind?'

'Mother made it impossible to keep Thin Bao in the house. She made ... *suggestions.*'

'I don't understand.'

Alice looked away. 'She suggested Thin Bao was interested in me.'

'Oh!'

'Thin Bao couldn't stay after that.' Alice shook her head. 'So, father promised never speak to Thin Bao again. But he kept in touch. I shouldn't be surprised …'

'What?'

She bit her lip. 'If father hadn't paid him to kill Foster.'

'What? Why?'

'Foster was blackmailing him. He had compromising letters from a woman to Ian, and Foster threatened to release them. Can you imagine what that would do to the family? To the business?'

Archie was full of confusion - yes, and guilt. She had made him complicit in the family's secrets, and now …

Now he was caught. He didn't want to make Alice unhappy. She had been so quiet, as though on the brink of tears. When they danced, she smiled bravely, but he could see her eyes brimming.

Her half brother had murdered Foster. Archie had recognised the hat immediately. And likely Thin Bao had done so because Alfred Winton had asked him to.

Archie couldn't keep that secret. But what could he do?

Back in his office, Rod was told that Dubois had called. He was soon connected to the Sûreté.

'I am glad to speak to you, my friend,' Rod said. 'I have news, I think. We have captured a man claiming to be from the French Settlement. He was demanding protection money when we caught him.'

'Do you know his name?'

'He claims to be called Chen. All we know is, the witness he killed said that he was collecting for the Green Gang.'

He could hear Dubois's tone change, as if he was suddenly sitting upright. 'The Green Gang?'

'Yes. Why?'

Rod could hear papers being shuffled. 'I have photos of men within the Gang. I would like to see this man of yours, and see if he is known to us.'

It took little arrangement. Although Dubois offered to come to Central Station, Rod said he would bring Chen to the Sûreté. An idea was forming in his mind. News of the witnesses had got to the assassins. It was likely that the killers had come from the Green Gang, and the Chinese witnesses died after Rod had told

Dubois about them. Had Rod mentioned to him before that it was the two from the shop? He could not remember.

Within the hour the prisoner was shackled to a vertical pole that supported the canvas roof of a police lorry, and was jolting along the roads with two guards and O'Toole. The lorry raised a hellish cloud of ochre-coloured dust, and the men were soon coughing and blinking furiously as they rode along.

Dubois was waiting at the door as they arrived, and they soon had Chen in Dubois' office, sitting in a hard wooden chair with his wrists handcuffed.

'You are here because of your membership of the Green Gang and your activities with them,' Dubois said. 'You asked to be brought here. Why?'

'I am from the French quarter. I want to be tried here. I have a lawyer, I want to speak to him.'

'Listen carefully,' Dubois said. 'You have no rights here. If you have broken the law, you must ...'

'I am Chilean. I have Chile passport.'

'What?' Dubois said.

Rod was as astonished. 'You did not mention this before?'

The man ignored him. 'Chile consulate will confirm. Ask. I talk to Consul.'

'Detective?' Dubois said, looking at me.

'Why did you not tell us before?' Rod said.

'In Frenchtown, safe,' he sneered.

O'Toole clenched his fist. It looked like a brick, and about as unforgiving. Rod pushed him away before he could punch, just as the Head of the Chinese Detective Squad walked in. His pockmarked face held its usual affable smile.

'I – oh, you have a suspect?'

Huang Jinrong smiled down at the man.

There are times when a policeman has a sudden intuition. This was one such. Rod had expected to see the gangster look away, or at least appear alarmed. Pockmarked Huang was known to all the criminals in Frenchtown, after all. He was the most senior police officer in the Chinese force, a man of authority. Chen must surely know that.

Yet there was no flinching away. Instead, he met Huang's smile without fear. He knew Huang.

Rod didn't know whether Dubois had seen the look that passed between the two. Did Dubois know that the two knew each other? After all, corruption was not unique to Asians. Even in the SMP there were men who lived suspiciously well on meagre salaries, and a number were suspected of offering protection or accepting bribes in order to look away when a crime was committed. Dubois would not be the first, if he was so inclined.

Huang rattled off a series of questions. Chen responded. Both were talking so quickly that it was hard to follow them, but Rod got the impression that Huang was telling the man he would soon have his consul.

'He states he is a Chilean national, and asks to have his consul come here to confirm his identity. It is ridiculous, of course, but there it is.'

'The Chilean consul?' Rod asked. Huang's French was very good, but Rod could understand most of it – while O'Toole looked simply bemused.

Dubois nodded, and turned to Huang. 'When will he be here?'

'Very soon.'

'I see.'

Huang left shortly afterwards, and Dubois and Rod walked outside. O'Toole remained in the room.

'Well?' Rod said, barely controlling his anger. At least Dubois had seen his suspect. They could still check Chen's face with the photos of past suspects.

'This is a strange matter,' Dubois said. He looked pensive and anxious.

'The Chileans are like the Mexicans. They offer passports – for a fee. I'm not surprised that this man could have access to a foreign passport. It protects him from the Chinese police.'

'This is so. We have many who claim nationality from a number of countries,' Dubois said. 'But of more import was the fact that my chief of detectives knew the man was there before he walked into my office. He said that he had already called the Chilean consul. How did he know to do that, when you and I did not know the man was going to claim Chilean nationality?'

'I saw the look they exchanged when your chief entered the room. They know each other.'

'Yes.'

'I hesitate to ask,' Rod said – he didn't want to make Dubois an enemy. 'But when I told you about the two Chinese witnesses to Foster's death, did you tell anyone?'

'I told Huang Jinrong. Why?'

'It was that same day that they were killed. Their deaths so soon after I told you seems a remarkable coincidence.'

Dubois nodded. 'I will see what I may do to investigate. I think I mentioned my own suspicions before? This could be the end of Huang Jinrong.'

# Chapter Forty-One

Rod's faith in Dubois was restored. He left Chen with him and started back to his office, but found his feet taking the road to Doctor Babu.

The doctor himself opened the door. Smiling, he led the way to the rear room once more. Once Rod was sitting, he said, 'Is it grown bad again?'

'Yes,' Rod said, trying to put his symptoms into words. 'Doctor, I am not sleeping well, I am tired all the time ... concentrating is difficult ... I cannot keep my mind on my work. I need more cocaine to clear my head.'

'It is as I feared,' the doctor sighed. He came to a decision. 'Very well. I shall give you more to clear your head, but it is a very powerful drug. If a man becomes addicted, it is difficult to give up the habit. If he gradually reduces his intake, the cravings will assail with ever greater force. And as the body grows accustomed to the drug, he will need more and more to satisfy his cravings. This is why those who are keen to stop taking the drug are so often unsuccessful. You have only a minor wish for it now, because I have given you only a quarter grain at a time. Were you to increase your dose even a little, the desire for ever more, day after day, would devastate you.'

Rod considered. 'Are there other side-effects?'

'You will find you will lose all desire for food, and will not feel sleepy. Many people find that a pipe or two of opium will allow them a refreshing sleep. For the appetite, perhaps brandy will make you hungry again. If you are happy to try this, I can help you.'

He walked from the room for a short period. When he returned, he carried a small morocco case, inside which sat a small syringe and a needle. Next to these was a glass vial of tablets. 'Be most cautious. This is strong medicine. I will let you have this case. You can arrange your own dose, but be careful.'

Rod shivered. Uppermost in his mind was the intoxicating vision of a needle holding the comfort of Doctor Babu's magical drug. Babu smiled at Rod, as he thought, benevolently. This was one man Rod could trust entirely.

Holding his arm up, he unbuttoned his cuff, straightened his arm and held it out to him.

Back at Central Station, Rod reopened his files on Foster's murder, the notes he had taken of his meetings with Eva, her husband, Alice and Maurice. He was thinking of Maurice's words on Yevgeny Bugayev: something about the Russian being happy for a while.

He was unsure what Maurice had meant. That Bugayev was trying to win back his wife's affections? It seemed unlikely; the man's only interest was alcohol. His wife paid for that because he had no money, and if he were to get money, he would buy more vodka. Rod doubted he cared. It was not kind, but it was how a young, rich man like Maurice would look at a poverty-struck alcoholic who couldn't hold on to his wife. But how did Maurice know Bugayev?

Who would pay Bugayev? And for what? Why would a man employ him? He would have to be desperate: an alcoholic made an unreliable employee.

Doctor Babu had told him to make sure he ate sensibly, for he would feel little hunger, so Rod went to the canteen. It was between shifts, and the place was empty apart from Bert Shaw. Rod joined him.

'Oh, hello,' he said. He was pale.

'You look like you need to sleep for a week,' Rod said.

'Thank you. You look pretty marvellous, too.'

He smiled quickly, but it faded.

'What is it, Bert?' Rod asked. To his discomfort he saw Bert had a tear in his eye. Muttering, 'I'm sorry, Bert. I'll ...' He scraped his seat back, but Bert caught his sleeve.

'Don't, old fellow. I am sorry, but stay a moment and I'll explain.'

It took him a few moments to compose himself. Rod didn't want to stay, other men's problems were ... *hard* to cope with. He had enough problems of his own without involving himself in those of others, but he owed Bert some sort of duty. He had become a friend on the long journey here.

'It is a girl,' he said at last.

'You don't have to tell me,' Rod said.

'You were good enough to tell me about your girl. I feel I should repay the debt.'

'Which is?'

'I am not a bad man, Rod. I hope you realise that.'

'Well, of course.' Rod felt an unaccountable irritation. If he was going to confess to a crime, Rod didn't want to know. He made an effort to rise, but before he could, Bert was speaking.

'I came out here because I couldn't stay at home. You see, my family is rather rich. Especially now. I always knew that there was money in the family, but never really ... well, these things come to one after the War, don't they?'

Rod wasn't sure what Bert was saying. 'We all have secrets. Few have unblemished pasts.'

'It's not like that, Rod. After the War, I had an opportunity to leave everything behind, to make a new life. I swear to you, Rod, it didn't take more than a second's thought to seize it with both hands.'

'What are you saying? If you have done something –'

'Me? No. It was my father. You see, he was profiting from selling weapons.'

Rod felt disgust settle on his stomach like greasy suet. After the horror of life in the trenches he could not forgive those who made the weapons they had faced.

Bert nodded at Rod's expression. 'Strange, isn't it? We both feel the same about those responsible. But all my life, through Harrow, then Oxford, all I wanted was to make him proud. I took the money and enjoyed myself. They were happy times, Rod. But then the War came. I saw my friends go, and one by one they died. You know how it was. And all the while, as the shells rained down, and the machine guns rattled, and my chaps were mown down, all that time, all I could think was, my own family was making these infernal devices. You know, I was raised as a good Church of England fellow, but since then, I've not prayed. Not once.'

'So after the war, you came out here.'

'Yes. after one last joke at my expense. It was the tenth of November, and we were fighting in a horrible place. Cold, wet, and we were exhausted. That evening, I went out to review the chaps. It was a filthy night. The Germans had been giving us gyp for most of the day, and they had just stopped for a while. We needed some air, my soldier-servant and I. So out we went, and while we were, they sent a massive *hate* of artillery. Mortars, ten and a half centimetres, fifteen centimetres, the lot. And a big one landed right slap-bang beside us.'

Rod had seen it so often: the sudden gout of flame, the hideous uprush of mud, wire, wooden slats, limbs and bodies. Everything shattered or blasted to pieces. The men who were chatting one moment, and in the next, vaporised in a burst of obscene fire.

'All my fellows caught it,' he continued quietly. 'All of them - even my soldier-servant, a lively fellow called Albert. And the thing was, when I came to, all I could think of was my family, and the fact that our wealth was built on exactly this: shells and bombs killing fellows like mine. And me too, nearly, I suppose. I was lucky. I'd had most of my clothes blown from me, but when I started hunting, I soon learned that I was the only survivor. It was a miracle. And I started to have an idea.'

He moodily took a bite of food. 'It was ridiculously easy, really. There was no one to argue the case with me. I was the sole survivor, so I swapped my neck tags with Albert's. Then I took my red disc.'

Rod nodded. Every soldier had a green tag on a string around his neck with his name, number and religion printed on it. Tied to it was a red disc with the same information. When a soldier was found dead, his red disc was taken, leaving his green one behind. The green tag meant he could be identified; the missing red one meant someone else had already reported the man's death.

'I was all done up. Albert's tunic was a mess, but I pulled it on, and soon some soldiers took me to the doctor. I told him my name was Albert, and my officer was dead. I gave him the red disc to be registered. I explained my tunic was shredded and I'd taken another man's. He wasn't going to argue. He was happy to learn that I had most of my marbles. I was there a week, and in that time the Armistice was implemented, and I was moved back fairly speedily. When I reached London, I took a room in a cheap hotel and planned my escape. I didn't want to confront the old man. And my mother … I didn't want her to know that I despised everything the family was built upon. No, it seemed better to up stumps and leave. They could pass everything on to my younger brother, and all would be well. Apart from my girl. She is the thing I …' He stopped, blinking heavily. 'Anyway. I saw an advert for the SMP, and thought, "why not?" Not part of the Empire, a certain amount of excitement, and safer than life at the Front. And then I got here, and realised nothing is ever that easy.'

'So what is your real name?'

'Albert Shaw,' he said seriously. 'You will never know me by any other name, old chap. Bert is my name now. And it might always have been.'

'Is this all true?'

'My dear fellow - what *is* the truth? After one's been in the front line, and thrashed, and then read about the glorious victory later in the newspapers, one begins to dimly appreciate how flexible the truth really is.'

The knock was a mild rap.

Billy Qian looked up from his papers as his Number One Boy ushered in his guest. 'Ah. Thin Bao. How can I help you?' he said.

Thin Bao walked in with the confidence of a man who knew his own worth. He didn't look at the paintings on the walls or the valuable vase over by the window; he fixed his gaze on Billy.

The two shook hands, and Thin Bao stared at the servant, until Billy motioned and said, 'Tea, please.'

He didn't have to specify what sort. Number One Boy had been with Billy for long enough to know his preferences.

Thin Bao took his seat and said nothing until Number One Boy had served them tea and silently left the room.

'Well?' Billy Qian said.

Thin Bao lit a cigarette. 'My cabaret was raided by the police.'

'I know. I was there.'

'Someone told the police. I have been asking who could have been responsible.'

'Have you been successful?'

'The only person mentioned is you.'

Billy Qian smiled, leaned forward, and opened his humidor. He selected a cigar, snipped off the end and unhurriedly lit it with a gold lighter. 'And these people who mentioned me, these are reliable men? Really, Thin Bao! You and I are like brothers. We have been since we met in the orphanage, haven't we? We are in business to make ourselves rich, and can only do so by joining forces. We both know that. You wish to advance in your organisation, and I want to make money from my investments. We both benefit by working together. That is why we joined forces with Maurice, it is why we are working towards the same objective with our bank. Shanghai has many charlatans and gangsters, but you and I together can be successful.'

'Did you alert the police?'

Qian held his hands apart in a gesture of openness. 'Would I alert the police, and then go to your cabaret to be arrested? I was there, my friend. You know that.'

Yes, Thin Bao did know that. And more.

'My friend,' Qian said, 'we are as good as brothers. When we met at the orphanage, before I was sent away, we were friends.'

Thin Bao remembered. The first boy to befriend him was Billy Qian. Then, when one or other was victimised, the other always came to his assistance. Billy, who had no friends because he was half-caste, Thin Bao because he was small, so easy to bully. But together they could protect each other.

'I saved you from that orphanage, didn't I? I saved you from the she-devil Hyland. I got you a place with the Wintons.'

Thin Bao nodded. 'Why would men say you set the police on me?'

Qian shrugged expansively. 'Brother, we know other men are jealous of us. We work together, and others notice.' He went to the window, staring down at the street with a frown. 'Could someone in your organisation could have done this? Someone who watched your rise through the Gang and was jealous? Someone who wanted to set you against me, to hurt us both, so that he could take over your interests?'

Thin Bao nodded. Several in the Gang would be keen to destroy him, and if they knew of his connection with Billy Qian, that would give them an easy weapon.

'We have a good thing going,' Billy Qian said. 'Don't let some fool who wants to hurt us succeed! You would be helping our enemies!'

Thin Bao nodded, but later he had doubts. He had known Billy Qian for much of his life. They had been friends for many years, but both had streaks of ruthlessness. Neither could trust the other entirely.

Billy was right. He had been there in the cabaret when it was raided and the gambling was discovered, but he was wealthy, and had powerful friends to guarantee that his arrest would be a minor embarrassment – nothing more, while for Thin Bao, it meant great loss of face. Du Yusheng would be less likely to trust him. But how could Billy profit by Thin Bao's injury? No, it would not help him to see Thin Bao destroyed.

It must have been someone else.

## Chapter Forty-Two

Rod was still thinking about the sad, quiet figure as he walked back to his office. His head ached, but the cocaine had taken the edge from it. His mind still seemed remarkably clear.

It was depressing that Bert Shaw, a man who seemed more composed and self-assured than most, had such a story. It was convincing; why would he invent such a tale? After the War, many could not return home. Rod was himself one. It was surprising how far Bert had been prepared to go to lose his past. It made Rod wonder how many others had been similarly provoked – Foster and his letters from different women sprang into his mind. Foster had changed his name and left the country too.

But even as he had the thought, Maurice saying that his brother was less an angel than others realised came to mind.

And made Rod catch his breath.

He pulled out the letters from the tin box and went through them again. He had no way to tell who had written them, but as he read, he didn't get the feeling they were addressed to a chauffeur with aspirations. They were from a well-to-do woman, communicating with someone from her social circle. She spoke of her garden, her children's suits, and the nanny, who caused problems with her slovenly ways, the difficulty of the gardener plainly stealing carrots and cabbages. It was possible that a man like Foster could attract a woman of a higher class, but it didn't ring true. To meet such a woman implied a man with time on his hands. Maurice had pointed him towards a different recipient of these letters; could they have been addressed to Ian?

If so, Foster had kept these letters – hoarded them. That implied a motive. Had he threatened to expose Ian Winton as a womaniser, possibly an adulterer? That would be embarrassing to the Wintons. Perhaps worse than embarrassing, if there was a little bastard.

Rod fanned himself with a handful of the letters.

Foster had collected them. He was keeping them to blackmail the Wintons.

When she appeared, a foul cloud of black coal smoke pouring from her funnel and drifting along the waterfront, no one paid much attention. Only the old beggar, who sat with his hand held out hopefully. Few glanced at him. To acknowledge the beggar would demean them.

Tim Burton dropped his hand. The contempt of these Chinese made him want to smash them in the face. He was a white man, damn them! How dare they look down on him, when he was good as ten of them? His gaze fell to the foul cloth that enwrapped him. It was a sickening. He was no longer a white man; he was an outcast. This was where he would die, here, in the roadway, perhaps this summer, perhaps next winter. No longer British, he was a *nothing*. A nobody. A mere grasping hand pleading for money.

He'd been here all day. There was nowhere else to go. His room was gone since he hadn't paid rent for a month. The Chinese owner had all but kicked him from the door. At least in summer it was no hardship sleeping outdoors. Occasionally an SMP officer would move him, but for the most part they left him. Some even gave him coins in memory of the days when he had been one of them.

Through a haze of rum, Burton remembered Rod Cottey expressing interest in a steamer. This was one such, an old tramp, with a coat of paint that must have been pre-War where it still clung to the rusting metal-work. Such paint as remained was coated liberally in soot and grease and oil.

She coughed and belched her way to the Bund, nudging past warships and steamers. Sailors moved about her with the languid efficiency of matelots who knew their vessel, and in a short space of time, the *Lucky Strike* was moored. Soon officials and dockyard workers were moving aboard.

The beggar was surprised to see an automobile rumble along the Bund and draw up near the ship, waiting. Nearby a lorry waited.

As the officials left the ship, meandering back to their offices, the lorry moved to the rear of the *Lucky Strike*.

Two men climbed out of the automobile, one a short, grubby man with moustache and beard, the other a taller, dapper man in a linen suit. The two were soon talking with the captain. A small derrick was collecting crates from a rear hold, while the captain and two visitors watched. The crates were stowed in the lorry, making the suspension creak, and then the lorry moved away while a second took its place.

In all, the beggar counted six lorries. Not a huge number, but all were taking heavy loads. When the last was loaded, the two men shook hands with the captain and returned to their automobile, setting off in pursuit of the lorries.

Burton remained watching, until a large SMP officer, recently recruited and new to the territory, prodded him with an unfriendly boot. 'You: bugger off,' he said.

'You new here?'

The officer scowled down at him. 'You speak English?'

'I *am* English. Get a message back to Central Station, for Detective Sergeant Rod Cottey. Tell him his ship is in, and tell him to bring my rum.'

And all the while the coolies trudged up the gangplank and back, bent under their loads, dogged and relentless as a parade of ants.

When Rod arrived, the *Lucky Strike* was sitting quietly, an occasional puff of sooty smoke rising from her funnel like the last rattling exhalations from a cancerous throat. An officer stood at the top of the gangplank, a crowd of coolies before him waiting to hear whether they would be allowed to offload his cargo. It was pathetic to see the scrawny figures so desperate for the back-breaking work that they would stand patiently like dogs waiting for a scrap to fall from the table. The officer pushed his cap to the back of his head and pointed to a number of men and then cursed the others, telling them to search for a job somewhere else.

'Good morning. Are you the Captain?' Rod asked as he walked up the gangplank.

'Who you?' the man said. He was short, with a bull-like neck and the shoulders of an Atlas. He had a strong slavic accent.

'I am a Detective with the Shanghai Municipal Police. I would like to see your cargo lists.'

'Why?'

Rod allowed a little asperity into his voice. 'Because it will save me the effort of arresting you. That would create paperwork.'

Glancing at the list, he saw muslins, linens, cotton cloth, a number of agricultural goods, some tons of rice, and other goods to be taken on up-river.

'How much of this has been unloaded already?'

The captain pointed. 'We have cargo to take up river. Then we unload, take on more to bring here and then sail on to Hong Kong.'

'I see.' What had Maurice said he was importing? Whisky and cigars, and no doubt other goods. 'Which godown has your cargo?'

He directed Rod to a couple at the Soochow Creek. Rod made a note of their names, thanked him, and was about to leave the ship, when he had a thought. 'Are you Russian?'

'Yes.'

'White?'

He smiled sadly at that. 'Why you think I'm on ship?'

'There is a man here, Yevgeny Bugayev. He was an admiral in your Imperial Navy. He needs work and money.'

'I know him.'

'How?'

'He was here. He came to translate and left with his companion.'

'Who was his companion?'

'Big man, German, white linen suit, hat.'

Rod made his way to the shore. The only German in Shanghai was Schreier. Why was Schreier here?

At the corner of the street opposite, a Chinese police officer was shouting at a beggar sprawled in the dirt.

'Leave him,' Rod said sharply. Then, 'Tim? Are you all right?'

'I'm fine. You want to know what happened?'

'Yes.'

'Did you bring my rum?'

'Not yet. I'll be back with it. And cigarettes.'

'There was a big Russian here. He was talking to the German. You know him: Schreier. They loaded boxes into lorries. I heard Schreier tell them to take the boxes to Honan Road.'

'Boxes? What was in them?'

'You think I can see through crates? There were six lorries. All loaded heavily with wooden cases. They took them all.'

The Honan Road godown was like a kicked hornet's nest. Men scrambled to pull crates from lorries, and carried them, four men to a box, into the building. When Rod reached the place, there was no sign of Yevgeny Bugayev or Helmut Schreier, but several large and impressive-looking Russian guards.

'Is Maurice Winton here?'

The man shook his head, and when Rod tried to step past him, a hand like a manhole cover was placed on his chest and pushed him backwards.

'Big man, if you do that again, you'll end up in hospital,' Rod said.

The Russian shook his head with a disparaging smile, as though there was nothing Rod could do which could possibly hurt him. Rod smiled back.

A blond Russian stepped between them. While he was about Rod's height, the span of his shoulder was half as wide again. He had an impressive scar on his left cheek, and a slight cast in the eye above. 'You want to talk Mr Winton, you must go his house. Not here.'

'How about Yevgeny or Helmut Schreier?'

'Not here.'

Rod took a short pace forward, his head jutting. 'I suggest you hurry and bring them. Now.'

'Which bit "not here" you not understand?' the Russian said truculently.

'Which bit "Shanghai Police" you not understand?' Rod said. 'Get them, unless you want to come to the Central Station.'

Behind him Rod heard a bell ringing. With relief he recognised the sound of a police car's approach. '*Now!*'

The man looked up at his friend uncertainly, and the two muttered. While they stood debating - Rod assumed - whether to pull his head off to use as a football, he could hear the bells approach. Finally the big man nodded and shuffled away, but by then the first of the police wagons was already hurtling up the road, an officer ringing the bell like fury.

Shouting over his shoulder, the blond reached under his jacket, but Rod was faster. As the Russian's hand reappeared gripping the familiar shape of a Browning, Rod already had his Colt's barrel at the man's forehead. 'Enough!'

The Russian glared, but allowed Rod to take the gun. Rod pushed him against the wall as the first of the police ran to help. Bert Shaw was in front, ordering a Chinese officer to bind the Russian and hold him there, before joining Rod running through the gates. Chinese and English officers bellowed to the men in the yard to stop working, while Bert and Rod made their way to the main door. Inside more men were stacking boxes, bare-chested in the sweltering heat, and as Rod stepped inside, he was almost choked by the cloying odours of sweat, urine, decay – and something else. The heavy, leaden odour of machine oil and grease.

'*Christ!*' Bert said.

Rod pushed a terrified coolie to one side. Grabbing a crowbar, he slipped the pry under the lid of the nearest box. It lifted with a squeak of nails, and inside he saw a line of neatly racked machine pistols. He went to the next box. Another row of Bergmanns. The next was smaller: it contained Mauser pistols.

'What you do?' a man shouted, and Rod turned to see Yevgeny Bugayev, swaying slightly at the turn of a flight of steps. He was well on his way, but something kept him upright. Perhaps the hope of another drink.

'Come here,' Rod called, but as he did, the immense Russian appeared behind Bugayev. He took in the sight and shoved Bugayev, who tumbled forward down the stairs, and sprang back.

Rod drew his pistol and made his way to the steps. He was about to clamber up them, when the Russian reappeared, but this time he held a machine-pistol, and as Rod sprang to take cover, he heard that hellish clatter once more.

## Chapter Forty-Three

The bullets striking the floor was deafening as he hit the ground and rolled behind a packing case. Bert had thrown himself sideways as the first shots roared.

Perhaps it was the humidity, or the narrow corridor, but the Russian's Bergmann sounded like an elephant gun. The flash from the muzzle lit the place like a flare, and Rod heard bullets slamming into wood and brick, and some horrible, wet impacts as men were struck, one of them setting up a loud wailing.

In his left hand Rod still held the other Russian's Browning, and he held it over the case, blasting away like billy-oh in the hope that it would persuade the Russian to keep his head down. When it was empty, he dropped it. The machine-pistol was silent at last.

Rod was more confident with his Colt, and he pulled the slide partway open, checking there was a round up the spout, before risking a glance up the stairs.

The Russian had gone. Rod glanced left to make sure Bert was unhurt. He was sitting just beyond a doorway with his back to a cupboard, and stared back with the pale, excited expression Rod had seen so often in the trenches: it was the face of a man who knew the danger, but would not retreat. He nodded, and both darted to the bottom of the stairs. Rod climbed as silently as he could, but the boards creaked. He felt the sweat spring from every pore. It was like walking along a trench while rifle fire whizzed overhead, looking out for booby traps, keeping his eyes fixed on the next corner waiting for bullets from a machine pistol to cut him in two. Rod held his gun two-handed, crouching low, watching the next level, expecting at any moment to see the Russian appear and start shooting.

Bugayev was still on the staircase, moaning. Blood was pouring from a gash in his brow where he had hit the wall. He looked pathetic, a confused, huddled figure. Rod carried on to the half-landing.

More men were arriving. Rod heard O'Toole bellowing at coolies to leave the boxes alone and step away from them. Content that the way behind was secured, Rod called to him that there was a man with a machine-pistol on the next floor, and continued up the stairs. The half-landing where the Russian had appeared gave on to a flight of stairs that rose with a wall on the left, but which was open on the right. Rod would be visible and vulnerable on that side as he climbed. He crouched lower, keeping his head down until he was almost level with the floor, and then snatched a quick glance.

It was most of the upper floor. Windows kept it bright and airy. There were bare boards on the floor, and a series of crates and boxes had been stacked neatly. Rod paused, breathing deeply, and then launched himself up the last of the stairs, aiming for the protection of the boxes.

As he broke cover, there was that hideous noise again, and bullets hummed and sang about him as he dived for the ground and slid to safety behind a number of crates. Not a moment too soon – he was glad to hear bullets clattering against something metal in the case behind him. He felt the draught as five bullets tore over his head, slamming into the wall.

Rod turned in time to see Bert Shaw peer over the floor from the stairs. As he did so, a sharp burst of three or four bullets ripped into the floor near him, and Rod saw him flung back, little puffs of red mist appearing where the bullets caught his breast and head.

At the Front Rod had occasionally seen red. When it happened, it was almost as though his mind was smothered by a fog of rage. In that state a man could hurl himself into battle without a care. Afterwards, a black reaction always set in, but just then he was not of a mood to rationalise anything. Bert was wounded and, Rod feared, mortally.

Rod was overwhelmed with a fury so intense, it felt as though his heart was on fire. He fired once to distract the Russian, and heard more bullets pass close by, but then he was moving. The

Russian was kneeling beside an open box of guns, and quickly turned to aim at Rod, but Rod squeezed his trigger twice more, quickly, and the Russian winced and ducked away as a slug hit the crate beside him, cringing as a third bullet bit into his shoulder, and he was flung aside, crying out, the gun falling from his hand and clattering on the floor. Rod ran full-pelt at him, his gun trained all the while. The Bergmann's snail-type magazine could hold at least thirty shots, and Rod had no intention of giving him time to grab it again.

He was sitting with his back to the case, desperately trying to reach the Bergmann. When Rod saw him, he almost fired on the instant.

'Leave it,' he shouted.

The Russian looked up with loathing, and Rod thought he might try to grab the gun anyway, but then he held his good hand up, leaning back and tapping at the packing crate. Rod glanced quickly at it, and saw rows of Bergmanns inside. There was a second case a few feet away, and Rod was about to investigate it, when he realised the Russian had been distracting him.

His other hand was in his pocket, and Rod saw the pocket move. He had another gun, and Rod fired even as he tried to point it. The bullet tore a hole through his upper arm, and he gave a shriek of pain, grabbing at his fresh injury with his other hand. Rod kept his gun fixed on the man's upper chest as he reached down and pulled a wicked-looking automatic from his jacket. He threw that to join the Bergmann on the floor, then ordered the man to stand, and forced him back to the stairs.

Bert was not dead. Blood oozed from a gash in his skull where a bullet had torn a three-inch slash in his scalp, and another bullet had ripped into his left breast. Rod's prisoner was turned quite pale as he was pushed down the stairs without sympathy. Downstairs, Rod passed him to three Chinese officers and instructed them to bind him and watch him, before grabbing two other men. There was a door leading to a rear chamber, and Rod grabbed one of the pry bars and pulled the door from its hinges, telling the two to carry it upstairs. It would suffice as a makeshift stretcher. Rod holstered his pistol and went to fetch the Russian's guns, studying the Bergmann as he walked back down the stairs. It was a German army weapon, with the little crown symbol to prove it had been proof-marked.

He pulled the magazine free and glanced at the empty breech as he walked out of the warehouse and into the yard.

He was tingling all over. His belly felt as if it had been sucked empty, and he was overly aware of everything in the aftermath of action, the sounds of birds, the wind in the air, men's voices, all seemed preternaturally clear and sharp in his ears. The red mist had left him, to be replaced by a heaviness and exhaustion.

The wounded Russian was being held with his comrade, both watched closely by O'Toole, and Rod gave him the Russian's guns before walking over to Yevgeny Bugayev.

'You are in a great deal of trouble, Yevgeny,' he said.

Bugayev's eyes bulged with fear. He exuded panic.

Rod said, 'You are a foreign national with no papers. You have no rights here. You have been discovered helping smuggle weapons into China, and the officials here will punish you. You will go to the International Mixed Court, but without the protection of a consul or ambassador, you will be subject to Chinese law. You understand this?'

He nodded mournfully. 'Perhaps I find new job, and ...'

'No. The Chinese will treat you as they would any Chinese. You have no rights.'

'What will happen to me?'

'It is likely that the Chinese will demand the strongest sentence for you. They have little love for foreigners, as you know.'

'What will happen to Eva, if they kill me?'

Rod had no words of comfort.

'What if I had information?'

'If you tell me all you know, it may make a difference, but I cannot tell until you speak to me. And you have to tell me everything. I can try to obtain clemency. But only if you tell me all.'

He shivered, stroked his moustache, peered about at the police officers, then back at Rod. He looked like a lost child, desperately seeking a face he recognised. 'You know I have nothing? All I ask is you help my wife. She doesn't deserve to live like this. Eva is good woman, but I have failed her. She wanted honourable man, but when the Czar ...' He snivelled, wiped his face with a hand, rubbed it with the sleeve of his shirt.

'Tell me about this,' Rod said, jerking his head towards the milling police officers. Men were manhandling crates, moving them inside the godown where they could be secured under police guard.

He nodded. 'I knew nothing about guns. I knew there was something to be brought, but I didn't know what it was. They said I would be paid well if I help people bring in something. No one told me guns!'

'You knew it was illegal?'

'No! No!' he said, but his eyes slid away. 'Not at first. It was put as favour, just helping friend. And I would be paid, too, because I was helping.'

'Who suggested this to you?'

'It was a German, Helmut Schreier. He was seeking to help his friend, he said: Maurice Winton.'

'Schreier told you this?'

'Yes, but he didn't tell me it was guns!'

'What else did he tell you?'

'Only he was trying to help friend, but didn't want friend to know. Schreier wanted his name quiet, so Maurice would have a pleasant surprise, so he said.'

'How did you help?'

'I spoke to Chinese friend of Maurice's. Schreier told me address and how to speak to him. I met Chinese in cabaret over towards Hongkew.'

'What was his name? Qian?'

Bugayev shook his head. 'No: Thin Bao. He is slim man, for a Chinese. With a cold, hard face.'

'He wears a fedora?'

'Yes. Grey, with a chequered band.'

Scenes flashed into Rod's mind: a slim figure in the roadway as he left the tobacconist's; a face in the doorway of his apartment. He imagined the same man at the shop while the old man and his daughter were tortured and killed, and at Foster's car, reaching in and shooting, then carving Chinese characters onto Foster's brow. 'You saw him often?'

'When Schreier had news: when it was due to arrive, what the ship was, where it would dock ... Schreier came to tell me, and I told Thin Bao.'

'But you had no idea it was guns?'

'If I knew it was guns, would I risk my life, my wife, for them?'

Yes, you probably would, Rod thought. An alcoholic would risk everything for a chance to rebuild his fortunes - or for a single bottle of vodka. This could have been the gamble of his life; the gamble for his life. 'How much did Schreier promise you?'

'He said a thousand dollars.'

'And you didn't think it was illegal?'

'He was persuasive,' he whined. 'I didn't understand. When I did, it too late.'

'You say that you were told this was all for Maurice, but you didn't speak to him about it?'

'No. Only to Thin Bao or Schreier. Schreier wanted it a surprise.'

'Where did these Russians come from?'

'I have met them here. Like me, they have nothing. They wanted a little money, that is all.'

'They were keen to shoot Bert and me.'

'They were told to protect this shipment. They did what they thought was best. That is all.'

Rod could have hit him then. The memory of Bert hitting the wall, the obscene little bursts of red spray where the bullets hit, made his fists clench. But there was no point hitting him. Bugayev was speaking the truth as he saw it.

Rod took his anger with him back to the station.

Writing up his report, Rod was suddenly assailed by a feverish shivering. He was forced to set his pen down and clench his fists to contain the shakes. And then there was the black reaction. Seeing a friend injured always brought the worst after-effects. He was overwhelmed, tears coursing down his cheeks. He had seen men with their bellies ripped open, and he saw those scenes again in his mind's eye, but now it was Bert trying to push his bowels back into his belly.

Rod forced himself to stand, but the shaking wouldn't leave him.

It was normal, he told himself. The events of the last days had caught up with him: the attempt to assassinate him, the shoot-out at the Honan Road godown, seeing Bert injured; all had taken their toll. He walked about the room, trying to still the trembling. Perhaps this was how Bugayev felt every morning, he thought, and almost chuckled: maybe Bugayev had an idea, resorting to alcohol? Even as Rod's eyes strayed to the drawer containing his bottle of whisky, he rejected that. He wasn't going to become an alcoholic because of a couple of shootings. He had experienced worse.

Calling to Mickey Hi for a fresh pot of tea, he sat and stared gloomily at the papers on his desk. He was beginning to understand what had happened. Maurice had arranged a simple transaction – either to impress his father or make money for himself – importing cigars and whisky. He had rented the godown, arranged finance somehow, – but someone else saw an opportunity. Maurice likely didn't know what the cargo was. If he had known it was guns, he would never have told Rod the name of the vessel, and would probably have redirected the ship rather than have it dock.

Schreier was involved. Rod's guess was, he had set up the deal deliberately to implicate Maurice. Schreier used Bugayev as a go-between, and was using the Chinese assassin Thin Bao too.

The two Chinese witnesses had said two Green Gang members had killed Foster. The Gangs were always on the lookout for weapons. It was likely that Thin Bao came from the gang, or was at least a go-between with the Gang and Schreier.

Why had Thin Bao tried to assassinate him? Because of the gun shipment or the murders? Perhaps someone had decided to remove him because he was getting close to the truth.

Thin Bao: Rod was sure he was the man who had killed Foster; the man Rod had seen at Dewitt's office; the man who killed the two Chinese witnesses; the man Rod had seen at his apartment last night. These must be the same man. The question was, how to find him?

O'Toole knocked and poked his head in, gazing suspiciously about the room. 'Oh, I thought you had concealed a girl in here.'

'What?'

'It's gone ten o'clock. You're still at your desk. Surely after the day you've had, a rest would be in order?'

'I have too much to do.'

'You had damn all sleep last night, and today you've been in a gunfight. Look at yourself! You look like the walking dead, man! Bert is recovering. You need rest too.'

'Yes,' Rod said. But the thought of returning to his apartment was unappealing.

O'Toole understood immediately. 'There are beds upstairs, if you want. Or you can come to Gordon Road and doss down there. There're a couple of spare rooms.'

Rod gave in. O'Toole could be stubborn as an Irish mule. 'Yes. Thank you.'

He put his papers away and locked the desk before slipping his pistol into his holster, pocketing two magazines. The revolver was still on his belt. The morning's cocaine was wearing off, and Rod couldn't help thinking of the beneficial comfort that a fresh dose would bring. While O'Toole's back was turned, Rod took up the morocco case Doctor Babu had given him and slipped it inside his jacket.

Rather than head back to Gordon Road immediately, they visited the Astor House and drank a soothing martini or two. The waiters were attentive, and Rod could feel the drink easing its way along his nerves. O'Toole was a master at dealing with officers who had been involved in shootings. There was a need to wind down, to accept the shock, and process the fact that death had been miraculously avoided. The music was calming – waltzes or some soothing, reflective jazz – the lighting was muted, and the overall atmosphere enough to tranquillise a charging boar. Rod felt himself relaxing.

'How is Bert?' he said.

'They pulled a bullet from his shoulder, but he'll be all right. He may have concussion from the head wound - it was a glancing blow - but the doctors won't know until later.'

Rod was about to reply when Billy Qian appeared. Qian nodded to O'Toole in a friendly manner, but spoke to Rod. 'I heard about your officer. I hope he is not badly injured?'

'What would it matter to you?' Rod demanded, standing. 'You were involved, weren't you?'

His rage returned, as swift and uncompromising as a light switch flicked from "off" to "on", as though all the anger of the previous week was bursting from the dams that had held it back. Rod lunged, but O'Toole stepped between them, hands up placatingly. 'Hold on, Rod.'

Qian was so calm, he might not have noticed Rod's sudden grab. 'No, Detective. I had nothing to do with the shipment. Eva told me about your conversation. You must understand I was trying to ensure that Maurice was safe. I like the fellow. But he would not listen to my advice.'

'You wanted the Honan Road godown.'

'Yes. But, as you know, Maurice won it. Not in partnership with me, but on his own behalf.'

'How?'

'I beg your pardon?'

'How did you learn he had taken it?'

Qian smiled. 'Where there is a lawyer, there is a secretary; where there is a secretary, there is a man who needs money. When I learned who had taken the godown, I employed Eva to become Maurice's friend. She learned of his ship, and the possible import of goods. With the secrecy involved, it was obviously not goods that he wanted others to know about.' He shrugged expansively. 'And that is that.'

'Who arranged for the guns to come into Shanghai?'

'As to that, the arms are all German. Only one man in Shanghai has such contacts. I feel sorry for Schreier, for he has truly lost everything – wife, wealth, business – still, it is an unpleasant business, selling guns to criminals.'

'So you think Maurice knew what he was bringing into the city?'

'Maurice? Dear me, no! He is the easiest fellow to dupe in all Asia. Maurice assumes that all others are as transparent as he, or that they are fools to be gulled. He little realises that he is the fool.'

'What of the arms? Where were they to be sold?'

'I have no idea. Perhaps to a warlord. There are many of them.'

'What of the Green Gang?'

'They would be keen to acquire guns, I am sure.'

'Do you know anyone in the Gang?'

Qian shook his head mildly. 'I keep away from such fellows, Detective. They are too dangerous for the likes of me - and you. I would avoid them if at all possible.

# Chapter Forty-Four

*Thursday 3rd August, 1922*

Next morning Rod's head felt like an overused wrecking ball: battered and dented. He opened a bleary eye to meet the expressionless face of a Chinese houseboy. The light through the window burned like a flare. 'Damn!'

'Sir, tea,' the man said calmly, and set a tray on the bedside table, pouring tea with practised economy. He bowed, and left. The servants at the barracks were used to dealing with hungover police officers.

Rod sat up gingerly and drank the tea while it was still scalding hot, then poured a second. His throat hurt, and he coughed a few times. He must have smoked an entire packet of cigarettes last night. With that thought, he pulled out the crumpled packet. There was one left. He struck a light, inhaling deeply. After the initial hacking cough passed, Rod sat back. He knew what he must do today, and he knew permission would be refused, were he to ask Hibbard. He must carry on without permission.

The houseboy had sponged down and ironed his suit, and washed his shirt. His shoes gleamed in the sunshine. Rod dressed, poured the last of the tea and drank it off before hunting for his pistols. O'Toole had placed them both in a chest of drawers at the farther side of the room. The Colt's magazines were in with it, and one loose cartridge, while the revolver had also been emptied, its ammunition lying beside it. It was sensible to leave guns out of reach of officers who were as drunk as Rod had been. He reloaded both and pushed both into their holsters before grabbing his hat and jacket and making his way downstairs to the mess. He patted his pocket. The morocco case was still there - he wouldn't need it today. His headache was bearable, with aspirin, but it was good to feel the little case in his pocket. It was like a hip flask: a precaution in case of need.

Rod ate four rashers of bacon and three fried eggs, with a slice of fried bread. By the time he finished, he felt ready to wrestle a bear.

It was fortunate. His next interview would be difficult.

The Winton house was quiet. It was early, not a good time to disturb a man as important as Alfred Winton, but after seeing Bert shot Rod didn't care. He felt close to a breakthrough and knew the last elements of the case were almost in his grasp.

At the door he was confronted by Crowther. 'You wish to speak to Mr Alfred, sir?'

'No. I want to speak to Maurice. Bring him to me on the terrace.'

'Sir?'

Rod slid some steel into his voice. 'You heard, Crowther. Fetch him, and do it quickly.'

Rod walked through the French windows onto the terrace. Lighting a cigarette, he let the smoke trickle from his nostrils. On hearing steps approach, he didn't turn, but said, 'You have to be the most splendid fool I have ever met.'

His words were greeted with a sharp intake of breath.

'What the devil do you mean?' Alfred Winton demanded. 'I thought it was clear you were to confine yourself to investigations away from my house!'

'I am sorry to come unannounced, sir. How is the Bank?'

He flinched. 'I do not intend to discuss my business with you.'

'You were happy enough after Gracie Gale put your chit in the collection.'

'Yes, well. She is not someone I will ever see again, I expect.'

Alfred Winton clutched a handkerchief and held it to his mouth when he coughed. Rod could see the blood. When Rod first met him, he had been a taipan – now he looked as though the life had been sucked from him by a vampire: weak and elderly.

'Where is your son?'

'He is engaged. What exactly do you mean by insulting me in my own house?'

'I thought I was speaking to your son. I told your butler to bring him.'

'Crowther has a better sense of propriety than you.'

'Fetch your son, and while I speak to him you can listen, if you like. Or, if you prefer, I can leave…'

'Good.'

'And return with a warrant to arrest your son for attempting to smuggle firearms. If you attempt to obstruct me, I will arrest you as well. Now, fetch your son!'

'What do you mean, firearms?' he said, his mouth falling open.

'I mean pistols, machine pistols, and ammunition for both. I must know to whom he intended selling them, and when he hatched this plan.'

'You cannot be serious!'

Rod stepped closer, intimidatingly. 'My patience is wearing thin. In the course of confiscating your son's illegal guns yesterday, an officer was shot. He is a friend of mine. I do not intend to dally while those responsible escape justice.'

'Surely there is some way we can …'

Rod threw away his cigarette, pushed him aside, and stalked back to the house. Crowther stood at the bottom of the stairs like a plump Cerberus.

'Either you get him now, or I will,' Rod snapped.

'Sir, I …'

'I am not listening to any more attempts to delay me. Get him now, or I will, and if you try to stop me, I will use all necessary force.'

Crowther was breathing stertorously, and he made a movement which Rod interpreted as the prelude to an attack. He took a short step back, preparing to knock the butler down if need be, but before he could, Maurice Winton's voice came from the staircase above.

'Don't, Crowther. You'll only get yourself into trouble. This isn't your fight. It's mine. I am coming down, Detective.'

Maurice was anxious. He had pulled on a light smoking jacket, and held a cigar in his hand. As he came down the steps, he rested a hand on Crowther's shoulder briefly. He had been found out.

'You wanted to talk on the terrace, I think?'

The detective's eyes were bloodshot and he looked like a man teetering on the brink of nervous exhaustion. 'I don't care where we talk. I only care that you answer my questions.'

'I will. I've been waiting for you ever since I heard about my godown.'

Maurice walked to the terrace, where his father stood. There was a pair of white-painted benches, and when Rod sat on one, Maurice lifted the other and brought it opposite. He sat, his father standing behind as though the seat could protect him from what he was about to hear. Maurice looked up at his father, thinking, *if only you had trusted me, this wouldn't have happened. I only ever wanted to make you proud of me.*

'Mr Winton,' Rod said, and Maurice faced him. He placed his elbows on his thighs, took a pull of his cigar, and blew the smoke towards the ground despondently.

'It was me. All me. I wanted to earn some money.'

He had at last found a kind of peace. There was little point in bluster. It was humiliating, but this blasted policeman knew all about his failures and foolishness. Maurice had no fight left. He kept his eyes on the ground; he could not meet Cottey's.

'Your contact was a man called Thin Bao?'

'Yes. He let me know he desired to bring some goods into the city.'

Maurice heard his father's sharp intake of breath.

'Did you know what these goods were?'

'I thought I did: whisky, brandy, tobacco and cigars. All innocuous stuff. I was a fool!'

'Yes, you are,' his father said with feeling. 'I cannot believe you could be so stupid!'

Maurice looked round at him. He was silent for a long moment, his face fixed in a frown of hurt. 'I only ever wanted to make you happy. All I wanted was a little support, perhaps a word of encouragement. But, no. You had nothing for me, did you? It was all for Ian. He could do no wrong and I could do nothing right.'

'You picked a bloody silly way to try to do it!'

Maurice turned back to Rod. He had crossed his Rubicon. He had hoped so much, for so long, that he might win over his father, but the dream was gone. What was the point of trying to please a father who was so antagonistic?

'You arranged for the godown?' Rod said.

Maurice shrugged. 'Yes. When the *Lucky Strike* arrived, I was to open the godown so that the goods could be stored, and to let him know. He would have the goods brought in. Well, I arranged the rent of the godown, and yesterday the ship docked. You know the rest.'

'What happened yesterday?'

'The go-between came to tell me I was implicated. He said that I would be punished if I got cold feet or told the police.'

'Good *God!*' his father exclaimed. He strode into the sitting room, and Maurice heard a cutter snip the end from a cigar, then the tinkle of a decanter rattling on a glass. He returned, blue smoke trailing.

'Where is this Thin Bao?' Rod said.

'In the French zone. I don't know exactly.'

'How did you get in touch with him?'

'By notes. He would write to me here, and I would send my messages to him at the Montmartre Café on the Rue Hué.'

Alfred muttered, 'You bloody fool!'

'I did what I could to make you see me as a man.'

'A man? A rank idiot!'

'You should be glad. I am following in your footsteps, after all.'

'What is that supposed to mean?'

Maurice gave a twisted grin. 'You smuggled opium, I smuggled guns. There is little difference.'

'You're bringing guns in to arm the Chinese, and you think that's remotely similar to me supplying a little opium?'

'No – the guns won't cause as much misery as your drugs,' Maurice said, standing and facing his father over the bench.

'You are a fool with *no* understanding!'

'I'm weary of being insulted by you. What of your German bonds?'

His father slapped him, and Maurice felt fingernails scrape down the side of his cheek as he flinched.

'Enough!' Rod said. 'Tell me about these bonds.'

'He doesn't know what he's talking about,' Alfred snapped.

Maurice gave a humourless chuckle. 'Schreier had a lot of investments, especially in Krupp, the German arms-makers. Of the guns and shells that killed our fellows, most were from Krupp. Father took those bonds and shares when he put Schreier out of business.'

'Hold your tongue!'

'Why? Because you'll cut me off? I daresay you'll do that anyway. Nothing I ever did, nothing I ever could do would ever be good enough. You prefer a son who lied, seduced married women, and finally ...'

This slap was startling, terribly loud in the still air. Alfred's open hand turned Maurice's face, raising an angry red welt. Maurice said nothing, but took a step back, looking at his father with loathing.

'Thank you, Father. I will leave now.'

'Don't think this is the last you've heard of this,' Alfred blazed.

'This is the last time I will speak to you. Good day,' Maurice said, and walked into the house.

He felt as though he had lost a heavy anchor that had held him back all his life. In part it was his father's contempt, but as he crossed the library, he realised it was more than that. It was the responsibility that he had always carried on his shoulders, the responsibility to compete and win against his brother.

He knew he was likely to go to prison for his involvement in smuggling guns. It felt like a kind of freedom.

Thin Bao was angry and bitter. No matter how hard he had dug, he had not learned who had brought him down. Rumours suggested Billy Qian was responsible, but Thin Bao was as sure as he could be that it wasn't Billy.

Their partnership was strong. It began when Billy Qian spoke of Alfred's troubles with the bank and business. Idly, Thin Bao had said that his master would be pleased to own a bank. It would make a safe haven for spare money. That was when both started speculating how much it would cost to create a bank. It would require investors, Billy Qian had said, almost dismissively, but Thin Bao could see the idea appealed. Over a few days they mapped out how it might be done. This would be a bank for the many, not only foreign devils. Many thousands of small investors with small amounts to deposit would soon add up to vast sums. And Du Yusheng would be keen to participate. In fact, when Thin Bao mentioned the idea, Du Yusheng had gazed at him with a sudden intensity that was a proof of his active mind seeing the potential.

Yes, Billy Qian had contacts, but he knew how dangerous Du Yusheng would be as an enemy. Du Yusheng controlled much of Shanghai. And in this, Thin Bao was Du Yusheng's comprador as well as Billy Qian's partner. Du Yusheng didn't know that Thin Bao was looking to the future, when he would be powerful enough in his own right to challenge Du Yusheng and take over the Green Gang.

However, now, at last, he had a sniff of someone who might been the leak that destroyed his cabaret.

He was a young man working for a fruit importer. Thin Bao had heard that he had a gambling habit, and when he found the man, he was bent over *mahjong* tiles in an alley behind an opium shop.

Thin Bao stood behind the man as he played and, aware of a shadow over his shoulder, the man looked up.

Opening his jacket, Thin Bao let him see the Mauser in its holster. The boy's eyes widened, and he lurched to his feet. 'What do you want?'

'To talk,' Thin Bao said, his gaze flicking over the other players. They showed a distinct disinclination to notice him. 'Come with me.'

With a reluctant glance at his tiles, the man followed Thin Bao.

'I've heard you know something about the raid on a gambling house last week.'

The fruit seller was emaciated, perhaps seventeen. His eyes were downcast as he spoke, as though he didn't want to challenge Thin Bao. 'I heard a man speaking to a police officer, telling him about a new gambling house.'

'Who was this?'

'The German. He said the place had been set up pretending to be a cabaret, but if they would raid it, they would find gambling and drugs.'

'What did you do?'

'Nothing. I didn't know who owned it. If I knew that, I would have warned him. I am a gambler, I don't see why the foreign devils want to stop our pleasures. What is it to them, that we test our courage?'

Thin Bao questioned him a little more, but the boy had nothing else to impart. He knew nothing of the German himself, only that he had been telling the police about the cabaret.

Thin Bao knew the German – who didn't in Shanghai? There was only one. And he was useful for arranging some goods, occasionally, but Thin Bao didn't care about that. What he cared about was losing his cabaret. If Schreier was responsible, Thin Bao would see to it that he never spoke to the police again.

## Chapter Forty-Five

Alfred Winton chewed his lip, his cigar forgotten. He felt more weary than ever. 'He's been a bloody little fool, I know, but don't make him suffer more than he need. Leave him here, and I will …'

Rod interrupted him. 'Mr Winton, I am waiting to hear how my friend fares after being shot in the head and chest by one of the guns your son imported. Not only that, someone involved with this shipment killed Foster and the lawyer Dewitt, and tried to kill me. Your son has been a fool, yes. But he is complicit in four murders and my own attempted murder.'

'He wouldn't kill anyone!' Alfred protested. He had lost one boy, he *couldn't* lose Maurice as well.

'But he could instruct someone else. This Thin Bao is an assassin.'

'Good God!' Alfred felt a sickening lurch in his belly. A cough began to stir, and he slapped the cloth over his mouth.

'And consider this: when Foster died, was it not after an argument with you?'

Alfred gave himself to the coughing fit. He couldn't meet the policeman's stare.

'That killer may have been intended to kill you, not Foster.'

Alfred watched as Rod walked in through the French windows, and then collapsed onto a seat.

Thin Bao was discovered. The guilt was returning. What he had done all those years ago was coming back to haunt him.

Rod found Crowther sitting in the hall, looking like an iceberg that had been in the tropics too long. He made no effort to stand, but watched the detective as he walked to the front door. There, in the open doorway, staring up at the sky, was Maurice. He gave no indication he had noticed Rod, but as the door closed, he murmured, 'So that is that, then.'

'Yes,' Rod said. He wanted to vent his anger on Maurice for the injuries done to Bert, and for the terror Rod had experienced when the two gunmen tried to kill him, but it felt pointless.

The two set off, Maurice looking about him with a kind of wonder, like a man who had lost his sight and only now had it returned. 'You know, this sort of end to the matter never occurred to me,' he said as they approached the gates.

'How do you mean?'

'It never crossed my mind that I should be arrested. I suppose I always considered myself above the law. And to be convicted because of stupidity, that is the real irony. I thought I was bright, but I've had the wool pulled over my eyes.'

Rod was fairly sure that he would be safe enough. Schreier was guilty: Maurice's offence was more that of foolishness. Besides, Maurice Winton was one of the privileged. The Council would not want to see one of their own brought low. That would have a devastating effect on the prestige of the British and Foreign community, and the community would tolerate nothing that could bring them down in the eyes of the Chinese locals. That way lay disaster.

'Why did you want the money? Was it just independence?'

'That and the chance of doing something my father would be proud of. But I should have realised: nothing I could do would make him proud of me. I was never going to win his love. He loved Ian too completely. And Alice. He had nothing left for me.'

'So you sought to become a trader in your own right?'

'It was a simple enough plan: win his trust and affection, and take over the business. He understands money; nothing else. Everything exists to be bartered or traded, and only a fool will give away something for less than he need. I thought, if I could only prove myself ...'

The gates opened, and Maurice stopped, staring back towards the house. 'I wonder ...'

'What?'

'I just wondered whether I shall ever see the old place again?'

Archie and the others were late for tiffin. The exercise on pistol maintenance and how to fix a jammed gun ran over, so the three did not reach the canteen until twenty minutes after all their colleagues.

'We'll be lucky to get the slops,' Peter said dismally.

Peter and Archie blamed John, for it was his gun that had caused their problems: an overloaded cartridge, so Dan Fairbairn said, leading to a swollen case. There was no blame attached to the recruit, for any batch of ammunition could occasionally have one over- or under-loaded case, but that didn't make Peter feel any better. They were all hungry.

Taking their food ('Aye, little more than the slops,' Peter noted), they took their seats and began to eat hurriedly so they wouldn't miss the next lesson, Shanghai Chinese, when a servant bowed and presented Archie with an envelope of pale lavender.

'Go on, man, open it!' Peter demanded. 'Eh, but I'll bet it even smells of her!'

Archie ostentatiously sniffed the note. 'Yes, it reeks of her perfume,' he said judicially.

'Will you open it?'

'Not quite yet. I'm enjoying your torment,' he said with a grin, but pulled out his jackknife and slit the envelope.

'She wants to see me tonight,' he said.

And for the first time, he felt a hollow sense of loss, rather than expectation.

Hans Schreier was sitting with a bottle of absinthe, celebrating the news of the shipment's arrival and the destruction of Maurice Winton's hopes. It was enough to make him smile broadly, thinking of the shame and embarrassment that were heaping on Alfred Winton's head like burning coals.

With a chuckle, he poured another glass and added water, taking half the glass in one, cleansing draught. There was still the matter of the items for the French officer, but that could wait. Perhaps tomorrow, if God spared him, he could take them to the French settlement. There was no hurry. Just now, he wanted to savour this victory. Small it may be, but it was sweet, ah, so sweet.

A man appeared and sat opposite him. A Chinese who wore a fedora with a black and white band about it.

'You are German.'

'Yes.'

'You send police to destroy my cabaret.'

Schreier focused his good eye on him. 'You are Thin Bao? Yes, I recognise you. I was asked to give a message to the police. I had no idea you were involved.'

'You destroyed my cabaret. Now I have nothing. You insult me, and you insult my master.'

'It had nothing to do with you or your master. I was told by a member of the Green Gang to tell the police. I was told to make sure it was raided, and I was paid for relaying that message.'

Thin Bao's features were impassive, but his voice betrayed his rage. It sounded like steam released from an engine. '*Who*?'

'Billy Qian. He told me to make sure that the cabaret was raided.'

'Dear Heavens, Cottey, what the *hell* did you think you were doing?'

For once, Sub-Inspector Hibbard was standing when Rod entered, his hands on his hips, a cigarette dangling from his lip and spraying ash. He walked to his window. 'Come here, Cottey. Look, do you see how far down it is there? I understand reincarnation and spirituality is all the rage in England. Do you think, if you jumped out of the bloody window, you might die and come back as a policeman? Christ, I wish so!'

'I'm sorry, sir.'

'I told you to clear this mess, not break up the most prominent family in the damned city!' He sucked hard on his cigarette, coughed, and viciously stubbed it out. 'You didn't have to bring in Maurice bloody Winton, did you? He said he had no idea he was bringing in weapons!'

'He arranged for the godown, he was responsible for unloading the ship and bringing guns into the city.'

'But he thought it was tobacco and ...'

'He said that after I questioned him. He may be innocent. However an SMP officer is in hospital as a result of his actions.'

'You don't need to remind me Bert's in the hospital. I'm aware of the fact. However, "May be innocent"? I think you mean, "Maurice Winton is innocent". Dear God, man!'

'I'm sorry, sir. I had no choice.'

'Well I would start looking at choices pretty damn quickly, Cottey, because the Chief will have your guts for garters, and then he'll go to town on your remains!'

'There is one aspect you may not have considered, sir. The man, Thin Bao, acted as middle-man between Maurice and the Chinese buyers. He's removed two witnesses already, and tried to murder me. Maurice Winton is a vital witness. Thin Bao may consider it expedient to kill him as well. At least while he's in our gaol, he's safe.'

'Christ! He's as much of a fool as you, isn't he?'

Rod said nothing. Hibbard picked up his pipe and began to thumb tobacco. He sat at his desk. 'Right, tell me again what you think happened.'

'Schreier wanted revenge. He was wiped out by Alfred Winton, and dreamt up a scheme for revenge, smuggling surplus German army weapons and selling them on the black market. To get his own back on Alfred, he involved Maurice. He felt the Winton family caused his suffering. Winton's eldest son had an affair with Schreier's wife, so she left him; Alfred bankrupted his business. Schreier wanted Winton's remaining son in return.'

'He's a particularly twisted sort of devil, this German.'

'He's lost everything - wife, business, money – everything. And he blames Alfred Winton.'

'A bit harsh. Doesn't he care that Winton lost his older son in the War?'

'It was Ian Winton who seduced Schreier's wife. Besides, Ian died fighting Schreier's people. I wouldn't expect much sympathy from him.'

Hibbard frowned at his pipe's bowl, then fished a match from the box and lit it, shaking his head. 'All right. First things first. Speak to your friend in Frenchtown, see if he can help track this Thin Bao, and perhaps we can get something that will stop the Commissioner's wife having kittens. For now, get out of my sight!'

Rod had only been at his desk for a couple of minutes when there was a knock and Mickey Hi peered in. He tried his usual anxious smile. 'Mrs Winton come for to talk.'

'Tell her I'm busy,' Rod said.

Mrs Winton strode in.

She was not the quiet, fretful figure she had been when Rod walked with her in the Municipal Gardens, or when he last saw her at her home. This was no timid dormouse, but a tigress ready to rend a man limb from limb in the defence of her cub. 'Detective Constable, I demand to see my son at once!'

'Please take a seat, Mrs Winton,' Rod said.

'Did you hear me? I demand that you bring my son to me!'

Rod pulled a message sheet from his drawer, and quickly wrote a request to speak to Dubois on the telephone in ten minutes. He hoped to be free of Mrs Winton by then. He walked to the door, pushing the inquisitive Mickey Hi out.

'Arrange this call,' he said and closed the door firmly. 'You can demand all you wish. The fact is, your son smuggled weapons into the city. As you know, that is illegal, opening the Municipal Council to the danger of armed uprising. He denies knowing the goods were weapons, but he is helping us to find those responsible.'

'You realise my husband could have you –'

'He could have me fired, yes. I am sure you're right. However, your son will remain in custody.'

She suddenly collapsed into a chair, her eyes bright with tears. Sitting with a poker-straight back, she held them in, her only concession being a brief dab with a white cotton handkerchief. 'He is my son, Detective. You cannot understand what this means, my only living son arrested. It was probably the effect of losing his brother. He was terribly affected by Ian's death. Alfred never realised just how badly.'

'But you were concerned, weren't you, Mrs Winton? You feared that Ian's – shall we call them misdemeanours? - might become common knowledge, if the letters Foster held ever saw the light of day.'

She looked up with a quick calculation. 'You knew?'

'You told me. You kept expressing interest in Foster's correspondence. That made me look at them in a new light. I had thought the letters were addressed to Foster. I hadn't realised they were your son's.'

'Foster found them when ... when Ian was killed. My poor boy must have been desperate to seek solace with that sort of woman.'

'"That sort"? She was an ordinary woman, and he was far from home and lonely,' Rod said sharply.

She inclined her head. 'He was always a kind boy. He would have done all he could to give comfort to those whom he felt deserved it, but she seduced him.'

'I doubt you believe that any more than I do,' Rod said. 'He was a womaniser. He seduced Schreier's wife. That was why you feared the letters – they would have made your family a laughing stock, and exposed his memory to ridicule. You had to keep them secret. Did others in your family know of them?'

'Not even Alfred. I couldn't burden him.'

'So you paid Foster, because you knew he could ruin Ian's memory. He blackmailed you.'

'What would *you* have done?' she snapped. 'Ian was Alfred's hope for the future. When we received that telegram ... he was devastated. You cannot imagine! And now …'

'Yes?'

'Alfred has cancer,' she whispered. 'He doesn't have long. I want to destroy them. At least then Ian's memory will be secure. The newspapers won't get wind of his little peccadilloes. And Alfred need never know. He can die easy.'

She held out her hand. In the other was the handkerchief, with which she dabbed at her eyes.

Rod reflected. He saw little reason to refuse her. The letters had been sent to her son, so technically they were hers. Rod saw no good reason to damage her son's reputation. The man could not defend himself, and the letters might harm the woman who wrote them. She may still be married. In the heat of the war many women had thrown themselves at soldiers, either to provide them with some solace, or seeking comfort themselves. What good could come of telling their stories? There were enough secrets in the city already. Did it matter if one more secret was held?

Rod reached into his drawer. 'I ask that you do not read them. They are from a good woman, I am sure. Whatever she wrote should be between her and him. It can do you no good, and might bring you misery.'

'I will not promise. I cannot. This woman knew my boy. She may have said something that matters to me.'

Rod hesitated, but the grief in her eyes was persuasive. He sighed and passed her the bundles. 'Very well. I can't stop you. And now, I must get back to work.'

'Arthur will still want to have Maurice freed.'

'I should have thought the last thing on his mind was freeing Maurice. I was there at their last conversation. Your husband cut Maurice off from the family, and Maurice accepted his fate.'

She made a moue. 'He was angry. You think Alfred so foolish that he would cut off his nose to spite his face? He is already enquiring about the best King's Counsel to represent our son.'

'He is only considering the family reputation, then.'

She flushed angrily. 'You truly do not understand, do you, Detective Constable? He has lost one son, and now you have taken away his second! He will fight with all his strength until he has one son back - and so will I!'

## Chapter Forty-Six

'*Bonjour*, Thomas Dubois.'

Rod rubbed his forehead. His headache had grown during the meeting with Mrs Winton. As soon as this call was done, he would open the little morocco case and take a dose of the cocaine. 'Hello? This is Detective Constable Cottey. I have news.'

There was a grunt from the other end. Rod had the impression that Dubois had given an emphatic Gallic shrug. 'I have news for you. Our man was released this morning.'

'*What?*'

'The Chilean Consul demanded to know why his national was being held. There were shouted conversations, and lawyers, and a group of most determined people saying this would cause an international incident. I was informed by my Commissioner that it would be best if the man was released.'

Rod clenched his jaws, not daring to speak.

Dubois sighed. 'What could I do? I was arguing against so many people. And in the end, after as long a delay as possible, I had to release him.'

'I see,' Rod said. He was ready to explode with anger, when Dubois chuckled quietly.

'In that time, I arranged five reliable constables to follow him.'

'Follow him?'

'We will learn who he meets, where, everything.'

'Where did he go?'

'To a restaurant at the Rue Hué. Well, less a restaurant, more a café.'

'Wait!' Rod said, turning the pages in his note book. 'What was the name of the café?'

'The Montmartre Café. It is a small …'

'It's the place where Maurice Winton communicated with this man Thin Bao,' Rod said, and explained about the gun-smuggling. 'Schreier wanted revenge on the Wintons, and used this cargo to entrap Maurice.'

'Do you have evidence against this German?'

'Only the word of a Russian.'

'That German must be keen to ruin the Wintons.'

'He is. Originally I had wondered whether someone paid to have Alfred Winton killed, and when that failed the killers executed the driver instead. If so, perhaps that was when Schreier put the second plan into operation – to set up Maurice Winton.'

Dubois was quiet for a few moments. 'What of the killers from the French Settlement?'

'There were two. One could have been the man I delivered to you, but with both witnesses dead, we will perhaps never know. The other I will recognise if I see him again,' Rod said.

'Our Chilean friend went into the café and met a man. We know him, he is called Du Yusheng, and is supposed to lead the Green Gang. There was another with him, but my men did not recognise him.'

'What does he look like?'

'A little below the height of an ordinary Chinese, very slender, but strong-looking, square face. Dresses well, like a man who has money.'

'Does he have a grey fedora with a black and white ribbon?'

'No, a plain panama. He went to Du Yusheng to pay homage, and it appeared that he spoke to the other man, the big one. Then the big man and Chen left the café. My officers tried to follow them, but the two separated, and they lost both.'

'I see.'

'We shall continue seeking them and let you know when we learn any more.'

'I am grateful. Meantime when I find Schreier. I shall let you know what he says.'

Schreier was sitting at a table when Rod Cottey walked in. Schreier saw him and remained sitting. He knew why the policeman was there. It was the reason for his drinking. He had consumed a lot of absinthe, and before that two bottles of wine.

'Mr Schreier, I would like to speak with you.'

'I am sure you would, but I have little to say.'

'I want to talk about the guns brought into the city yesterday.'

'I know nothing of guns.' Simple denial. That was best for now.

'You were there with Yevgeny Bugayev and the captain of the *Lucky Strike*. You arranged for the guns to be taken to the Honan Road godown where Maurice Winton had arranged storage.'

'I know nothing of this.'

'You were watched. You left the ship. What did you do, go and celebrate?'

'I have nothing to celebrate.' This man was so slow he was infuriating. With roles reversed, Schreier would have arrested him by now.

'Come, you wanted revenge on the Wintons, and you successfully put the responsibility onto him. He wanted money; you helped him set up a perfect little deal, except he knew nothing of the real goods, did he? The icing on the cake was leaving him with the guns, the costs, and the blame, wasn't it?'

'Me? How would I do that?'

'You tried to have Alfred Winton murdered, but they killed his driver. That must have been frustrating. Was that when you hatched this plot?'

Schreier gave a chuckle. 'Oh, excuse me,' he said, emptying his glass once more. He refilled it. 'I should not laugh. I know it is galling when a man laughs in your face, yes? But you suggest I could negotiate a trade of weapons in a matter of days? How long would it take for the arms to arrive here, do you think? Where did they come from? Europe, would you say? Such guns would take weeks to reach here. You say I arranged for them to be sold? To whom? It takes time to negotiate the rental or purchase of a building but you say I did all this in a matter of days, since the attempt on Alfred Winton's life? This sounds like the work of many weeks.'

'No: you had planned it long before,' Rod said.

'How, then? I am no arms dealer.'

'You had stocks in Krupps.'

'So? I dealt in shares and stocks. That does not mean I touched a gun,' he said dismissively. He sipped again.

Rod nodded. 'We shall work out how. For now, you were responsible for bringing a number of guns into the city against the International Arms Embargo Agreement of 1919. These guns are prohibited under Chinese law, and the City does not condone smuggling.'

'So I am to be punished for something I have had nothing to do with?'

'You were on the ship.'

'I do not deny it. I was there to oversee the import of five cases of whisky.'

'What whisky?'

'Whisky for Huang Jinrong. You may know him. He's the head of the Chinese detective force in the Sûreté.'

'Where is the paperwork?'

Schreier swayed slightly as he reached into his inner pocket, pulling out a black wallet. Inside was a letter confirming that he had collected five cases of whisky from the *Lucky Strike*.

'This proves that you had one consignment on the ship, but does not show you were not involved in the guns.'

Schreier could not prevent a little petulance entering his voice. 'How does a man prove a negative? I have demonstrated the reason why I was on the ship. Your *English* justice would not prosecute an innocent man, I am sure. I am trying to make a slight living from the few resources I have left. I have already been robbed of all. All I can do is scrape by with an occasional deal. The Chief of Chinese Detectives is good enough to commission me to bring in certain luxuries every so often.'

'You will come with me to the police station. I have more questions for you.'

'Certainly, officer. Please be good enough to ask the barman to keep this excellent absinthe for my return, and I will be with you.'

Schreier watched him carry the bottle to the bar. He tipped the last measure into his mouth and sat staring at the glass in his hand, admiring it. He had enjoyed this last glass. It had been pleasant to sit here and drink to his memories: to his business, to his life here in Shanghai, to his family, wherever they were.

'Mr Schreier?'

'Of course.' He rose with the careful dignity of a duke being led to the scaffold. Rod took his elbow, but Schreier stared at his hand until Rod released him. Schreier straightened his back, pulled his shoulders back, and marched out like an elderly warrior. Outside, Schreier waited while Rod hailed a rickshaw. As the coolie ran to them, Schreier heard something: a metallic snap. He glanced across the road. At the entrance to an alleyway there were two men.

One, he knew, was Chen, and at his side was Thin Bao. They stood in the half-darkness of the alley's mouth. Schreier saw the blue-grey oily gleam of metal in the light, then the vicious flashes, and felt each hammer blow as he was struck. He toppled back to the wall, pushed himself upright, but two more bullets found their mark. They were like enormous wasp stings, he thought, and fell back once more, his head striking the wall.

He saw Rod throw himself sideways, rolling, his pistol thundering twice rapidly, then twice more, and Schreier saw Chen flung into the alley, but then Thin Bao was shooting again. Rod returned fire, and the yellow flashes from the alley ceased.

Schreier's legs would not support him. *I must have drunk more than I realised*, he thought, sliding to the ground. There was a feeling of bruising in his belly, and when he looked down, there was blood all over his suit. It didn't concern him. He felt only slightly nauseous, and acid was rising in his throat. Probably the absinthe. There was no pain, but the breath was harsh in his throat, and there was a bubbling and crackling in his lungs. He considered it curious, but he was too tired to wonder at it. The absinthe was repeating on him, and he rested his head back against the stonework, but then he began to shiver, his legs were uncontrollably shaking.

It was then that his eyes snapped open, when he realised he was dying, but by then it was too late to cry for help.

Rod dropped the magazine and reloaded before rising to his feet, keeping his gun trained on the alley. There was a choking, sobbing sound coming from there, and he crossed the road cautiously, while all about him he heard screams of panic.

Chen lay slumped, his European suit splotched with blood. Three shots had struck home, and the thin man who claimed he was Chilean was dying. Rod knew that from the rattling in his lungs as he struggled to breathe. A revolver lay beside him, and Rod picked it up before glancing behind him.

Schreier was dead. It looked as if someone had painted red carnations on his white suit, and each grew as Rod watched. His face was already slack and grey, his eyes fixed in a thousand-yard stare. There were three men with him, two with the coolie, another with a wailing woman. A bullet had shattered her leg. All gazed at Rod with horror. He shouted that he was a policeman, that they should fetch the police, but he could see they didn't understand him, or perhaps didn't hear him. They were too shocked.

It didn't matter. Rod's duty was clear. He slid along the wall and peered up the alleyway. He could neither see nor hear anything. Diving in, he bolted to a doorway, and waited for gunfire, but nothing came. He counted to three, took a deep breath and ran to another doorway. Still no bullets, so he kept on going, faster, as quickly as he could, every nerve, every fibre straining.

A sudden rattle, and dust was thrown into his face. A sharp pain in his cheek, and he dropped to the ground, the Colt leaping in his hand as he went, but he heard the pattering of leather-soled shoes, and he clambered to his feet and set off again, feeling his cheek. It seemed little more than a scratch, although whether from a ricochet or fragments of stone shrapnel, he couldn't tell.

A sudden noise made him drop behind a box. It would afford little protection, but he felt safer, catching his breath. He peered over the top, and saw that he was close to the end of the alley. There were bright lights, people moving to and fro past the alley's entrance. Quickly he ran to it, the Colt in his hand, but there was no sign of Thin Bao.

Rod cursed long and loudly. He flicked up the safety and holstered his gun, making his way back along the alley.

The dead gangster was still slumped at the wall, and a policeman standing guard over him, while two more Chinese officers and a Sikh guarded Schreier's body.

Schreier was dead.

It had surprised Rod that Schreier had been happy to go with him. He must have known he would be interrogated. Rod would have expected him to protest his innocence more loudly, rather than quietly submitting. Perhaps it was the quantity of alcohol he had taken, but Rod wondered whether he had anticipated an attempt on his life? Had he drunk himself into a state of inebriation on purpose?

Why did he die? Rod put his feet on his desk. The obvious conclusion was, to prevent him talking to the police. But others could talk, from Maurice to Thin Bao. Maurice denied knowing anything except what he had heard from Thin Bao, and Rod guessed the German had been the main conduit of information.

He knew what the goods were, how they had been ordered, and he had deliberately implicated Maurice. The least Maurice could expect would be to be thrown from the settlement; anyone else would be imprisoned for a lengthy period. The fact he was a Winton would save him that indignity, but Alfred would still be devastated to lose his remaining son.

There was one other reason why someone could killed Schreier. If his buyers realised he had caused the guns to be discovered by the police, they would want revenge. That would be exacerbated if they had paid him for his services. Gangsters loathed disloyalty, but they hated losing money even more.

Either way, someone had decided that Schreier would not survive. Who?

Rod's only thought was Thin Bao. Surely he would want to keep his own involvement secret. Rod considered: if Thin Bao wanted to prevent the police learning more, he would also want to kill Maurice Winton and Yevgeny Bugayev, the two men who knew most about the affair.

Rod went to the phone and called Dubois. 'Thomas? We have had some developments,' he said, and ran through what had happened. 'The Chilean is dead. He and the man we spoke of earlier, Thin Bao, murdered Schreier. Can you keep searching for him?'

'The thin man? We have men watching the café and Du Yusheng. If Thin Bao appears, we shall let you know.'

The thin man …

Suddenly Rod felt a tingle. 'Thank you,' he said, and hung up the receiver.

He opened his drawer, and hunted through his notes. Then he thought hard for two cigarettes, before calling Mickey Hi and asking for Maurice to be brought from the cell.

'Mr Winton,' Rod said. 'I want to confirm a few details with you.'

Maurice Winton sat before the desk and looked about him with a kind of shock at the bare boards of the floor, the plain desk, the squeaking, all but useless ceiling fan. Rod's words drew his attention back to him.

'Certainly, although I don't know there is anything more I can tell you,' he said. He looked and sounded exhausted. Rod felt a certain sympathy for the man.

'How did your brother get on with your family?'

Maurice gave a sardonic smile. 'Ian was the bright one, the golden boy. He was the charming one, the man who could flatter and smarm, who could talk to the Chinese like a fifty-year-old taipan. Everyone loved him.'

'Everyone? Women?'

'Yes. He loved women, but in France, well, when on leave in England, I suppose, he fell in love.' He subjected Rod to a suspicious stare. 'What are you getting at?'

'Foster held letters which showed that your brother had an affair with a woman in England. But you knew that.'

'Yes.'

'Your mother was very proud of him. She would walk through flames to protect his memory, wouldn't she?'

'Yes. She adored Ian.'

'She would protect him and his reputation to the bitter end.'

'I don't know about that. She is not entirely ruthless, you know. She isn't like father.'

'But someone is.'

He shrugged. 'Most people have a streak of ruthlessness, don't they? I do, but I'm just not competent. I think I'm driving a hard bargain when I am being nailed to the wall. I'm useless.'

'I think it makes you a better man.'

'You think so?' he said, and his lip curled into his characteristic sneer.

'How many shipments have you arranged before this?'

Maurice gave him an enquiring look. 'What do you mean?'

'There have been many shootings with machine pistols, so you must have brought them in before.'

'No, this was my first trade.'

'Lying to me will not help, Mr Winton. You need to tell me everything.'

'I am! I don't know of any other shipments for guns!'

Rod mulled that over. Then, 'Tell me: when Thin Bao needed to contact you, how did he do so?'

'I told you. He would write.'

'But sometimes he would visit in person?'

'Occasionally.'

'Like the time he visited you about the shipment, and said you must keep quiet.'

'He was very *persuasive*. A man like him, with a gun in one hand and a knife in the other can be ... highly convincing.'

'I am sure,' Rod said. 'Where was this?'

'What do you mean?'

'I doubt he walked into your house to tell you, did he?'

'Why not? He was often there.'

'At your house?'

'Yes, he was an orphan. Mother's orphanage looked after him, and when he was old enough, he came to work for us. He became rather like a brother to me. We all liked him.'

'All of you?'

'Yes.'

He was about to continue, when Mickey Hi knocked, a telegram in his hand. Rod slit the envelope and pulled out the message. It froze him.

The murder of Foster; the murder of Dewitt; the murder of Schreier; the attempt on his own life. There was an enthusiasm for violence. Thin Bao didn't worry his own part might become apparent. Almost as if he felt safe.

It was late, and Rod was bone-weary. There had been too many deaths, too many secrets. He sent Maurice back to the cells, pulled on his jacket, tucking his guns away in their holsters.

He had another man to see.

## Chapter Forty-Seven

Rod took a ride to the Bund, and bought a tin of fifty Three Castles cigarettes and a bottle of rum. With the rum in one hand, the cigarettes in his pocket, he began searching for Tim Burton. There was no sign where he would usually sit begging, but it was late now, almost eight o'clock, so Rod started looking in the doorways and side alleys. A beggar might get lucky with dancers and drinkers on their way home.

It was more luck than good police work when Rod found him.

He lay, a huddled shape more like a hessian sack of garbage than a human. Rod glanced, but didn't think it was Tim. A moment later the door opened, and a furious little man almost fell over him, and took to berating him in pidgin.

Tim woke, startled, and hurried away with his few belongings wrapped in a cloth that he huddled to his breast, like a woman shielding her child.

'Tim, hold on!' Rod called, and he turned with such an expression of fear that Rod's voice was stilled. To feel such terror on hearing his own name, was shocking.

Recognising Rod, Burton glanced about him quickly, as if reassuring himself that he was safe, and waited for Rod to join him. 'You want to join me for a meal?'

'Maybe for a smoke,' Rod said, and gave him the cigarettes and rum. 'Thanks for your help, Tim.'

He looked at the bottle, salivating at the sight. 'I'd ask you into my parlour to share a drink,' he said after a moment. 'But you're already in it.'

Rod glanced up. 'A good view from your apartment,' he said, and Tim joined him staring up at the sky. It was a clear evening. The cook fires had gone out long since, and the smoke from the municipal power station was being blown in the other direction, leaving the sky clear for once. Here the buildings were two and three storeys, and the two had a fine view of the stars.

'Yes, well, better than some,' Tim said. 'You know, there was a time when I used to look up at the stars and think I could be anyone, do anything. But life changes you.'

'The sky is still there; so are you. You could get a job, start again. There's always hope.'

'For a beggar?' he sneered. 'Try it some day! You know how people look down on me? Especially Europeans: they see trash, not a man. The Chinese will sometimes give me a little food or drink. This,' he said, holding up the rum, 'is the first drink a white man's given me in weeks.'

'I could see if there's a job. There are plenty of ships. Maybe one would …'

'I wouldn't sail with a captain who took *me* on as crew.' He opened the tin and shoved a cigarette into his mouth, waiting expectantly for a match. Rod lit it for him, and another for himself, before giving him the matchbox.

'You caught the German?' Burton said after a few moments.

'Not for long. He was murdered.'

'You don't look after your resources very well, do you? Did the Chinaman find you?'

'What Chinaman?'

'The day you spoke to me, a Chinese came and asked me where you were going. I said to the Honan Road, and he said he'd find you there.'

'What was this man like?'

'Oh, skinny, short, dressed like an Englishman. You know the sort.'

Rod did; he stared. 'Did he have a grey fedora?'

'Yes, with a black and white ribbon. Very pretentious.'

'When was this?'

'Just after you stopped talking to me, I think. Why?'

Rod was thinking. He had been followed on the way to see Tim Burton. Why? In order to kill him? Or to get information before the guns were offloaded, so that he could make sure none of his own men were there at the Honan Road godown when the police arrived?

'It was odd, though. I mean, there was a time I'd have said all Chinese looked the same. But this one, he reminded me of a man, a murder victim. I fished his body out of the Whangpoo. His son went to the orphanage.'

'Was that Bao Xiu?'

'Yes! There was talk of a gangland hit, but I think it was just money. He owned some waterfront, and other folks wanted it.'

'Who?'

'You can see for yourself. It's the godown with Liverpool and Asiatic on the boards.'

'Alfred Winton's company?'

'You're quick.'

Rod made his way back to Gordon Road keeping a wary eye open for ambushes. Hiring a rickshaw, he bellowed at the poor coolie to take a circuitous route, while Rod glanced behind them every few seconds. He felt bad giving the fellow a hard time, but he was not taking risks. Foster's ambush was on his mind the whole way. Rod arrived at the Gordon Road depot without any ill effects and made his way down to the mess. O'Toole was there, and two other sergeants relaxing after their duties.

'How is it?' O'Toole said.

Rod bought a round for them, and beckoned for the chit.

'No, no, you're our guest here,' O'Toole said. 'You can't sign for our drinks. I'll do it.' He took the chit and signed his name with a flourish.

'Can no guests ever pay?'

He smiled as Rod sipped his drink. 'Don't be daft. Guests can't sign chits. And no money is allowed in the Mess. A fellow mustn't sully his hands with real money.'

'That was why the chits were in different names,' Rod realised. 'Foster couldn't buy drinks.'

'Eh?'

'When Foster died, I found a large number of chits signed at different places. He wasn't a member at casinos like The Wheel. Garcia wouldn't want a mere chauffeur going into his casino. So Foster needed someone else to buy his drinks for him.'

'Was he likely to have that many friends who'd stand him drinks?'

'No, but he would have been with someone else,' Rod said.

'Like who? Alfred Winton?'

'He wouldn't have bought his chauffeur a drink!' Rod remembered Alfred Winton's disdain for his servants.

'Then who?'

'I don't know. Maurice Winton? Alice?'

'Were they friendly with him, then?'

Maurice had been scathing about Foster, but Alice was his dancing partner. Alice could not have paid for the drinks herself in the rarified circles of Shanghai society, but if she offered to reimburse others, such as Dewitt, they might have allowed her to use their names. If so, it would be natural for Alice to keep the chits to keep track of the sums she owed. And Dewitt being a lawyer, she may well have gravitated to him in preference to other men in the casinos and cabarets she visited with Foster. If Alice feared someone might go through her papers, what would be more natural than that she left them in the care of the man she was seeing - Foster?

'Maurice can't have had much to do with it,' Rod mused. 'He was the fall-guy in Schreier's plot to make money at Alfred's expense and simultaneously hurt the family.'

O'Toole shook his head. 'You can't trust a Boche.'

It was a common view. Rod sipped his whisky, thinking.

Maurice had been seeking a mentor to help him. When Rod questioned him, Maurice had blurted out the ship's name and cargo he thought he was importing. At the time Alice's expression showed she thought he should keep quiet. Anyone dealing with the police tended to hold their tongues. The principle that a man should be careful and not divulge much to the police had been missed by Maurice.

Later, in bed, after he turned off the light, Rod's thoughts were of Thin Bao. He was still out there, a shadowy figure with a Mauser pistol. The news he was still following Rod the day after he had tried to kill him in his apartment had been a shock. Perhaps he was tracking him even now? Until Rod caught him, Rod could not know real peace.

Thin Bao was in a bar in the French settlement.

Schreier had been convincing. It was Billy Qian who had destroyed Thin Bao's investment. The bar was to have launched his career, and Billy Qian had taken it away. There was a special hell for devils who betrayed their friends.

Should he go and kill Qian now? No, he must first report to Du Yusheng, and let him know that the foreign devil from

Germany had paid for his betrayal, but that there was one other who must be made to pay.

His own brother, Billy Qian.

# Chapter Forty-Eight

*Friday 4th August, 1922*

Next morning, Rod woke in a foul mood - he had not slept well, constantly alert to any sound in case it was another assassin. His head hurt, and he was desperate for a pipe of opium. He kept going round and around the same question: why had he been targeted by the assassin? If Maurice's contacts in the Green Gang knew Rod had uncovered their gun smuggling, they might have tried to kill him - or had Rod annoyed someone else with no connection to the Gang?

In a rickshaw, Rod sat back, eyes half-closed against the dust and glare. His headache was worse, and the shivering had returned. He had to clench his fists to stop the shaking.

Arriving at the Station, he went to the washroom and feverishly pulled out the syringe. A scant five minutes later, he was greatly refreshed and smiled when Mickey Hi appeared in the doorway.

'Miss Hyland sent this,' he said.

Rod slit open the envelope. Inside was a sheet of paper with perfectly regular copperplate in lavender ink. It even had a faint odour about it.

*Dear Detective Cottey,*

*I was sorry that you were detained and could not visit the orphanage for the party on Wednesday. You would have been most welcome. It was a delight to see their little faces light up. The children have so little to look forward to.*

*When we first spoke, I did say that I would let you know if I saw that man again. I am sorry to say, I did today. He marched up the lane as bold as brass, as if he knew my poor Barney was dead and wouldn't bark. And I saw him talking to the lady again. It was over towards the next garden, where the Wintons live ...*

There was a knock at his door.

'Yes?'

'May I come in, sir?' Archie said.

He had also slept badly. That morning, when the recruits met for their morning's exercise, Archie found it hard to keep up. He was too tired.

'Sir, I don't rightly know ... It's like this, sir.'

He began to talk. He told Rod about Alice, her half-brother, her suggestion that he had been Foster's murderer, and that her father could have been guilty of paying Thin Bao to kill him.

'You're sure of this?'

'I saw him. It was the fedora with a black and white checked band. He was the man I saw shooting Foster.'

'I see,' Rod said.

'I didn't want to tell you, sir. You can understand, can't you? She asked me to keep it secret.'

'Of course. And she said she knew what it was like to have love taken away? Did she explain that?'

'No, sir.'

'Are you still sweet on her?'

Archie looked at him. 'She's a lovely girl, sir, but she's far above my league. She asked me to see her last night, and I ... well, I wrote to say I couldn't.'

'I think you were wise, Lane.'

'Thank you, sir.'

After he left Rod sat contemplatively tapping a pencil against his teeth.

Alice had said Edith Winton threw Thin Bao from the house. But Miss Hyland's note showed that Mrs Winton was herself maintaining contact with him. Archie had reported what Alice had told him, but she was repeating what her mother had said. Alfred was ruthless in business, but he was also a philanderer. His wife knew of his visits to the Line, if her reaction in the church was any indication. Was she manipulative enough to spread stories about Thin Bao, and then keep in touch with him after throwing him from the house? Perhaps even ask him to kill Foster?

Or her husband?

'Detective, how nice to see you again,' Miss Hyland said as he walked in. 'Would you like a little tea? Or something stronger?'

'A cup of tea, please,' he said quickly. 'Miss Hyland, I understand you saw the man again. You are sure it was him?'

'Oh, yes. He had the chequered band on his hat.'

'You didn't mention his chequered band when we spoke before,' he said.

'Didn't I? It was the same fellow. European suit with those silly, wide lapels, and a grey fedora pulled low.'

'You think he was concealing his identity?'

'What else?'

'Miss Hyland, do you remember a boy called Thin Bao? He was orphaned.'

'Oh yes, I remember him. He was very quiet. Shy and anxious. He never seemed to fit in. It was such a relief when Mrs Winton asked for him as a houseboy.'

'Mrs Winton?'

'She was most determined. She thought the boy would flourish in her household, and it was preferable to leaving him at the orphanage. She was a trustee, so we knew he would be looked after.'

'Did he stay long?'

'He was there quite a while, but he did leave, yes.' She sighed. 'You have to understand: the Winton boys were away at school, and there was only Alice in that great house. Sometimes without other boys with whom to play, with a different culture, and the hard work …'

'Did that happen?'

She was quiet for a moment. 'I fear not,' she said at last. 'No, Alice made … *accusations* against him. Accusations the parents could not ignore.'

'Of what nature?'

She pursed her mouth. 'Accusations of a deeply intimate nature. He took advantage.'

'You think Mrs Winton believed them?'

She looked shocked. 'Of course!'

'But since then, you have seen Mrs Winton talking to him, haven't you?'

'I never said that.'

'You hinted at it. It *was* Mrs Winton you saw with Thin Bao, wasn't it?'

'I couldn't see her face - but yes, it was her, I'm sure. She is a distinctive lady.'

The General Hospital was a bright, airy, and smelled of disinfectant and bleach. When Rod entered Bert's ward, the sunshine made him look pale and washed out. He had a sling on his left arm, and thick bandaging swathed his skull, but his grin was the same as usual. 'Did you bring an Old Fashioned? The matron here's a gorgon. Won't allow any drink into the ward.'

'Sorry, Bert. I didn't think to bring it.'

'Blast! Next time you're passing, slip a bottle into your pocket, won't you?'

'How is it?'

He lifted a hand towards his head. 'Little more than a scratch. It itches like blazes, though. The doc says I'll have a fascinating scar to show the ladies. There's not much damage there. It's this one here,' he said, tapping his chest, 'that nearly put paid to my rent charges. Missed my heart by a half inch. A little nearer, and the shock would have … well, you know. Thanks for getting me out of there.'

'Can't leave an injured officer behind. You'd have had coolies going through your pockets and taking your ill-gotten gains.'

'And my bevy of cabaret beauties, don't forget them,' he said lightly, coughing and wincing.

Rod helped him to a glass of water.

'You know, I find it hard to believe Maurice Winton was so foolish,' Bert said.

'I don't think Maurice had anything to do with the weapons. He was just the patsy.'

'Why?'

'Out of the Wintons, Maurice seems the least messed up. He just had a lot to live up to with his older brother.'

'You said he was killed at the front, I think?'

'You know better than me. Why didn't you tell me about Ian Winton?'

Bert sighed. 'It wasn't my story to tell.'

'You weren't in the Dorsets. How did you get involved?'

'You think my mind's wandering, eh, old chap?' he said. 'No, I was 2nd Battn of the Manchesters. We were in the 14th Brigade of the 32nd Division, same as the Dorsets. After a particularly nasty little battle, the Manchesters lost almost all their officers, and I was sent over to help. Winton died when I happened to be duty officer, and I had to write the letter of condolence to his parents.'

'Hard?'

'Very. I had to do the decent thing by the family. You know, remove anything potentially secret; burn the more risqué things - French post cards and the other things that appeal to a fellow - and basically make everything tickety-boo. Trouble was, he had written a pretty explosive letter to his parents, and left half his brains on it. I couldn't send that, so I burned it and wrote my own note. It seemed kinder.'

'I checked. He committed suicide.'

'Did it say why?'

Just then the terrifying Matron appeared, accusing Rod of tiring her patient, and shooed him from the room like a hen herding chicks. Bert rolled his eyes as Rod gave him a wave, but then she pulled a thermometer from her breast pocket and approached him with the weapon held aloft like a bayonet, and Rod fled.

Rod reached the Winton house just after noon. The butler opened it.

'Detective.'

'Where is Mr Winton?'

'The family is enjoying their midday meal, sir.'

His tone indicated that any man of breeding would have known that.

'Good. Bring Mr Winton.'

'When he has finished his meal, I shall inform him.'

'You will tell him I am in his sitting room now. I do not expect to be kept waiting,' Rod said. 'Because if I leave, this affair will become public. Neither Mr Winton nor his wife will want that.'

He lit a cigarette. The chain of logic which he had built was faultless, but the coming interview was daunting. He poured himself a brandy and sat in a wing-backed chair.

It took Winton a long time and then the door opened quietly.

'I am glad,' he said. 'I wasn't sure who I would get to see first.'

Alice Winton appeared very demure and relaxed, but for the way that she pulled at a loose thread at her jacket's collar. 'You are very persistent. What would it take for you to leave us alone?'

'First you would have to see me fired from the police,' Rod said. 'And then, probably, that I was dead.'

'That is a silly thing to say.'

'Perhaps.' He leaned forward to light the cigarette she had taken from her case.

'You know, this will ruin my father. He is already broken, and seeing his remaining son in court will do him more harm.'

'I am sorry.'

'What will you do?'

'When Thin Bao left here, is it true that you accused him?'

'Accused him of what? I loved him! He was another brother to me!'

'But he was sent away because he grew intimate with you.'

'He wasn't sent away – he decided to go.'

'And now he is a gangster and assassin for hire.'

# Chapter Forty-Nine

'Alice, leave us,' Alfred said.

When Rod last saw him he was as grey as an old smoker. Now his flesh was greenish-yellow, like that of a two-day corpse. His eyes glittered. He wore a red house coat that boasted the Shanghai Club badge at his breast as though to flaunt his wealth, but these were false trappings. He knew he had lost the aura of power.

'Father, I am an adult. If it affects the Bank, I want to hear it. It is my future too.'

'Alice, just go!'

Alice glared and flounced from the room.

Edith had entered behind her husband. 'What is this about, Detective?'

Rod ignored her. 'I am sorry to return after arresting your son, sir, but you realise I had no choice. Just as I have none now.'

Alfred Winton dropped into a chair. 'Well? What do you want?' He sounded petulant, like a demented old man deprived of his evening cocoa.

'Foster was marked out and assassinated by Thin Bao. But you know that, don't you?'

Alfred said nothing but stared through the window.

'Foster was killed to keep your son's secret.'

Edith Winton snapped, 'You know how upset we were at Ian's death, but still you rake it up,' she said, adding viciously, 'We'll see you *broken*!'

'Your upset doesn't excuse Foster's murder. Thin Bao was paid to remove an embarrassment.'

'You're mad,' Edith Winton said. 'They tried to kill Alfred.'

'Yes, and since I wasn't there, they killed Foster instead. It was probably that damned Hun, Schreier. I told you he had reason to want to hurt me.'

Rod nodded. 'Yes, and he did a good job of it. It's likely he smuggled the guns which Maurice warehoused. Not that we will ever know; he was murdered yesterday. Schreier thought you would be ruined when Shanghai heard Maurice had smuggled the guns for the Green Gang.'

'Who killed Schreier?' Winton said.

Edith shot him a look that must burn like a blowtorch.

'Thin Bao. He is a competent assassin. Ruthless and unemotional, he doesn't care whom he kills, only that he is paid. He killed Foster because he was paid to do so.'

'Who?'

'By someone who wanted him punished. Because Foster had letters your family didn't want published. Because they proved your son to be an adulterer.'

'Oh, my poor, poor boy,' Winton said, and cupped his face in his hands. Edith sat stiffly, pale with hatred.

'Thin Bao was paid to kill Foster by someone desperate to protect your son's memory, someone who would do anything to protect your dead son.'

'Who would do such a thing?'

'Your wife, because Foster's blackmail grew intolerable. That was why they aimed at the driver, why they gave him the *coup de grace*, and why they carved *er guizi*, "traitor" into his forehead.'

'He is talking nonsense!' Edith declared.

Alfred stared at him. 'You're mad!'

'You deny it?' Rod asked.

She glared, then lifted her chin defiantly. 'If only it were only blackmail. He wanted a seat on the board, and expected Alice's hand to achieve it.'

'You decided Foster must die. You paid the assassin, and arranged for the car to take that route.'

Alfred shook himself. 'Could you not just forget all this?' he said. 'I am a wealthy man, and … She's not a murderer, for God's sake!'

'I cannot forget it, no. I'm truly sorry.'

'Let me help you,' he said, reaching for a chequebook, but Rod shook his head curtly.

'I will not accept a bribe, Mr Winton. I swore an oath to uphold the law, and I will do so.'

'I could offer you many times your salary.'

'I'll pretend I didn't hear that.'

'What if I speak to the chief commissioner? I drink with him at the Club! I could destroy your career like that!' he said, snapping his fingers.

'I am sure you could, sir,' Rod said. 'But the secret has to come out.'

'What secret?'

'Your son's suicide.'

'What?' Alfred said. 'I don't understand!'

'I couldn't tell you,' Edith said. 'That was what Foster knew.'

'I am sorry, Mr Winton,' Rod said.

'You're sorry? So am I,' Winton said. He yanked open a drawer on his side table and pulled out a military revolver.

Edith Winton gaped. 'Alfred, what are you -'

'I have killed men before, you know. I can do it again.'

'This is Ian's revolver. Foster brought it back. It's fitting that the man destroying his memory should die by his weapon.'

'His memory is not mine to destroy,' Rod said. 'How you and your family remember him is all that matters. Put it away. You're not shooting anyone with that.'

'I can stop you ruining his memory. I can take your life,' Winton said.

Rod looked at him. He was shivering like a man with malaria. The Webley was gripped tightly, but shaking. 'Mr Winton, you are not a well man. Put the gun down.'

In answer, Alfred tried to squeeze the trigger. While Rod watched, he strained at it, and then set his thumb to the hammer.

'That is a Webley Fosbery. Some of my friends had them,' Rod said, rising. He plucked it from Alfred. 'It is an automatic revolver. You won't fire it pulling the trigger.' Rod pressed the latch and tipped the cartridges into the palm of his hand, pocketing them. 'I will forget this,' he said, placing the gun out of Alfred's reach.

Edith Winton was pale as a wraith. She took a handkerchief from her sleeve and dabbed her eyes. 'I'll tell you what happened.'

'What brought matters to a head?' Rod asked. Outside an automobile started. He glanced through the window in time to see a small car hurtling along the drive.

'Foster's greed,' Edith's face hardened. 'When he spoke of a seat on the board. I said, "You're mad! My husband would never consider you!" He told me he enjoyed Alice's company, and would marry her. And then he would take a seat.'

'He said that?' Alfred said. His cheeks had coloured.

'He was foul,' she said. 'I had to stop him.'

Rod said, 'You searched his room for the letters after he died.'

'Yes.'

Alfred coughed, and covered his mouth with a handkerchief. 'How did you know I wouldn't be in the car?'

She had the grace to look away. 'I did what was necessary, Alfred. I didn't want you to get hurt.'

'What did you give your husband to make him unwell?'

'I beg your pardon?'

'You didn't want him to die when Foster was killed. How did you ensure he was safe?'

'I told Thin Bao not to hurt him,' she said.

'That is all?' Rod said, and he could hear the disbelief in his voice.

She lifted her chin defiantly. 'Yes.'

'But, with bullets flying, he would have been killed too.'

'You left me in the line of fire?' Alfred said.

'You were unwell that morning,' she said.

'What if I hadn't been? I could have been killed!'

'What did Foster have?' Rod interrupted.

'Letters. Saucy, risqué letters from married women, which he said would ruin Ian's reputation. They would show a different side of him, Foster said, that Ian was a cad, and no right-thinking man or woman would celebrate a cad's memory. I was distraught! I couldn't tell Alfred, because I knew how he – you – would be hurt. I'm sorry, Alfred. I did what I thought was best. I paid him, and he swore to keep the letters hidden, but refused to sell them to me. I had to keep paying, larger and larger amounts. It was intolerable.'

'Mrs Winton, what did you think would happen when he died? All his papers must be discovered.'

'I thought to find them. They're safe now,' she said with a sly smile. 'They are destroyed, as they should have been before Foster got his hands on them.'

'There is still this,' Rod said and brought the telegram from his pocket.

'What is that?' Alfred demanded.

'The report of your son's death, sir.'

'But he died attacking the enemy!'

Alfred's eyes moved from the paper to his wife.

'That's enough!' she said. 'You would ruin our boy's reputation, for justice for a *blackmailer*?'

'No, Mrs Winton, for justice for an old Chinese man, his young daughter, and a solicitor who did nothing to deserve a bullet. I will do it for them.'

'I don't understand!' Alfred said. He coughed, the handkerchief over his mouth again.

'Your son shot himself.'

'*Go*!' Edith spat. She was at her husband's side now. 'I hope you're satisfied! Two Chinese and a lawyer, you say? What of them? Our *son* died! He's *dead,* just like the other poor boys in that stupid, pointless war!'

'Is this true? Edith?'

'Don't blame him, sir. He was in the trenches too long. It affected all of us differently. You can't imagine the horrors. But that doesn't give anyone the right to assassinate Foster – nor the others.'

Alfred shook his head. 'Leave now. You have made wild allegations. You have no evidence, no proof of my wife's complicity, and by the time I have instructed a King's Council to handle the matter, you will have no career either. Get out!'

She smiled then, and Rod knew that Alfred was right. Without the letters, without proof that she had been paying Foster, Rod had no case, only circumstantial evidence. A tenuous chain, in which every link would be feeble under the forensic eye of a barrister. Rod felt a grim conviction he would never see her in court.

He stood, but before he reached the door, Alfred called him back.

'You came here to accuse my wife; you tormented us with news of Ian's death. I will speak with the Commissioner and make a formal complaint. If these matters are raised in the press or elsewhere, I shall sue you personally. I hope that is clear enough? Now, you have my property. Give me back my bullets.'

And he held out his hand for his bullets.

## Chapter Fifty

As Rod closed the door, he saw Alfred break the Webley open and begin to insert the cartridges one by one into the cylinder.

Crowther materialised at the door to his pantry, and watched Rod stalk to the door. He remained still as a hangman's scaffold when Rod struggled to operate the door's two handles.

Alfred was right. Without the letters there was no evidence of blackmail. So what if their son had committed suicide? If it became common knowledge, it would affect the family, but for what purpose? Rod had discovered a nasty secret which was probably best kept private. Broadcasting it would help no-one, only destroy the reputation of a soldier. Others had succumbed to despair and committed suicide. Rod could not condemn them. The Front was a uniquely hideous experience.

Rod had no case.

Alfred Winton could have Rod thrown from the Force, but Hibbard at least should know the truth. Later, while Rod was pecking out his report on the office typewriter, Eric Leigh appeared in the doorway.

'Just when I thought my day couldn't get any worse,' Rod grunted.

'You know you like me really,' Eric grinned.

'What do you want?'

'Anything. My editor's giving me a hard time, and I have to give him something. I was hoping you would tell me what's happening with the Wintons,' he said hopefully.

It was tempting. Rod would have liked to, but it would only serve to get him fired more quickly. And then he had a thought.

He stared through the window. Bert had said that his family had been involved in arms. He felt so disgusted that he ran here, to Shanghai. How much worse for Ian Winton, learning his father profited from companies making weapons aimed at him and his men?

'Rod? Are you listening?'

'What?'

Rod heard shouts and running feet.

'What is it, a raid? Sounds like there's been some kind of incident,' Eric said.

Rod suddenly had a horrible premonition. Seeing Mickey Hi running past, he called, 'Mickey, what's the flap?'

'Murder, sir. Horrible news, sir, the Winton family.'

Death can strike at any time, but those inflicted within a family home are surely the worst. To find bodies lying in the midst of their possessions, shattered and ruined, adds a hideous dimension to the scene.

Rod ran up the steps. Crowther was sitting in the hallway. Red-rimmed eyes stood out in his ashen face. Officers were moving about in the sitting room. Rod pulled a chair to Crowther's side.

'I am very sorry, Crowther. What happened?'

When he focused on Rod's face his features were tugged into a fist of grief: tight and sore as a picked scab.

'Soon after you left,' he said, 'they rowed. I heard Mr Winton say that he would be damned, and Mrs Winton cried out. I knocked, but Master Alfred told me to … to go away. I took the servants to the kitchen so they would not hear, and I myself remained with them. Until I heard the gun.'

'How many bullets did you hear?'

'Five, I think. They were loud. Terribly loud. First one, and Mrs Winton screamed, and then three or four more. It was horrible.'

'What then?'

'I knocked, but there was no answer. I went to seek for Mrs Winton, but she was not in her dressing room or … Well, I knew the worst, I suppose. I entered, and found … It was horrible, sir. Horrible!'

'Did anyone move anything?'

'No, sir. Poor Mr Winton! It was all too much for him! First his son, then Master Maurice, and now his wife …'

'What of her?'

'It was you, sir. Telling Mr Winton that she had ordered someone to kill Foster. He said she could have killed him. His own wife! Your talk made him kill his wife.'

Rod left Crowther weeping and entered the sitting room.

Mrs Winton's chair was overturned, her body beside it. Bert Shaw had said a bullet in a room made a hell of a mess, and he was right. Three bullets had hit her, one shattering her shoulder, another puncturing her throat, one more striking her left breast. The smell of blood was everywhere; flies drank at the wounds.

Her husband remained in the same wing-backed chair. His bullet had passed through his right cheek. His skull and brains spattered the chair, the wall and rugs.

O'Toole was standing with his lips pursed as if whistling silently. He glanced up. 'Nasty one, Rod.'

'I've been talking to the butler.'

'I couldn't get much out of him, except it was your fault.'

'That's what he said.'

'Well,' O'Toole shrugged, glancing about him. 'This isn't your fault. He was clearly deranged.'

'I suppose.' Rod stared at Edith Winton's body. He felt a stab of responsibility, of guilt.

Crouching at her side, Rod studied her injuries as if they could speak and remove a little of his self reproach. There was a large exit wound at the rear of her throat. She must have turned slightly, because the bullet didn't strike perpendicular. Perhaps panic took over, and she tried to escape even as her husband fired and the massive .455 calibre bullets caught her?

'The butler said you thought his wife tried to kill him?'

'I wondered that, yes,' Rod said.

'Poor bastard believed you, didn't he?'

'Perhaps.' Rod was about to speak when there came a scream. '*No! Daddy! Daddy!*'

He turned to see Alice Winton, her face rent in grief, held back by Crowther and Eva.

'Sweet merciful heavens,' O'Toole muttered, and Rod hurried to the doorway, blocking the scene and pushing Alice away. He pulled the door shut.

Alice looked about her as though she didn't recognise her home. Crowther helped lead Alice to a small dining room, and poured a stiff brandy. Alice held a handkerchief to her eyes, trying to get a grip, breathing slowly and deeply, then suddenly sobbing again. She grabbed the glass from Crowther like an opium addict snatching his pipe, drinking half in one draught.

'What's happened?' she wailed.

Rod thought she was about to faint, or perhaps vomit, but she lifted the glass and took another gulp.

'Weren't you here?' Rod said.

'No, after father spoke so rudely, I went to meet Eva. I've only just returned.'

'I'm very sorry, but it looks as though ...'

'Someone killed them both, didn't they?' Alice said. She finished the drink, a small, pale childlike figure. 'I can't believe it! Who would ... was it robbery?'

'I'm sorry, I don't think anyone else was involved.'

'What does that mean? What are you saying?'

'It looks as though ...' He couldn't find the words. To say, *your father killed your mother, and then turned the gun on himself* was too blunt, too cruel.

He was saved by a dawning horror in her eyes. 'No! *No!* He wouldn't do that! He couldn't!'

'He has been under a lot of stress.'

'No, no, he wouldn't. He loved mother.' She stared about her, her eyes wild. 'I didn't mean for this to happen!'

Alice Winton sobbed quietly into a handkerchief. She started her story several times, only to dissolve into racking sobs. 'Oh, God!' she said again and again, until Rod was tempted to shake her.

'I'm sorry! It's just ... I can't believe they're dead!'

'You must try to calm down,' he said firmly.

She snivelled a little, and nodded. At last she managed to speak more coherently.

'It was hard to lose Ian, but he was determined to go. He used to write often, you know. He was a good letter-writer. Always had been. First his letters were full of excitement, learning how to be a soldier, leading his men ... but gradually they grew bleak. A shell landed in the middle of his company and killed most of the men. He said, *the others were awfully shattered, their limbs blown away, their lives destroyed in a flash of explosive.* It was so horrid, I remember it word for word.'

She looked at Rod, tearful. 'In his letters, he said that he had never known such affection as he had for those men. He loved them. *Really* loved them. And then they were wiped out. And he felt guilty.'

'Why so?'

'Father wrote telling him all that happened here. He felt he knew Ian so well, and wanted to keep Ian informed … Father told him about the business, how he broke Schreier. He didn't know Ian had enjoyed an affair with Mrs Schreier. It must have made Ian feel terribly guilty.'

'Because he deprived the man of his wife?'

'Yes, and now father had taken Schreier's livelihood. And then Ian learned he was profiting from the very weapons that had helped kill his men. It was in his last letter. It was horrid. Ian said that if the family was profiting from German weapons, he would have nothing to do with it.'

'And he died a little later?'

'You don't have to skirt around it. I know he killed himself.'

'Did Ian say he would commit suicide?'

'No, but his horror was so clear, it was no surprise.'

'What then?'

'Foster arrived with his story of serving Ian loyally right to the end. Mother offered him a job, and he accepted, promising never to mention Ian's suicide. But it wasn't enough that he had a well-paid job. He wanted more.'

'More money?'

She gave a brittle laugh, like a car's windshield when a body goes through it. 'You could say that. He wanted a better job, and to seal it, he decided he wanted me as his wife. What better way to seal a contract? As his wife, I would have to be obedient to his wishes.' Her voice was bitter.

'You looked content enough when out dancing.'

'That was before I realised. He and I were … intimate. He promised to marry me, until … one day, I discovered letters. Letters from his wife. I realised Foster was an adulterer, or possibly a bigamist. I told mother, and said I wanted him out of the house, but she told me we couldn't … he had something. I had to pretend I didn't know about his wife, so that we could think of a means of ensuring his silence. And I told Maurice. I didn't realise how it would affect him …'

Eva looked across at Rod as Alice poured more brandy.

'And?'

'Maurice said I shouldn't encourage him. I was happy to agree. I couldn't bear to feel his hands on me!'

'What of Thin Bao?'

'He was one of mother's orphans. Sometimes she would give them work. Thin Bao came, but he hasn't worked here for ages. I think Maurice met him again a little while ago.'

'Thin Bao killed Foster. He has killed many: the lawyer Dewitt, two Chinese, Schreier – he tried to kill me.'

She subsided into deep, racking sobs that threatened to tear her throat. 'But … how could he? Oh, but this is *terrible*. Poor father, poor *mother*! It's all my fault! All because I spoke to my brother for help!'

Rod leaned forward. 'What are you saying?'

'Maurice hired Thin Bao to kill Foster!' She collapsed into floods of tears.

'Listen, Alice, this is not your fault. You were the victim. Now, promise me you'll tell no one. Nor you, Eva. Do you understand? Tell no one about Maurice, Foster, nor about Thin Bao. When I find him, you will be safe. Tell me, how did Maurice contact him?'

'I think it was a café in the French Settlement. The Montmartre.'

## Chapter Fifty-One

Two hours later, Rod and Dubois were in a small room overlooking the Café Montmartre.

'You are sure you will recognise him?' Dubois asked.

'He's not the sort of man you forget. Not when he has pointed a Mauser at you.'

'He made an impact!'

Dubois was firm and reliable, and Rod was glad of his company.

'I worried that news might get to the man himself,' he said. 'When the witnesses were gunned down, I felt sure there must be a spy in our ranks - or in yours.'

'There are many, I believe,' Dubois said. 'When our Chilean friend recognised Huang Jinrong, I was told to leave him alone. They think one rotten apple is safe if wrapped about with bureaucracy. They don't realise one rotten apple can infect the whole barrel.'

'You think he is giving information to the gangs?'

Dubois gave a Gallic shrug. 'Some view his profit-taking as an expense of law and justice. He does catch the criminals, but not the Green Gang. I wonder - do we permit the Green Gang to flourish? Are we creating a monopoly, where gangsters with certain contacts must squeeze out all others?'

'That is the counsel of despair,' Rod said.

'It is the counsel of pragmatism, my superiors would say.'

Rod wiped his brow. It was blazingly warm in the small room, like sitting in a roaring inglenook in mid-summer. He fanned his face with his hat.

'Thin Bao wants to kill me. Perhaps because I disrupted the flow of guns. He had thought to make money from the smuggling -'

'There he is!' Dubois said, pointing.

Rod saw a slender, short Chinese, with a light-coloured fedora and dark suit. He walked with a rolling swagger, and other people took one look and moved from his path. As he watched, Thin Bao approached the Café Montmartre's doors, and paused, glancing around as if struck by something.

'*Viens*!' Dubois said, and hurried to the door.

Thin Bao stood, his hand on the door handle, staring in. Du Yusheng stared back impassively, but one of the men at the table gave a curt nod. Thin Bao walked in.

'You have learned?' Du Yusheng did not look at him. His cadaverous features faced the road.

'Yes. Schreier told the police, but Billy Qian told him to. Qian was behind the raid on my cabaret.'

'Why would he do that?'

'Because he wants to compete with you.'

'You are a fool!'

'I ...'

'He is a member of the Gang.'

'But ...' Thin Bao felt a fist clench about his heart. 'Why would he risk my cabaret?'

'You are why,' Du Yusheng said. 'You wanted power. You wanted control. You forgot that you swore to me personally, didn't you?'

'I never broke my oath to you.'

'You have no honour.'

Rod and Dubois walked idly, like two clerks on a lunch break. The men inside the restaurant did not glance at them as they passed the glass windows. Dubois and he leaned against a wall and watched, trying to remain inconspicuous.

At a circular table sat a number of Chinese. Facing the road was a thin man with the features of a committed opium addict. Behind him stood two bodyguards. Thin Bao bowed and the two spoke.

And then all went mad.

A portly figure, Huang Jinrong, stood bowed at the thin man, and walked from the room. An instant later, two gendarmes burst in from the back. There was a moment's paus, then gunshots, and Rod heard a scream, cut short. The window at the front of the café erupted as a chair was hurled through it, and Thin Bao followed close behind, landing heavily, and ran towards the Chinese old city.

Dubois and Rod drew their weapons and set off in pursuit. Behind them Rod heard shouts and bellows as police stormed the restaurant.

Thin Bao was thirty yards ahead, but they were gaining. Rod was tempted to try to bring him down, but he dare not risk killing him outright; he wanted Thin Bao alive. He would not be an easy man to catch. He was determined.

Thin Bao span, the gun in his hand.

'*Damn*!' Rod cried, and as he did, Dubois shouted at him to drop his weapon.

Thin Bao crouched, the Mauser flashing. Rod didn't hear it, only saw the muzzle flares, and threw himself to the ground as bullets tore over his head. He aimed, his first two shots going wild. Dubois fired slowly and deliberately, still standing. The Chinaman pulled a fresh clip of bullets from his pocket and pressed them into the Mauser's magazine, releasing the bolt and lifting his gun to aim just as the Frenchman ran out of bullets. Dubois released the cylinder, swung it out and ejected the cases. Rod saw him fumble two cartridges, and then the Mauser was up. Rod squeezed his trigger and fired three times, dropped the magazine and reloaded, firing two more.

He saw Thin Bao step back as though punched. His gun dropped a little, and his next shot went into the road, but then he tried to lift the barrel again, and Rod had no choice. He fired twice more. Thin Bao staggered and fell onto his rump. He put his left hand on the ground, surprised. Then he rolled to a knee and tried to push himself up, but toppled backwards, and the hand holding the Mauser was on the ground too, as if he needed both arms to support himself. He remained there, panting, while Rod turned to Dubois.

He was standing with a hand pressed to his flank. Blood already soaked his shirt and jacket. 'Please, capture him,' he hissed, teeth clenched against the pain.

Rod nodded.

'Leave go your weapon,' he said.

'I should have killed you in your apartment,' Thin Bao spat.

'Yes. Now you will stand trial for murder.'

'I will stand no trial.'

Rod's bullets had found their mark. Thin Bao's face was yellow as jaundice, and a shivering fever ran through his frame.

'Was it you murdered Alfred Winton and his wife?'

'Tell Alice ... Tell Alice ... *er guizi* ... Tell her ...'

But even as he spoke, Thin Bao's head dropped until his chin was resting on his breast, and he remained there as French officers hurried up, one kicking away his gun, another pushing him over, and then there was a scrimmage of officers congratulating each other about their successful operation.

Rod helped Dubois lie, balling his jacket to make a pillow and setting it under his head. He was blinking and breathing quickly, but his injury didn't look deadly. Rod placed a hand on his chest. 'You'll be fine.'

Dubois peered up through the fog of pain, recognising the conviction in Rod's voice. He attempted a smile as two medics appeared with a stretcher. They deftly lifted him onto it and set off at a trot to their ambulance. Rod paused only to pick up a single brass case from the Mauser, and then followed them. It took him two attempts to holster his pistol as the reaction kicked in. Passing the restaurant, he saw a portly figure: Huang Jinrong.

'Good day,' Rod said.

'A sad day, to see my colleague Dubois so injured,' he said, bowing and smiling.

'You must be very upset,' he said.

'Yes, of course.'

'The brandy and cigars you ordered from Schreier. You didn't receive them, did you?'

'Ah, no. Sadly Mr Schreier died before he could deliver them.'

'You were with the men at that table when Thin Bao came in.'

'Yes. I was speaking to my good friend Du Yusheng. He is a businessman here in the French settlement.'

'And Thin Bao used to work for him.'

'I do not think so. I think Thin Bao used to work for himself. He was a free lance.'

'So he could be employed by anyone?'

'Only those who could pay him!'

Rod peered inside the café. Du Yusheng still sat at the table. His black eyes met Rod's briefly, as though the sight of the detective was unappealing. With his suit scuffed from rolling on the road, that was hardly surprising, but Du Yusheng had the arrogance of a man who wielded authority.

Rod would keep an eye on him in future.

Rod badly needed a rest; not the electric thrilling of cocaine, but sleep. He walked to the opium den, standing outside until he was convinced that no one was watching. The scent of burning opium came to him, and he felt like a hound who smells the spoor of a deer.

He crossed the road. Soon he was inside, following the man to a spare chamber, and lay back with a good pipeful.

The world took on a more pleasant aspect. About him the smoke swirled and moved, forming faces and scenes. He saw Eva and Alice, and was instantly aroused. Eva, in particular, was beautiful. She smiled at him, and the light glinted from her hair. She lifted her hands to it and ran her fingers through it, then ran her hands down her body, like one of the whores in Gracie Gale's establishment. He would like to lie with Eva. She was lovely: entrancing.

That was his last thought as he drifted off: that she was entrancing. A wonderful young woman.

## Chapter Fifty-Two

*Saturday 5th August*

When Rod visited Bert, he brought a basket of fruits and sweets, with a bottle of whisky concealed beneath. When the matron wasn't looking, he lifted it from the basket. Bert grinned, shoving it beneath his pillow. 'Thanks, old Cock. You're a sport.'

'I do my best.'

'I heard that you got the man who killed Foster. You should be at Dan's, celebrating.'

'Yes,' Rod said. 'It's good to take one gangster out of the city.'

'Why aren't you more cheerful, then?'

Rod grinned wearily. 'It's only a start. What were you going to say yesterday? Something about Ian Winton's suicide?'

'Yes.'

'I've already learned it,' Rod said. 'Alice said his father told Ian he had acquired shares in Krupp's. Ian lost his men to a shell, so when he heard his father was profiting from German weapon sales, he couldn't live with the shame.'

Bert looked at him. 'Does that strike you as likely?' Bert shook his head. 'I told you that there was a letter there.'

'Yes. He said he couldn't live with the knowledge. Alice told me.'

'She never saw it.'

'I'm sorry?'

'I told you: he blew his brains out over the letter. I couldn't send that home. So instead I wrote a letter speaking of his courage, determination, and his honourable conduct. I didn't copy his own.'

Rod was frowning in confusion. 'What was in the letter, then?'

'It was rambling, but mentioned of David and Uriah. The meaning was clear enough.'

'David and Uriah the Hittite?'

And then Rod understood. The letter Pamela Grey had written to Ian. She had said she despaired of life and must die without Ian. How had she put it? 'If only I had not married. I could be free to live with you, to love you. Sometimes I think I should be so happy, were I to hear that George were dead. Do not think badly of me. It is only my love for you. You must surely feel the same for me.'

Bert gave a twisted grin as the realisation dawned. 'Yes, old cock. Dearest Ian, the epitome of the "Perfect, Gentle Knight" was an adulterer and murderer. I checked. Lieutenant George Grey was in his company. Ian was sleeping with Grey's wife, and succumbed so far to her charms, that he sent Grey over the top on a raid. Grey and two others were killed. His men knew. Grey was popular, and no rifleman likes to think his officer would throw him into danger for no reason. Especially not that late in the war. To his credit, I suppose, Ian was consumed by guilt and blew his brains out.'

He paused a moment, peering through the window thoughtfully. 'It was probably a good thing. If he hadn't, one of his men would have done it for him.'

Bert began yawning. Rod felt in need of another quarter grain of cocaine. He left Bert dozing, Passing Kiangse Road, he walked to number 52.

There was a party in full swing. A tall, dark-haired beauty was dancing on a table to music from a gramophone player, wearing little and clutching a bottle of champagne to her breasts. She smiled at Rod, and the look alone was enough to send the blood coursing faster through his body.

'Hey, fella, you can't afford her *or* the wine,' Gracie Gale said with a chuckle in her voice.

'Can I speak with you for a moment?'

'Sure. Come into my office,' she said. Her breath was pure cognac. He felt intoxicated merely by inhaling. She led the way to her sanctum, and he closed the door, accepting a glass of cognac. It was exquisite.

'What brings you here, Detective?' she asked, nipping the end from a cigar.

'I have found the murderer.'

'Yeah, and you found out about the guns in time to stop Maurice Winton being an asshole.'

'Well, I think he was played by others.'

'You do? Maybe. He wasn't the brightest.'

'You knew them well?'

'I knew Alfred and Ian. Alfred was a good client until that unpaid chit. He brought Ian for his first experience.' She cocked an eyebrow. 'What, am I shocking you?'

'After witnessing your dancer just now, I don't think I can shock so easily.'

'I'll bet I could shock you easily enough. No,' she chuckled, 'not the way you're thinking. I knew about the Wintons before you did.'

'How do you mean?'

'You came in here with your wild talk of a Russian girl called Eva. Well, Shanghai isn't that big, and there ain't that many taipans. It didn't take above a handful of seconds to know you were talking about Alice.'

'And what have you heard?'

'Plenty. The girl is a real peach, and bright as a new-minted Mexican dollar; her brother's a fool who tried to compete with her to take the business.'

'She could hardly have done that.'

'Couldn't she?'

'Would anyone trade with a company headed by a woman?' Gracie stiffened. 'If you reckon …'

'I am thinking of the Chinese and taipans.'

'No one will deal with her, but they'd deal with her Comprador, and be happy.'

'I suppose she almost succeeded.'

'Almost? She has the business sewn up, pretty much. Not that it'll do her any good. The bank is almost out of funds, and there'll be a run.'

When Rod left her a little later, he couldn't help but reflect on her words.

Alice was a clever little thing, but she was not ruthless like her father or Schreier. Both were determined men capable of any extreme to promote themselves and their businesses. Her father hinted as much when he threatened Rod with his son's revolver. Schreier was capable of violence against Alfred and his family. Schreier had got the guns to the warehouse, yet Rod didn't know how he communicated with Maurice. Rod had learned that Maurice had notes from the assassin via the café. Perhaps Maurice kept in touch with Schreier the same way.

Gracie reckoned Alice was not an innocent, and was as determined and ruthless as her father. Rod found that hard to believe. Alice detested Foster because he blackmailed the family, and wanted to marry her to take a seat on the board, but that didn't make her ruthless.

There were aspects that still puzzled him. How had Thin Bao known to hunt Rod down, following him until he found his apartment? Rod was surprised he had managed that – Rod was careful to ensure that he was not followed – yet Thin Bao knew where he lived.

Or someone who knew where his apartment was had told him.

Alice was there when Maurice told Rod about the ship. Alice had known Rod's address – she had asked him. Alice knew of Eva's search for documents, too.

Was Alice involved in the shipment?

His blood was suddenly chilled. Could Alice - not Edith - have ordered Foster's murder? Edith took the blame – she would do anything to protect her children, but she had not thought quickly enough about Alfred being in the car.

But Alice ... She wanted Foster removed, both because of the threat he posed to Ian's memory, and the threat he posed to her personally. What would a woman not do to protect herself from a gold-digger who wanted her money and would deprive her of her liberty to gain it? Had she ensured Alfred didn't take the car that day?

At Dan Bailey's, Eric sat nursing a drink. Rod took the stool next to him.

'I hear congratulations are in order,' he said. 'Not that the spirit of our agreement was honoured. I trusted you to let me have the scoop.'

'I will,' Rod said.

'A bit late!'

Rod sipped. 'There's possibly more to come.'

Maurice and Alice, he thought, both communicating by that little café. One to hire an assassin, the other to smuggle guns. Both dealing with the man who had once worked in their house, who had remained their friend.

And then Rod realised what had been staring him in the face. Both were communicating with the same place – perhaps about the same deal? If Alice was as ruthless as Gracie said, maybe the gun deal was cooked up to ruin Maurice's reputation not bySchreier, but by *Alice*. As Gracie said, other companies would deal with her comprador, no matter what they thought of her.

'Eric, do you keep registers of ships, who owns them and so on?'

'In the office, yes.'

'I need you to look into the ownership of the *Lucky Strike*. See how often Alfred Winton used it.'

'Why?'

'I think you'll have a story that could double the paper's sales.'

It was the last time Rod would look up at the house with its incongruous tower. After Dan Bailey's, he returned to the Station and the little morocco case. Now his mind was clear as spring water. He could see it all perfectly clearly - Ian's death, Foster's threats, the decision to kill him, the smuggling - everything fell into place.

Crowther opened the door. He nodded and invited Rod inside.

'How are the staff?'

'Shocked, sir. We have asked a cleaning company to … well, you can imagine, sir. It would be cruel to ask the house staff to clean the blood of their master and mistress.'

'Of course. And how are you?'

'I am well enough, sir. It was horrible, but my job is to keep the house running. I will do that for as long as Miss Alice wants me.'

'You are fond of her, aren't you?'

'I have known her since she was a child.'

'Was she always wilful?'

'I don't know that I would say that. What is the purpose of your visit, sir?'

'The Webley. Was it taken by the police yesterday?'

'Yes, sir. They said it was material evidence.'

'I see. The thing is, Crowther, something is niggling at me.'

'Yes, sir?'

'The Webley was Ian Winton's, wasn't it? I know the type: a Fosbery. It was quite popular in the trenches. The standard Webley was perfectly serviceable, but the Fosbery was faster to fire. Every shot recocked the gun and turned the cylinder.'

'Yes, sir.'

'I'll come to the point. You know pistols. The Fosbery hammer has a very strong spring. It is much more difficult to cock than a normal revolver. As Alfred discovered. He used both thumbs and still couldn't cock it in his weakened state.'

'Really, sir?'

'So someone else cocked it. Was that you?'

'No, sir.'

'Was Alfred a keen shooter?'

'Not at all. No, he practised, naturally, as any man must, but he was not a terribly good shot. Not like Miss Alice.'

'Miss Alice?'

'She is a very competent pistol shooter. She uses a service revolver.'

He had stiffened, as if he expected Rod to accuse him of murder.

'Crowther. You know guns. You told me that you heard one shot, a scream, then three or four in a group.'

'Yes, sir.'

'You are quite sure?'

'Yes, sir.'

'You see, I think the first shot killed Mr Winton, and that made his wife scream, and shortly afterwards the other shots were fired at his wife.'

'You don't think he shot her and committed suicide?'

'Think: one shot, then three or four? If he committed suicide, there would have been a flurry of shots, then a single one.'

Crowther gave Rod his best patronising smile. 'But if the first shot killed Mr Alfred, sir, he would not have been able to shoot Mrs Winton.'

'No, Crowther. He wouldn't.'

Crowther's smile sidled away from his face. 'But …'

'When you found the bodies, were the French windows unlocked?'

'In this heat we leave them open.'

'Someone entered through the French windows. I want to look to see if there is a cartridge case: a bottle-necked casing, of the sort a Mauser fires.'

Crowther was staring at him as if he had sprouted horns and a tail. 'A Mauser, sir?'

'I think you heard a Mauser kill Mr Winton. You heard Mrs Winton scream, and then a series of shots. That was the murderer killing Mrs Winton. The murderer, Thin Bao. Will you come and help me look?'

'Yes, of course, sir, but I don't know that there will be much to see.'

They entered the sitting room. The rugs had been removed, as had the chairs, and the only evidence of the horror of yesterday was streaks on the wall where heavy washing had smeared blood. Rod walked to the French windows. The wingback chair had stood there, on his left. To his right was the patch where Mrs Winton's body had lain. A bullet passing through Alfred's head from here would have sprayed blood in that direction. On the wall in a direct line from here were streaks of stained paint. It was not proof, but it was supportive. Standing where Alfred had been, he looked towards where Mrs Winton had been seated, and immediately realised something was not right.

'What are you doing here?' Alice demanded.

## Chapter Fifty-Three

'Aren't you *satisfied*?' she asked. 'Because of you my parents are dead, and still you cannot bear to leave me alone!'

'I am sorry, Miss Winton,' Rod said.

She stood in the doorway, two bright patches of red high on her cheeks. 'What is this? "Miss Winton" now, am I? Crowther? What are you doing?'

'We are looking for a cartridge case, Miss Winton,' Rod said.

'I don't understand.' She looked from him to Crowther as Eva joined her in the doorway.

'A revolver like your father's Webley holds all the cartridge cases after firing. You know that. All six are ejected at the same time when you break the barrel. But the Mauser throws out each cartridge as it fires. And because of the way it is made, they can be flung in any direction.'

'What of it?'

'If a Mauser was fired here, there will be a cartridge case,' Rod said. 'If a man like Thin Bao, perhaps, walked in and saw your father holding a gun he might have fired first.'

'You think so?'

'I am sorry, Miss Winton. This must be painful.'

'If you are saying that Father didn't kill mother and shoot himself, that is a great relief.'

'If Thin Bao came in and shot your father, that would make your mother scream. He might have walked to your father, taken the pistol, and shot your mother with it.'

'And left the gun to make it seem that Father did it.'

'Yes.'

'What a horrible man!'

But something was adrift. Rod knew it. 'Where did you go while I was talking to your parents?'

'Pardon?'

'Yesterday: when I was speaking to your parents, you drove off and returned with Eva. Where did you go?'

'I often go for a drive when I am angry or frustrated.'

'Are you often very angry?'

'Isn't everybody in this heat? I met Eva at the Astor House.'

Rod nodded, crouching and peering under tables and a display cabinet. There was no sign of a cartridge case. Rising, he said thoughtfully, 'It was just something that made me think. You see, that day Maurice told me about the *Lucky Strike*, that same evening Thin Bao tried to murder me. Somehow he learned where I live.'

'So?'

'Thin Bao saw Maurice that day, too. Maurice discovered that he wasn't importing tobacco and other goods, but guns. Thin Bao warned him not to speak to the police about the ship, then hunted me down. Someone told Thin Bao of my conversation in here with Maurice.'

'Yes,' Alice said. She ran a finger over a book case.

'But the only people privy to that conversation were Maurice, me, and you.'

'You suggest that I planned your murder, Detective?'

'I think you made it clear he could be in danger if I wasn't killed.'

Alice shook her head. 'Crowther, could you fetch me tea, please? I think we'll drink it on the lawn.'

Rod followed Alice and Eva to the table where he had seen her with her mother only a week and a half ago. It seemed months since he had stood in the sitting room and thought how Alice and Edith could have been sisters, both with the same poise and elegance. That was why Miss Hyman had mistaken the daughter for the mother when she saw Thin Bao with her.

Alice took her seat and motioned to Rod to sit opposite her. Eva sat near.

'Well, Detective?' Alice said.

'Did you shoot them yourself?'

She gasped, and her hand rose to her throat. 'Me?'

'You know about guns. I know you spoke to Thin Bao. I have a witness to that. The whole train of events was set in motion by you. I assume because you learned about Foster's wife.'

'Oh, I wouldn't have minded that. No, it was his assumption that he could marry me and take control. I wasn't going to allow that. I may look a foolish girl, Detective, but I know my value. I am not some frippery to be traded. So I determined to destroy him. I already knew Mr Schreier, and asked for his assistance. He told me to write to the café, and a day later Thin Bao came to visit me. We discussed the affair.'

'What then?'

She gave that enigmatic shrug again, the shoulder rising, head tilting. 'I bought some Chinese medicine to make father feel liverish. I gave him quite a lot, and he felt so unwell he could not face work. Meanwhile I instructed Foster to go to the dressmaker's. Thin Bao was waiting. It was easy.'

'What of the lawyer?'

'I have no idea.'

Rod did, though. Basil Ross had said that the man trying to buy the Honan Road godown was angry. Thin Bao was sent to demonstrate his frustration, no doubt.

'And then you had your parents killed.'

'What else could I do? Father was determined to prevent me having more than a minority share. Mother supported him. They thought I was too frivolous. And now, ironically, Father has driven the business into the ground!'

'So you left while I was talking to them, and arranged for Thin Bao to kill them?'

'I thought it would be easier if everyone thought that Father had killed Mother and himself.'

She stopped. Crowther and a maid had appeared. The maid carried the butler's tray, while Crowther himself bore a stand. When he reached the group he pulled the legs apart and set the stand near the table, before taking the tray from the maid and carefully placing it on the stand. He busily set out plates, cups and saucers on the table, adding cakes on a tiered stand as a centrepiece.

'Thank you, Crowther,' Alice said. He backed away obediently and left with the maid.

'So you planned for everyone to assume your father was a murderer.'

'Why not? He had been quite a pirate in his youth.'

'He threatened me once, saying it wouldn't be the first time he had killed someone. I didn't believe him.'

'You should have. He killed Thin Bao's father. Yes,' she chuckled at the sight of Rod's expression. 'Father was ruthless. Bao Xiu owned godowns that Father wanted, but refused to sell. Father had no compunction about killing him and marking him like a series of murders at the time. I told Thin Bao. Father told me lots,' Alice said. 'He ... he was rather infatuated with me.'

'Why kill them?' Eva gasped. 'They were your parents!'

'Neither trusted me. They thought I was too foolish, too silly, to run a bank and the rest of the business. And yet I was more capable than them. I took the hard decisions. Ian wasn't as determined as me. He could take advantage of others, certainly, but he lacked the instinct to kill.'

Rod finished his tea. 'This was very pleasant. However, I must ask you to come with me, Miss. You have confessed to murder, and I have to place you under arrest.'

'I thought you might. Would you object to my fetching my coat?'

'I will come with you.'

'How ungallant!'

At the broad, marble staircase, Alice ascended, Rod following. Alice led the way to the second door on the right. The bedroom would have accommodated two of Rod's apartments with ease. A large dressing table, a huge bed, and Rod stood bemused by the opulence of the fittings as Alice crossed to the dressing table. He should have realised something was amiss – she was moving with such easy confidence.

The first warning was the triple click of a hammer being cocked. Rod turned to find himself staring into the barrel of a Webley. 'I thought the police had the Fosbery,' he said stupidly.

'They do. This is mine. I prefer Ian's Fosbery. It's more gentle on recoil, but this is adequate.'

'Put it down before –'

'Before someone gets hurt? It won't be me, Detective. If only you hadn't been such a pest, this would never have happened.'

'What do you intend to do?'

'We will go for a drive, and you won't come back.'

'You can't get away with another murder, Alice. Eva here knows: my friend Thomas Dubois knows, Crowther knows ...'

'You won't have to worry about it,' she said, and waved the pistol's barrel. 'Take your pistol out, very carefully, and throw it onto the bed.'

Rod had no choice. He carefully pulled the Colt free and tossed it onto the bed. She told him to raise his hands, and Eva too, and they slowly descended the stairs.

Alice sent them to the front door, and Rod reached for the two locks, fumbling with them.

'Hurry!' she snapped.

'What is it, Miss?'

Crowther had been in his pantry, and he stood in the doorway now, jacket off, an apron over his swelling belly, a cloth in one hand, a part-polished silver teapot in the other.

'Nothing, Crowther,' Alice said. 'We are going out for a drive.'

'Miss Alice,' Crowther said, 'Please put the weapon down. That is a police officer. You cannot threaten him.'

'Leave me alone, Crowther,' Alice said.

'Miss, I cannot allow you to hurt them. Please.'

'Open the door and get outside,' Alice said. 'Hurry!'

Rod felt one lock move. At his belt, he still had the little revolver in Dan Fairbairn's holster. There was a chance he could draw that. He took a deep breath, pulled the door wide, and stood aside to allow Eva through. As she passed, he hissed, '*Run!*' and span, crouching, drawing the pistol.

Alice shouted '*No!*', lifting her revolver. Behind her, Rod saw Crowther drop the cloth, and there was a nasty-looking, squat pistol in his hand. Alice was about to fire, and Rod threw himself sideways, desperate to avoid her bullet. A gun went off and he heard a scream, and he thought Eva had been hit, but he kept low, rolling, his pistol pointing at Alice.

But even as he aimed, he saw she was no threat. She had dropped her gun and gripped her belly with both hands. The blood was spurting in quick, sharp jets, and she stared down in dumbfounded horror.

And Rod saw Crowther go to her, holding her gently and rocking her, his voice hoarse as the life ran from between her fingers.

The next hours were confused.

Maurice Winton arrived. Someone had thought it a good idea to release him without considering the effect on him of finding mother, father and sister all dead. He looked like a wraith, with a face like tragedy. Alice's body had been removed by then, but her blood lay thickly about the hall.

'My God!' he said, over and over again. Rod managed to drag him through to the library and tried to have him sit down, but Maurice refused, pacing fretfully, chain-smoking cigarettes. When Rod poured him a large brandy, he drank it off in one gulp. A moment later, he started sobbing. He put glass and cigarette down, and covered his face in his hands.

'It was her idea,' he said at last. 'All hers. I thought we were bringing in tobacco and brandy. I didn't realise what she was up to, not until Thin Bao threatened me. It was a horrible shock!'

'You knew Thin Bao from his time here?'

'Yes. He was one of mother's favoured orphans, one of her cheap servants.'

'She often had them?'

'Oh, yes. Thin Bao, Billy Qian …'

'Qian?'

Maurice shrugged. 'What of it? Thin Bao was our playmate until Alice grew to puberty. Father wouldn't let an adult native stay near her after that.'

'And then?'

'Alice made me meet him in the Wheel. She said he was a businessman. That was all I knew, I swear! I told you about the ship – would I do that if I knew it held guns?'

'Why was that?'

He drew his hands away, blew his nose into an enormous silk handkerchief, and sighed. Taking up glass and cigarette again, he walked to the window, as though expecting to see his family enjoying tea in the shade of the great tree. 'Billy Qian told me. When I mentioned Thin Bao, he told me he was a dangerous man, he served a dangerous master. He said that I should be wary of him. When Alice saw Eva searching through my papers, she realised that Eva must be working for Billy, and hoped you would arrest Eva for attempted theft. When it all went sour, I sought to protect her.'

'She counted on that, I think.'

'What do you mean?'

'She wanted the company. She knew you would lie to keep her safe, so she set up the shipment and expected you to carry the blame when it went wrong. If it went well, she would have taken her profit happily.'

'No, Alice would not betray me like that.'

He raised his chin. Once more the petulant schoolboy. He looked away, finished his brandy. 'You cannot understand, Detective, because you don't come from a family like ours. There are ... bonds of affection and loyalty.'

'You're right. I have been in the army, and fought alongside men who I knew would fight and die for me. I can't understand how a family could be so broken that a daughter would see her parents murdered, her brother imprisoned, just so that she could have still more.'

But her wealth and privilege wasn't enough.

## Chapter Fifty-Four

*Monday 7th August, 1922*

Doctor Babu was in his consulting room when Rod visited.

'And how are you this wonderful day?' he asked.

'I have a question for you, Doctor,' Rod said.

'Oh, this sounds like a serious meeting,' the Doctor said, smiling. He sat in his chair with his hands in his lap. 'You are become a policeman, not a patient. How may I help you?'

'You contacted me to say you could help me. Someone directed you to speak to me. Who was it?'

'I cannot tell say. There is confidentiality involved in this matter.'

'Was it Alice Winton? She is dead now, so no confidentiality exists.'

'I do not know this lady.'

'I need to know, Doctor. Someone sent you my name. They paid for my drugs, too.'

'Call it medication. It is essential for your health, Detective. You are suffering the result of deprivation and fear.'

Rod bridled. 'I am not …'

'My friend, you see me in this splendid apartment, and you think I have never left Shanghai. Yet I spent the War not far from you, I expect. I was with Fane's Horse, the 19th Lancers, serving as medical orderly. I saw at first hand how the shelling affected my comrades. I felt it myself. That was why I developed an interest in medication, and how it could help me. It was not only for them, it was for myself as well.'

'You served?'

'Yes. I understand how you suffer.'

'You said it was malaria.'

'Yes, you had some symptoms. But you were also suffering nervous exhaustion, which exacerbated the symptoms. The cocaine will help with that.'

'I am a police officer. I should have you arrested.'

'I do not think so, my friend,' he smiled. 'You cannot arrest me, because my practice is here, in the French Settlement. Of course, you could report me to the French authorities, but naturally I will admit to prescribing for certain patients, such as you. The authorities know that I operate within their laws. Besides, if you could stop me dispensing, you would no longer have access to your own medication.' He smiled, infuriatingly. 'So it is surely better that you and I continue to our mutual benefit.'

His unflappable confidence appeared unshakeable. Yet Rod was still struck by one question. 'Someone is paying you for the drugs. It must be someone with money.'

'It is someone who knows the benefits of good medical practice with a man who, like you, has suffered. You are on a course of treatment, Detective. You are benefitting from it. Accept the gift.'

Rod Cottey was to meet Billy Qian again that summer.

It was a broiling day, the last truly hot day of that year, and Rod was wilting at the race course. On race days, the whole commercial life of Shanghai closed down. Taipans mingled with coolies, ladies with amahs, and bets were made, slips noted, only to be thrown down with a groan when the wrong horse came in. It was while Rod was following a thin, scrawny Chinese whom he suspected of picking pockets, that he met Billy Qian once more.

'Detective, I am glad you could find time to watch the horses,' Billy said.

'I am glad you both could,' Rod responded, but he wasn't watching Billy, he was looking at Eva, who clung to his arm like a soldier clinging to his rifle. She looked away: not with resentment, but a kind of weary patience, as though waiting for death to come and collect her. 'How are you, Eva?'

'Since his death? I am alive.'

The same day Bugayev had been arrested, he hanged himself in the prison. Few, apart from perhaps his widow, had mourned him. No one mourned the dispossessed in Shanghai. What was the point, when there was another party to go to?

'You managed the Winton affair well,' Billy said conversationally. 'It wasn't easy, I am sure. And successfully bringing down Thin Bao, that was a good deed. He would have killed many more.'

'You knew him well?'

'We were almost brothers. I met him in the orphanage, and then we both went to live with the Wintons. But then, of course, I was sent away.'

Rod nodded. 'Because you were Alfred's son.'

'Yes. And I think Edith could not bear to have me in the house, so I was sent abroad, while Thin Bao remained, but he was never happy.'

'Alice said Thin Bao was Alfred's son, too.'

'It is possible, but I doubt it. Besides, he went when Alice complained to her mother about the nocturnal visits to her bedroom. Too much affection going on there, old chap.'

'Thin Bao tried to rape her?'

Billy gave a loud guffaw, and Eva shot him a look. 'Good lord, Detective, no! Thin Bao looked on her as a sister. He adored her, which was why he took her orders so willingly - although at first he believed they were from Alfred himself. No, it was my father, Alfred, who was incontinent. He not only raped my mother, he sought to do the same to his own daughter. These taipans, eh? They assume just because they are filthy rich, they can do whatever they want. Edith didn't want Thin Bao hearing of such things and spreading rumours. She knew Alice talked to him.'

Rod had heard and seen much in his years as a policeman, but this sent a shiver through his frame. 'Good God! Poor Alice.'

'Certainly: poor Alice.'

'I thought you were his son, but I was surprised by the will.'

'Yes? He and I came to an understanding. I invested in his bank, so I own more or less fifty-five percent. I saved him from going under, because he knew he was dying. He had cancer, and wanted to ensure his family were not destitute. With the money I injected, the bank was secure, and his family would have been able to enjoy many years of comfort. Of course, now only Maurice will be able to enjoy that.'

'The fool will drink himself into an early grave,' Rod said sombrely.

'I fear so. My half brother is not as moderate in his drinking as he is in his intellect.'

'One thing still confuses me.'

'What is that?'

'Thin Bao was close to the family, until Edith Winton threw him from her door. Yet he found it easy enough to kill Edith and Alfred. That seemed curious to me.'

'Eva?'

She kept her eyes on the horses parading. 'Alice was clever. She knew how to make a man do her bidding. Once she told me that her father had taken over Thin Bao's father's godown and company. His father's business was strong and profitable. But Alfred murdered him and orphaned Thin Bao. Alfred once told her that he had killed Thin Bao's father to take over his godown because it was a prime location. He used a corrupt lawyer to take over the business for little money.'

'And the "traitor" carved into his head?'

Billy chuckled again, but this time without humour. 'There were other killings at the time. The police thought it was all gang-related. If a man turned up dead, with that on his forehead, what would the police think? That a gangster had done it for some slight, or a prominent businessman?'

Eva continued, 'Alice told him. He already hated Edith, and now he had reason to kill Alfred too.'

'And that was why he wanted me to tell Alice *er guizi*. He was calling her the traitor, because she saw to his death,' Rod breathed.

'Very likely.'

'What of you, Billy?'

'Me? I shall enjoy profits from my ventures, especially the bank. I shall promenade with beautiful women, and impart an indulgent smile on all those who deign to speak with me, and all the while,' he said, his smile disappearing like chalk wiped from a board, 'I will know that behind their backs they laugh. The English will call me the Chinaman, the chap with a touch of the tar-brush, while the Chinese will look at me with disgust and make the sign to ward off evil spirits, and I shall always know that I have no friends, none. Only acquaintances who want to make use of me. But I shall keep smiling, happy to know that my house is more sumptuous than theirs'.'

He smiled again.

'What of you, Eva?'

'While my friend pays, I will be his companion,' she said. 'And then, who knows? Perhaps I will marry an American and go back to his country with him. Better that than staying here, where I am nothing.'

'You see, Detective? She and I are ideally suited.'

When the racing was done, Rod went to Dan Bailey's and drank a lot more than usual.

Alice Winton had pulled the wool over his eyes, and everyone else's. She had persuaded them that she was a poor innocent, but she was more dangerous than the snakes infesting Shanghai's Foreign Settlement. As ruthless as any business taipan, she had no feelings for anyone. She was interested only in herself.

She had set up her own brother, to remove him from the field. At least it meant he was alive. As for the others: Thin Bao was hired by her to kill Foster, and he had killed the two Chinese witnesses to show that punishment would quickly be visited on those who betrayed him, just as Dewitt was killed for thwarting the attempt to buy the godown. Schreier took their money, and had to be killed because – well, perhaps the gangsters thought he had told the police about the guns, although in fact he was innocent of that. The leak of the ship's name had come from Maurice.

Maurice, poor Maurice, the man who would be taipan, but had little idea of business, and who had lost his family in a matter of days. Qian's information was correct: Alfred's gambles had failed, and if Billy Qian had not invested large sums, the firm would have gone bankrupt. It made Rod wonder again where his money came from.

He was still sitting at his table when Eric entered ordered himself a pink gin, and sat next to Rod. He slapped his notepad and pencil down on the table. 'Well?' he said.

'What?'

'You promised me a scoop. Where is it?'

It was late when Rod returned to his apartment. He took out his morocco case and tightened a cord about his arm as Doctor Babu had shown him. The tablet was dissolved, the syringe filled, and Rod held the needle denting the skin over the vein. There was a sensation of resistance overcome, and the needle slipped in.

The cocaine was like a comet that flooded his entire being with wellness and happiness. He was brighter, full of energy as he set the syringe and needle into a pan of water and boiled them as the doctor had instructed. A dirty needle could lead to gangrene, and Rod had seen enough of that in the War.

Someone had asked the doctor to treat him, someone who could afford to pay for his services, yet Rod had no idea who. Only that it was someone who had themselves made use of the Doctor.

Rod feared he could be compromised. If the man paying for Doctor Babu's services was a criminal, he might expect some form of payment in future. And that Rod was anxious to avoid. The doctor's protestations that he understood Rod because of his own service was hardly convincing.

And yet …

The cocaine was marvellous. It gave him a wonderful clarity of thought. A fresh thought occurred: the doctor said he had been medical officer to the 19th Lancers. Perhaps, Rod could find out who else had been in the Lancers, or a nearby battalion, and could have come to know the Indian?

Over the coming days Rod investigated Fane's Horse, as they were known. They'd been engaged in the Somme and Cambrai, but so many units were involved in both battles, almost any serving soldier could have met Babu. He extended his search; Fane's Horse had been resting near the Manchesters after the first week of the Somme. There were many cases of shell shock after that battle.

And Bert Shaw had been in the 2nd Battalion. He could have met the Doctor. Rod could easily imagine the Doctor happily sharing his knowledge about medicines after the terror of that assault.

Bert Shaw had endured a similar war to Rod. He bore the same scars.

Rod could confront him. But if he was wrong, he would be admitting to a fellow officer that he was making use of powerful drugs. And if so, he would be putting a strain on his friend. Perhaps it was better not to look into the matter any further.

It was his little secret.

# Epilogue

Secrets. Alfred's visits to Gracie Gales' house and his daughter's bed; Ian's deliberate murder of Lieutenant Grey; Alice's murder of Foster and her own parents.

Shanghai was built on secrets. They were the bedrock of the city. The piles were driven into the secrets like stakes impaling vampires, as though they could pin them there. And, like marsh gas, every so often secrets would emerge.

And when they did, like marsh gas, they could flare and burn, and scorch all those standing near.

\* \* \*

# Author's Note

## Shanghai - the world of W.E. Fairbairn

In recent years Shanghai has gained an almost legendary flavour. "Empire of the Sun," and J.G. Ballard's autobiography "Miracles of Life", as well as films such as "Indiana Jones and the Temple of Doom" all caught the public's interest - the city is known as a place where drugs, alcohol and debauchery ruled.

Often thought to have been a British imperial city, in fact Shanghai was an international community, in which a Municipal Council ruled with British, American and German representatives (after the First World War the German was replaced with a Japanese representative). There was a French settlement, which was integrated into the French colonial service, but this operated separately. The Chinese section surrounded the two foreign free trading areas.

From the 1800s, when the city was founded on the muddy shores of the river, Shanghai grew rapidly. The free-wheeling foreigners could make millions from opium and other goods, especially arms and military hardware, which were sold to any warlord with money. By the end of the First World War, with a world-wide glut of weapons on the open market as European governments disbanded their armies, many of these guns began to appear in Shanghai.

The Shanghai Municipal Council had a small police force for the settlement. It was largely composed of white, British officers, and a large number of local Chinese recruits, along with a number of Sikhs. Pay was dreadful, which led to a number of the British police officers resorting to extortion, protection rackets, getting involved in selling drugs, and borrowing money from Sikh officers.

In much the same that Al Capone cemented his relationships through the political and law enforcement communities in Chicago, Du Yusheng, head of the Green Gang, bolstered his position with bribery. A small man brought up as an orphan, he was fiercely ambitious. Huang Jinrong was similarly ambitious, but he had a comfortable position in the Sûreté. As a racketeer, gangster and policeman, he was installed as a thief set to catch thieves, and in ten years he became one of the three leading criminal commanders in Shanghai, along with Du Yusheng and Zhang Xiaolin.

It is not surprising that the streets grew increasingly dangerous. The ready supply of guns, the interest of gangs in drugs, gambling, prostitution and smuggling, all formed a potent mix. The Shanghai Municipal Police (SMP) in the International Settlement, as well as the French and Chinese forces, found themselves forced to deal with growing violence. There was a need to fight fire with fire, which bred a particularly tough form of police officer. For example, there were exchanges organised between various international police forces and the men of the SMP, whose officers were keen to learn from other forces. This had mixed success. During an exchange with officers from Chicago, the visiting policemen soon demanded to return to the US: the streets of Shanghai were too dangerous for them. They were happier in Al Capone's city.

In many ways the two cities were formed by prohibitive legislation. Prohibition in the US led to vast criminal profits, in the same way as the ban on opium in Shanghai led to the gangs' expansion. The difference was the lack of government in China. Warlords fought each other, seeking to capitalise on the country's political vacuum. With civil war erupting, the police had too many calls on their time and attention.

However, there were men who were determined to help protect their officers. W.E. (Dan) Fairbairn was one. A keen martial artist, he had been a Royal Marine, but discovered a fascination for Shanghai and joined the Municipal Police Force. He developed his own systems for unarmed combat, and taught the police recruits how to protect themselves on the streets. This system he called "gutter fighting" or "Scientific Self-Defence", and he wrote several books on the subject (one with an enthusiastic preface by Douglas Fairbanks).

He believed in training his officers to use whatever weapon might be at hand. The modern sport of Practical Pistol Shooting is thought to be his creation, as is the concept of the Special Weapons and Tactics (SWAT) units, the use of body armour, the use of automatic pistols, and even daggers.

At the outbreak of the Second World War, Fairbairn and one of his colleagues, Eric "Bill" Sykes, were recalled to Britain. These two were tasked to train a new breed of soldier, Churchill's commandos. It was in honour of the two men that the commando dagger became known as the Fairbairn-Sykes dagger - the dagger they invented for fighting on the streets of Shanghai. During the war the two trained many special forces personnel, the SOE, and, after the war, Fairbairn moved to the US. There he took over training for the OSS and the Marine Corps.

One last person deserves mention in this note. I did not intend to make much of Gracie Gale and the ladies who entertained down The Line, but Gracie began to take over the story. Her history as portrayed in the story is accurate. The system by which Shanghai started to try to close down prostitution is also correct - an annual ballot to see which licensed premises could continue to operate versus which would be closed, was an innovative idea. American evangelists were as determined to stop prostitution as they were to prohibit drugs and alcohol, and Gracie could see the end coming. When the situation grew difficult, she took one last journey home to San Francisco and, sadly, on the way she took her own life.

*Further reading*:

Empire Made Me by Robert Bickers

The Shanghai Green Gang by Brian G. Martin Shanghai Policeman by E.W. Peters

Mao by Jonathan Spence

The Bund by Peter Hibbard

Scientific Self-Defence by W.E. Fairbairn

Shooting to Live by W.E. Fairbairn

Underworld of the East by James S. Lee

Policing Shanghai by Frederick Wakeman

Old Shanghai by Lyn Pan

Shanghai by Stella Dong

The World's First SWAT Team by Leroy Thompson

# About the Author

After 13 years as a computer salesman, Michael Jecks turned to crime.

He is the author of 50 mystery novels. His work encompasses the highly acclaimed *Templar* series of historical thrillers, humorous *Bloody Mary Tudor* series, the *Vintener* trilogy, the modern *Art of Murder* series, and a modern spy story, *Act of Vengeance:* 'an instant classic British spy novel' - Lee Child. His stories are grounded in real life and real people: what motivates them, and what makes them turn to violence.

*Death Ship of Dartmouth* (Headline, 2006) was short-listed for the Theakston's Old Peculier Crime Novel of the Year Award, and he has been published by HarperCollins, Headline, Simon & Schuster, Canongate and Severn House.

The founder of Medieval Murderers, he has served on the committees of the Crime Writers' Association, Historical Writers' Association, and The Detection Club. He has taught writing at Swanwick, Evesham, and tutored for the Royal Literary Fund at Exeter University. He works with Smithsonian Journeys as their expert on the Mystery Lover's England tour.

In 2014 he was the International Guest of Honour at the Bloody Words festival in Toronto, and Grand Master of the first parade in the New Orleans Mardi Gras.

Michael lives in north Dartmoor with his wife and two dogs.

Printed in Great Britain
by Amazon